Pneumatology at the Beginning of the Third Millennium

THEOLOGY AT THE BEGINNING OF THE THIRD MILLENNIUM

Series Preface

Theology at the Beginning of the Third Millennium is a series of theological monographs which seek to examine the *status quaestionis* of various sub-disciplines within the field of theology in this second decade of the third millennium and some half a century after the conclusion of the Second Vatican Council. While the initial impetus for the series came from scholars at the University of Notre Dame (Australia), the Catholic Institute of Sydney, and Campion College (Sydney), contributors to the volumes come from a diverse array of theological academies. A feature of the series is the fact that although the majority of the contributors are situated within the Catholic intellectual tradition, scholars from other traditions are also welcome.

The various sub-disciplines which form the subject of each volume are examined from the perspective of scripture scholarship, fundamental, systematic and dogmatic theology, spirituality, historical theology, ecumenical and pastoral theology and the theology of culture. This is consistent with the Balthasarian metaphor that "Truth is Symphonic" and thus created by a harmonious integration of different disciplines or "sections" of the theological orchestra. Consistent with the charism of St. James, the contributors share a high degree of respect for the deposit of the faith, a Johannine interest in integrating spirituality and mystical theology with dogmatic and fundamental theology, a Pauline sensitivity to the influence of the Holy Spirit, a Petrine interest in official magisterial teaching and, above all, a Marian disposition of receptivity to the Divine *Logos*.

Pneumatology at the Beginning of the Third Millennium

THEOLOGY AT THE BEGINNING OF THE THIRD MILLENNIUM

Edited by

KEVIN WAGNER

PETER JOHN MCGREGOR

and

M. ISABELL NAUMANN

PICKWICK *Publications* · Eugene, Oregon

Pickwick Publications
An Imprint of Wipf and Stock Publishers
199 W. 8th Ave., Suite 3
Eugene, OR 97401
www.wipfandstock.com

PAPERBACK ISBN: 978-1-6667-7286-9

HARDCOVER ISBN: 978-1-6667-7287-6

EBOOK ISBN: 978-1-6667-7288-3

Cataloguing-in-Publication data:

Names: Wagner, Kevin [editor]. | McGregor, Peter John [editor]. | Naumann, M. Isabell [editor].

Title: Pneumatology at the beginning of the third millennium / edited by Kevin Wagner, Peter John McGregor, and M. Isabell Naumann.

Description: Eugene, OR: Pickwick Publications, 2023 | Series: Theology at the Beginning of the Third Millennium | Includes bibliographical references.

Identifiers: ISBN 978-1-6667-7286-9 (paperback) | ISBN 978-1-6667-7287-6 (hardcover) | ISBN 978-1-6667-7288-3 (ebook)

Subjects: LCSH: Holy Spirit. | God (Christianity). | Theology, Doctrinal. | Catholic Church—Doctrines.

Classification: BT121.3 W34 2023 (paperback) | BT121.3 (ebook)

VERSION NUMBER 11/28/23

CONTENTS

CONTRIBUTORS

Mario Baghos is an Academic Sessional at the University of Notre Dame (Sydney) and Adjunct Lecturer in Theology in the Faculty of Arts and Education at Charles Sturt University. From 2010–17 and 2020–22, he taught Patristics and Church History at St. Andrew's Greek Orthodox Theological College (Sydney College of Divinity). He has also lectured in the discipline of Studies in Religion at the University of Sydney and has published extensively in the disciplines of patristics and Byzantine studies. His most recent publication is entitled *From the Ancient Near East to Christian Byzantium: Kings, Symbols, and Cities* (Cambridge Scholars Publishing, 2021).

Mariusz Biliniewicz currently serves as Director of the Liturgy Office in the Archdiocese of Sydney. He has worked at the University of Notre Dame Australia as Senior Lecturer in Theology and Associate Dean of Research and Academic Development. He has studied and taught in Poland, Ireland and Australia and has spoken and published internationally on a number of theological topics. His interests include contemporary Catholic theology, liturgy, sacraments, Second Vatican Council, intersections between ecclesiology and moral theology, faith and reason and general systematic theology.

David Collits is an independent scholar and Sydney-based lawyer. His undergraduate degrees were in history and law. He was awarded a PhD in theology from the University of Notre Dame, Australia. His thesis explored the hope-history debate in fundamental theology and the cleavage in contemporary theology between the Communio and Concilium schools. He has been on the personal staff of the Archbishop of Sydney, (Most Rev.) Anthony Fisher, OP, and has been Lecturer in Catholic Theology at the University of Notre Dame, Australia.

Adam Cooper is Associate Professor of Theology at Catholic Theological College and teaches in the departments of Systematic Theology and Church History. He has taught Greek at the University of Durham (NT), patristics at the Melbourne Institute of Orthodox Christian Studies and Theological Anthropology, Historical Theology, and Moral Theology at John Paul II Institute for Marriage and Family.

Paschal M. Corby is a priest of the Order of Friars Minor Conventual. He is a Lecturer in Moral Theology at the University of Notre Dame, Australia (Sydney) and the University of Divinity/Catholic Theological College (Melbourne). With a background in Medicine, he has a particular interest in Bioethics. He is the author of *The Hope and Despair of Human Bioenhancement* (Pickwick, 2019).

Sr. Susanna Edmunds, OP, is currently the Dean of Studies at the Seminary of the Good Shepherd, Sydney. She has a degree in Education (Secondary) and has completed a range of other studies in philosophy and theology. Sr Susanna has recently submitted a Masters thesis in Biblical Theology at the University of Notre Dame, Australia.

Joseph Hamilton is a priest of the Catholic Archdiocese of Sydney and Associate Professor of Theology at the Pontifical University of St. Tomas (Angelicum) in Rome. He gained his license in Patristic Science from the Pontifical Institute Augustinianum and completed doctoral studies in Patristics at Christ Church, University of Oxford. His principal areas of research are patristic pneumatology, angelology, and the understanding of charismatic phenomena in the early Church.

Robin Koning is a Jesuit priest of the Australian Province and an Honorary Fellow of Australian Catholic University. He has taught systematic theology and philosophy at the United Faculty of Theology in the Melbourne College of Divinity. His main areas of research have been in the work of Bernard Lonergan and Robert Doran as well as inculturation and culture as a category in theology, grounded in his work in a remote Aboriginal a community in the 1990s. In recent years his research has also turned to Ignatian spirituality. He currently serves as Provincial Assistant for Vocations for the Australian Jesuits and is much involved in young adult ministry. He offers spiritual direction and retreats as well as workshops on Ignatian prayer and the Rules for Discernment of Spirits.

Robert Krishna, OP, is a Dominican friar and Catholic priest. He has a BSc (Hons), and a PhD from Sydney University in History and Philosophy of Science, and a BTheol and MTheol from the University of Divinity. He is a member of the Dominican Province of the Assumption (Australia and New Zealand), and is currently studying for a License in Sacred Scripture at the Ecole Biblique in Jerusalem. He was ordained a priest in 2017, and has served as the Catholic Chaplain at the University of Technology Sydney and Monash University (Clayton, Vic). His research interests include the Twelve Prophets, Biblical Intertextuality, and Christian and Jewish interpretation of the Scriptures in late antiquity.

Benjamin Johnson, OFMCap, is a Capuchin Franciscan of the Province of Australia. In 2022, he completed his doctorate at the Pontifical Lateran University in Rome on the relationship between the sacraments of the Eucharist and Marriage in the thought of Saint Bonaventure of Bagnoregio. His research interests include the relationship between Franciscan theology and Christian experience, and scholastic sacramental theology. Br. Ben lectures in sacramental theology at the University of Notre Dame, Australia.

Matthew Levering holds the James N. and Mary D. Perry Jr. Chair of Theology at Mundelein Seminary. He is the author or co-author of over thirty-five books and editor or co-editor of over twenty books. His most recent book, published with Cambridge University Press, is *Reconfiguring Thomistic Christology* (2023). Matthew is the director of the Center for Scriptural Exegesis, Philosophy, and Doctrine; past president (2021–22) of the Academy of Catholic Theology; and a longtime member of Evangelicals and Catholics Together. He serves as co-editor of two scholarly journals, *Nova et Vetera* and *International Journal of Systematic Theology*.

Peter John McGregor is a lecturer in Dogmatic Theology and Spiritual Theology at the Catholic Institute of Sydney and the University of Notre Dame Australia. He is the author of *Heart to Heart: The Spiritual Christology of Joseph Ratzinger*, and a co-editor of *Healing Fractures in Contemporary Theology* and the *Theology at the Beginning of the Third Millennium* series. He is also a contributor to the forthcoming *Cambridge Companion to Joseph Ratzinger* and the *Joseph Ratzinger Dictionary: Central Concepts*. His current research interests include the theology of Joseph Ratzinger, the relationship between theology and spirituality, theological anthropology, fundamental theology, postmodern theology, and missiology.

M. Isabell Naumann, ISSM, is the President of the Catholic Institute of Sydney (Ecclesiastical Faculty of Theology) and a Professor of Systematic Theology. She is a Member of the Secular Institute of the Schoenstatt Sisters of Mary (ISSM) where holds the position of provincial for Australia and the Philippines. For over ten years, she served as the Academic Dean of Studies at the Seminary of the Good Shepherd, Sydney and taught Systematic Theology at the Catholic Institute of Sydney. She is also an Adjunct Professor in Systematic Theology at the University of Notre Dame,

Sydney. She has served, and currently serves, on various national and international academic boards and councils, including two terms at the Pontifical Council for Culture. She has been a member of the International Theological Commission since 2021.

Peter Pellicaan currently serves as the Executive Director of Evangelisation Brisbane, an Agency of the Archdiocese of Brisbane. He is involved with the Archdiocesan Centre for Catholic Formation in Brisbane teaching courses on scripture and the sacraments. Peter completed his PhD in Theology at the University of Notre Dame Australia developing a theology of confirmation from the canon of scripture. Peter has been involved in leadership in the Church for over twenty years, is a Deacon and is married with five children.

Tracey Rowland holds the St. John Paul II Chair of Theology at the University of Notre Dame (Australia). Her civil doctorate (PhD) is from the Divinity School of the University of Cambridge and her pontifical doctorate (STD) is from the Lateran University in Rome. She was a member of the IXth International Theological Commission (2014–19) and is currently a member of the Pontifical Academy of the Social Sciences. Her most recent book is *Beyond Kant and Nietzsche: The Munich Defence of Christian Humanism* (Bloomsbury, 2021) and she is a co-editor of *Joseph Ratzinger in Dialogue with Philosophical Traditions* (Bloomsbury, 2024).

Matthew John Paul Tan is the Dean of Studies at Vianney College, the seminary of the Diocese of Wagga Wagga, and Adjunct Senior Lecturer in Theology at the University of Notre Dame Australia. He completed his Doctorate in Theology at the Australian Catholic University, and did his License in Sacred Theology at the Pontifical University of St. Thomas Aquinas in Rome. He has published two books, *Justice, Unity and the Hidden Christ* (Pickwick, 2014) and *Redeeming Flesh: The Way of the Cross with Zombie Jesus* (Cascade, 2016).

Pamela Van Oploo is a Lecturer at the University of Notre Dame, Sydney who has a background in Earth and Environmental Science, having completed a Bachelor of Science and Mathematics (Hons) and a PhD in Science and Technology. She is currently completing a second PhD on the educational philosophy of St. Thomas Aquinas and the pedagogical implications of this as gleaned from his writings.

Joseph Vnuk, OP, is a Dominican friar whose theological motto is "taking every thought captive and rendering it obedient to Christ." Joseph has an STL from Catholic Institute of Sydney and a doctorate from the University of Nottingham. His doctoral thesis focused on sacraments and grace according to Thomas. Joseph has taught both in Papua New Guinea and at CTC Melbourne.

Kevin Wagner is the principal convener of the *Theology at the Beginning of the Third Millennium* conference series and co-editor of the eponymous book series. He is a Senior Lecturer in Theology at the University of Notre Dame, Australia, specializing in patristics, early Church history, and Scripture. Kevin was previously the Director of the Emmanuel School of Mission in Rome, a role he shared with his wife.

Nigel Zimmermann is Director of Catholic Mission and Identity at Melbourne Archdiocesan Catholic Schools (MACS). He is an Adjunct Lecturer with the Institute for Ethics & Society at the University of Notre Dame Australia and Senior Fellow with the PM Glynn Institute, Australian Catholic University. Nigel has authored numerous works in theology and bioethics including *Levinas and Theology* (Bloomsbury, 2013), *Facing the Other: John Paul II, Levinas, and the Body* (Cascade, 2015), and *The Great Grace: Receiving Vatican II Today* (T. & T. Clark, 2015).

PREFACE

Kevin Wagner

THE THEOLOGY AT THE Beginning of the Third Millennium book series began with a chance encounter in 2015 between three lay theologians of the Emmanuel Community (*la Communauté de l'Emmanuel*), a Public Association of the Faithful. Members of the Emmanuel Community have a special devotion to Mary, and each prays a daily consecration to her. Inspired by the thought to place Mariology back on the radar of Australian theologians, the three conspired to organize a conference on the topic. The quality of the papers delivered meant it was an easy decision to publish the best of them in a monograph, entitled *Mariology at the Beginning of the Third Millennium*.

What began with a desire to give the theology of Mary a more prominent place in academia, has become a biannual conference series, as well as a series of books published by the good folks at Wipf and Stock. Thus far we have taken up the topics of ecclesiology, theological anthropology, and pneumatology. And it is this final topic that is the theme of this book.

As is usual in this series, we begin with a chapter detailing the *status quaestionis* of our theme. Here, Peter McGregor, one the "founding fathers" of the Third Millennium series, draws on both his extensive experience in the Catholic charismatic renewal and his theological prowess. McGregor presents a fascinating and useful account of the development of pneumatology from the rise of Pentecostalism in the nineteenth century and its early appropriation by Catholics, through the Catholic Charismatic Renewal of the 1960s, and up to the current time. His chapter concludes by raising two important points. First, he muses on the role of the Spirit in resolving the apparent conflict between history and ontology. Second and finally, Peter emphasizes the place of the gifts of the Spirit for theologizing.

Chapters 2–4 are explicitly scriptural contributions. Chapter 2 begins by asking the question "What was the Holy Spirit doing when Jesus died on the

Cross?" Drawing on patristic and contemporary witnesses, Zimmermann offers a compelling argument that the Spirit plays a cooperative role in the sacrifice of Jesus on the Cross.

Next, in chapter 3, Naumann shows how Mary cooperated with the Holy Spirit at the time of Pentecost and continues to do so today through her mediatory role in the Church. Indeed, the Mother of God is presented to the readers as a model both for the individual Christian and for the Church; the *homo viator* (person on pilgrimage) and the *homo spiritualis* (the spiritual person).

Chapter 4 examines the corpus of the minor prophets—the Book of the Twelve—in order to show how God's Spirit disrupts the life of the prophet such that he or she is inspired to act as a conduit for God's salvific purpose. But this work of the Spirit continues, Krishna shows, in the time of Christ and is evidenced in Luke-Acts. This observation from the Dominican, should give us hope that the Spirit can continue to disrupt prophets for our own time!

Chapters 5–8 may be classified as works of patristic pneumatology. Cooper leads the way by wrestling with the complicated character of Tertullian and his flirtations with the New Prophecy. This chapter is particularly insightful and helpful for the light it shines on the different ways Tertullian and modern liberals understand openness to the Spirit.

Hamilton, in chapter 6, also offers an account of the Spirit's role in prophecy, but here the focus is on the particular phenomena of dreams and visions. Focusing on early Latin texts, Hamilton offers a scholarly survey of the oneiric experiences of Tertullian, Perpetua, and Cyprian. In the process, Hamilton demonstrates admirably that the Spirit is manifested to some through such experiences.

My own chapter, chapter 7, is motivated by the desire to deepen our reflections on the image of the Holy Spirit as dove. It strikes me that the dove is too often presented in modern catechesis in a cursory or banal way, such that the Spirit—who the dove usually represents—is emasculated and stripped of all Its divinity. Here I seek to remedy this somewhat by drawing on the collective genius of Origen and Gregory of Nyssa as expressed in their commentaries on the Canticle. I can only hope that the enjoyment I had in reading these works deeply can stimulate further reflection on the Holy Spirit as dove.

Chapter 8 draws on two orations of St. Gregory Nazianzen in order to demonstrate that history is pneumatological; that is, it is guided by the Holy Spirit. In this chapter, Baghos argues convincingly for a view of history that takes seriously protology and teleology. This alone makes his chapter an important read for those disheartened by the state of many modern approaches to historiography.

Chapters 9–12 take us on a journey through the Middle Ages through to the Council of Trent. Johnson gets us started with his account of Bonaventure's insights on mystical experience, the theological virtues, and the role of the Spirit in leading the soul towards union with God. Here we are introduced to the Seraphic Doctor's reflections on the crucified One and on the work of the Spirit in St. Francis, that great founder of Bonaventure's order who sought so admirably to imitate Him. What we discover in Johnson's account of Bonaventure is a rugged and attractive spirituality that places poverty and humility at the center of the Christian's life. And this is all for the sake of better imitating the incarnate and crucified One.

Chapter 10 is a masterful piece of Catholic theology from a veritable master of Catholic theology, Matthew Levering. *Contra* to some who over-emphasize the division between Logos and Spirit Christologies, Levering argues that a true Logos Christology is also a Spirit Christology "because the Word . . . is never present without the Spirit." Levering takes the reader through a spirited engagement with Aquinas' Trinitarian Christology and some of Thomas' more important interpreters, including Suarez, Garrigou-Lagrange, and Legge. This chapter is a fine demonstration of a theological method that preferences holding truths in tension over the easier path of falling to one or other side of an argument.

Van Oploo, in chapter 11, draws on Aquinas for a different end. Her primary objective is to show that God is our Primary teacher and that the Father, Son, and Spirit each have their own particular pedagogies. Having established this, van Oploo goes on to show that the Spirit and the Spirit's gifts are key in the classroom. Her insights, drawn both from her studies and classroom experience, are invaluable in an age where education is focused more on *techne* than *eudaimonia*.

Chapter 12 focuses attention on the apparent "paucity of explicit references to the Spirit" in the *Spiritual Exercises* of St. Ignatius of Loyola. Koning begins his chapter by showing that Ignatius was strongly influenced by his historical context (particularly the rise of the *Alumbrados*) and by his various encounters with the Inquisition. This context alone goes some way to understanding why Ignatius steers clear of explicit references to the Spirit in the *Exercises*. Koning then introduces the reader to the pneumatology of the founding documents of the Society of Jesus and of the *Exercises*. The end result of his efforts is a convincing argument that the *Exercises* is replete with allusions to the Spirit and that the *Exercises* stand in continuity with Ignatius' other writings.

Chapters 13 and 14 should be required reading for all who teach the sacrament of confirmation or prepare people for its reception. In the first of these chapters, Pellicaan sets himself the task of answering the question "What is the role of the Holy Spirit in confirmation?" Drawing first on the Scriptures and then on the documents of the Church—principally the *Catechism*—Pellicaan shows that confirmation is ordered to the mission of building up the Church.

The Dominican, Joseph Vnuk, takes a different, though compatible, approach in seeking to show that confirmation is concerned with transformation; a transformation rooted in the unity of Christ and the Spirit. Taking the reader on a journey through the scriptures, patristic literature, and the writings of the scholastics, Vnuk demonstrates that baptism and confirmation are indeed both Christic and pneumatological, and that this realization should impact our pastoral approach to preparing confirmands.

The remaining chapters of this book deal with a somewhat eclectic array of topics. Chapter 15 offers an overview of key milestones in pneumatology between the publications of *Divinum Illud Munus* (1897) and *Dominum et vivificantem* (1986). Rowland presents a survey of a veritable who's who of Catholic theologians—Rahner, Congar, La Soujeole, Bouyer, Balthasar, Daniélou, Guillou, John Paul II—and their work in the field of pneumatology. In the process, Rowland not only affirms Vnuk's assumption that pneumatology and Christology are inseparable, she reminds us of "the importance of understanding the bridges or links between pneumatology and ecclesiology and pneumatology and theological anthropology."

The topic of scriptural inspiration takes center stage in Chapter Sixteen. Here, Edmunds brings Thomism and the Pontifical Biblical Commission's *The Inspiration and Truth of Sacred Scripture* into dialogue in order to better understand revelation, inspiration, and prophecy, and the relationships between these. Edmunds is particularly concerned with showing how the prophet is a model for understanding the writer of the scriptures. Her efforts in the chapter reveal that an inadequate understanding of prophecy can leave "the historicity of biblical events in ambiguity." What we discover in Edmunds' work is a key to re-affirming the veracity of the doctrine of scriptural inerrancy. Needless to say, this is of great importance today.

Chapter 17, written by the Conventual Franciscan Paschal Corby, places the Holy Spirit at the center of a Christian moral theology. Corby expounds on the work of Servais Pinckaers, who proposed a revolution in moral theology away from a morality of obligation and towards a morality of "self-fulfilment in beatitude." This self-fulfilment is not an exercise in self-will devoid of grace. Rather, Corby shows, it is attained through the welcoming of the Holy Spirit into the heart of believer such that the New Law inscribed thereon conforms the believer to the living God.

Biliniewicz, in chapter 18, dives into the age-old controversy concerning the procession of the Holy Spirit. Rather than engaging with the standard debates over the inclusion or exclusion of the *filioque* in the Creed, or how one ought to interpret the Second Ecumenical Council of Constantinople, or other such matters, Biliniewicz prefers to simply pose the question, does this doctrine influence ecclesiology? What we find in Biliniewicz's chapter is not so much a downplaying of the classic problems, but rather, a call to turn our attention to fundamental theology and to theological method. It is by doing this, the author suggests, that we may find more points of agreement with theologians across the divide, and thus, I would suggest, more hope of a way forward in ecumenical dialogue.

It is a truism to say that the writers of the scriptures could not have imagined cyberspace, nor could they have envisioned online liturgical participation! This being so, what can Jerusalem have to say about this new Athens that exists in this virtual space? In chapter 19, Tan poses two interrelated questions: "Is . . . encountering the person of Jesus Christ attainable in a real way in cyberspace?" and "is there a proper dogmatic basis on which we can justify an internet end-user having a real encounter with the body of Jesus Christ on the net?" Through a strong engagement with the work of Chiara Lubich and her concept of Christ abandoned, Tan convincingly argues in the affirmative, though perhaps not in the way we might expect!

The so-called Joachimite expectation that the Spirit will usher in a new age in which the visual church is superseded by a spiritual one, is compelling both for opponents of organized Christianity and for those enthralled by utopianism. Our final chapter, by David Collits, brings Augustine's theology of history into conversation with that of Joachim of Fiore—through the interlocutor, Joseph Ratzinger—in order to demonstrate the "enduring value of the Augustinian vision of history." Augustine's genius on this point, expounded convincingly by Collits, is that it affirms the teleological dimension of history and the salvific work of the Holy Spirit in and through the Church.

It is the editors' hope that this book will contribute to the discussion on the place of the Holy Spirit in the theologate, in the sacramental and liturgical life of the Church, and in the lives of individuals. We leave it to the Spirit to determine the fruits you may each experience in partaking of this product of our collective labors!

1

INTRODUCTION TO PNEUMATOLOGY AT THE BEGINNING OF THE THIRD MILLENNIUM

Peter John McGregor

IN THIS FIRST CHAPTER I wish to present something a little different from what one would expect to find in an introduction to a specific theological subject. In its second half I will be looking at how Pneumatology has developed in the twentieth and twenty-first centuries, contrasting its character before the Second Vatican Council with what comes after the Council. This will be followed by an identification of eight *quaestiones disputatae* in contemporary Pneumatology. Finally, I will look at two pneumatological topics that are of particular interest to me. Yet I wish to begin this chapter with a more than cursory account of something different from Pneumatology as a theological topic. This is an account of the action of the Holy Spirit in the Church from the late nineteenth century until today, under the headings of (1) Pentecostalism, (2) Pope Leo XIII and Elena Guerra, and (3) the Catholic Charismatic Renewal. I will reveal the reason for this approach in due course.

PENTECOSTALISM

Let us look at the beginnings of a movement that has become very influential within contemporary Christianity, a movement called Pentecostalism.[1]

1. For an introduction to the history of Pentecostalism in the twentieth century, see Synan, *Century of the Holy Spirit*.

During the nineteenth century, radical evangelical revival movements began to appear in the United States of America and Great Britain, the most important of these being the Wesleyan Holiness movement. Within this radical evangelicalism, themes such as restorationism, premillennialism, faith healing, and greater attention to the person and work of the Holy Spirit emerged. Believing that the second coming of Christ was imminent, these Christians expected an end-time revival of apostolic power, spiritual gifts, and miracle working. As expectation grew, especially in the Great Britain, some Protestant ministers began to investigate reports of manifestations of charismata, believing that they would be signs that the return of Christ was imminent. For example, one Edward Irving, the pastor of a prestigious London Presbyterian church, travelled all the way to Scotland to investigate reports of miraculous healings and glossolalia. In 1831 he established the Catholic Apostolic Church, wherein speaking in tongues and prophesying were encouraged.[2] About twenty-five years later, people such as the British Baptist minister C. H. Spurgeon and the British Methodist minister William Arthur, were preaching and writing about a coming new outpouring of the Holy Spirit.[3] Some twenty years later, preachers in the USA such as Dwight L. Moody, R. A. Torrey, and A. B. Simpson, began to speak of an experience available to all Christians which would empower believers to evangelize the world. This experience was called "baptism in the Holy Spirit."[4]

Ultimately, no one person or group founded Pentecostalism. Instead, isolated Christian groups experienced charismatic phenomena such as divine healing and speaking in tongues. The Methodist holiness movement provided a theological explanation for what was happening to these Christians, and they adapted Wesleyan soteriology to accommodate their new understanding. As it happens, the Wesleyan understanding of salvation is very like the Catholic one. Hence the Pentecostal understanding of salvation and sanctification are often like the Catholic understanding.

An important figure in the emergence of Pentecostalism was Charles Fox Parham, an independent holiness evangelist who believed in divine healing. He was important for the emergence of Pentecostalism as a distinct Christian movement.[5] In 1900, he started a school near Topeka, Kansas, which he named Bethel Bible School. There he taught that speaking in tongues was the scriptural evidence for the reception of the baptism with

2. Synan, "Pentecostal Roots," 22–25.

3. Synan, "Pentecostal Roots," 25–26.

4. Synan, "Pentecostal Roots," 29–32.

5. For what follows about Parham and the Azuza Street Revival, see Owens, "Azuza Street Revival," 39–68.

the Holy Spirit. On January 1, 1901, after a vigil service, the students at this school prayed for and apparently received the baptism with the Holy Spirit with the evidence of speaking in tongues. Later, Parham received this same experience as his students and began preaching about it in all his services. Parham taught that the baptism with the Holy Spirit was a third experience, after conversion and sanctification. Sanctification cleansed the believer, but Spirit baptism empowered for service.

At about the same time that Parham was spreading his doctrine, the Welsh Revival of 1904 to 1905 saw thousands of conversions and also exhibited speaking in tongues.[6] In 1905, Parham moved to Houston, Texas, where he started a Bible training school. One of his students was William J. Seymour, a one-eyed black preacher. Seymour travelled to Los Angeles where his preaching sparked the three-year-long Azusa Street Revival, beginning in 1906. Worship at the racially integrated Azusa Mission featured an absence of any order of service. People preached and testified as moved by the Spirit, spoke and sung in tongues, and fell in the Spirit. The revival attracted both religious and secular media attention, and thousands of visitors flocked to the mission, carrying the experience back to their home churches. Crowds of blacks and whites worshiped together at the Mission. This set the tone for much of the early Pentecostal movement. From 1906 to 1924, Pentecostals defied social, cultural, and political norms vis-à-vis racial segregation. As the Azusa participants carried their new experience back to their own churches, sometimes whole churches were converted to the Pentecostal acceptance of charismata. But more often Pentecostals were forced to establish new religious communities when their experience was rejected by their own churches. It was not until 1960 that the use of charismatic gifts à la Pentecostalism began to be accepted in many Protestant Churches.

From such small beginnings, by 2011, there were about 280 million Pentecostal Christians worldwide, making up nearly 13 percent of the Christian population. Other charismatic Christians, including Catholics, numbered some 305 million, or about 14 percent of the Christian population, making an overall total of 27 percent.

POPE LEO XIII AND ELENA GUERRA

As the Pentecostal movement was coalescing during the nineteenth century, what was happening in the Catholic Church? Certainly, there was no equivalent expectation of an imminent return of Christ. However,

6. Owens, "Azuza Street Revival," 41–42.

theologically, there was some movement vis-à-vis Pneumatology. Most notable is the work of two theologians, Johann Adam Möhler and Matthias Scheeben. In 1825, Möhler published his *Unity in the Church, or, the Principle of Catholicism*. Therein he stressed that the Church was more like an organism than a juridical society, and that the principle of this organism's life was the Holy Spirit.[7] In the second half of the century, Scheeben brought a renewed focus to the role of the Holy Spirit in the *theosis* (divinization, deification) of the Christian.[8] However, these theological advances were not accompanied by the kind of spiritual activity witnessed in Protestantism.

The next stage in the story of the manifest activity of the Holy Spirit in the Catholic Church begins at the end of the nineteenth century. Between 1895 and 1903 a religious sister called Elena Guerra wrote twelve confidential letters to Pope Leo XIII. The purpose of these letters was to urge the pope to renew the Church through a return to the Holy Spirit. In one of these she wrote:

> Pentecost is not over. In fact, it is continually going on in every time and in every place, because the Holy Spirit desired to give himself to all men, and all who want him can always receive him, so we do not have to envy the apostles and the first believers; we only have to dispose ourselves like them to receive him well, and He will come to us as he did to them. ... The mystery of Pentecost is a permanent mystery. The Spirit continues to come to all souls who truly desire Him. ... If they only want Him ... if they only invoke Him ... if they only prepare a place for Him in their hearts. ... Who is hungry enough? Who is thirsty enough? Who is humble enough? Who is zealous enough? ... It is necessary that we return to the Holy Spirit so that the Holy Spirit may return to us.[9]

Leo XIII took these letters seriously, so seriously that he wrote three documents in response to them. After the first letter he published *Provida Matris Caritate* in 1895, in which he asked the entire Church to celebrate a solemn novena to the Holy Spirit each year between the feasts of the Ascension and Pentecost. After the third letter, he wrote the encyclical *Divinum Illud Munus* in 1897 on the doctrine of the Holy Spirit. Following the ninth letter the pope wrote a letter to the bishops, *Ad Fovendum in Christiano Populo* in

---

7. Möhler, *Unity in the Church*, 79–205.

8. See especially Scheeben, *Glories of Divine Grace*; Scheeben, *Handbook of Catholic Dogmatics*. The *Handbook* is currently being published in English, for the first time in an unabridged form, by Emmaus Academic.

9. Mansfield, "Blessed Elena Guerra," para. 4–5. For more on Elena Guerra, see Abbrescia, *Elena Guerra*.

1902, reminding them of the obligation to make the novena annually.[10] Also, in this ninth letter to Pope Leo XIII, written on October 15, 1900, Elena begged the pope to exhort all Catholics to pray for the new century and to place it under the sign of the Holy Spirit. She wrote, "Most Holy Father, I humbly present with confidence to your Holiness that the new century may begin with the hymn *Veni Creator Spiritus* to be sung at the beginning of the Mass of the first day of the year."[11] As a result of this request, the pope intoned the *Veni Creator Spiritus* in the name of the whole Church, on January 1, 1901, the same day that Parham's students experienced their "baptism in the Holy Spirit."

THE CATHOLIC CHARISMATIC RENEWAL

I will now look at the beginnings of what is called the Catholic Charismatic Renewal. In a homily on Pentecost Sunday in 1959, Pope John XXIII expressed his desire that the upcoming ecumenical council would convene like a new Pentecost. On September 23rd of that same year, he prayed for the council with the words, "Renew your wonders in this our day as by a new Pentecost." On October 11, 1962, the Second Vatican Council opened with the praying of the *Veni Creator Spiritus*. But it was not until February 1967 that there was any public manifestation of a dramatic answer to this prayer. I say "public" deliberately, for we do not know what private manifestations may have been occurring. I remember an Australian Marist priest telling me that as a young seminarian in Rome at the time of Vatican II he had privately and spontaneously experienced something that he identified as a "baptism in the Holy Spirit," which included praying in tongues.

In 1967, David Mangan was a graduate student at Duquesne University in Pittsburgh. He belonged to the Chi Rho society, a group of Catholic students who met before classes to pray and study Scripture. In February of that year, they went away together on retreat at The Ark and The Dove retreat center. Mangan recounts that, "We were given a little paperback book called *The Cross and the Switchblade* by David Wilkerson, who was a Pentecostal pastor who worked with drug addicts and, in miraculous ways, brought them to healing and salvation merely through prayer."[12] Another student, Patti Mansfield, recalls,

---

10. This letter is not available on the official Vatican website.

11. Mansfield, "Blessed Elena Guerra," para. 10.

12. Wilcox, "Exploring the Roots," para. 25. For more on the beginning of the Catholic Charismatic Renewal, see Mansfield, *As by a New Pentecost*.

I kept saying, "This is happening today? Well, why aren't these things happening in my life?" I thought, "Here I am, I'm baptized, I'm confirmed, I've received the Holy Spirit. Why isn't the Holy Spirit doing this in my life?" And, we were told to do three things, first, pray with expectant faith. The next thing was to take the Bible and read the first four chapters of the Acts of the Apostles. To tell you how ignorant I was of Scripture, I had no idea where to find the Acts of the Apostles. I figured it was in the New Testament because I knew the Apostles were in the time of Jesus.[13]

Returning to Mangan's account,

The students opened each session of the retreat with the hymn "Veni Creator Spiritus"—"Come, Holy Spirit"—the same hymn Pope Leo invoked over the 20th century. One of the speakers taught from Jesus' words in Acts 1:8, "but you will receive power when the Holy Spirit comes upon you." The word for power is the same Greek word where we, in English, would get the word dynamite. And He (Jesus) likened the coming of the Holy Spirit to dynamite, And, that struck me extremely deeply, because I'd been raised a good Catholic boy, and I was with the Lord. He hadn't abandoned me at all and I knew that's where I belonged and where I was but, I don't think I could have used the word "dynamite" as an adjective to describe my spiritual life at that point.[14]

David joined his small group session and asked a question: "Where is the dynamite?" He later recorded in his notes his desire to hear someone speak in tongues. "And then I put a dash. And I put 'me!' with an exclamation point."[15] David went off by himself to reflect on the teaching. He recalls,

When I opened the door and walked into the chapel, the presence of God was so powerful, I could hardly move. The only way I could say this, "I was lost in Christ, and happy to be so." And, I forgot—completely forgot—about all my pushing to say, "Where's the dynamite? Where's the dynamite?" And that's exactly what it felt like. It felt like little explosions in my body were going off as part of this whole experience. I don't even know how to describe it beyond that. So, I started opening my

---

13. Wilcox, "Exploring the Roots," para. 26.
14. Wilcox, "Exploring the Roots," para. 27–28.
15. Wilcox, "Exploring the Roots," 29.

mouth to thank God for what he had done, and I started praying in another language.[16]

Later Patti joined David in the chapel. She remembers,

I began to tremble. I remember thinking, "But God is here. And he's holy, and I'm not holy." And so, just kneeling there in the quiet of my heart . . . I said, "Father, I give my life to you. Whatever you ask, I accept it." I was lying there prostrate, and I felt immersed in the love of God. I felt like I was swimming in the mercy of God. I remember thinking, just [whispering] to Him, "Stay, stay, stay."[17]

Other students were drawn into the chapel. Mansfield recalls,

"Some people were laughing for joy, others were weeping for joy. Some said they felt like they wanted to praise God, but they didn't know if it was going to come out in English. We were there and just in awe of the sovereign God." Mangan remembers, "Everything changed at that point . . . Now, I didn't spot it all right away, but I mean everything was different, as it turned out—after this happened to me."[18]

Please note that the experiences recounted above are not just about the reception and exercise of charismatic gifts, but also about experiences of God himself: his presence, his love, his mercy, and his holiness. As of 2013, this Catholic charismatic renewal, which began in 1967, was estimated to have affected over 160 million Catholics, mostly in third world countries.

CATHOLIC PNEUMATOLOGY PRIOR TO VATICAN II

Now, why am I talking about all this in an introductory chapter on the theology of the Holy Spirit at the beginning of the third millennium? It may be interesting, even inspiring, but what does it have to do with Pneumatology today? It is because I want to contrast the apparent work of the Holy Spirit in the lives of so many Christians in the twentieth century with the relative paucity of theological reflection on the Holy Spirit, at least for much of that century. In Catholic circles prior to the Second Vatican Council there is very little. This situation does not begin to change until the time of the Council itself. Just a cursory glance at Catholic Pneumatology

16. Wilcox, "Exploring the Roots," para. 31.
17. Wilcox, "Exploring the Roots," para. 33.
18. Wilcox, "Exploring the Roots," para. 35–36.

in the six decades before the Council reveals almost no awareness of what could be called widespread and growing pneumatological phenomena. Perhaps this is because these phenomena were Protestant phenomena. When there was a Catholic response, it was usually along the lines of Ronald Knox's *Enthusiasm*, published in 1950, where, in his chapter entitled "Some Vagaries of Modern Revivalism," he gives the following opinion.

> We have seen Quaker and Camisard and Wesleyan so carried away in prayer as to behave like automata rather than human beings; we shall be more ready to believe it when we find the Irvingites speaking with tongues. . . . Perhaps the most striking thing about the claim to speak with tongues is its infrequency. All enthusiastic movements are fain to revive, in a more or less degree, the experience of Pentecost; a new outpouring of the Holy Spirit has taken place, and a chosen body of witnesses is there to attest it. What is more likely than that they should aspire to imitate Pentecost in this, its most characteristic manifestation? Accordingly, if you consult the works of reference, you will find a long litany, copied from one encyclopaedia into another, purporting to show that all the enthusiastic movements have in fact given rise to glossolaly.[19]

Regarding "enthusiasm" in the twentieth century, Knox says no more than, "In our own island [Britain], for the last century, revivalism has shown a law of diminishing returns; each new wave, as it recedes, registers less of a high-water mark—Moody and Sankey, Torrey and Alexander, Aimée Macpherson."[20] Of these, only the last was Pentecostal.

Typical of Catholic Pneumatology in this period is a 1937 work by Fr. Edward Leen of the Congregation of the Holy Spirit entitled *The Holy Ghost and his Work in Souls*. This book looks at the Holy Spirit as God's loving kindness to his creatures, as divine love subsistent, the work of the Holy Spirit, the relation of the Holy Spirit to the Incarnation, the Holy Spirit as the Fount of Life and the Gift of God, the Mission of the Holy Spirit, the relation of the Holy Spirit to Baptism, the Holy Spirit as the Spirit of Adoption, the principles of supernatural growth, and the gifts, fruits, and beatitudes. The sources most frequently referred to in the footnotes are Sacred Scripture, Thomas Aquinas' *Summa Theologica*, *Sentences*, and *Summa Contra Gentiles*, and Aristotle's *Nicomachean Ethics*.

It is both necessary and important that we broaden and deepen our theological reflection upon the Holy Spirit. We should not be theologizing just

---

19. Knox, *Enthusiasm*, 550.
20. Knox, *Enthusiasm*, 578.

about what has happened in the past, but also about what is happening now. Pope Francis speaks of this in *Evangelii Gaudium* when he says, "Expressions of popular piety have much to teach us; for those who are capable of reading them, they are a *locus theologicus* which demands our attention, especially at a time when we are looking to the new evangelization."[21]

CATHOLIC PNEUMATOLOGY AFTER VATICAN II

However, even during Vatican II, things do start to get moving. One theologian who jumps right in is a German Council *peritus* named Heribert Mühlen.[22] For Mühlen, his engagement with Pentecostalism and the Catholic Charismatic Renewal led to a broadening of his early speculative theology in a practical direction. For example, while he is quoted as saying that "The doctrine and person of the Holy Spirit is not one doctrine among others, but a fundamental doctrine and reality in the church,"[23] he also states that "As I looked into the charismatic renewal I was amazed to see many of my theological observations of the Holy Spirit happening in the daily lives of people."[24]

Better known in the Anglosphere than Mühlen's theologizing about the Holy Spirit are the pneumatological writings of Yves Congar. His magisterial three volume work, entitled *I Believe in the Holy Spirit*, was published between 1979 and 1980. The first volume focused on the experience of

21. Francis, *Evangelii Gaudium*, sec. 126.

22. In 1963, he published his doctoral dissertation, *Der Heilige Geist als Person* (*The Holy Spirit as a Person*). In 1964 he published, as his habilitation thesis, *Una Mystica Persona* (*One Mystical Person*), which looked at the relationship between Christ, the Trinity, the Holy Spirit, and the Church. After becoming involved in the ecumenical dialogue between the Catholic Church and Pentecostal churches, he published *Die Erneuerung des christlichen Glaubens: Charisma, Geist, Befreiung* (*The Renewal of the Christian Faith: Charism, Spirit, Liberation*) in 1974, *Einübung in die christliche Grunderfahrung* (*Practicing the Basic Christian Experience*, translated into English as *Charismatic Theology: Initiation in the Spirit*) (1976), and in 1979, *Erfahrungen mit dem Heiligen Geist* (*Experiences with the Holy Spirit*). Following these come *Geistesgaben heute* (*Spiritual Gifts Today*) (1982), *Gemeinde: Erneuerung aus dem Geist Gottes I* (*Community: Renewal from the Spirit of God*) (1984), *Gemeinde: Erneuerung aus dem Geist Gottes II* (*Community: Renewal from the Spirit of God II*) (1985), and *Befreiende Gemeninschaft im Geist* (*Liberating Communion in the Spirit*) (1986). For an introduction to Mühlen's theology, including his Pneumatology, see Vondey, *Heribert Mühlen*.

23. Vondrey, *Heribert Mühlen*, xv. Unfortunately, the source of this quotation is not clear in the accompanying footnote. It may be from the work quoted in the next footnote, *Kirche wächst von Innen*.

24. Martin, "Interview with Fr. Mühlen," 4.

the Holy Spirit as recounted in the Sacred Scriptures and throughout the history of the Church. The second looked at how the Holy Spirit animates the Church and the individual believer, as well as giving an assessment of the Charismatic Renewal and Pentecostalism. The third investigated the Holy Spirit from the perspective of the development of the doctrine of the Holy Spirit in the Trinity and in the Sacraments. Here, particular attention was given to the issue of the *filioque*. In 1984 he published *The Word and the Spirit*, which looked specifically at the relationship between Pneumatology and Christology. Earlier than the Council, but not to be neglected, is his *Esquisses du Mystère de l'Eglise* (*Outline of the Mystery of the Church*), first published in 1941.

Other important theologians who take an interest in Pneumatology are Karl Rahner, Hans Urs von Balthasar, Louis Bouyer, and Walter Kasper. Published in English as *The Spirit and the Church* in 1979, this book of Rahner's is composed of three earlier works, *Erfahrung des Geistes*; *Das Charismatische in der Kirche*; *Visionen und Prophezeiungen* (*Experience of the Spirit* from 1977, and *The Charismatic in the Church* and *Visions and Prophecies*, both published in 1962). One could say that Rahner, in these last two mentioned works, was ahead of his time, in that, as yet there was no widespread manifestation of visions, prophecies, or other extraordinary charisms in the Catholic Church. Von Balthasar's more explicit work on the Holy Spirit is to be found in the third and fourth volumes of his five-volume *Explorations in Theology*. These are *Spiritus Creator* (1967) and *Pneuma and Institution* (1974). Yet he too seems to have been unconsciously ahead of his time, as in 1954 he published *Thomas und die Charismatik* (*Thomas and the Charismatics*). With Louis Bouyer the pnuematological *foci* are two, the Church and the Trinity. He addresses the first in his 1970 *The Church of God: Body of Christ and Temple of the Holy Spirit*. The second is addressed as one of three volumes on the Trinity, the third being *Le Consolateur: Esprit-Saint et Vie de Grace* (*The Consoler: Holy Spirit and Life of Grace*) in 1982. Finally, we have Walter Kasper's 1976 *Kirche: Ort des Geistes* (*The Church: Place of the Spirit*).

Departing briefly from Catholic shores, we should not neglect the works of important Orthodox and Protestant theologians such as Sergius Bulgakov's 1939 *The Comforter*, Paul Evdokimov's 1969 *L'Esprit Saint dans la Tradition Orthodoxe* (*The Holy Spirit in the Orthodox Tradition*), James D. G. Dunn's 1970 *Baptism in the Holy Spirit*, and Jürgen Moltmann's 1975 *The Church in the Power of the Spirit*.

Besides the work of these top tier theologians, we should pay attention also to that of some lesser, albeit shining, lights. From France we have the contribution of three biblical theologians, François-Xavier Durrwell with *The Holy Spirit of God: An Essay in Biblical Theology*, Ignace de la Potterie with *The Christian Lives by the Spirit*, and Stanislaus Lyonnet who, with de la Potterie, wrote *Life according to the Spirit: The Condition of the Christian*. From Italy we have the work of the sometime preacher to the Papal Household, Raniero Cantalamessa, with his two-volume *Sober Intoxication of the Spirit*, as well as *Life in Christ: A Spiritual Commentary on the Letter to the Romans*, *The Holy Spirit in the Life of Jesus*, and *Come, Creator Spirit*. And from Australia we have the work of a Professor Emeritus of the Catholic Institute of Sydney, David Coffey, with *The "Incarnation" of the Holy Spirit in Christ*, and *Grace: The Gift of the Holy Spirit*. We have liberation approaches to the Holy Spirit, such as Leonardo Boff's *Come, Holy Spirit*, and Joseph Comblin's *The Holy Spirit and Liberation*, feminist approaches such as Elizabeth Johnson's *Women, Earth, and Creator Spirit*, ecological approaches such as Denis Edward's *Breath of Life: A Theology of the Creator Spirit*, and something called Spirit Christology in the work of people like David Coffey, Ralph Del Colle, Myk Habets, Frank Macchia, and Piet Schoonenberg.[25] Finally, we have the work of theologians in the USA who themselves became involved in the Catholic Charismatic Renewal, such as the biblical scholar George Montague, as well as the theologians Donald Gelpi and Kilian McDonnell.[26]

I will not sail any further on this tack since, as the Finnish, sometime Pentecostal, now Lutheran theologian Velli-Matti Kärkkäinen wrote in 2010, "In recent years, one of the most exciting developments in theology has been an unprecedented interest in the Holy Spirit."[27] I think that anyone wanting a good introduction to this development could do worse than read the work of Kärkkäinen.[28] As a very recent example of a renewed interest in the Holy Spirit, I refer the reader to an article published in the *Irish Theological Quarterly* on June 7, 2022, by John Stayne. It is entitled, "Post-Conciliar Developments in the Catholic Doctrine of Charisms: *Lumen Gentium* and *Iuvenescit Ecclesia* Compared." As of the end of June 2023 it had over 550 views and downloads, an extraordinary amount of interest in such a short time.

25. See O'Byrne, *Spirit Christology and Trinity*; Del Colle, *Christ and the Spirit*; Habets, *Anointed Son*; Macchia, *Jesus the Spirit Baptizer*; Schoonenberg, "Spirit Christology and Logos Christology."

26. For example, see Montague, *Holy Spirit*; Gelpi, *Divine Mother*; McDonnell, *Other Hand of God*; McDonnell and Montague, *Christian Initiation and Baptism in the Holy Spirit*.

27. Kärkkäinen, *Holy Spirit and Salvation*, 1.

28. See Kärkkäinen, *Holy Spirit*; Kärkkäinen, *Spirit and Salvation*; Kärkkäinen, *Pneumatology*.

Taking all these above-mentioned theologians together, we find the following *foci*: the Holy Spirit and experience, the charismatic gifts, conversion, biblical theology, Trinitarian theology, Christology, Ecclesiology, Grace, Theological Anthropology, Social Justice, Women, and Creation. We can see that, as with all theology, it is not possible to focus on Pneumatology in isolation from every other aspect of theology. To speak about the Holy Spirit means also speaking about the theology of Revelation and Inspiration, the Trinity, the Christ, the Church, the sacraments of the Church, the mission of the Church, the human person, grace, human morality, creation, eschatology, spiritual theology, the work of the Holy Spirit outside the Church, and so on.

It also means speaking of not just the "content" of theology, but the "method" of theology as well. What role does the Holy Spirit play in how we theologize? At the very beginning of his book *Engaging the Doctrine of the Holy Spirit*, Matthew Levering quotes Graham Tomlin, who says that "today we need not just a theology *of* the Holy Spirit, but theology done *in* the Holy Spirit."[29] St. Paul tells us that we are to "live according to the Spirit" (Rom 8:2). Since theologizing is a part of living, this must mean that we are to theologize in accord with the Holy Spirit. Related to this need is a current division between what could be called spiritual or mystical theology on the one hand, and fundamental and dogmatic theology on the other. Various diagnoses have been given regarding the causes and chronology of this split, but many theologians indicate sometime in the Middle Ages, some placing it pre-Aquinas and Bonaventure, while others place it post. Thinking of this split as one that is gradually evolving can help to explain this divergence in opinion.[30] By way of a contemporary example, I am slowly working my way through the theology of Lieven Boeve, a postmodern Catholic theologian, who advocates what he calls a recontextualizing theology of interruption. Amongst the numerous deficiencies in this theology, one thing that strikes me is its thoroughly *a*-pneumatic character, both in method and content. Although Boeve occasionally mentions the Holy Spirit, he does not theologize about the Holy Spirit, nor does the Holy Spirit play any discernible role in how he theologizes.[31]

29. Levering, *Engaging the Doctrine of the Holy Spirit*, 1.

30. See McGregor, "Theology and Spirituality."

31. For example, see Boeve, *Interrupting Tradition*; Boeve, *God Interrupts History*; Boeve, *Lyotard and Theology*.

EIGHT DISPUTED QUESTIONS IN CONTEMPORARY PNEUMATOLOGY

I will now very briefly introduce some of the *quaestiones disputatae* in contemporary Pneumatology. Some of these will be addressed in subsequent chapters of this book. I will not be mentioning some issues that are not so much matters of dispute as of development. Many such issues will also be covered in this volume.

My disputed questions are eight in number. They are:

1. How should the Holy Spirit be named? For example, can he be named as Love and Gift?[32] This question is also related to how the Holy Spirit should be named in the Trinity. For example, is the triad Creator-Redeemer-Sanctifier a valid alternative to Father-Son-Holy Spirit?

2. Is Spirit Christology opposed to Logos Christology? This question draws us into the work of Catholic theologians such as Piet Schoonenberg, David Coffey, and Ralph Del Colle, as well Protestant theologians such as the Baptist Myk Habets, and the Pentecostal Frank Macchia.

3. Is there any solution to the Filioque controversy?[33]

4. What role does the Holy Spirit play in *theosis*?

5. Are the missions of Christ and the Holy Spirit separable?[34]

6. How is the Holy Spirit at work outside the visible temporal Church? These last two questions are especially related to the issue of the significance of non-Christian religions.[35]

7. Is Confirmation a sacrament in search of a theology?

8. How does the Holy Spirit inspire people? This includes the question of how the Holy Spirit inspires the Holy Scriptures.

---

32. For example, see Levering, *Engaging the Doctrine of the Holy Spirit*, 51–71.

33. On this question, see the Dicastery for Promoting Christian Unity, *Greek and the Latin Traditions*.

34. For example, see Kanjamela, "*Redemptoris Missio* and Mission in India," 203; McGregor, "Universal Work of the Holy Spirit."

35. For example, see Dupuis, *Toward a Christian Theology of Religious Pluralism*.

TWO PERSONAL INTERESTS

Since I do not get to give my own more specific chapter, I beg your indulgence in allowing me to finish with two points that have become particularly interesting to me. The first is a brief reflection on how the Holy Spirit might help us overcome what Joseph Ratzinger has called the "fundamental crisis of our age," which is "coming to an understanding of the mediation of history in the realm of ontology."[36] Is it possible that the Holy Spirit can help us overcome the apparent conflict between history and ontology? Ratzinger points out that while Christ has assumed human *nature*, the Holy Spirit is given to each *person*.[37] From this I conclude that the Holy Spirit is able to make the ontological Christ present in us in the historical now by transforming an ontological presence of Christ into a relational abiding presence. The Holy Spirit is new each day, and makes Christ present, the same yesterday, today, and forever (cf. Heb 13:8).

Another way of saying this is that the Holy Spirit can make the historical Christ present in us. There is only one Christ, who is both ontological and historical. On this point, I would like to quote Hans Urs von Balthasar's *Theology of History*. So von Balthasar writes,

> This carving out of a section of history in order to make it relevant to the whole of history is a process involving several factors, all interconnected in their dependence upon the Holy Spirit, but nonetheless distinguishable. The first concerns the working of the Spirit upon the Incarnate Son himself. . . . A second factor is the working of the Spirit as he relates to Christ, thus transformed, to the historical Church of every age, which is expressed typically in the sacraments, and most fully in the Eucharist. A third completes this relation by creating the missions of the Church and individual as applications of the life of Christ to every Christian life and the whole life of the Church.[38]

Of this passage Tracey Rowland says, "Prescriptively Balthasar observes that the task of making the historical existence of Christ the norm of every individual existence is the work of the Holy Spirit."[39]

The second point is a reflection on the seven gifts of the Holy Spirit. While these gifts were part of the standard fare of pre-Vatican II Pneumatology,

---

36. Ratzinger, *Principles of Catholic Theology*, 160.

37. Ratzinger, "Holy Spirit and the Church," 69–70.

38. Balthasar, *Theology of History*, 80.

39. Rowland, *Benedict XVI*, 111.

after the Council they seem largely to have disappeared from the menu. Yet these gifts are not just important, but crucial for living a life in the Spirit, which includes theologizing in the Spirit. Any attempt to theologize without the gifts of wisdom, knowledge, and understanding will not get very far.[40] This is because, as St. Francis de Sales tells us in his *Treatise on the Love of God*, these gifts are the very means by which we love God. While it is true that knowledge inspires love, the gifts of the Holy Spirit remind us also that love inspires knowledge. I will let St. Francis have the final say.

> Now, [these gifts] are not only inseparable from charity, but, all things well considered, and speaking precisely, they are the principal virtues, properties, and qualities of charity. For:

> *Wisdom* is in fact no other thing than the love which relishes, tastes, and experiences how sweet and delicious God is;

> *Understanding* is nothing else than love attentive to consider and penetrate the beauty of the truths of faith, to know thereby God in himself, and then descending from this to consider him in creatures;

> Science or *knowledge*, on the other hand, is but the same love, keeping us attentive to the knowledge of ourselves and creatures, to make us re-ascend to a more perfect knowledge of the service which we owe God;

> *Counsel* is also love, insomuch as it makes us careful, attentive, and wise in choosing the means proper to serve God holily;

> *Fortitude* is love encouraging and animating the heart, to execute that which counsel has determined should be done;

> *Piety* is the love which sweetens labor, and makes us, with good heart, with pleasure, and with a filial affection, employ ourselves in works which please God our Father;

> And to conclude, *Fear* is nothing but love insomuch as it makes us fly and avoid what is displeasing to the divine Majesty.[41]

---

40. The classic theological expositions of the gifts are to be found in St. Bonaventure's *Collations on the Seven Gifts of the Holy Spirit*; Aquinas, *Summa Theologica*, I–II, q. 68; Denis the Carthusian, *Gifts of the Holy Spirit*.

41. Francis de Sales, *Treatise on the Love of God*, book 11, chap. 15; emphasis added.

BIBLIOGRAPHY

Abbrescia, Domenico M. *Elena Guerra (1835–1914): Profetismo e Rinnovamento.* Brescia: Queriniana, 1970.

———. *Elena Guerra: Prophecy and Renewal.* Makati: Society of Saint Paul, 1982.

Aquinas, Thomas. *Summa Theologica.* Notre Dame: Christian Classics, 1981.

Balthasar, Hans Urs von. *Pneuma and Institution.* San Francisco: Ignatius, 1995.

———. *Spiritus Creator.* Einsiedeln: Johannes, 1967.

———. *A Theology of History.* London: Sheed & Ward, 1964.

———. *Thomas und die Charismatik: Kommentar Zu Thomas Von Aquin Summa Theologica Quaestiones II II 171–182: Besondere Gnadengaben und die zwei Wege menschlichen Lebens.* Einsiedeln: Johannes, 1996.

Boeve, Lieven. *God Interrupts History: Theology in a Time of Upheaval.* New York: Continuum International, 2007.

———. *Interrupting Tradition: An Essay on Christian Faith in a Postmodern Context.* Dudley, MA: Peeters, 2003.

———. *Lyotard and Theology: Beyond the Christian Master Narrative of Love.* London: Bloomsbury, 2014.

Boff, Leonardo. *Come, Holy Spirit: Inner Fire, Giver of Life, and Comforter of the Poor.* Maryknoll, NY: Orbis, 2015.

Bonaventure. *Collations on the Seven Gifts of the Holy Spirit.* Translated by Zachary Hayes. Works of St. Bonaventure 14. St. Bonaventure, NY: Franciscan Institute, 2008.

Bouyer, Louis. *The Church of God: Body of Christ and Temple of the Holy Spirit.* Chicago: Franciscan Herald, 1982.

———. *Le Consolateur: Esprit-Saint et Vie de Grace.* Paris: Cerf, 1982.

Bulgakov, Sergius. *The Comforter.* Grand Rapids: Eerdmans, 2004.

Cantalamessa, Raniero. *Come, Creator Spirit: Meditations on the Veni Creator.* Collegeville, MN: Liturgical, 2003.

———. *The Holy Spirit in the Life of Jesus: The Mystery of Christ's Baptism.* Collegeville, MN: Liturgical, 1994.

———. *Life in the Lordship of Christ: A Spiritual Commentary on the Letter to the Romans for a New Evangelization.* Kansas City, MO: Sheed & Ward, 1990.

———. *Sober Intoxication of the Spirit: Filled with the Fullness of God.* Cincinnati: Servant, 2005.

———. *Sober Intoxication of the Spirit, Part 2: Born Again of Water and the Spirit.* Cincinnati: Servant, 2012.

Coffey, David. *Grace: The Gift of the Holy Spirit.* Manly: Catholic Institute of Sydney, 1979.

———. *The "Incarnation" of the Holy Spirit in Christ.* Sydney: Catholic Institute of Sydney, 1984.

Comblin, Joseph. *The Holy Spirit and Liberation.* Maryknoll, NY: Orbis, 1989.

Congar, Yves. *Esquisses du Mystère de l'Eglise.* Paris: Cerf, 1941.

———. *I Believe in the Holy Spiri.* 3 vols. New York: Seabury, 1983.

———. *The Word and the Spirit.* London: Chapman, 1986.

Del Colle, Ralph. *Christ and the Spirit: Spirit-Christology in Trinitarian Perspective.* Oxford: Oxford University Press, 1994.

Denis the Carthusian. *Gifts of the Holy Spirit.* Dublin: Columba, 2013.

Dicastery for Promoting Christian Unity. *The Greek and the Latin Traditions regarding the Procession of the Holy Spirit?* http://www.christianunity.va/content/unitacristiani/en/documenti/altri-testi/en1.html.

Dunn, James D. G. *Baptism in the Holy Spirit: A Re-examination of the New Testament Teaching on the Gift of the Spirit in Relation to Pentecostalism Today.* London: SCM, 1970.

Dupuis, Jacques. *Toward a Christian Theology of Religious Pluralism.* Maryknoll, NY: Orbis, 2001.

Durrwell, François-Xavier. *The Holy Spirit of God: An Essay in Biblical Theology.* London: Chapman, 1986.

Edwards, Denis. *Breath of Life: A Theology of the Creator Spirit.* Maryknoll, NY: Orbis, 2004.

Evdokimov, Paul. *L'Esprit Saint dans la Tradition Orthodoxe.* Paris: Cerf, 1969.

Francis. *Evangelii Gaudium.* Strathfield: St. Pauls, 2013.

Francis de Sales. *Treatise on the Love of God.* Translated by Henry Benedict Mackay. Blacksburg, VA: Wilder, 2011.

Gelpi, Donald. *The Divine Mother: A Trinitarian Theology of the Holy Spirit.* Lanham, MD: University Press of America, 1984.

Habets, Myk. *The Anointed Son: A Trinitarian Spirit Christology.* Eugene, OR: Pickwick, 2010.

Johnson, Elizabeth E. *Women, Earth, and Creator Spirit.* New York: Paulist, 1993.

Kanjamela, Augustine. "*Redemptoris Missio* and Mission in India." In *Redemption and Dialogue: Reading Redemptoris Missio and Dialogue and Proclamation*, edited by William R. Burrows, 195–205. Maryknoll, NY: Orbis, 1994.

Kärkkäinen, Velli-Matti. *The Holy Spirit.* Louisville: Westminster John Knox, 2012.

———, ed. *Holy Spirit and Salvation: The Sources of Christian Theology.* Louisville: Westminster John Knox, 2010.

———. *Pneumatology: The Holy Spirit in Ecumenical, International, and Contextual Perspective.* 2nd. ed. Grand Rapids: Baker Academic, 2018.

———. *Spirit and Salvation.* Grand Rapids: Eerdmans, 2016.

Kasper, Walter. *Kirche: Ort des Geistes.* Freiburg: Herder, 1976.

Knox, Ronald. *Enthusiasm: A Chapter in the History of Religion.* Oxford: Clarendon, 1950.

La Potterie, Ignace de. *The Christian Lives by the Spirit.* Staten Island, NY: Alba House, 1971.

La Potterie, Ignace de, and Stanislaus Lyonnet. *Life according to the Spirit: The Condition of the Christian.* Staten Island, NY: Alba House, 1971.

Leen, Edward. *The Holy Ghost and His Work in Souls.* London: Sheed & Ward, 1937.

Leo XIII. *Divinum Illud Munus.* https://www.vatican.va/content/leo-xiii/en/encyclicals/documents/hf_l-xiii_enc_09051897_divinum-illud-munus.html.

———. *Provida Matris Caritate.* https://www.vatican.va/content/leo-xiii/it/briefs/documents/hf_l-xiii_brief_18950505_provida-matris.html.

Levering, Matthew. *Engaging the Doctrine of the Holy Spirit.* Grand Rapids: Baker Academic, 2016.

Macchia, Frank D. *Jesus the Spirit Baptizer: Christology in Light of Pentecost.* Grand Rapids: Eerdmans, 2018.

Mansfield, Patti Gallagher. *As by a New Pentecost: The Dramatic Beginning of the Catholic Charismatic Renewal.* Steubenville, OH: Franciscan University Press, 1992.

———. "Blessed Elena Guerra: Apostle of the Holy Spirit." *Renewal Ministries*, May 24, 2022. https://www.renewalministries.net/blessed-elena-guerra-apostle-of-the-holy-spirit/.

Martin, Ralph. "An Interview with Fr. Mühlen." *New Covenant* 4 (1974) 4.

McGregor, Peter John. "Theology and Spirituality." In *Healing Fractures in Contemporary Theology*, edited by Peter John McGregor and Tracey Rowland, 1–40. Eugene, OR: Cascade, 2022.

———. "The Universal Work of the Holy Spirit in the Missiology of Pope John Paul II." *Irish Theological Quarterly* 77 (2012) 83–98.

McDonnell, Kilian. *The Other Hand of God: The Holy Spirit as the Universal Touch and Goal*. Collegeville, MN: Liturgical, 2003.

McDonnell, Kilian, and George Montague. *Christian Initiation and Baptism in the Holy Spirit: Evidence from the First Eight Centuries*. Rev. ed. Collegeville, MN: Liturgical, 1994.

Möhler, Johann Adam. *Unity in the Church, or, the Principle of Catholicism*. Edited and translated by Peter C. Erb. Washington, DC: The Catholic University of America Press, 1996.

Moltmann, Jürgen. *The Church in the Power of the Spirit: A Contribution to Messianic Ecclesiology*. London: SCM, 1977.

Montague, George. *The Holy Spirit: The Growth of a Biblical Tradition*. New York: Paulist, 1976.

Mühlen, Heribert. *Befreiende Gemeinschaft im Geist: Persönliche Zeugnisse aus Familie, Orden, Lebens gemeinschaften: Weg aus der Krise III*. Mainz: Matthais-Grünwald, 1986.

———. *Einübung in die christliche Grunderfahrung*. 2 vols. Mainz: Matthais-Grünwald, 1976.

———. *Erfahrungen mit dem Heiligen Geist*. Mainz: Matthais-Grünwald, 1979.

———. *Die Erneuerung des christlichen Glaubens: Charisma, Geist, Befreiung*. München: Don Bosco, 1974.

———. *Geistesgaben heute*. Mainz: Matthais-Grünwald, 1982.

———. *Gemeinde: Erneuerung aus dem Geist Gottes I: Berichte au seiner Großstadtgemeinde*. Mainz: Matthais-Grünwald, 1984.

———. *Gemeinde: Erneurung aus dem Geist Gottes II: Zeugnisse, Berichte, Hoffung für die Ökumene*. Mainz: Matthais-Grünwald, 1985.

———. *Der Heilige Geist als Person: Beitrag zur Frage nach der dem Heiligen Geiste eigentümlichen Funktion in der Trinitat, bei der Inkarnation und im Gnadenbund*. Münster: Aschendorff, 1963.

———. *Una Mystica Persona: Die Kirche als das Mysterium der heilsgeschichtlichen Identitat des Heiligen Geistes in Christus und den Christen: Eine Person in vielen Personen*. Paderborn: Schöningh, 1964.

O'Byrne, Declan. *Spirit Christology and Trinity in the Theology of David Coffey*. Bern: Lang, 2010.

Owens, Robert. "The Azuza Street Revival: The Pentecostal Movement Begins in America." In *The Century of the Holy Spirit: 100 Years of Pentecostal and Charismatic Renewal*, edited by Vinson Synan, 39–68. Nashville: Nelson, 2001.

Rahner, Karl. *The Spirit and the Church*. London: Burns & Oates, 1979.

Ratzinger, Joseph. "The Holy Spirit and the Church." In *Images of Hope*, 63–73. San Francisco: Ignatius, 2006.

————. *Principles of Catholic Theology: Building Stones for a Fundamental Theology.* Translated by Mary Frances McCarthy. San Francisco: Ignatius, 1987.

Rowland, Tracey. *Benedict XIV: A Guide for the Perplexed.* London: T. & T. Clark, 2010.

Scheeben, Matthias. *The Glories of Divine Grace.* Saint Meinrad, IN: Grail, 1946.

————. *Handbook of Catholic Dogmatics.* Steubenville, OH: Emmaus Academic, 2019.

Schoonenberg, Piet. "Spirit Christology and Logos Christology." *Bijdagen* 38 (1977) 350–75.

Stayne, John. "Post-Conciliar Developments in the Catholic Doctrine of Charisms: *Lumen Gentium* and *Iuvenescit Ecclesia* Compared." *Irish Theological Quarterly* 87 (2022) 192–211.

Synan, Vinson, ed. *The Century of the Holy Spirit: 100 Years of Pentecostal and Charismatic Renewal.* Nashville: Nelson, 2001.

————. "Pentecostal Roots." In *The Century of the Holy Spirit: 100 Years of Pentecostal and Charismatic Renewal*, edited by Vinson Synan, 15–37. Nashville: Nelson, 2001.

Vondey, Wolfgang. *Heribert Mühlen: His Theology and Praxis: A New Profile of the Church.* Lanham, MD: University Press of America, 2004.

Wilcox, Cheryl. "Exploring the Roots of the Catholic Charismatic Renewal." *Christian Broadcasting Network*, December 10, 2022. https://www2.cbn.com/article/holy-spirit/exploring-roots-catholic-charismatic-renewal.

2

THE WORK OF PNEUMA IN THE EMPTINESS OF GOLGOTHA

Nigel Zimmermann

INTRODUCTION

What was the Holy Spirit doing when Jesus died on the Cross? According to Christian tradition, the Pneuma of God is associated with the events of Pentecost, some fifty days after the resurrection. Christians do not normally associate the images of the Spirit—breath, fire, the dove—with the stark symmetry of the Cross, in its sorrow and hope, and the emptiness it bears in Christ's death. And yet, Trinitarian theology insists upon a purposeful work of unity between the persons of the Godhead which, logically, requires of the Spirit a role at the Cross. In the emptiness of Golgotha, the "place of the Skull," the death of Jesus marks the moment of paradox in which a new kind of life begins, one that is robustly spiritual in nature. Our understanding of the points of continuity between the Crucifixion and the life of the Spirit after the Resurrection is not always well defined.

The problem of soteriology's relationship with pneumatology will be studied as the context in which these questions can be considered. Some possibilities for a "cruciform Pneumatology" are weighed in light of a broader tradition including post-Vatican II language from St. John Paul II, and the patristic theology of St. Maximus the Confessor. While we might give our theological attention to the Second Person of the Trinity in the narratives of the Passion, death and Resurrection, there is a work of the Spirit at the Cross deserving of closer analysis and better understanding.

"AN INTIMATE BOND": SOTERIOLOGY AND PNEUMATOLOGY

The narrative of the Cross centers upon the Second Person of the Trinity, by whose sacrifice the course of salvation is made possible. Logically, theologies of salvation take up their foci in the person and work of Christ, whereas in pneumatology, our theology shifts focus to the work of the Third Person of the Trinity. There is an overlooked relationship at work, one that can remain both focused on Christ and the Spirit, without detriment to the work of the Cross. It is helpful to begin with the Biblical witness, as Mark's Gospel describes:

> And they compelled a passer-by, Simon of Cyrene, who was coming in from the country, the father of Alexander and Rufus, to carry his cross. And they brought him to the place called Golgotha (which means the place of a skull). And they offered him wine mingled with myrrh; but he did not take it. And they crucified him, and divided his garments among them, casting lots for them, to decide what each should take. And it was the third hour, when they crucified him. And the inscription of the charge against him read, "The King of the Jews." And with him they crucified two robbers, one on his right and one on his left. And those who passed by derided him, wagging their heads, and saying, "Aha! You who would destroy the temple and build it in three days, save yourself, and come down from the cross!" (Mark 15:21–30)[1]

In Mark's Gospel, the derision aimed at the crucified Jesus is indicative of weakness and loss, culminating in the mocking voice of power calling for Him to "come down from the cross." When the Christian believers give witness to the Cross in some fashion, do they derive significance of the work of the Holy Spirit in that narrative, or simply rely on the power of the Spirit as it has been given at Pentecost?[2] The ancient Jewish conviction that God's breath—His πνεῦμα—was given freely and powerfully to form a People, cannot simply be negated or fall away at the moment of divine suffering. A question persists about the appropriate and the best way to understand the work of God's Spirit in the events of Christ's relenting to suffering and

---

1. Biblical references in this chapter are from the New Revised Standard Version Catholic Edition.

2. A good signifier of the theological problem here is that in many spiritual works about the Passion and the Cross, scant attention is given to the Holy Spirit. For example, in the classic spiritual text by A. G. Sertillanges, *What Jesus Saw from the Cross*, no mention is made of the Spirit throughout.

death. John Paul II provides a partial answer in *Dominum et Vivificantem*, emphasizing the unbreakable bond between the three persons of the Trinity:

> Between the Holy Spirit and Christ there thus subsists, in the economy of salvation, an intimate bond, whereby the Spirit works in human history as "another Counselor," permanently ensuring the transmission and spreading of the Good News revealed by Jesus of Nazareth. Thus, in the Holy Spirit-Paraclete, who in the mystery and action of the Church unceasingly continues the historical presence on earth of the Redeemer and his saving work, the glory of Christ shines forth, as the following words of John attest: "He [the Spirit of truth] will glorify me, for he will take what is mine and declare it to you."[3]

For John Paul II, it was important to emphasize the living union of the three divine persons, but he gave particular attention here to the work of the Spirit in the world. Such a work is a witness to the truth, out of which unfolds a concrete unity, thus offering a vision that makes the Spirit an essential element to mission and *ecclesia*. John Paul II's emphasis is upon a living Spirit whose union with the other persons of the Godhead is the "supreme source" of unity for Christian disciples who are bound together in the same truth from the same source.[4] As Jean Daniélou puts it: "There is no unity save in truth possessed in common."[5] The notion of the Holy Spirit as "another Counselor" sent by the Father and the Son provides a permanence to the possibility of transmitting and sharing the Gospel as the fundamental fruit of that truth.

Lumen Gentium says that "discernment in matters of faith is aroused and sustained by the Spirit of truth."[6] The Second Vatican Council taught of the ongoing and continuous life of the Spirit, "sustaining" the life of faith in a way that requires a "sensitivity" to the Spirit's movement in the world.[7] There is no place in the Conciliar theology of the Holy Spirit for a static account of the Spirit or of its effectual life in the Church. A life of active listening, reflection, and prayerful engagement with the Spirit is a consequence if any human life is to effectively give witness to the life-changing event of the Incarnation. While it could be argued that Western Catholic theology has not always shone as strong a light as it should have upon the work of the Holy Spirit, it can be equally argued that the Spirit

---

3. John Paul II, *Dominum et Vivificantem*, sec. 7.

4. John Paul II, *Dominum et Vivificantem*, sec. 2.

5. Daniélou, *Scandal of Truth*, 111.

6. Second Vatican Council, *Lumen Gentium*, sec. 12.

7. Second Vatican Council, *Apostolicam Actuositatem*, sec. 29.

has certainly been "experienced" regardless as to how much He has been written of.[8] The giving of witness is not abstracted by the Persons or Persons who grant the means by which that work is undertaken. Witness is not ethereal and unanchored in the world, but instead it is intimately given as a presence of Christ himself, as Gerald O'Collins has argued: "Any and every acceptance of saving grace and the Holy Spirit, whenever it takes place, is an acceptance of Christ."[9] By "acceptance," O'Collins outlines a notion of active engagement with the person of Christ, and of an energetic echoing of Christ's presence within one's own life and activities. The perspective of post-Conciliar Catholic mission is such that the Spirit is an essential ingredient and an ongoing one both to the Triune life in and of itself, as well as to the life of discipleship in Christ Jesus.

Turning to Christology in a way that values Christ's self-offering and centrality to the Christian life requires a precise Pneumatology, for the witness of Christ is to a Kingdom in which the Spirit acts fully and freely. T. F. Torrance says:

> How can we undertake this without a thorough reassessment of the whole doctrine of the Spirit, especially in relation to the humanity of Christ, but also in relation to the doctrine of the Trinity? It does not seem possible to undertake a very radical reconstruction of christology without a far deeper and more exacting pneumatology. The spectrum of thought runs, *from* the Father, *through* the Son and *in* the Spirit, so that *through* the Son must be thought out not only in respect of *from* the Father but in respect of *in* the Spirit.[10]

Here, Torrance builds upon a Christo-centricity with a view to a complete spiritual transformation that begins in the emptiness of Golgotha. The paradox becomes clear: An intimate union for each of us with the divine Son becomes possible because of his self-emptying love for all Creation, and the beginning of a new life in the Spirit. Such a different and redeemed path is both manifest in the world at the same time that the Spirit remains invisible, hidden, discrete, known only in the immateriality of spiritual things. Edith Stein called such a knowing a "permanent possession" gained by a "continual engagement" with the Holy Spirit.[11] Hans Urs von Balthasar took from John Paul II's encyclical on the Holy Spirit a particular focus upon the freedom that emerges from such engagement. He refers to "the spirit of

8. Boulding, "Doctrine of the Holy Spirit," 253–54.

9. O'Collins, *Christology*, 301.

10. Torrance, *Incarnation*, 86.

11. Stein, "Activity of the Spirit," 116.

truth" (John 16:3) and the spirit "of freedom" (2 Cor 3:17) of which New Testament Christianity speaks, of the one who creates the space in which we become liberated.[12] For Balthasar, a key to understanding the Holy Spirit in John Paul II's thought can be found in his encyclical on the divine Father, *Dives in Misericordia*:

> At the core of this work stands the declaration not only that the Incarnate Son is the revelation of the Father's love to the world, but that his surrender to the Cross and God-forsakenness, his having "been made sin," brings to light the whole depth of this love as mercy for mankind in its guilt.[13]

The point Balthasar makes, so crucial to the soteriology/pneumatology relationship, is that when the Spirit comes to us, it is as a result of the Father's own love, revealed in the event of the Cross and "God-forsakenness." The depths of the Father's love are endless and invisible, but made visible through the finite means of the Cross through the power of the Spirit.[14] John Paul II taught profoundly of an intimate union in which the activities of the Son and the Spirit are always manifestations of the Father's love, and as such, the work of the Spirit also has a soteriological dimension. The line between the Cross and the Spirit is both essential and lacking in clarity, which if paradoxes are a central aspect of Christian belief, could be described as entirely keeping within character.

TOWARDS A CRUCIFORM PNEUMATOLOGY?

An Australian theologian, Carolyn Tan, has written in support of a *"pneumatologia crucis."*[15] Tan's essential claim regarding the relationship between Pentecost and the Cross is this: "The Holy Spirit cannot be separated from the incarnate Son. Pentecost cannot be separated from the cross, because Pentecost would not have been possible without the cross."[16] The work of the Holy Spirit is one of intimate union with the Son, to the point of Jesus' death upon the Cross, in which the cooperative work of the Spirit is witnessed, by sign and activity, as the one giving life in circumstances of kenotic loving witness to the Father. The Holy Spirit, therefore, has a role, perhaps even a mission, at the site of the Cross, and is present in the

---

12. Balthasar, "Commentary," 851.
13. Balthasar, "Commentary," 842.
14. John Paul II, *Dives in Misericordia*, sec. 2.
15. Tan, *Spirit at the Cross*, 29.
16. Tan, *Spirit at the Cross*, 285.

emptiness of Christ's death. How can we describe this presence? What can we say of the work of the Spirit at Calvary?

For Tan, an active involvement of the Spirit at the Cross can be defended biblically, especially on the basis of the "pneumatological context of Hebrews," in which the Spirit unites believers to the Father and makes possible the birth of a new humanity.[17] Tan's work draws modern theologians into a question that is not perhaps at the forefront of contemporary religious debate, but it is not without significance. The three writers Tan makes most use of are John Vernon Taylor (1914–2001), Jürgen Moltmann (1926–), and John Zizioulas (1931–). These voices, an Anglican clergyman, a German Reformed Christian and a Greek Orthodox bishop, are not a comprehensive cross section of modern theologians, but they do represent various perspectives from the East-West Christian expanse, and they are marked by the language and concerns of a post-World War II mindset, bearing the marks of modernity's struggle with Christian faith after a magnitude of death and international disorder. These are important voices to consider, but outside of St. Augustine, Tan does not give ample consideration to a longer history of theological debate about the Person and Work of the Holy Spirit.

Tan's work is important because of its depth, at a time when the soteriology/pneumatology relationship is commonly not given a critical evaluation, or simply taken for granted. Her approach is through a de-sacramentalized and largely Barthian lens, but a key point being that "the Holy Spirit is the Spirit of Jesus Christ."[18] The term most important here with regard to the kind of activity displayed by the Spirit is that of power; of the capacity to take on human flesh by its own will and to sustain the very existence of the cosmos out of an indescribable love, and of an empowerment given to the Christ so that he "lives, teaches, performs miracles, dies, and lives again."[19] Tan links the power of Christ's spiritual conquering of sin and death to his role as the ultimate judge, and in his authority over the end of time and of history.[20] Because of her engagement of Barth's Calvinist Christology with figures like Taylor, Moltmann, and Zizioulas, Tan's work is an insightful and helpful study of how we can understand the Cross and the Holy Spirit in reference to the fullness of Christ and the sheer gift of grace. Helpfully, Tan outlines what she calls a "multifaceted *Pneumatologia Crucis*," identifying numerous sub-categories in which to theologize about

17. Tan, *Spirit at the Cross*, 284.

18. Tan, *Spirit at the Cross*, 232.

19. Tan, *Spirit at the Cross*, 233.

20. Tan, *Spirit at the Cross*, 244–47.

the Spirit's place at Golgotha, including "Spirit as 'Bond of love,'" "Spirit as Coworker with the Son," "Spirit as Unifier," culminating in a description of the Cross as "Crucible" under which the following categories are relevant: "Spirit as Divine Power," "Spirit as Divine Unifier," and "Spirit as Consuming Fire."[21] Each of these are compelling accounts of the Spirit at work, always intimately expressing a union of divine nature with the Son, on *missio* from the Father. There are elements of Tan's work that might be developed from a richly Catholic perspective, such as the place of Mary at the foot of the Cross who, in her own way, gives witness to the Spirit and to Christ, or to the Eucharist in its re-presentation of the once-and-for-all events of the Passion among God's People in the power of the Spirit. In both Mary and the Eucharist, the sacrifice of the Cross and the life of the Spirit are essential aspects of a broader narrative in which God meets his people in the risen Body of the Son, while still bearing his wounds in love (cf. Luke 24:40).

Tan has opened up an important conversation about the Spirit and the Cross, but we are far from a conclusion on the topic. A significant patristic voice helps to situate the work of redemption in a broader context, and in this respect the Byzantine St. Maximus the Confessor (c. 580–662) can help us.

MAXIMUS THE CONFESSOR ON SIN AND THE REDEMPTION OF THE CROSS

Maximus has been a point of connection between Eastern and Western traditions, emphasizing in his teaching that all of creation is dynamic and destined to glory, which Christ assumed in its fullness so that he might restore "the entire cosmos in a united harmony."[22] Hans Urs von Balthasar writes of Maximus' "evangelical love, which has renounced all power of its own," and of a charity that emerges powerfully from his "passionate vulnerability."[23] Maximus is known particularly for his account of the cosmic liturgy, of a hierarchical reality in which we participate in mediations of divine glory, recalling others around us to that same divine life.[24] The cosmic order in which we live is one of graduated glory in a vertical and upwards direction (this language is obviously analogical), but one also subject to the corruption resulting from sin. The First Adam let not only humanity but all of Creation into an environment in which sin corrodes in subtle and pervasive habits of

21. Tan, *Spirit at the Cross*, 250, 251, 252, 255–63.
22. Meyendorff, *Living Tradition*, 130.
23. Balthasar, *Cosmic Liturgy*, 30.
24. Louth, *Maximus the Confessor*, 75.

fragmentation and dis-unity; the conditions of which can only be overcome by the Word of God.[25]

Henri De Lubac writes of Maximus' account of sin and redemption:

> Maximus the Confessor considers original sin as a separation, a breaking up; we might even say, individualization, in the bad sense of the word. While God acts unceasingly in the world to make everything work in unity, by sin (which is man's deed) "the one nature was broken into a thousand pieces," and humanity, which ought to constitute a harmonious whole with mine and thine unopposed, became a dust of individuals with violent discordant tendencies. "Now," Maximus concludes, "we tear one another like wild beasts." "Satan has scattered us," Cyril of Alexandria used to say in explaining the Fall and the need for a Redeemer. And in a curious passage, in which there can still be heard the echo of an ancient myth, Augustine gives symbolically an analogous explanation. After associating the four letters of the name of Adam with the four points of the compass in their Greek form, he adds: "Adam therefore hath been scattered over the whole world. He was in one place and fell, and as in a manner broken small, he filled the whole world."[26]

Maximus offers a poetic rendering of the notion of the fruit of sin being a scattering to the far ends of the earth, of a fragmentation in brokenness and disunity, of the opposing pole to harmony and concord. As de Lubac shows, Maximus is in good company on this point with Cyril of Alexandria and Augustine. Elsewhere Maximus refers to the union of everything with God as achievable only after the human person deals with its "own division," leaving it behind as intermediate steps are taken towards a higher goal of unity in God, in which there is "no division."[27] The division of which Maximus speaks is that of original sin, and it is no accident that he uses violent imagery to convey the fruit of that division. Its result is a scattering of Adam in all of Adam's children, and of a distance that arises as each part separates from its counterparts. The division intermingles with divisiveness, and disunity becomes the interruption of good order and human flourishing. The alternate to the division and divisiveness of sin is the one pure nature of God, "simple, of one form, unqualified, peaceful, and undisturbed."[28] Only by a clear rendering of sin and its bad fruits, and of the

25. Louth, *Maximus the Confessor*, 64.

26. Lubac, *Catholicisme*, 10–11.

27. Maximus the Confessor, "Difficulty 41," 157.

28. Maximus the Confessor, "Four Hundred Chapters on Love," 9.

Byzantine theological emphasis upon sin as *division*, can the good work of the Cross be seen for what it is in Maximus, and the concordant witness of the Spirit of God at Calvary.

While Maximus does not dwell at length upon the Cross, its importance cannot be understated. The Cross, for all the witness of its inflicted pain and misery, is also the site of emptiness and death, of a letting-go and a kind of non-being, the site in which the "Word of God was crucified for us out of weakness" in the midst of the whole work of Incarnation.[29] As much as the positive activity of walking the way of the Cross captures our imagination, it reaches its pinnacle in the giving up or the "yielding" of the Spirit (Matt 27:50). The ultimate purpose of the Incarnation, insofar as human destiny is concerned, is no less than the consummation of our whole selves with the inner life of God, referred to by Maximus as an "ecstasy."[30] For Hans Urs von Balthasar, the beginning of Creation's salvific re-unifying towards such an ecstatic objective begins, in light of Maximus' account of the Incarnation, with the work of the Cross:

> The Incarnation—put more sharply, this means the descent into suffering, the Cross, and the grave and the resurrection of the creature who has been burned out in death and so has become transparent for God—is thus the final form of the world, the one that reshapes all other natural forms. Everything takes its decisive meaning and its ultimate justification only from here.[31]

The transparency of the creature, in which God chooses to be seen and witnessed, is made possible by the death of the self, which only the path of the Cross provides. In this sense the cosmological drama centers history upon the Cross, giving it a decisive part in the beginning of the new Creation. Such a moment is foreshadowed before all the ages (1 Cor 2:7; Col 1:26; 1 Pet 1:20) in the pre-eminence of Christ who perceives all stages of the history in his gaze, oriented as it is as the beginning and the end.[32]

For our purposes, Maximus becomes of interest because of the important role of the Holy Spirit in relation to the revelation of Christ, albeit understated and, possibly, underdeveloped in comparison with his

---

29. Maximus the Confessor, "Chapters on Knowledge," 153.

30. While it is not a focus of the present chapter, the Eastern distinction, going back to St. Gregory Palamas, is crucial to remember, in which the divine essence (unknowable and unseen) is distinct from divine energies (in which the life of God acts in the world and human affairs). See Meyendorff, *Christ in Eastern Christian Thought*, 146–47.

31. Balthasar, *Cosmic Liturgy*, 278.

32. Blowers and Wilken, "Introduction," 34.

Christological emphases. For Maximus, what happens in the person of Christ does not convey any conceptualization of change or movement in God himself, for such change belongs only to movable creatures like ourselves, as he puts it:

> This is the great and hidden mystery, at once the blessed end for which all things are ordained. It is the divine purpose conceived before the beginning of created beings. In defining it we would say that this mystery is the preconceived goal for which everything exists, but which itself exists on account of nothing. With a clear view to this end, God created the essences of created beings, and such is, properly speaking, the terminus of his providence and of the things under his providential care. Inasmuch as it leads to God, it is the recapitulation of the things he has created.[33]

The unmoved mover, we might suggest, who created all things, is the point of focus and orientation in the person of Jesus Christ. The great mystery of Christ's incarnation, of the participation of the supernatural in the fallenness of nature, is something "known solely to the Father, the Son, and the Holy Spirit before all the ages."[34] While only one knowledge is shared between the three persons of the Godhead, the manner of that knowledge can be distinguished, in that the Father first knows the mystery, the Son carries out its work, and the Holy Spirit cooperates with it.[35] The cooperation of the Holy Spirit does not wax and wane according to different modes of work undertaken by Christ, but is rather one of consistent energy and conviction. We have to keep in mind that for Maximus, Christology is the convergence of apophatic and cataphatic theology, in which God's work in Christ is the work of the unmoved mover who, paradoxically, can only be known to us via the language of "movement."[36] The movement, reflecting as it is the unmoved Son, is the beginning of a work which is ultimately experienced within the human person as conversion, redemption and, ultimately, deification.

Adam Cooper has argued for the crucial part of the body in a comprehensive understanding of deification.[37] Cooper does not find in deification an unlimited possibility for anthropological change and development, but a means by which the limited and conditioned body is

33. Maximus the Confessor, *On the Cosmic Mystery of Jesus Christ*, 124.

34. Maximus the Confessor, *On the Cosmic Mystery of Jesus Christ*, 127.

35. Maximus the Confessor, *On the Cosmic Mystery of Jesus Christ*.

36. Louth, *Maximus the Confessor*, 52.

37. Cooper, *Body in St. Maximus the Confessor*.

transfigured; changed gradually in light of that which does not change. Cooper notes Maximus' realism about human living, that the body, like all visible or material realities, needs a "cross" of some kind to avoid the lie that it is without limit.[38] A boundary experience is necessary for things in the world, creating clearly the space in which that living thing can find purpose and flourish, and in which it experiences a suffering or, perhaps minimally in most cases, a kind of deprivation. The body seeks after its end in the plenitude of Trinitarian life, experiencing the nature of the Cross, of suffering and finitude, not as the *end* but as a *means* by which it can find its way home in God. Cooper says: "There alone is the purpose of the universe fulfilled, and God 'proclaimed to be truly a Father by Grace.'"[39] The path of deification begins in the person and work of Christ, and on this point, the work or the role of the Holy Spirit at the place of the Cross is significant. If the work of the Cross is the beginning of salvation, then the Holy Spirit's cooperation with that task will need to be consistent and invested, spurring on the event of re-Creation in the world.

The role of the Cross is also for Karl Barth a witness to the unity of the Spirit with Christ. Barth maintains a strict adherence to the Trinity as the preeminent foundation for theology, holding to an Augustinian principle: *omnia opera Trinitatis ad extra sunt indivisa* ("all the outward works of the Trinity are undivided"). The Triune God, revealed in Christ Jesus, is an operation of perfect personal unity, undivided and indivisible. For Barth, there is no contradiction between the specificity of the Persons of the Trinity and a unity of their works, thus "the Father is the Creator, but the Son and the Spirit are also Creator with him."[40]

While readers of Barth will be conscious of his focus on Christology, Philip Rosato has observed that his pneumatological insights become progressively pronounced in his later works.[41] The reconciling work of the Cross is, for Barth, the primary point of revelation about the meaning of Christ's work, but the Spirit as the bond of love in the Godhead is a point of focus given increased attention by him in his later works.[42] Barth says:

> Just as the Holy Spirit, as Himself an eternal divine "person" or mode of being as the Spirit of the Father and the Son (*qui ex Patre Filioque procedit*), is the bond of peace between the two, so in the historical work of the reconciliation He is the One

38. Cooper, *Body in St. Maximus the Confessor*, 252.
39. Cooper, *Body in St. Maximus the Confessor*, 254.
40. Tan, *Spirit at the Cross*, 223.
41. Rosato, *Spirit as Lord*, 121.
42. Tan, *Spirit at the Cross*, 241.

> who constitutes and guarantees the unity of the totus Christus,
> ie of Jesus Christ in the heights and in the depths, in His
> transcendence and in His immanence.[43]

The Spirit, according to Barth, is not only a bond of peace but an active guarantee of the unity of Christ in himself, of his "heights and in the depths," of what might be called the vertical with the horizontal dimensions of Christ's work. This approach returns us to Maximus' insight of the dialectic at work in the revelation of God, of a "dark radiance" that draws close to human experience.[44] In the Incarnation, the divine transcendence appears as the wholly other of God "precisely in this burgeoning immanence" of the meeting of earth and heaven.[45] The Spirit, whose work in Christ reaches its summit in the self-offering of the Cross, is the one whose greatness does not belong in the world, and yet makes itself present in that strangely meagre place. It is for this reason that the Cross, and the whole work of Christ and His Spirit in the world, bears a cosmic significance and not merely an anthropocentric one. The Christ is the Logos who is all-in-all, uniting and not dividing the fragility of human persons with the whole cosmic order in which they live, bearing out the meeting of the horizontal-vertical cross. Maximus refers to the "spiritual configuration of the kingdom which has no beginning, a configuration characterized, as has been shown, by humility and meekness of heart."[46] Glory appears darkly radiant, not altogether obvious without the eyes of humility and meekness, and it performs its work in the ordinary and material stuff of human activity. The beginning of such humility, shining perfectly in a spirit of proclamation in the cry of the Cross, can be located in Golgotha, in which emptiness and self-offering become—without any movement or change within the Godhead—the event of the Father's "innermost depth" on display in the "whole mystery of Christ." That is to say, the depths of God's love, despite their unfathomable nature, are shown in the person and actions of Jesus upon the Cross. God's inner life does not change, but it is revealed and shared in the Son of God.

For Maximus, as with Barth, the Spirit was not merely present at Golgotha, but active from the depths of the Father's heart, displaying his love through the wounded flesh of the Son. The logic of Barth, as with Balthasar and with John Paul II, is defined by the perfection of love as it emerges from the Father's own being, and which we perceive in the Incarnation. Much

---

43. Barth, *CD* 1/2:241.
44. Balthasar, *Cosmic Liturgy*, 81.
45. Balthasar, *Cosmic Liturgy*, 85.
46. Maximus the Confessor, *Selected Writings*, 111.

more can be said on such a mystery, and it remains a topic worthy of richer analysis and consideration.

CONCLUSION

With Maximus the Confessor, we have a means of perceiving the irreducible relationship of the Holy Spirit *with* the Father and the Son, and in terms of the Incarnation a role, in the patristic witness, of *cooperation*. In this sense, the Holy Spirit is the one who cooperates with the sacrifice of the Cross, insofar as the divine person of Christ self-empties himself in that task. What is contemplated as divine in Jesus of Nazareth is also prayerfully recognized as the Spirit of the Father and of the Son. The work of the bloody nails, of the piercing crown of thorns, the cynical bartering of the soldiers, the entire pilgrimage of sweat and aching along the path of the Cross acts concordantly as a dramatic witness not just to the Son but to the Spirit who, invisibly— almost inconceivably—irreducibly, and utterly indivisibly, is present, active, and invested in our salvation.

BIBLIOGRAPHY

Balthasar, Hans Urs von. "A Commentary on John Paul II's *Dominum et Vivificantem*." *Communio* 47 (2020) 839–61.

———. *Cosmic Liturgy: The Universe according to Maximus the Confessor*. Translated by Brian E. Daley. San Francisco: Ignatius, 2003.

Barth, Karl. *Church Dogmatics*. Translated by Harold Knight et al. Edinburgh: T. & T. Clark, 2010.

Blowers, Paul M., and Robert Louis Wilken. "Introduction." In *On the Cosmic Mystery of Jesus Christ: Selected Writings by St. Maximus the Confessor*, translated by Paul M. Blowers and Robert Louis Wilken, 13–43. New York: St. Vladimir's Seminary Press, 2003.

Boulding, Mary Cecily. "The Doctrine of the Holy Spirit in the Documents of Vatican II." *Irish Theological Quarterly* 5 (1985) 253–67.

Cooper, Adam G. *The Body in St. Maximus the Confessor: Holy Flesh, Wholly Deified*. Oxford: Oxford University Press, 2005.

Daniélou, Jean. *The Scandal of Truth*. Translated by W. J. Kerrigan. London: Lowe and Brydone, 1962.

John Paul II. *Dives in Misericordia*. https://www.vatican.va/content/john-paul-ii/en/encyclicals/documents/hf_jp-ii_enc_30111980_dives-in-misericordia.html, 1980.

———. *Dominum et Vivificantem*. https://www.vatican.va/content/john-paul-ii/en/encyclicals/documents/hf_jp-ii_enc_18051986_dominum-et-vivificantem.html, 1986.

Louth, Andrew. *Maximus the Confessor*. London: Routledge, 1996.

Lubac, Henri de. *Catholicisme: Les Aspects sociaux du dogme*. Paris: Cerf, 1938.

Maximus the Confessor, St. "Chapters on Knowledge." In *Maximus the Confessor: Selected Writings*, translated by George C. Berthold, 129–80. New York: Paulist, 1985.

———. "Difficulty 41." Translated by Andrew Louth. In *Maximus the Confessor: Selected Writings*, translated by George C. Berthold, 155–62. London: Routledge, 1996.

———. "The Four Hundred Chapters on Love." In *Maximus the Confessor: Selected Writings*, translated by George C. Berthold, 35–98. New York: Paulist, 1985.

———. *On the Cosmic Mystery of Jesus Christ: Selected Writings by St. Maximus the Confessor*. Translated by Paul M. Blowers and Robert Louis Wilken. New York: St. Vladimir's Seminary Press, 2003.

———. *Maximus the Confessor: Selected Writings*. Translated by George C. Berthold. New York: Paulist, 1985.

Meyendorff, John. *Christ in Eastern Christian Thought*. New York: St. Vladimir's Seminary Press, 1975.

———. *Living Tradition*. New York: St. Vladimir's Seminary Press, 1978.

O'Collins, Gerald. *Christology: A Biblical, Historical, and Systematic Study of Jesus*. Oxford: Oxford University Press, 1995.

Rosato, Philip. *The Spirit as Lord: The Pneumatology of Karl Barth*. London: T. & T. Clark, 1981.

Second Vatican Council. *Apostolicam Actuositatem*. https://www.vatican.va/archive/hist_councils/ii_vatican_council/documents/vat-ii_decree_19651118_apostolicam-actuositatem_en.html, 1965.

———. *Lumen Gentium*. In *The Sixteen Documents of Vatican II*, 123–95. Boston: Pauline, 1964–65.

Sertillanges, A. G. *What Jesus Saw from the Cross*. Translated by Ernest Flammarion. Manchester, NH: Sophia, 1996.

Stein, Edith. "The Activity of the Spirit." In *The Science of the Cross*, translated by Josephine Koeppel, 111–20. Washington, DC: ICS, 2018.

Tan, Carolyn E. L. *The Spirit at the Cross: Exploring a Cruciform Pneumatology*. Eugene, OR: Wipf & Stock, 2019.

Torrance, T. F. *Incarnation: The Person and Life of Christ*. Milton Keynes: Paternoster, 2008.

3

HOPE AND EXPECTATION

Mary's Co-operation with the Holy Spirit in the Church

M. Isabell Naumann, ISSM

IN THIS CHAPTER, MARY'S co-operation with the Holy Spirit within the ecclesial *communio* will be discussed from a hermeneutical-centered, mariologically ecclesial perspective. The key event of Pentecost consists of a number of relevant constituents of the topic—the concept of fellowship with the exulted Lord, Mary's place at the center of the community at Pentecost, and the correlation between *homo viator* and *hope*. These will be considered in order to elucidate the definite mariological underpinnings, because it is these that give Pentecost a unique, novel setting and dynamic. Furthermore, the continual expectation of the Holy Spirit within the Church will not only be discussed alongside Mary's exemplary persona, but within a much more profound Marian dimension and Marian consciousness. In this we will discover that Mary is not only a symbol of pneumatological-ecclesial interaction but is the anthropological model of the individual member of the Church in his/her pneumatological-ecclesial communion, and that Mary generates through her co-operation with the Holy Spirit a covenanted inter-relation among the members of the ecclesial *communio*.

As the concluding act of the Ascension, the Pentecost event (cf. John 7:39; 16:7) inaugurated a new era, the era of the Church, of the *new people of God*, paralleling the birth of the Old Testament people of God through the Law given at Sinai.[1] Pentecost is the expected event for the Apostles and the wider circle of the disciples of Jesus. With the coming of the Holy Spirit the Church started out to be the bearer of *Christian hope*, a hope, rooted in the Resurrection and the exalted Christ; and this hope is nurtured and sustained by the ongoing outpouring and activity of the Holy Spirit.[2] The Spirit not only manifested the centrality of the Resurrection and the exulted Christ but through it also the universal promise of salvation (cf. Acts 4:12).[3]

> The Christ event, death and resurrection, was interpreted as part of the divine purpose [Acts 2:23]. Yet, Luke also recorded Peter's words that Jesus was killed by the hands of lawless men. The tension involved in this juxtaposition is characteristic of Luke's soteriology. The significance of such a claim was to establish that neither the salvation provided by Jesus nor the salvation offered to men and women happened accidentally.[4]

FELLOWSHIP WITH THE EXULTED LORD

Integral to the Spirit's activity is the manifestation and substantiation of authentic discipleship to Jesus, the exalted Lord. Luke's concept of discipleship to Jesus, so prominently given in his Gospel and so effectively verified in his Acts, is closely bound up with *faith*, *repentance*, *conversion*, and *baptism*. Here we will briefly discuss these constituents.

The best description of *faith* in the Lukan concept is given in the parable of the sower, "in the seed fallen into good soil" (Luke 8:15). Here the disciples are described as "those who listen to the word and hold on

1. Dockery, "Theology of Acts," 45–46. For a salvation-historical structure and approach, see Conzelmann, *Theology of St. Luke*, 12–17, 149–69.

2. "The activity of the Spirit in Acts universalized the mission of Jesus. What the apostles did, in fact whatever was done by the church, was seen to be the work of the Spirit. Initially Luke indicates that his book was the result of the Spirit's teaching from the resurrected Lord to the apostles (Acts 1:2)." Dockery, "Theology of Acts," 45–46. For the concept of God's רוּחַ (ruah) and πνεῦμα (pneuma/spirit), see Sherry, *Spirit and Beauty*, 87–91.

3. Dockery, "Theology of Acts," 46–48. Christ's resurrection is the foundation of the believer's resurrection (Acts 4:2; 13:32–33; 17:18, 29–32; 23:6; 24:21; 26:23). Dockery, "Theology of Acts," 49–50.

4. Dockery, "Theology of Acts," 50–51. For a more detailed study of the Pentecost context and the eschatological community, see Levering, *Jesus and the Demise of Death*, 65–83.

to it with a noble and generous mind: these yield a crop through their persistence." As a response to the Christian *kerygma*, the following of Jesus Christ "along the way of life" is always marked by divine initiative.[5]

Faith as the fundamental condition for salvation is often referred to in Luke's Gospel (cf. 7:30, 8:48, 17:19). In addition to the parable of the sower (this addition is not in the Marcan version) it is said that the devil removes the word of God "from their heart, lest believing they should be saved" (Luke 8:12). "Luke's editing of this text underscores his basic theme of salvation through faith, in which salvation results from the presence of the word of God in one's heart."[6]

In Luke's writings, *epistrephein* (ἐπιστρέφειν/conversion) is always a "turning towards" the "Lord" or "the living God."[7] Thus, the person "who turns towards the Lord" will begin to walk the "way of the Lord." This conversion is dynamic and leads the person to an ever-deeper faith, closer to Christ. *Metanoia* (μετάνοια/repentance) signifies the total change of attitude from which stems the profound awareness of sinfulness in the past.[8]

The person who believed in Christ and "wanted to walk the way of the Lord" had also to be *baptized* in the name of Jesus. There is no actual mention of the baptism of the original apostles or disciples. For them Pentecost was the occasion where they received "the Father's promise," the Holy Spirit, which enabled them to preach the Good News and baptize others in order that they too would receive "the gift of the Holy Spirit" (Acts 2:38).

Along with the basic responses to the Christian message, Luke also indicates the way in which the Christian life should be lived. It is the following of Jesus in undivided loyalty, which means detachment from all other allegiances and total allegiance to Jesus (cf. Luke 14:26–27). It is significant to note that Luke avoids the word *mathétés* (μαθητής/disciple) from Gethsemane onwards, only taking it up again in Acts 6:1 and applying it to the wider community in Acts.[9]

Discipleship is a "coming after Jesus" as illustrated in the person of Simon of Cyrene who carries the cross "behind Jesus" (cf. Luke 9:23–26; 14:26–27). The way of Christ to his final destiny—Jerusalem, with death

---

5. Luke 1:26–28; 5:1–4; 10:1–3; Acts 9:1–22; 10:1–48.

6. Navone, *Themes of St. Luke*, 145. For Luke, the new community, the Church, was "the sphere in which the forgiving and re-creating presence of God was experienced." Dockery, "Theology of Acts," 50–51.

7. See ἐπιστρέφω, ἐπιστροφή, in Kittel and Friedrich, *TDNT* 7:722–29.

8. Hezel, "Conversion and Repentance in Lucan Theology," 2596–602. Dockery, "Theology of Acts," 50–51. See also Acts 2:37; 3:19, 26; 5:31; 10:43; 13:38, 39; 15:9, 36.

9. For the use of μαθηταί and μαθητής, see Trebilco, *Self-Designations and Group Identity*, 208–46.

and resurrection—which is the way to the Father, has to be followed by his disciples, because discipleship for Luke is not only the acceptance of the teaching of the "Master," but also the "identification of oneself with the Master's way of life and destiny in an intimate, personal following of him."[10]

Jesus *must* go the way designated for him. The word Δεῖ (must)[11] frequently used in Luke, expresses Jesus' submission to the will of the Father[12] and the follower's obedience to the same divine will.[13] However, it is only through the power of the Holy Spirit that Jesus' followers are able to walk his way.

Linked with the undivided loyalty to Jesus is another important criterion for discipleship, that of *poverty*. In Luke's Gospel the poor "are associated with prisoners . . . the downtrodden (Luke 4:18), or with those who hunger, weep, are hated, persecuted and rejected (Luke 6:20b–22), or with blind people, cripples, lepers and deaf people. . . . [T]hey represent generally the neglected mass of humanity."[14] Luke sees poverty as a *fundamental sign of blessedness* (cf. Luke 6:20). The blessedness of the poor derives from the kingdom of God and not from the resources of this world. The lack of these resources becomes a blessing when it leaves Christ's hearers free and disposed to accept the Good News of salvation. Disciples have first to set their hearts on his kingdom, then all their other needs will be satisfied.[15]

The dynamics of the pre-Resurrection follower of Jesus changes in the Pentecost event. As mentioned earlier, the Lukan Gospel account of what makes a true follower of Christ is only authenticated after the coming of the Spirit at Pentecost. Pentecost thus marks the transition from being called into fellowship with Christ to that of *authentically being and becoming a true follower of Christ*. It is the Holy Spirit, the Spirit who was with Jesus, who enables the disciples to become true *mathétés*. In an ongoing experience the Spirit leads the way,[16] empowers and guides the apostolic community

---

10. Fitzmyer, *Gospel according to Luke*, 241.

11. Grundmann, *Evangelium nach Lukas*, 21–25. See also Navone, *Themes of St. Luke*, 100–101; Cosgrove, "Divine Δεῖ in Luke-Acts," 168–90.

12. Luke 4:43; 9:22; 13:33; 17:24; 22:37; 24:44.

13. Acts 5:29; 9:7; 16:14, 22.

14. Fitzmyer, *Gospel according to Luke*, 250–51.

15. Navone, *Themes of St. Luke*, 107. See also in this context: DooHee, *Luke-Acts and "Tragic History*," 214–36.

16. Luke 1:14; Acts 16:6–10.

in giving *witness*,[17] in living a life of *prayer*,[18] and in practicing *poverty*. Indeed, the Spirit "gives continuity to the acts of God in the ongoing course of history."[19]

Acts leaves no doubt that the Church is essentially a community of the Holy Spirit and is guided by the Spirit. The Spirit united the believers into a fellowship that could not be paralleled in any other group, in order to create in individuals and in the church a quality of life that would otherwise be beyond their ability (cf. Acts 1:8). Directly following the Spirit's descent on the community, it grew significantly in a surprising manner (cf. Acts 2:41).[20]

What has been said so far may be summed up in the fact that Pentecost signifies a defining moment in salvation history. The Spirit's activity at Pentecost was seen as the fulfillment of the prophecy of Joel "the coming of the day of the Lord" (Joel 2:1–2, 30; 3:14) and by the "outpouring of the spirit" (Joel 2:27, 28–29) on all believers, as a corporate body;[21] Luke's theology is clearly indicating that the *eschaton* ($\check{\epsilon}\sigma\chi\alpha\tau\sigma\varsigma$)—"the last days"—has been inaugurated, but is still *awaiting a future consummation*.[22] And this time of waiting for the *parousia* ($\pi\alpha\rho\sigma\nu\sigma\acute{\iota}\alpha$) was for the early Church an

17. The *witness* is one who had been chosen beforehand by God. However, it is the Holy Spirit with his gifts who enables the receiver to fulfil the mission of witnessing to the Lord in word and action. Fitzmyer, *Gospel according to Luke*, 243; Luke 24:49. See in particular Acts 1:8; 2:38–41; 8:12, 36; 16:15; 19:5; 22:16. Dockery, "Theology of Acts," 51–52.

18. "Discipleship requires that union with God which Jesus manifested in his *prayer*, and this must be learnt from Jesus himself (Luke 11:1). Jesus' precepts on prayer imply that we must pray to the Father because he is good and will give us the Holy Spirit, the fullness of his gifts (Luke 11:9–30) and the cause of Christian joy." Navone, *Themes of St. Luke*, 129.

19. Navone, *Themes of St. Luke*, 188–98. The picture of the early church presented in Acts 2:42–41 combined worship, fellowship, proclamation, and concern for physical and social needs, e.g., Acts 1:14; 2:42; 3:1; 4:24; 12:12; 13:3. Dockery, "Theology of Acts," 51–52.

20. Dockery, "Theology of Acts," 46–48. "It is the promise of Christ that the Spirit will direct the expanding ministry of the church (Acts 1:8). After Pentecost the Spirit was active in many aspects of the Christian community. The Spirit's power was specifically noticed in preaching, in prophecy, in witness, in joy, and in the making of decisions. Yet the primary emphasis of the work of the Spirit in Luke's second volume was mission. His theological emphasis demonstrated that the Spirit who dwelt in the Messiah of Israel now was available to the citizens of Rome." Dockery, "Theology of Acts," 46–48.

21. Dockery, "Theology of Acts," 45–48.

22. Dockery, "Theology of Acts," 45–46. See Peter's sermon on the day of Pentecost, Acts 2:14–42; see also Acts 17:31. Dockery, "Theology of Acts," 55.

"*object of hope* [2 Cor 5:4; 1 Cor 15:51)] for hope is not a passive attitude but a dynamic stance by which we are moved to attain that for which we hope."[23]

Thus Pentecost, the outpouring of the Spirit, and the birth of the Church inaugurate a development from waiting for the *parousia* to what constitutes true *Christian hope*. The Holy Spirit enables the followers of Christ to transcend their expectancy of the return of Christ to a life lived in genuine hope in the awareness of the "already and not yet." At Pentecost the Church becomes the sign and instrument of supernatural hope and in that becomes an answer to one of the fundamental questions of humanity: What do we hope for?

In my opinion, it is precisely this concept of *hope* that facilitates the presence of Mary, the Mother of the Lord, within the group of the believers at Pentecost. In her, as the first *new creation in Christ* (the *Immaculata*) and as the true *Daughter of Sion*,[24] hope has triumphed already in the person of Christ at the Annunciation and in the Incarnation, and in Mary's own lifelong undivided commitment to the triune God. In Mary we see the true *homo viator* who as the Spirit-endowed person, the *homo spiritualis* (πνευματικός/*pneumatikos*), becomes a "sign of sure hope."[25] Having indicated this, mariologically-ecclesiologically it will be valuable to point here to the important link between the Annunciation and Pentecost.

MARY AT THE CENTER OF THE COMMUNITY AT PENTECOST

Acts 1:12–14 mentions Mary in the upper room among the followers of Jesus.[26] All the eleven persevered, with a "single heart" (ὁμοθυμαδὸν/ homothymadon) in prayer with the women disciples—Mary, the Mother of Jesus (Μαριὰμ τῇ μητρὶ τοῦ Ἰησοῦ)—and his brothers.

Only Mary is *named* with the Eleven. She is situated between the two groups of disciples: the Eleven, and the women and family, since she belonged to both. With them she is in prayer and awaits the promise of

23. For an extensive and interesting distinction between the concepts of "awaits" and "hopes for" see Entralgo, *Espera y la Esperanza*; 56–70, 299–313, 580–601 are worth noting. See also Gonzáles-Carvajal Santabárbara, "Esperanza Humana y Esperanza Cristiana," 201–12; Candido. *Theology of the Beyond*, 88–89.

24. John Paul II, *Redemptoris Mater*, sec. 24.

25. Second Vatican Council, *Lumen Gentium*, sec. 68, 69.

26. According to John's Gospel she was in Jerusalem during the Passion (cf. John 19:25–27), according to Luke she does not seem to leave the city before the time of the Ascension or Pentecost (cf. Acts 1:14). Laurentin, *Court traité de théologie mariale*, 120.

Christ—the Holy Spirit—who would make of this praying community a Church (Acts 1:8).

She has a role proportioned to that of the Annunciation (*before* Christ), for a new transition, now (*after* the life of Christ), at the birth of the Church through the Spirit. As Mary, through her belief, conceived Christ by the power of the Holy Spirit at the Annunciation, so, after Christ's Ascension, Mary prays for the coming of that same Holy Spirit, so that the Church might be born at Pentecost.[27]

Mary, as the *Immaculata*, is at the center of the scene. It is she who figuratively becomes the focal point of Pentecost. In her, and in her representation of the "original Church," is concentrated the dynamic interaction between the Holy Spirit and her, and between the Spirit and the ecclesial community. Further, in her is concretized the time before Christ, the time of Christ and the time of the Church. Her immaculate *Fiat* of the Annunciation becomes at Pentecost the pure *Fiat* of the nascent Church. *Redemptoris Mater* rightly states:

> In the redemptive economy of grace, brought about through the action of the Holy Spirit, there is a unique correspondence between the moment of the Incarnation of the Word and the moment of the birth of the Church. The person who links these two moments is Mary: Mary at Nazareth and Mary in the Upper Room at Jerusalem. In both cases her discreet yet essential presence indicates the path of "birth from the Holy Spirit." Thus she who is present in the mystery of Christ as Mother becomes— by the will of the Son and the power of the Holy Spirit—present in the mystery of the Church.[28]

In viewing Mary in this context, we have to understand discipleship in terms of an attitude of heart and mind in relation to Jesus. There is a significant link between Pentecost and the Annunciation: Mary's first response to the Good News—"Behold the handmaid of the Lord. Let it be done to me according to your word" (Luke 1:38)—re-echoes in Acts 1:14 (although Acts provide no further explicit information about Mary) in a way that demonstrates that Mary kept the word of God in her heart and acted on it—she has not changed her attitude.[29] In hope she advanced on her journey of faith as the *homo viator* and *homo spiritualis*.

---

27. Second Vatican Council, *Lumen Gentium*, sec. 58; John Paul II, *Redemptoris Mater*, sec. 24.

28. John Paul II, *Redemptoris Mater*, sec. 24.

29. Bearsley, "Mary," 461–504; Hochschild, "John Henry Newman," 1007. Kurz indicates that "Luke seems to have created a deliberate intratextual link between his

What the Spirit did for Mary in the Annunciation (cf. Luke 1:35) was done for her at Pentecost by that same Spirit, together with all who were present in the upper room; all were "filled with the Holy Spirit" (Acts 1:14; 2:1–13). Could Mary, who had already received the Spirit at the Annunciation, receive the Spirit again? According to Acts, the Apostles themselves, "filled with the Holy Spirit" at the day of Pentecost (cf. Acts 1:5; Acts 2:4; 11:16), were "filled" again in Acts 4:31 for a new stage in the life of the Church. It is the same for Mary, who is and remains the object of God's favor (cf. Luke 1:28); the outpouring of the Spirit renews from plenitude to plenitude,[30] for this is the *new reality* of the *new person in Christ.*

The Russian theologian Bulgakov captures this reality so pertinently when he writes:

> The one full of grace received *the fullness* of the Holy Spirit with the indivisible totality of His gifts. But Mary's reception and assimilation of these gifts were also characterized—according to the general law of life in the Spirit—by degrees of growth. Her growth in the Spirit progressed from Her birth and Her presentation in the Temple to the Annunciation; and then from the Annunciation—through Golgotha and the Pentecost—to Her Dormition and Her Assumption, which attests to the fullness of spiritual receptivity and spirituality that She had attained in Her glorification and deification. Without being God or the God-Man, Mary communes with the Divine life in the Holy Trinity in Her perfect spirituality. She follows, like Her Son, the path of kenotic diminution and maternally participates in His salvific passion. To this is added Her apostolic ministry after the Ascension: Her silent and self-sacrificing work for all of Christianity.[31]

---

statements in Luke 2:19 and 51, about Mary recalling and reflecting on the meaning of Jesus' origins, and Mary's presence in the Jerusalem community awaiting Pentecost." Kurz, "Mary," 808–9.

30. "The absolute sovereignty of God who in Jesus Christ alone establishes his New and eternal covenant with man and women . . . had to be made by Mary at the incarnation (and for all its implications*) loco totius humanae naturae*—in place of the whole human nature—especially as kernel of the new Church." Balthasar, *Reader,* 217–18. At Pentecost she became a member of the nascent Church, in the visible Church, an unequaled member, prefiguring the ecclesial future.

31. Bulgakov, *Comforter,* 247. Gregory of Nyssa describes pertinently this movement: "Every good thing and every good name, depending on that power and purpose which is without beginning, is brought to perfection in the power of the Spirit through the Only-begotten God." Gregory of Nyssa, On *"Not Three Gods";* and in Sherry, *Spirit and Beauty,* 90–91.

Cardinal Journet gives the positive indication that Mary's role of the perfection of the Church is in the order of divine life and holiness (not in the order of ministry) when he writes:

> She lifted up the nascent Church by the power of her contemplation and by her love. She had been more useful to it than had been the apostles who acted from without. She was for it the hidden root, where the sap works and bursts forth in the flowers and in fruit.[32]

To enter into the mystery of the Incarnation means to respond to God's calling, to receive the living Word and to carry it effectively into the world, to receive Christ *virginally* in the heart and bring Christ to the world in a continuous way. Mary did this precisely in the Annunciation, from the moment she was taken into the mystery of the Incarnation and again, when the Holy Spirit overshadows and empowers the nascent Church at Pentecost, she is there.[33] As the *homo viator* she is and remains as the Spirit-empowered person, the *homo spiritualis*.

Pope John Paul II refers to this:

> That first group of those who in faith looked "upon Jesus as the author of salvation," knew that Jesus was the Son of Mary, and that she was his Mother, and that as such she was from the moment of his conception and birth a unique witness to the mystery of Jesus, that mystery which before their eyes had been disclosed and confirmed in the Cross and Resurrection. Thus, from the very first moment, the Church "looked at" Mary through Jesus, just as she "looked at" Jesus through Mary. For the Church of that time and of every time Mary is a singular witness to the years of Jesus' infancy and hidden life at Nazareth, when she "kept all these things, pondering them in her heart" (Luke 2:19, 51).[34]

Redemptoris Mater, elucidating further *Lumen Gentium's* teaching, stresses the importance of Mary's presence in the nascent Church:

> At the first dawn of the Church, at the beginning of the long journey through faith which began at Pentecost in Jerusalem, Mary was with all those who were the seed of the "new Israel." She was present among them as an exceptional witness to the

---

32. Journet, *L'Eglise du Verbe incarné*, 120.

33. Augustine attests to this in *Sermon* 215 (Augustine, *Sermon* 215, in *Sermons* [184–229Z]).

34. John Paul II, *Redemptoris Mater*, sec. 26.

mystery of Christ. And the Church was assiduous in prayer together with her, and at the same time "contemplated her in the light of the Word made man." It was always to be so. For when the Church "enters more intimately into the supreme mystery of the Incarnation," she thinks of the Mother of Christ with profound reverence and devotion. Mary belongs indissolubly to the mystery of Christ, and she belongs also to the mystery of the Church from the beginning, from the day of the Church's birth. At the basis of what the Church has been from the beginning, and of what she must continually become from generation to generation, in the midst of all the nations of the earth, we find the one "who believed that there would be a fulfillment of what was spoken to her from the Lord" (Lk 1:45). It is precisely Mary's faith which marks the beginning of the new and eternal Covenant of God with man in Jesus Christ; this heroic faith of hers "precedes" the apostolic witness of the Church, and ever remains in the Church's heart hidden like a special heritage of God's revelation. All those who from generation to generation accept the apostolic witness of the Church share in that mysterious inheritance, and in a sense share in Mary's faith.[35]

Integral to this link between Mary at the Annunciation and Pentecost and her advancing in faith is, as mentioned earlier, that important facet of theological anthropology, the *concept of hope* which in turn corresponds to the purpose of the outpouring of the Spirit at Pentecost. For Pentecost inaugurates the Church's journey *in hope* toward its heavenly homeland. This dynamic image of the Church corresponds to the very nature of the human person as the *homo viator*.

For an applicable exposition of what it means to be a *viator* we will turn here to J. Pieper.

The Correlation between *Homo Viator* and *Hope*

A *viator* is someone who is on the way; theologically speaking, the viator makes progress toward eternal happiness. To have encompassed this goal, to be a *comprehensor*, means to possess the Beatific Vision, beatitude—primarily understood as the fulfilment objectively appropriate to our nature and only secondarily as the subjective response to this fulfilment. Both concepts *status viatoris* and *status comprehensoris* designate the natural states of being of all creatures—above all of man. Until the moment of

35. John Paul II, *Redemptoris Mater*, sec. 27; Second Vatican Council, *Lumen Gentium*, sec. 65.

his death, the human person remains in *the status viatoris*, in the state of being on the way.[36] As this state refers to the innermost structure of created nature, it is the inherent 'not yet' of the finite being and thus it "includes both a negative and a positive element: the absence of fulfilment and the orientation toward fulfilment."[37]

The "way" of *homo viator*, of the human person being "on the way," leads toward being and away from nothingness. It leads to realization, not to annihilation, even though this realization is "not yet" fulfilled and the fall into nothingness is "not yet" impossible.[38] "The only answer that corresponds to the actual existential situation [of the human person] is hope."[39] This is so, as "the virtue of hope is preeminently the virtue of the *status viatoris*; it is the proper virtue of the 'not yet'."[40] In hope, we reach "*with restless hearts*, with confidence and patient expectation, toward the *bonum arduum futurum*, toward the arduous 'not yet' of fulfilment, whether natural or supernatural."[41]

What directs hope to its true possibilities is *magnanimity*, while *humility*, with its gaze fixed on the infinite distance between God and us, reveals the limitations of these possibilities and preserves them from fake realization and for true realization. From this inner action of magnanimity and humility is borne the proper ordering of natural hope.[42] Indeed, "implanting in man the new 'future' of a practically inexhaustible 'not yet,' supernatural hope lays the foundation for a *new youthfulness* that can be destroyed only if hope is destroyed."[43]

36. Pieper, *Faith, Hope, Love*, 92. See in this context the thorough study by Schumacher, *Philosophy of Hope*, 11–63.

37. Pieper, *Faith, Hope, Love*, 93.

38. Pieper, *Faith, Hope, Love*, 97–98.

39. Pieper, *Faith, Hope, Love*, 98.

40. For the biblical concept of hope, see Kittel and Friedrich, *TDNT* (abridged) 2:229–32. For a theological exposition of hope, see Kasper et al, *Lexikon für Theologie und Kirche*, 5:198–207. See also Benedict XVI, *Spe Salvi*; Doyle, "*Spe Salvi*," 350–79; Pieper, *Faith, Hope, Love*, 98. "In the virtue of hope more than in any other, man understands and affirms that he is a creature, that he has been created by God." Pieper, *Faith, Hope, Love*, 98.

41. Pieper, *Faith, Hope, Love*, 100.

42. Pieper, *Faith, Hope, Love*, 102. "Man flees from God because God has exalted human nature to a higher, a divine, state of being and thereby enjoined on man a higher standard of obligation. *Acedia* is, in the last analysis, a 'detestatio boni divini,' [Aquinas, *Quaestiones disputatae de malo* 8, I] with the monstrous result that, upon reflection, man expressly wishes that God had not ennobled him but had 'left him in peace.'" Pieper, *Faith, Hope, Love*, 119–20.

43. Pieper, *Faith, Hope, Love*, 100. Aquinas, *Summa Theologica* II–II, q. 21, a. 3.

Opposed to the theological virtue of hope is *presumption* which is the individual's perverted attitude toward the fact that eternal life is the meaning and goal of our earthly "way."[44] It is an attitude of the mind that fails to accept the reality of futurity and of arduousness. These realities constitute the formal nature of the object of hope. Should one of these characteristics be missing or ceasing to be genuine, hope is no longer possible.[45] Presumption, thus,

> destroys supernatural hope by failing to recognize it for what it is; by not acknowledging that earthly existence in the *status viatoris* is, in a precise and proper sense, the "way" to ultimate fulfilment, and by regarding eternal life as something that is "basically" already achieved, as something that is "in principle" already given.[46]

As long as we remain in the *status viatoris* there is hope that we can escape our ultimate existential uncertainty, the root of which is the ever-present possibility of voluntary defection, into an absolute certainty. "Absolute certainty is unattainable, even 'in principle,' for *homo viator*. ... The uncertainty of human existence cannot be totally removed. But it can be 'overcome'—by hope, and only by hope."[47]

The Church, inaugurated at Pentecost, resembles precisely this most human state of being—the community of those who are in the *status viatoris*, the pilgrim people of God—living in the uncertainty of human existence but who in the power of the Holy Spirit have "overcome" the uncertainty by hope—hope in the eschatological fulfilment. The concept of "pilgrim people of God" is inconceivable without the continual expectation of the Holy Spirit and his gifts that sustain this people on this journey. The manifestation of this reality is well attested by *Lumen Gentium*.

---

44. Pieper, *Faith, Hope, Love*, 124.

45. Aquinas, *Summa Theologica* I–II, q. 40, a. 1.

46. Pieper, *Faith, Hope, Love*, 125. Aquinas, *Summa Theologica* I–II, q. 40, a. 1. Augustine calls the essential nature of presumption "a *pervarsa securitas* [Augustine, *Sermones* 87, 8], a self-deceptive reliance on a security that has no existence in reality. In the last analysis, what appears to be a 'superhuman' element in the anticipation of fulfilment is, in reality, none other than a yielding to the, if not exactly 'heroic,' yet certainly not despicable weight of man's need for security. In the sin of presumption, man's desire for security is so exaggerated that it exceeds the bound of reality." Pieper, *Faith, Hope, Love*, 125–26.

47. Pieper, *Faith, Hope, Love*, 128–29.

THE CONTINUAL EXPECTATION OF THE HOLY SPIRIT'S PRESENCE IN THE CHURCH

Consideration of Vatican II's description of the dynamics of the Church verifies the root characteristics of the effects of the outpouring of the Spirit on Pentecost and the Church's continual expectation of the Spirit in guiding her in her mission and in nurturing her hope centred on the Paschal Mystery of Christ. In order to establish an appropriate approach to the Holy Spirit's activity within the Church, it seems beneficial to point out Yves Congar's contribution in regard to an appropriate pneumatology within the Church. For Congar, both the Spirit and the Word institute the Church. He insists that the Spirit is the co-instituting principle of the Church and the Spirit is the constantly animating principle of the Church, always bringing it to life. Sacred Scripture speaks of a mission of the Word and a mission of the Spirit. Congar builds on this theology of a two-fold mission.[48]

In this,

> Congar builds on Aquinas's profound theology of the missions, which includes the visible missions of Word and Spirit in salvation history, and the invisible missions by which they are present to us in grace. The Church exists because of the visible missions of *both* the Word and the Spirit. ... The Church is dependent on the Spirit both for its foundation and its life. The Church is then both Christological and pneumatological.[49]

Based on this, Congar emphasizes a complementarity between institution and charism in the Church. He insists that the risen Christ and the Spirit are profoundly united in the New Testament theology of the Church, and they need to be held together in today's ecclesiology. In this, he speaks of the principal role of the Spirit concerning the Church's holiness, unity, apostolicity, and catholicity.[50]

According to *Lumen Gentium* the *people of God* are taken up in God's Trinitarian plan: coming from the eternal Father, revealed in Christ, and unfolded through the Holy Spirit toward the *eschaton*.[51]

---

48. Congar, *I Believe in the Holy Spirit*, 2:3–64. Edwards, "Correcting the Balance," 261.

49. Congar, *I Believe in the Holy Spirit*, 16; Edwards, "Correcting the Balance," 262.

50. Congar, *I Believe in the Holy Spirit*, 16; Edwards, "Correcting the Balance," 262.

51. Second Vatican Council, *Lumen Gentium*, sec. 2–4. The gradual unfolding of this plan is to be understood from its καιρος, the inbreaking of the εσχατον in Christ, "the image of the invisible God, the first-born of all creation (Col 1:15)," (sec. 2) in whom God spoke the ultimate word of revelation (cf. Eph 1:9–12), and who established the βασιλεια των ουρανων on earth. In the divine economy of salvation, the Church,

What we presented earlier in regard to the *homo viator* and the supernatural virtue of hope seems to be particularly pertinent within the context of the fourfold principle of activity of the Spirit in the Church. If the Church as community and in its individual members remains docile to the Spirit, it will prevail in a dynamic *youthfulness*. The Spirit's ongoing enlivening presence in the Church will guarantee the status of *homo viator* with the theological virtue of *hope*. In the human acknowledgement of being God's creature, and continuing on life's journey, in true humility and magnanimity, toward the God-given goal, the Church will *witness* to a Christian Resurrection consciousness, realizing an authentic faith directed toward a *hope* that has overcome all uncertainty.[52]

In this journey to the eschatological fulfilment, the Church, engaged with and sharing the sentiments of people and nations, is continuously called to look at Mary and adhere to her motherly influence and education. *Redemptoris Mater*'s nuanced iteration of *Lumen Gentium* demonstrates this:

> Given Mary's relationship to the Church as an exemplar, the Church is close to her and seeks to become like her: . . . by the power of the Holy Spirit, she preserves with virginal purity an integral faith, a firm hope, and a sincere charity. Mary is thus present in the mystery of the Church as a model. But the Church's mystery also consists in generating people to a new and immortal life: this is her motherhood in the Holy Spirit. And here Mary is not only the model and figure of the Church; she is much more. For, "with maternal love she cooperates in the birth and development" of the sons and daughters of Mother Church. The Church's motherhood is accomplished not only according to the model and figure of the Mother of God but also with her "cooperation." The Church draws abundantly from this cooperation, that is to say from the maternal mediation which is characteristic of Mary, insofar as already on earth she

---

as the βασιλεια του Χριστου already present in mystery, becomes visibly manifest in the world (sec. 3). The Church's presence in *salvation history* is foreshadowed from the beginning (sec. 2), prepared in the history of the covenanted people of Israel, established by Christ—symbolized by the blood and water that flowed from the open side of Jesus crucified (cf. John 19:34)—and in the outpouring of the Holy Spirit at Pentecost, as it journeys toward its eschatological completion (sec. 2, 3, 4). *Lumen Gentium*'s notion of the mystery of the Church refers to the design of God's wisdom, God's salvific plan for all creation in the mystery of Christ (cf. Rom 16:25–27; 1 Cor 2:7–10; Eph 1:5–12, 3:3–5, 8–10, 5:32; Col 1:15, 24–27, 2:2–3, 4:3–4]. See Second Vatican Council, *Lumen Gentium*, sec. 2. For μυστήριον, see Deden, "Mystère Paulinien," 405–42; Brown, *Semitic Background*.

52. Pieper, *Faith, Hope, Love*, 125.

cooperated in the rebirth and development of the Church's sons and daughters, as the Mother of that Son whom the Father "placed as the first-born among many brethren."[53]

BIBLIOGRAPHY

Acta Synodalia Sacrosancti Concilii oecumenici Vaticani II. Vatican City: Typis Polyglottis Vaticanis, 1970–86.

Aquinas, Thomas. *Summa Theologica.* Cambridge: Cambridge University Press, 2007.

Augustine. *Sermons (184–229Z) on the Liturgical Seasons.* Vol. III/6. Translated by Edmund Hill. New Rochelle, NY: New City, 1993.

Balthasar, Hans Urs von. *The Balthasar Reader.* Edited by M. Kehl and W. Löser. New York: Crossroad, 1982.

Bearsley, Patrick. "Mary, the Perfect Disciple: A Paradigm for Mariology." *Theological Studies* 41 (1980) 461–504.

Benedict XVI. *Spe Salvi.* New York: Pauline, 2007.

Brown, Raymond. *The Semitic Background of the Term "Mystery" in the New Testament.* Philadelphia: Fortress, 1968.

Bulgakov, Sergius, *The Comforter.* Translated by Boris Jakim. Grand Rapids: Eerdmans, 2004.

Candido, Pozo. *Theology of the Beyond.* 5th ed. New York: Alba House 2009.

Congar, Yves. *I Believe in the Holy Spirit.* Vol. 2. New York: Seabury, 1983.

————. *Le Christ, Marie et L'Église.* Paris: Desclée de Brouwer, 1952.

Conzelmann, Hans. *The Theology of St. Luke.* London: SCM, 1982.

Cosgrove, Charles Henry. "The Divine Δεῖ in Luke-Acts." *Novum Testamentum* 26 (1984) 168–90.

Deden, David. "Le mystère Paulinien." *Ephemerides Theologicae Lovanienses* 13 (1936) 405–42.

Dockery, David, "The Theology of Acts." *Criswell Theological Review* 5 (1990) 43–55.

DooHee, Lee. *Luke-Acts and "Tragic History"—Communicating Gospel with the World.* Wissenschaftliche Untersuchungen zum Neuen Testament 2. Reihe 346. Tübingen: Mohr Siebeck, 2013.

Doyle, Dominic. "*Spe Salvi* on Eschatological and Secular Hope: A Thomistic Critique of an Augustinian Encyclical." *Theological Studies* 71 (2010) 350–79.

Edwards, Denis. "Correcting the Balance: The Holy Spirit and the Church." *Australasian Catholic Record* 76 (1999) 259–69.

---

53. John Paul II, *Redemptoris Mater*, sec. 44; Second Vatican Council, *Lumen Gentium*, sec. 63–64. Through the office of her divine motherhood (Second Vatican Council, *Lumen Gentium*, sec. 57) and "her singular graces and gifts," Mary is "intimately united to the Church" and called "the *type of the Church* in the order of faith, charity and perfect union with Christ"; "our mother in the order of faith" (sec. 61–63). In this, according to Pauline theology, the highest order in the Church—that of love—is presented in Mary (1 Cor 13:1–3). Her maternal care toward humanity does not diminish Christ's unique mediation because it originates, rests upon, and draws everything from Christ's merits and mediation (sec. 60). See also: Congar, *Christ*, 20–26; Flórez, "Espiritualidad Ecclesial y la Virgen," 91–132; Laurentin, "Role de Marie," 43–62.

Entralgo, Pedro Lain. *La espera y la esperanza: Historia y Teoria del Esperar Humano.* 3rd ed. Madrid: Revista de Occidente, 1962.

Fitzmyer, Joseph. *Gospel according to Luke: Introduction, Translations and Notes.* 2 vols. Anchor Bible 28–28A. New York: Doubleday, 1981.

Flórez, Fulgado. "La Espiritualidad Ecclesial y la Virgen." *Estudios Marianos* 34 (1970) 91–132.

Gonzáles-Carvajal Santabárbara, Luis. "Esperanza Humana y Esperanza Cristiana." *Ephemerides Mariologicae* 62 (2012) 201–12.

Gregory of Nyssa. *On "Not Three Gods."* www.newadvent.org/fathers/2905.htm.

Grundmann, Walter. *Das Evangelium nach Lukas.* Theologischer Handkommentar zum Neuen Testament 3. Berlin: Evangelischer, 1966.

Hezel, Francis. "Conversion and Repentance in Lucan Theology." *Bible Today* 37 (1968) 2596–602.

Hochschild, Paige. "John Henry Newman: Mariology and the Scope of Reason in the Modern Age." *Nova et Vetera* 11 (2013) 993–1016.

John Paul II. *Redemptoris Mater.* New York: Pauline, 1987.

Journet, Charles. *L'Eglise du Verbe incarné.* Paris: Desclée, 1987.

Kasper, Walter et al., eds. *Lexikon für Theologie und Kirche.* Vol. 5. Freiburg: Herder, 1996.

Kittel, Gerhard, and Gerhard Friedrich, eds. *Theological Dictionary of the New Testament.* Translated by Geoffrey W. Bromiley. Grand Rapids: Eerdmans, 1964–76.

———. *Theological Dictionary of the New Testament: Abridged in One Volume.* Translated by Geoffrey W. Bromiley. Grand Rapids: Eerdmans, 1985.

Kurz, William. "Mary, Woman and Mother in God's Saving New Testament Plan." *Nova et Vetera* 11 (2013) 801–18.

Laurentin, Rene. *Court traité de théologie mariale.* Paris: Lethielleux, 1959.

———. "Role de Marie et de l'Eglise dans l'oeuvre Salvifigue du Christ." *Etudes Mariales* 10 (1952) 43–62.

Levering, Matthew. *Jesus and the Demise of Death: Resurrection, Afterlife, and the Fate of the Christian.* Waco, TX: Baylor University Press, 2012.

Navone, John. *Themes of St. Luke.* Rome: Gregorian University Press, 1970.

Pieper, Josef. *Faith, Hope, Love.* San Francisco: Ignatius, 1997.

Schumacher, Bernard. *A Philosophy of Hope: Josef Pieper and the Contemporary Debate on Hope.* Translated by D. C. Schindler. New York: Fordham University Press, 2003.

Second Vatican Council. *Lumen Gentium.* https://www.vatican.va/archive/hist_councils/ii_vatican_council/documents/vat-ii_const_19641121_lumen-gentium_en.html.

Segovia, Fernando. *Discipleship in the New Testament.* Philadelphia: Fortress, 1985.

Sherry, Patrick. *Spirit and Beauty: An Introduction to Theological Aesthetics.* Oxford: Clarendon, 1992.

Tanner, Norman, ed. *Decrees of the Ecumenical Councils.* 2 vols. London: Sheed & Ward, 1990.

Trebilco, Paul. *Self-Designations and Group Identity in the New Testament.* Cambridge: Cambridge University Press, 2012.

4

"I WILL POUR OUT MY SPIRIT UPON ALL FLESH"

The Spirit in the Book of the Twelve as the Solution to Prophetic Conflict

Fr. Robert Krishna, OP

INTRODUCTION

In the New Testament, and particularly in Luke-Acts, God is depicted as acting through agency of the Holy Spirit, who acts as a personal and volitional agent. The Spirit is disruptive to the person receiving it but directs the preaching of the kingdom both by the individual and by the Church as a whole. In this chapter, I will argue that this depiction builds on various aspects of the portrait of the workings of winds and storms in the Old Testament, and in particular God's use of the wind/spirit to redirect and recall his people to live in union with God and brings salvation to the nations. This idea of God redirecting his people and enabling them to fulfill their prophetic vocation through spirits, winds, or his Spirit in the singular, is particularly brought out in the Book of the Twelve in response to the conflict between prophets and prophetic corruption, and the end or universalization of prophecy which is presented as a solution to prophetic conflict and corruption. Having briefly laid out the reason for looking for the ancestry of the idea of a personalized spirit in the Book of the Twelve, this chapter will explore the theme of the conflict of prophets and prophetic corruption. I will then look at the responses which emerge to this conflict. Next, I will argue that this is connected to the idea of the spirit as a distinct means of divine action in the Holy Spirit. Finally, I will contend that this idea of the Spirit carries over into the New Testament.

LOOKING FOR AN ANCESTRY FOR THE SPIRIT

We see in the New Testament a strong association between preaching and the Spirit, and more broadly between the Spirit and the mission of Christ and the Church. The Spirit makes Zechariah prophecy (cf. Luke 1:67). The Spirit is present in Simeon, assures him that he will not die before seeing the Messiah, and brings him to the Temple, where he too prophesies (cf. Luke 2:25–27). The Spirit drives Jesus into the desert, and brings him into Galilee, where he himself begins to preach (cf. Luke 4:1, 14). In the book of Acts, the Spirit comes upon the disciples and drives them out to preach, and directs the mission of the Body of Christ, the Church, moving the disciples, preventing them from going to one city, or telling him to be set aside for another mission.

This should lead us to ask whether this idea has a prehistory. The question becomes even more acute in the light of some recent narratives of the story of the idea of the Trinity, which have highlighted how the divine Wisdom reveals to us something of the Word, and how a certain Binitarianism can be seen in the Son of Man in Daniel or Wisdom in Wisdom literature or the Logos in the works of Philo.[1] But the close association between the Spirit and the Word of God in both the Old and New Testament should lead us to ask whether the idea of an active divine Spirit has a history.

The New Testament's use of the Old Testament is a kind of pedagogy for Christians in reading the Old Testament. So, it is appropriate to begin a study of the Spirit in the Old Testament with those texts in which the New Testament writers themselves see the Spirit at work. We can identify many such texts, but one which is particularly of interest is the book of the Twelve, often called Minor, Prophets. One notable reference to the Twelve Prophets occurs during Peter's sermon after the descent of the Holy Spirit at Pentecost (cf. Acts 2:17–21). In the sermon, Peter appeals to the book of Joel (cf. Joel 2:28–31) to connect the coming of the Spirit with prophecy, and its universalization.[2] This association of ideas between the descent of

---

1. See, for instance, Hurtado, *Lord Jesus Christ*.

2. Mowinckel, *Spirit and the Word*, 83, quite unhelpfully, effectively narrows down

God's spirit and the universalization of prophecy occurs not just in Joel, but throughout the book of the Twelve. And in the Twelve it is intimately connected with another prominent theme: that of the failure of prophecy. Studying both themes and how one is connected to the other can help us appreciate what the New Testament is doing in its pneumatology.

THE BOOK OF THE TWELVE

The Book of the Twelve is the collection of the prophets sometimes referred to as the minor prophets. Though they seem to have been composed separately under different circumstances, they have long been read as forming a unit with several themes running through.[3] Recent biblical scholarship has tried to recover this reading.[4] While several themes have been identified as uniting the Twelve, I would like to highlight one of them, the problem of the failure of prophecy, and argue that the Spirit is presented in the Book as the solution to this problem. It should be noted that there are some differences both in ordering and content between the Hebrew (MT or Masoretic Text) and the Greek (LXX or Septuagint text) of the Twelve Prophets, and as a result, there are also theological differences between the two, but for the purposes of our study here, the differences do not change the nature of the depiction of prophecy or of the Spirit.[5]

---

the understanding of the role of the spirit to possession, when he makes the statement that the reforming pre-exilic prophets "rarely expressed a consciousness that their prophetic endowment and powers were due to possession by or any action of the . . . *ruaḥ YHWH.*"

3. Sweeney, "Place and Function of Joel," 189–90. See also Sweeney, *Twelve Prophets*, 1:xv–xvii, on the ancient reading of the twelve as a unit.

4. Cf. Sweeney, *Twelve Prophets*, 1:xix–xxvii. See Sweeney, "Sequence and Interpretation," 175–88. Kessler, "Twelve," 209–10, suggests a linkage by catchwords.

5. Henceforth in this chapter, LXX will be used to refer to the Septuagint text and MT for the Masoretic text. Also of note is the Vulgate text, which is a rendering of the Hebrew text with some attempt at harmonization between the Septuagint text more commonly used by Christians and the Hebrew texts to which St. Jerome had access. See Sweeney, "Sequence and Interpretation," 177–78. The LXX ordering is Hosea–Amos–Micah–Joel–Obad–Jonah–Nahum–Habakkuk–Zephaniah–Haggai–Zechariah–Malachi. The MT orders the last six books exactly as does the LXX, but the first six are ordered Hosea–Joel–Amos–Obadiah–Jonah–Micah. Mostly, this chapter will focus on the Masoretic ordering and text, but where relevant, I have noted differences created by the ordering and the interpretation. Sweeney, "Sequence and Interpretation," gives one account of the thematic factors which underlie the two different orderings.

WHO SHALL PROPHESY TO THE PROPHETS?

Conflict between prophets, and the problem of false prophecy, is a common theme in the prophetic literature.[6] In Jeremiah 23:34, the Lord, responding to false and mercenary prophets misusing him, says that he will fall silent, so that there will be no one to say, "the burden of the Lord." In Ezekiel 13:23, the Lord says in response to the same issue that there will be no more false visions. This theme runs through the Twelve Prophets, together with other themes such as the Day of the Lord, and the idea of Israel as a model for God's judgement of the whole universe. The idea of the corruption or rejection of prophecy emerges as a developing problem with a truly startling conclusion: the complete cessation of prophecy itself.

Thus, in Hosea the prophets share the weakness (LXX)/stumbling (MT) of the people (cf. Hos 4:5). They are dwelt in by the spirit of fornication (cf. Hos 4:12, 5:4). Prophecy either fails to turn the people around though God hews his people through them (cf. MT Hos 6:5), or the prophets themselves are hewn and slaughtered (cf. LXX Hos 6:5), in either case a shocking reversal of the normal relationship between a nation and its god(s).[7] Part of the judgement of Israel for her evil is that the prophet is a fool, and the man of Spirit is mad.[8] In all the prophet's ways is a fowler's snare, though he be a watchman of Ephrem (cf. MT Hos 9:7–8).[9] Hosea 9:9 then speaks of the prophets or Israel as deeply corrupt. In the LXX, the prophet shares the oppression and madness of Israel, and as in the MT, his ways are a snare. Later on, Hosea says that God used to work through the prophets (cf. MT Hos 12:10, 13) but he will now be punished, itself implying a failure of prophecy.

In Amos, it is said that the Lord does nothing without revealing it to his servants, the prophets, and that once the Lord has spoken, one cannot but prophesy (cf. Amos 3:7–8). But though God has hitherto taken prophets from the young men of his people, but now they tell the prophets

6. See Blenkinsopp, *History of Prophecy in Israel*, 186–88. For a view that where there are prophets, this conflict is normal and inevitable, see Grabbe, "Shaman, Priest, or Spirit Medium," 127.

7. Sweeney, *Twelve Prophets*, 1:72.

8. Sweeney, *Twelve Prophets*, 1:97, reads this as incompetence. He also notes that other commentators have read this as taunts directed at the prophet. For one such reading, see Peterson, *Roles of Israel's Prophets*, 62–63. Peterson reads it as a typical Israelite taunt against the Judean figure of a prophet, and therefore also reads Hosea as having a uniquely positive understanding of the prophetic movement.

9. Sweeney, *Twelve Prophets*, 1:97, reads this as the inadequacy of the prophet to prevent the people from falling into the snare. In either sense, this is an indictment of prophecy, but my version sharpens the indictment.

not to prophesy (cf. Amos 2:11–12). This is instantiated in Amos 7:12–16, when Amaziah tells Amos to go back and prophecy in Judah. Amos' own prophesying can be seen as a continuation of the Lord's faithfulness to his commitment to the institution of prophecy, but Amos disclaims being a prophet in Amos 7:14–16. Rather, he says that prophesying is inevitable to anyone to whom God reveals his words. A prophet is less a member of a guild as in 1–2 Kings, and more an individual whom the Lord chooses and sends to announce his will.[10] Another response to the brewing crisis is put forward in Micah 3:5–12, where God says that he will put an end to prophecy, because they are all mercenary.[11]

The crisis nonetheless continues to the later books of the twelve. For the most part, Zechariah (e.g., Zech 1:4–7; 7:7, 12), changes focus from prophetic corruption to prophetic ineffectiveness, arguing that prophetic preaching is ineffective and people don't listen to it. Zechariah still recognizes that prophecy is a continuing institution, and urges those who have been listening to the prophets to look to him in hope (cf. Zech 8:9). However, when the Lord cleanses Jerusalem, he also sweeps away prophecy (cf. Zech 13:2). The extent of the reaction against prophecy can be seen in the warning which follows, and its warning that if anyone claimed to be a prophet his own parents would run him through (cf. Zech 13:3). God says that if anyone is accused of prophesying, he will deny that he is a prophet much as Amos already has (cf. Amos 7:14), but here the reason for the denial is shame (cf. Zech 13:4–6).[12] The final word on prophecy in the Book of the Twelve is Malachi's foreshadowing of the return of the archetype of the prophet, Elijah (cf. Mal 4:5). But if we look at the history of versions of the prophet, we find that the Septuagint does not call Elijah "the prophet" but simply identifies him as "Elijah, the Tishbite." Whether the Septuagint represents a different tradition of the original text, or that this reflects a translation choice, again this change witnesses to a disenchantment with the institution.

In the Masoretic order, an alternative to the institution of prophecy is already foreseen in the second book of the Twelve, when the Lord announces (cf. Joel 3:1–2) that prophecy will be universalized.[13] In the Septuagintal order, the universalization of prophecy in Joel, the fourth book

10. Cf. Sweeney, *Twelve Prophets*, 1:260.

11. Sweeney, *Twelve Prophets*, 2:370–72. Andersen and Freedman, *Micah*, 361, notes that Micah is described as prophesying, but also as not being a prophet.

12. Sweeney, *Twelve Prophets*, 2:693–96, narrows down the concern here to false prophecy. Zechariah, I would argue, is being much more universal in this sweeping away of prophecy.

13. Crenshaw, *Joel*, 164–67.

of the Twelve, follows on the end of prophecy as an institution announced in Micah, the third book (cf. Mic 3:5–8).[14]

But universalization does not entirely solve the problem of prophecy as we see with Jonah, a prophet who, as has long been recognized, represents Israel.[15] In Jonah, we see Israel's rejection of its vocation of prophecy[16] and God having to drag the prophet/Israel back to that vocation through the sojourn in the belly of the whale which is a transparent metaphor for the experience of exile. But even so, the book ends with the prophet grumbling about the ways of God, and being called to recognize the need for his own conversion. Even if Israel/Jonah is a prophetic nation, it still needs someone to prophesy to it.

GOD'S RESPONSE THROUGH HIS SPIRIT(S)

The need for continuing prophecy to Israel is heightened by the presence of several other competing powers at work in the world, which hostile to Israel's integrity and to her God. A simple cessation of prophecy would be leaving the world to its chaos, from the Biblical perspective where creation was an act of bringing order to chaos, a reversal of creation itself. A world where the voice of God went unheard is indeed threatened in an extraordinary moment in Hosea 1:9, where Israel is identified as Not my people, and God says that he will not be (a direct contradiction of the name of God revealed in Exodus 3:19).[17] However, God relents from this to say that Israel is once again God's people, and he remains her God. But there is another aspect to the solution to the problem of prophecy within the book of the twelve. God's "repentance" does not happen in isolation from the repentance of human beings, and that repentance, in the book of the Twelve, results from God's gift of his spirit. This is also the case elsewhere in prophetic literature, as for instance in Ezekiel 26:37; 37:41, and Isaiah 44:3; 59:21. But in the book of the Twelve, the Spirit is shown in action in a way that anticipates the action of the Spirit in the book of Acts.

14. See Hillers, *Micah*, 44–46.

15. Sweeney, *Twelve Prophets*, 1:309. Sweeney has a very insightful reflection on Jonah Ben Amittai, as the dove (wavering, "senseless" and "fickle") who is nonetheless the son of "Truth" (*Amittai*), though he argues that part of what is at stake in the book is also God's faithfulness to Israel and the truthfulness of what he threatens (and thereby promises) in prophecy. See Limburg, *Jonah*, 59.

16. On the unprophetic behavior of Jonah and its connection to the rejection of his being an Israelite in favor of identification as a Hebrew, see Sweeney, *Twelve Prophets*, 1:313–14.

17. For this interpretation, see Blenkinsopp, *History of Prophecy in Israel*, 103.

The role of the spirit or spirits in the direction of prophesy is often obscured in the English translation which renders the Hebrew word, (rûaḥ), as wind rather than spirit (with or without a capital letter). But more is at stake here than merely the translation of a word.[18] Winds, whirlwinds, and tempests from God, all described using different Hebrew or Greek words, are the means by which God acts to direct prophecy.[19] In MT Hosea 4:19, a רוּחַ (rûaḥ) wraps Ephraim in its skirts, which will lead to their shame. The imagery suggests a wind which reveals the shame of a feminine Israel, but the wind is an agent that brings about that shame as well. But if this spirit seems to be responsible for the corruption of Israel, in Hosea 8:7, Ephrem's sowing of the wind (רוּחַ, rûaḥ) will beget a whirlwind (סוּפָה, sûphâ). The sowing of destruction in other words will meet a response in a greater disruption by God.[20] Likewise, in Hosea 12:2, Ephrem follows the wind (רוּחַ, rûaḥ), and chases the east wind (קָדִים, qādîm). The parallelism here suggests that Ephrem is chasing after destruction. The LXX renders this to harmonize with Hosea 8:7, where Ephrem is an evil wind chasing a burning wind. This is not just a case of bad bringing worse in its trail, because in Hosea 13:15, the קָדִים (East Wind, qādîm) is identified as רוּחַ יְהוָה (wind/ spirit of the Lord, rûaḥ YHWH).

Joel, as we have already seen, has God pouring out his spirit/wind upon all flesh. As in Hosea, however, this pouring out of the spirit which results in prophecy has a certain disruptiveness,[21] and this disruptiveness

18. For one example of narrowing down on רוּחַ, see Congar, *I Believe in the Holy Spirit*, 1:3. For the association of the spirit with prophecy, see Congar, *I Believe in the Holy Spirit*, 1:6–7.

19. This is often lost sight of when the focus is on the spirit as personally possessing and effectively dictating the prophecy, as in Mowinckel, *Spirit and the Word*, 84–86. Mowinckel, in contrast to what I argue here, sees the "literary prophets" as placing "power, justice, and might" which the true prophet has in contrast to the windiness, or even uncleanness, of the false prophet. Mowinckel has far too unitary an understanding of the spirit which takes no account of the several different kinds of spirits in action in the prophets, both positive and negative. For the idea of great storms as part of God's repertory of messengers, see Sasson, *Jonah*, 94.

20. Sweeney, *Twelve Prophets*, 1:89, interprets the wind as referring to the emptiness of the idols which will bring destruction. But that doesn't seem to account for the one-upmanship of the verse.

21. Congar, *I Believe in the Holy Spirit*, 1:9 recognizes the purifying activity of the spirit, but not entirely the destructive aspect of this. Likewise, Blenkinsopp, *History of Prophecy in Israel*, 258, sees a parallel here with Ezek 39:29, 26:26, 37:1–14, but not with the action of the spirits in the rest of the Twelve prophets which explains the cosmic disruption which follows. See also Sweeney, "Place and Function of Joel," 199–200. For a closer reading of the spirit to my own, see Sweeney, *Twelve Prophets*, 1:173–74. Sweeney sees the link between wind and cosmic transformation and prophecy as demonstrating "the interrelatedness of the natural and the human worlds." See also

has a creative aspect to it. The pouring out of the Spirit occurs after all in the midst not just of God's reassurance of his people that they will never be ashamed henceforth, but also in the context of God showing "portents . . . of blood and fire and columns of smoke" (MT Joel 2:28; 3:1–4). As Marvin Sweeney explains, the "dry desert wind" which "darkens the sun and causes the moon to appear red as blood is both destructive and transformative in that it marks the transition from one season to another; one reality is destroyed as another emerged."[22] It is only those who call on the name of the Lord who will escape the destruction wrought by God.

In Amos 1:14, Ammon is devoured by a סַעַר (gale, *sa'ar*) in the day of the whirlwind (יוֹם סוּפָה, *yôm sûpâ*).[23] Later, in Amos 4:13 God is identified as making the mountains and creating the spirit/wind (יוֹצֵר הָרִים וּבֹרֵא רוּחַ, *yôtzēr hārim ûborē' rûaḥ*). This phrase, with its echoes of Isaiah's description of God as "[forming] the light, and [creating] darkness; [making] peace, and [creating] evil" (Isa 45:7: יוֹצֵר אוֹר וּבוֹרֵא חֹשֶׁךְ, עֹשֶׂה שָׁלוֹם וּבֹרֵא רָע, *yôtzēr 'or ûborē' ḥošek 'ośeh šālôm ûbôrē' rā]'*) hints at God's destructive as well as his creative power.[24]

But it is in Jonah, the prophet who symbolizes the prophetic vocation of Israel, that the combination of the destructive and creative aspects of God's spirit is most clearly explored. Jonah is a prophet himself in need of conversion,[25] a conversion which the end of the book leaves as a question. But over the course of the book, we see that when Jonah runs away from his vocation, God hurls a רוּחַ (*ruaḥ*) upon the sea, thereby causing a tempest (סַעַר, *sa'ar*). Jonah's personal experience of God's disruptive spirit for his own actions brings down a disruption that extends beyond him.[26] And so too, the descent of the רוּחַ (*ruaḥ*) leads to the conversion of the sailors, who turn from praying to their various gods to praying to, fearing, and sacrificing and making vows to Lord (cf. Jonah 1:5, 14–16), all activities characteristic

---

Crenshaw, *Joel*, 167–68. The disruptiveness also militates against reading the text purely as a gift of the Lord's "life force" that animates and renews life, as Barton, *Joel and Obadiah*, 94–97, does. In line with the rest of his reading, Barton sees Joel 3:3–4 as a disconnected fragment of prophecy.

22. Sweeney, *Twelve Prophets*, 1:174–75.

23. Cf. Barton's comment in "Theology of Amos," 193, that the Lord "for Amos is above all the destroyer: a just destroyer, but a destroyer nonetheless."

24. Sweeney, *Twelve Prophets*, 1:230.

25. Blenkinsopp, *History of Prophecy in Israel*, 270–73, sees Jonah as a "sapiential critique of prophecy" implying that prophecy and the prophetic presentation of God does not limit God's freedom to save. But Blenkinsopp does not quite see that freedom as directed to a rectification of prophecy itself.

26. Sweeney, *Twelve Prophets*, 1:311, remarks on the disruptive aspect.

of the people of God.[27] Meanwhile, Jonah himself affirms that he reverences (MT: יָרֵא, yārē' / LXX: σέβομαι, sebomai) the Lord. And in order to put an end to the storminess (Jonah 1:11–13: סָעַר,[28] so'ēr) of the sea, he is thrown into the sea.[29] It is in the belly of the fish, a transparent symbol for the exile,[30] that Jonah prays (for the first time) in words which echo various verses of the psalms.[31] After the whale spews him out, Jonah fulfills his prophetic function which leads to the conversion of the city of Nineveh (Jonah 3). When Jonah is indignant at the conversion of the Ninevites as a result of his preaching and prays the prayer of Elijah to have his life taken from him (cf. 1 Kgs 19:4),[32] God again resorts to a vehement East wind (רוּחַ קָדִים, rûaḥ qādîm) to move Jonah out of his opposition to God's will.[33] Throughout the book of Jonah, we see God using the wind/Spirit in a way that is destructive and disruptive and nonetheless also as the Spirit brings conversion and renewal to Jonah and to the nations, bringing Israel to fulfill her prophetic role in obedience to God.[34]

In Micah 2:7, the Spirit of the Lord (רוּחַ יְהוָה, rûaḥ YHWH) is used as a metonym for the Lord, either as a way of expressing the anger of the Lord[35] or his (assumed) powerlessness, in either case as a rhetorical question addressed at those who would silence the prophets. In contrast to these, the people prefer "a man walking in the wind" (אִישׁ הֹלֵךְ רוּחַ, 'îš holēk rûaḥ)[36]

27. Sweeney, *Twelve Prophets*, 1:315–16; Limburg, *Jonah*, 57–59.

28. The LXX translates this with a circumlocution for the seas rising and falling.

29. Sweeney, *Twelve Prophets*, 1:314, points out that this is a further fleeing from his prophetic vocation towards death. The exile is the solution rather than extinction as Jonah had thought.

30. The parallel is highlighted by the ironic use of the word *qw'* (to spew out) for the whale's action in expelling Jonah, which echoes the threatened punishment for the misdeeds of the people of God in Lev 18:25, 28; 20:22.

31. For the echoes, see Sasson, *Jonah*, 171–214; Limburg, *Jonah*, 63–72.

32. Limburg, *Jonah*, 92–93. The function of wind in the Elijah episode is suggestive, but there is no corresponding note in Jonah as in the books of Kings that the Lord is not in the wind (cf. 1 Kgs 19:11).

33. Sweeney, *Twelve Prophets*, 1:330–31.

34. Cf. in contrast to this reading, Sweeney, *Twelve Prophets*, 1:305–7, for a reading which sees Jonah as presenting a question of theodicy about why God spares the evil nations, and God's sovereignty in this respect.

35. Andersen and Freedman, *Micah*, 309–11, has a discussion of the alternatives. He argues that it is rather the Lord's "Spirit . . . active in prophecy" with the negative implying that the Lord remains powerful. A very different reading is offered by Hillers, *Micah*, 34–37, where it is read as a response by the people assuring themselves that the Lord has not exhausted his patience.

36. The LXX Mic 2:7 retains the conflict but changes the sentence so that a spirit establishes lying. The Vulgate has instead "Would that I were not a man having the spirit and rather spoke lies."

who prophesies lies (Mic 2:11).[37] Announcing the cessation of prophecy on which we have remarked above, the speaker of the prophecy nonetheless declares himself filled with power by the spirit of the Lord (cf. Mic 3:8: אָנֹכִי מָלֵאתִי כֹחַ אֶת-רוּחַ יְהוָה, *ānokî mālē'tî koah et-ruah YHWH*).[38]

In Nahum, we witness once again the destructive aspect of the Lord's spirit directed at the enemies of Israel, appropriately enough for a book which reverses the sparing of the Ninevites in Jonah. Pointedly, the Lord is said in Nah 1:3 to be in the whirlwind and the storm (בְּסוּפָה וּבִשְׂעָרָה, *běsûpâ ûbiś'ārâ*),[39] rebuking the sea and making a full end of the place of his enemies (cf. Nah 1:8). Here it is the voice of the messengers of Nineveh, rather than that of God's prophets, which will no longer be heard (cf. Nah 2:14).

In Habakuk 1:11, it is, by contrast, the spirit of the invading Chaldeans which changes and overruns and causes him to fall (אָז חָלַף רוּחַ, *āz hālap rûah*) so that he worships his own strength. But the graven image the Chaldean worships has no breath (רוּחַ אֵין, *rûah 'ēn*) in it at all (cf. Hab 2:19). The idolatrousness of the Chaldean military, and its being devoid of real power in contrast to the Lord's might is again highlighted by describing them as storming to scatter the speaker of the book (cf. Hab 3:14), just as God scatters the mountains (cf. Hab 3:6).[40] On the other hand, in Haggai 1:14, the Lord stirs up the spirit (רוּחַ, *rûah*) of Zerubbabel, Joshua, and the remnant of the people so that they could do his work, much as earlier in the book of the Twelve, the Lord stirs up winds and storms.[41] And the Lord promises them that his spirit (רוּחַ, *rûah*) will dwell with them (cf. Hag 2:5)[42] and he will shake "the heavens, the earth, the sea, and the dry land . . . and all the nations" so that their wealth can flow to his house, the temple (cf.

---

37. Mowinckel, *Spirit and the Word*, 85.

38. Sweeney, *Twelve Prophets*, 2:370–72, highlights Micah's hostility to the other prophets, and argues that, since this is the only place where Micah presents himself as a prophet, it might well be a gloss explaining that Micah is indeed speaking from the Lord. He also notes that the "spirit" is appositional here, explaining how it is that Micah, despite not belonging to a professional guild, is a prophet. Andersen and Freedman, *Micah*, 376–77, point out the oddness of the Hebrew construction.

39. Sweeney, *Twelve Prophets*, 2:429 makes the point that this suggests the metaphor of an approaching army, but also that highlights the Lord's "power and capacity for destruction."

40. Sweeney, *Twelve Prophets*, 2:478.

41. As Sweeney, *Twelve Prophets*, 2:540–42, argues, Haggai's use of the prophetic language of "the remnant," and his identification of himself as "the messenger" of the Lord, is of a piece with this reference to the "stirring up of the Spirit," a term often used in relation to the Prophets.

42. This is a straightforward metonymy for the Lord himself. Sweeney, *Twelve Prophets*, 2:547.

Hag 2:6–7). The combination of the disruption, renewal, and the spirit of the Lord continues.

The theme of the conflict of spirits reaches its conclusion in Zechariah, which ends with the triumph of God and the destruction of the unclean spirit. In Zechariah 2:6 (LXX Zech 2:10), Zion has been spread as the four winds of heaven (כְּאַרְבַּע רוּחוֹת הַשָּׁמַיִם, *kĕarbaʿrûḥot hašā mayim*). In Zechariah 4:6–9, Zerubbabel is told that he will perform great works by the Lord's spirit, levelling mountains and building up God's house. In Zechariah 5:9, the mysterious women who transport the Ephah of wickedness to Shinar, are moved by the wind (רוּחַ, *rûaḥ*) beneath their wings. Zechariah 6:5 describes the four horses as the four winds/spirits of heaven, that go forth after presenting themselves to the Lord of all the earth, and a little later, the ones going to the North (from which invasions come, as noted in Jeremiah 1:14, or because the prophet is thinking of the restoration of Israel, in the North) are said to set the spirit of the Lord at rest (cf. Zech 6:8). It was the same spirit of the Lord that was at work in the former prophets (cf. Zech 7:12) to whom the people did not listen, and as a result he stormed and scattered them with a whirlwind (cf. Zech 7:14: סָעַר, *sāʿar*)[43] to alien nations.[44] In Zechariah 9:14, the Lord is said to go in the whirlwinds of the south (בְּסַעֲרוֹת תֵּימָן, *bĕsaʿărôt ṭēmān*) to sustain the sons of Zion as they execute God's vengeance on the Greeks (cf. Zech 9:13–15). Zechariah 12:1 reminds us that the God who created the heavens and the earth also formed the spirit of man (רוּחַ-אָדָם, *rûaḥ-ādām*). The use of *rûaḥ* becomes more significant at the end of the chapter, when God, destroying the opponents of Jerusalem, says that he will "pour on the house of David and the inhabitants of Jerusalem, the spirit of grace and supplication" (רוּחַ חֵן וְתַחֲנוּנִים, *rûaḥ ḥēn wtaḥănûnîm*) causing mourning for their misdeeds (cf. Zech 12:10). In Zechariah 13:3, God says that he will remove the unclean (רוּחַ הַטֻּמְאָה, *rûaḥ hatṭumâ*), significantly together with prophets, leaving a pure people who will call him "my God" and whom he will call "my people," fulfilling what is promised in Hosea 2:1, 25.[45]

Thus, through his use of winds and his spirit(s), God directs and corrects the prophesying of his people. There are a variety of spirits at work in the world, but God acts through his spirit(s), and is in ultimate control. The spirit(s) often serve merely as the means through which God works albeit a particularly powerful means, but is also sometimes portrayed as

43. The verb occurs only seven times in the Scriptures, five times in the book of the Twelve, and most notably here and in Jonah to refer to God's disturbing activity. Isaiah 54:11 uses it to mean "tempest tossed."

44. Sweeney, *Twelve Prophets*, 2:645.

45. Sweeney, *Twelve Prophets*, 2:673.

a personal agent, sometimes a metonym for the Lord. In either case, the spirit(s) of the Lord are powerful and unfailingly efficacious, and the spirit reveals the power of the Lord in guiding his people. This continues into the New Testament and its depiction of the Holy Spirit's action in guiding the mission of Christ and the early Church.

FROM THE PNEUMATOLOGY OF THE TWELVE TO ACTS

Thus far, we have seen that the book of the Twelve is concerned with the problems with the institution of prophecy, and prophecy either being ignored by the people or itself sharing in the corruption of the people. One emerging response to this "crisis of prophecy" is that God would put an end to prophecy and universalize prophecy to all his people. This solution still does not escape the problem of the corruption and hard heartedness of the people of God. In response to this, the book of the Twelve develops the theme of the action of God's wind/spirit which is destructive and disruptive but draws the prophet and the people to do God's work of prophesying. The presence of an active spirit in the book of the Twelve is not just a matter of the use of the word, *rûaḥ*, but a consistent portrayal of God's disruptive action through whirlwind(s) and spirits which draws the people to fulfill their prophetic function.

This aspect of the activity of the Spirit is also clearly evident in the New Testament.[46] In Luke-Acts, John is proclaimed as "going before the Lord in the Spirit and power of Elijah," a reference to Malachi 4:5–6, where Elijah's reappearance represents both the conclusion of a flawed prophetic tradition, and its renewal.[47] The coming of the Holy Spirit causes Mary to become the mother of the Messiah, Elizabeth to exclaim at the coming of Mary, and Zechariah to prophesy (cf. Luke 1:35, 41, 67). The Spirit is upon Simeon, has promised him the sight of the Messiah, and brings him to the temple and the prophecy he utters there (cf. Luke 2:25–32). But the Spirit also plays a disruptive role here, descending upon Jesus, and promptly leading him out into the wilderness (cf. Luke 3:22, 4:1) to be tempted. It is the Spirit who anoints him to bring the good news to the poor. There are also evil spirits here, over which Jesus has authority as revealed by his expulsion of them (cf. Luke 4:33, 36). The spirits are participants in a conflict in the Gospel of Luke much as in the book of the Twelve. At the same time, Jesus tells his disciples, not to rejoice because "the spirits are subject to you; but rejoice that your names are written in heaven." The Spirit is also the source

46. Rowland, "Prophecy and the New Testament," 412.
47. Rowland, "Prophecy and the New Testament," 413.

of God's direction and protection of his people. Jesus himself rejoices in the Holy Spirit and thanks God (cf. Luke 10:20–21). The Father will give the Holy Spirit to anyone who asks (cf. Luke 11:13). Likewise, Jesus warns his disciples that unclean spirits remain threatening even after they leave someone and can bring other spirits with them to afflict him again (cf. Luke 11:24–26). The Holy Spirit will teach the disciples what to say, and those who blaspheme against the Holy Spirit will not be forgiven (cf. Luke 12:10, 12). Jesus, dying, commends his spirit to the Father (cf. Luke 23:46). Spirits remain frightened. When Jesus' disciples see him again, they are afraid because they think he is a spirit (cf. Luke 24:37, 39).

In Acts, Jesus commands the disciples through the Holy Spirit, and promises them baptism in the Spirit and the power of the Holy Spirit to proclaim him (cf. Acts 1:2, 5, 7). The coming of the Holy Spirit, which Luke reminds us fulfills Joel, makes the disciples prophecy,[48] but is cosmically disturbing, and brings salvation to the people (cf. Acts 2:4, 17–21). Peter preaches about Jesus pouring out the Holy Spirit and calls his audience to repent and receive the Holy Spirit (cf. Acts 2:33, 38). When the Apostles pray, they are filled with the Holy Spirit, following a disturbance, and speak the word of God (cf. Acts 4:31). Ananias and Sapphira tempt the Holy Spirit, lie to him, and meet their death as a result (cf. Acts 5:3, 9). The Holy Spirit bears joint witness with the Apostles, and when they look to ordain deacons, they look for people who are full of the Spirit. Stephen is one such person, and being full of the Holy Spirit speaks with an irresistible wisdom (cf. Acts 6:3, 5, 10). As he is dying, the Spirit, it is implied, opens his eyes and let him see the heavens with Jesus standing at the right hand of God's glory (cf. Acts 7:55). He accuses the people of resisting the Holy Spirit, and when he dies, like Jesus, hands his own spirit into Jesus' hands (cf. Acts 7:51, 59). Much as with the corrupt prophets of old, Simon attempts to purchase the gift of the Spirit, but is rebuked for it (cf. Acts 8:15–24). The Spirit directs Philip to join the chariot of the Ethiopian eunuch, and after the Eunuch's baptism, transports Philip away (cf. Acts 8:29, 39). Ananias describes his mission to Paul as enabling him to "regain his sight and receive the Holy Spirit" (cf. Acts 9:17). In Acts 9:31, the Holy Spirit comforts the Church and multiplies it. The Spirit plays an active role in this multiplication. Much as with Jonah, it is the action of the Spirit who brings the Gentile Cornelius and his companions to the attention of Peter, and while he is preaching descends upon them to make them praise God (cf. Acts 10:19, 45–46; 11:12–16). Through the Spirit, Agabus foretells a great famine (cf. Acts 11:28). The

---

48. For the renewal of prophecy in Acts, see Rowland, "Prophecy and the New Testament," 411.

Spirit calls for Barnabas and Saul to be set aside for the mission, sends them out to Seleucia and Cyprus (cf. Acts 13:2, 4), and gives Paul insight to rebuke Elymas for trying to "make crooked the straight paths of the Lord" (cf. Acts 13:9). But the Holy Spirit also forbids Paul and Timothy from preaching in Asia and sends them through Phrygia and Galatia, forbidding them again from going into Bithynia (cf. Acts 16:6–7). The conflict of spirits remains a constant as Paul confronts a girl with a spirit of divination and expels it from her (cf. Acts 16:16, 18), an act which earns him hostility and imprisonment. But, like Jonah after his spell in the belly of the whale, Paul preaches, prays, and brings about the conversion of his jailer and his family (cf. Acts 16:16–35). Later, the garments which have touched Paul are able to expel spirits, but when Jews who are not followers of Christ attempt to use the name of Jesus to do the same, the spirits question who they are and end up afflicting them instead. This then leads to another great conversion and turning from idols (cf. Acts 19:11–20). Paul directs the course of his journeys in the Spirit (cf. Acts 19:21), and he will describe himself as "bound in the Spirit" who has told him of the imprisonment and the sufferings he must bear (Acts 20:22–23). The disciples tell Paul in the Spirit not to go to Jerusalem (cf. Acts 21:4), and later, Agabus, in the Spirit, prophecies Paul's imprisonment and being handed over to the gentiles (cf. Acts 21:11). At Jerusalem, it is the prospect of a spirit or an angel speaking to Paul that disrupts the unity between the Pharisees and Sadducees at Paul's trial (cf. Acts 23:8–9). Paul's last invocation of the Holy Spirit in the book is, intriguingly, a reference to the resistance of the ancestors of his interlocutors, rebuked by the Holy Spirit through Isaiah the prophet.

The portrait of the Holy Spirit in Luke-Acts is much more personalized than in the book of the Twelve, but at the same time carries forward the same idea of the conflict of spirits that we observe there. Likewise, the Spirit acts disruptively where necessary, and guides the prophetic action of the people of God as in the book of the Twelve. The Spirit controls the course of this prophesy and moves and binds the prophets to act according to God's will, as in the Twelve.

CONCLUSION

Thus, we see again and again in the New Testament, as in Luke-Acts, a presentation of the action of the Holy Spirit which is disruptive particularly to the person who receives it, but which also moves, directs, redirects, and enables the fulfillment of the prophetic function of the people of God to live in union with God, and bring salvation to the gentile nations. This is not an unprecedented claim. It builds on the depiction of God working through winds, spirits, and storms in the book of the Twelve Prophets to correct and redirect the people of God in their prophetic vocation.

BIBLIOGRAPHY

Andersen, Francis I., and David Noel Freedman. *Micah: A New Translation with Introduction and Commentary*. Anchor Yale Bible 24E. New York: Doubleday, 2000.

Barton, John. *Joel and Obadiah: A Commentary*. Louisville: Westminster John Knox, 2001.

———. "The Theology of Amos." In *Prophecy and Prophets in Ancient Israel: Proceedings of the Oxford Old Testament Seminar*, edited by John Day, 188–201. London: Bloomsbury, 2012.

Blenkinsopp, Joseph. *A History of Prophecy in Israel*. London: SPCK, 1984.

Congar, Yves. *I Believe in the Holy Spirit*. Vol. 1, *The Holy Spirit in the "Economy": Revelation and the Experience of the Spirit*. Translated by David Smith. London: Chapman, 1983.

Crenshaw, James L. *Joel: A New Translation with Introduction and Commentary*. Anchor Yale Bible 24C. New York: Doubleday, 1995.

Grabbe, Lester L. "Shaman, Priest, or Spirit Medium: The Israelite Prophet in the Light of Anthropological Models." In *Prophecy and Prophets in Ancient Israel: Proceedings of the Oxford Old Testament Seminar*, edited by John Day, 117–32. London: Bloomsbury, 2012.

Hillers, Delbert R. *Micah: A Commentary on the Book of the Prophet Micah*. Edited by Paul D. Hanson and Loren Fisher. Hermeneia—A Critical and Historical Commentary on the Bible. Philadelphia: Fortress, 1984.

Hurtado, Larry W. *Lord Jesus Christ: Devotion to Jesus in Earliest Christianity*. Grand Rapids: Eerdmans, 2003.

Kessler, Rainer. "The Twelve." In *The Oxford Handbook of the Prophets*, edited by Carolyn J. Sharp, 207–23. New York: Oxford University Press, 2016.

Limburg, James. *Jonah: A Commentary*. Louisville: Westminster John Knox, 1993.

Mowinckel, Sigmund. *The Spirit and the Word: Prophecy and Tradition in Ancient Israel*. Minneapolis: Fortress, 2002.

Petersen, David L. *The Roles of Israel's Prophets*. JSOT 17. Sheffield: JSOT, 1981.

Rowland, Christopher. "Prophecy and the New Testament." In *Prophecy and Prophets in Ancient Israel: Proceedings of the Oxford Old Testament Seminar*, edited by John Day, 410–30. London: Bloomsbury, 2012.

Sasson, Jack M. *Jonah: A New Translation with Introduction and Commentary*. Anchor Yale Bible 24B. New York: Doubleday, 1990.

Sweeney, Marvin A. "The Place and Function of Joel in the Book of the Twelve." In *Form and Intertextuality in Prophetic and Apocalyptic Literature*, 189–209. Eugene, OR: Wipf & Stock, 2005.

———. "Sequence and Interpretation in the Book of the Twelve." In *Form and Intertextuality in Prophetic and Apocalyptic Literature*, 175–88. Eugene, OR: Wipf & Stock, 2005.

―――. *The Twelve Prophets*. Vol. 1, *Hosea, Joel, Amos, Obadiah, Jonah*. Berit Olam: Studies in Hebrew Narrative and Poetry. Collegeville, MN: Liturgical, 2000.

―――. *The Twelve Prophets*. Vol. 2, *Micah, Nahum, Habakkuk, Zephaniah, Haggai, Zechariah, Malachi*. Berit Olam: Studies in Hebrew Narrative and Poetry. Collegeville, MN: Liturgical, 2000.

5

TERTULLIAN AND THE NEW PROPHECY

A Test-Case for the Contemporary Quest for Openness to the Spirit[1]

Adam G. Cooper

ALTHOUGH HE WROTE HIS earliest works in Greek, Tertullian of Carthage (d. ca. 220) is famously remembered in history as the father of Latin theology. He lived at a time when Christianity in northwest Africa was fast gaining a reputation of undiminished resilience in the face of persecution. An adult convert to Christianity, Tertullian was completely at home in the advanced intellectual and legal culture of both Rome and Greece. Yet his primary inspiration was Scripture and he filled Latin terms with new theological content. Tertullian was captivated by the Christian message of the crucified God, especially as recounted and proclaimed in the gospels and apostolic letters. Already a rhetorician of genius, he came to appreciate an even deeper sense of the power of words, "because Jesus Christ was for him a word-event."[2] Tertullian perceived the apparent folly and scandal

1. I would like to acknowledge the University of Divinity and Catholic Theological College for providing a small research grant towards the original delivery of this article as a lecture at the "Pneumatology at the Beginning of the Third Millennium" conference hosted by the University of Notre Dame Australia, Sydney, 2022.

2. Osborn, *Tertullian*, xiv.

of Christianity among his cultured contemporaries with its faith in a God glorified in humiliation. To the charge that catholic Christians embraced a superstition unworthy of a transcendent divinity, Tertullian responded: "In fact the whole of that which in my God is dishonorable in your sight, is a sign and token of man's salvation."[3]

THE NEW PROPHECY

Yet Tertullian is also remembered for his increasing sympathy for Montanism, that exuberant, charismatic movement which claimed the special inspiration of the Holy Spirit, and which was known at the time as the Phrygian movement or the New Prophecy. By the time Tertullian encountered it, the New Prophecy had already been underway for some forty years. Most of our knowledge about the initial emergence of the New Prophecy is based on later, critical accounts from the fourth century. According to a fragment recounted by Eusebius, its founder was given to "abnormal ecstasy," "frenzied babbling," "spurious utterances," and "new-fangled teaching." He and his movement were eventually judged heretical.[4] Epiphanius provided what appears to be an accurate list of utterances communicated by the Phrygian prophets, including oracles purporting to express the very voice of God.[5]

Nothing in those oracles, taken on its own, indicates any kind of doctrinal deviation from orthodox Christian teaching. The Church had always known the continuation of the prophetic office, even after the death of the apostles, and widely accepted the operation of ecstatic gifts and the possibility of the Spirit communicating in extraordinary ways, when and where he wills, by means of his chosen vessels. Nor in principle was the prominence of female leaders or prophetesses in Montanism a problem, even though more hostile critics often impugned the New Prophecy precisely for this reason. While the early Church reserved the functions of the presbyteral and episcopal ministry to suitably qualified and ordained men, women prophets had always been recognized right back to apostolic times.[6] The issue rather seemed to be one of practical interpretation,

---

3. Tertullian, *Marc.* 2.27.7, in Evans, *Tertullian*, 163.

4. Eusebius *HE* 5.16. For this passage along with a collection of relevant texts on Montanism, see Stevenson, *New Eusebius*, 102–8.

5. Epiphanius, *Pan.* 48–49, in Stevenson, *New Eusebius*, 107.

6. Cf. Tilley, "North Africa," 395–96: "Tertullian . . . opposed leadership roles for women, perhaps because of his association of women's leadership with gnostic theology. Not only was he at odds with African trends but also with members of the New Prophecy outside Africa." This claim needs qualification, in that Tertullian clearly accepted the

Church order, and the authoritative application of apostolic teaching in a new situation. Christine Trevett has argued that in the end the difference between Montanism and the catholic congregations from which it emerged was simply a matter of emphasis. Even though its followers either left or were expelled from the Church in due course,

> They shared in common with many Asian Christians Johannine incarnational orthodoxy, an anti-docetic/Gnostic stance . . . , prophetism (with appeal to New Testament and other prophets as forebears), Johannine Paraclete pneumatology, plus, perhaps, chiliasm. . . . The New Prophecy spread rapidly to Rome, North Africa and elsewhere. More rigorous (in fasting, for example) and less forgiving of failure and lapse, its followers were not at odds with apostolic tradition nor, in principle, with episcopacy.[7]

TERTULLIAN'S PNEUMATOLOGY

To what extent was Tertullian influenced by the New Prophecy, and what did that look like in his theology? His leaning towards the movement seems at one level to be connected with his opposition to Praxeas, a theologian who had attacked Montanism for being doctrinally deviant. Praxeas, whose name means "busy-body," had arrived in Rome toward end of the second century from Asia Minor. He taught a strict monarchianism, maintaining unity of the Godhead to the extent of declaring that the one who was crucified was none other than God the Creator and Father of all. The names Father and Son do not designate distinct persons, but simply reflect differing modalities of the one indivisible divinity. Praxeas was apparently strictured for his doctrine, yet not without persuading the "Bishop of Rome" to decide against the Montanist prophets.[8]

In his treatise against Praxeas, Tertullian complains that Praxeas not only "crucified the Father" and (so) "brought in heresy," but that he also "drove away prophecy" and "put to flight the Paraclete" (that is, he rejected the authenticity of the Montanists' *charismata*).[9] Tertullian was also critical of Praxeas' pneumatology, even though at this time (the first

leadership of women prophetesses, distinguishing it from the leadership of presbyters and bishops. See also Madigan and Osiek, *Ordained Women in the Early Church.*

7. Trevett, "Asia Minor and Achaea," 321–22. On possible weaknesses in Trevett's assessment and use of evidence, see Tilley's review of Trevett's *Montanism*, 726–28.

8. Tertullian's use of this somewhat minimalist title (see, e.g., *Prax.* 1) may indicate his ire about this turn-around decision.

9. Tertullian, *Prax.* 1 (Robert and Donaldson, *Ante-Nicene Fathers* [hereafter ANF] 3:597).

decade of the third century) pneumatology was "still at a very early stage of development."[10] In the baptismal liturgy, the doxologies, and the *regula fidei* of the Church, the Holy Spirit was named with the Father and the Son. And Irenaeus of course, whose works Tertullian had studied, had placed the Spirit alongside the Word in the *ad extra* acts of God and spoke of his special role in sanctifying the believer. Yet theologians to this time were "very little concerned to go on to define the Spirit's position within the divine sphere."[11]

In the works following his confrontation with Praxeas, Tertullian increasingly demonstrates special interest in the Holy Spirit. He is one of the earliest thinkers explicitly to call the Holy Spirit, God: "The Father is God, the Son is God and the Spirit is God, and each one is Lord."[12] Eastern theologians certainly treated the Spirit as divine, and lauded the divine character of his activity, but did not explicitly call him "God," *Theos*, it seems, until after the middle of the fourth century.[13] For Tertullian, the Spirit is the representative of the Son, who issues from the Father through the Son (*a patre per filium*), being "third from the Father and the Son, just as the fruit derived from the shoot is third from the root, and as the channel drawn off from the river is third from the spring, and as the light-point in the beam is third from the sun."[14] The Spirit also is a *persona*, a specific subsistent entity, so that the one God really is a *trinitas*, a "three," or a *trinitas unius divinitatis*, a threesome or triad of one divinity.[15] They are different only by way of disposition (*dispositio*), not by separation (*separatio*). In all these formulations, Tertullian's theology is drawn by reflection on the actual facts of the economy, not, like Praxeas' teaching, from the abstract idea of monarchy. God is indeed one, agrees Tertullian, but "through the Son and the Spirit" we have come to know God's unity "in a new way."[16]

---

10. Studer, *Trinity and Incarnation*, 72. See also Litfin, "Tertullian on the Trinity," 81–98; McGowan, "Tertullian," 437–57.

11. Studer, *Trinity and Incarnation*, 72.

12. Tertullian, *Prax.* 13 (ANF 3:608).

13. See Prestige, *God in Patristic Thought*, 92.

14. Tertullian, *Prax.* 8 (ANF 3:609). For discussion of this passage in the context of the development of Trinitarian doctrine, see Kelly, *Early Christian Doctrines*, 112–15.

15. Tertullian was the first to coin the term *trinitas* in theology. Theophilus was first to use the equivalent Greek term *triad*, which Hippolytus used after him.

16. Tertullian, *Prax.* 31 (ANF 3:627).

OPEN TO THE PARACLETE

For all his pioneering developments in pneumatology in the context of Trinitarian theology, it is especially in his ecclesiology and ethics that Tertullian pushes into new ground on the question of the Spirit's role in the divine economy and in the present life and well-being of the Church. Across a range of controversial pastoral questions—from remarriage of widows and absolution of grave sins to propriety in fasting, dress, and demeanor—Tertullian invokes the Holy Spirit, the Paraclete, as the giver of a strict, new, sanctifying discipline that exceeds the rigor of the New Testament writings. Recalling Jesus' promise that he had much more yet to teach his disciples, that only the Spirit would eventually enable them to bear, Tertullian writes: "The Paraclete has many things to teach which the Lord deferred until such time as he should come."[17] So, for example, the Paraclete, speaking through his appointed charismatic vessels, now forbids remarriage to those whose first spouse has died. The concessions the apostle Paul had made, which allowed remarriage to the widowed, the Holy Spirit now has abrogated, "so that in these days the flesh should be pinned down at last. . . . For now more than ever it is true that the time is short."[18] Does this not represent an innovation opposed to catholic teaching, a rule which imposes upon the faithful a burden beyond the "light burden" given by the Lord (Matt 11:42)? Quoting John 16:12, with its promise that the Spirit will guide the Church into all truth, Tertullian explains: in this way the Lord "sufficiently indicates that the Holy Spirit will reveal such things as may be considered innovations, since they were not revealed before, and burdensome, since it was for this reason that they were not revealed."[19]

In actual fact what the Holy Spirit now teaches on this question of remarriage (or digamy, as it was called then) is not a new but an ancient discipline. "It was already revealed in our Lord's chastity . . . and later by recommendation and example of his Apostles. . . . It is no novelty that the Paraclete reveals. What he foretold; he now fulfills. What he deferred, he now exacts."[20] The newness of these teachings consists in the fact that they have only just been revealed, and if they seem burdensome it is only because up until now they have not been required. "Nevertheless, their author is the very same Christ who said that he had yet many *other things* which the

---

17. Tertullian, *De monog.* 2 (*Treatises* [hereafter ACW] 13:75).
18. Tertullian, *De monog.* 3 (ACW 13:75).
19. Tertullian, *De monog.* 2 (ACW 13:71).
20. Tertullian, *De monog.* 3 (ACW 13:76).

Paraclete should teach, things which would be found no less a burden by men of our own day than by those who in his day could bear them not."[21]

Tertullian similarly invokes the authority of the Paraclete for his rigorist disposition towards those who, having fallen into fornication or adultery, now seek absolution and re-admission to the communion of the Church. It is true, admits Tertullian, that the Church has power to forgive sins. But citing the oracles recently given through the New Prophecy, Tertullian proposes a more cautious, less indulgent approach:

> I have the Paraclete himself in the persons of the new prophets, saying, "The church has the power to forgive sins, but I will not do it, lest they commit other sins because of it." . . . No doubt the Spirit of truth does indeed have the power of indulgently granting pardon to fornicators, but wills not to do it if it will involve harm for the majority.[22]

What then of the power to loose sins granted to Peter and through him to the bishops of the Church? Tertullian here argues that just as it is as a spiritual person that Peter receives the keys, so "it is to spiritual persons that this power will belong, either to an apostle or to a prophet." In other words, the power to forgive goes with the person, not just the office. All depends on the spiritual integrity of the office-holder concerned, on his charismatic receptivity to the Spirit whose power he is appointed to exercise.

> For the very Church itself is, properly and principally, the Spirit himself, in whom is the Trinity of the one divinity—Father, Son and Holy Spirit. The Spirit unites that Church which the Lord has made to consist in three. . . . And accordingly "the Church," it is true, will forgive sins; but it will be the Church of the Spirit, by means of a spiritual person; not the Church which consists in a number of bishops.[23]

Tertullian's point is that the vital spiritual power or energy by which sins are forgiven is not the automatic possession of the Church's bishops, but is given and expressed charismatically, in prophetic and apostolic works. The question is not whether or not God can pardon very grave sins. It is rather whether he wills to do so in those cases where it might undermine repentance and cause scandal to faith. The Church, instrument of the Spirit, is servant, not master, of this power expressive of God's will, and must therefore exercise due discernment, discretion, and deference in its

---

21. Tertullian, *De monog.* 2 (ACW 13:72).
22. Tertullian, *De pud.* 21 (ACW 28:120).
23. Tertullian, *De pud.* 21 (ACW 28:121–22).

administration. Only a spiritual person, acting in a spiritual Church, has the interior affinity with the Holy Spirit necessary for this undertaking.

THE SPIRIT IN THE ASSEMBLY

With this invocation of the Holy Spirit's direct authority in support of innovations in discipline and pastoral practice, we may wonder how precisely such revelations were given and corroborated in the concrete circumstances of Tertullian's ecclesial circle. We get a glimpse of how things worked in a remarkable and under-studied passage in Tertullian's treatise on the soul.[24] In the course of defending the materiality of the soul, a doctrine which may sound odd to us but for which Tertullian had consistent reasons, the African theologian refers to the assurance granted on the question not only by rational argument, but also by divine revelation. But the revelation he refers to is not to be found in the Scriptures, but in the prophetic oracle of a certain unnamed woman in Tertullian's Carthaginian congregation. He first explains the context by which the revelation came about.

> For seeing that we acknowledge spiritual *charismata* or gifts, we too have merited to attain the prophetic gift, even after the time of John (the Baptist). We have now among us a sister whose lot it has been to be favoured with various gifts of revelation, which she experiences in the spirit by ecstatic vision during the sacred rites of the Lord's Day in the church. She converses with angels and sometimes even with the Lord. She both sees and hears mysterious communications [*sacramenta*]. She sees into some people's hearts, and to those who are in need she distributes remedies. Whether it be in the reading of the Scriptures, or in the chanting of psalms, or in the preaching of sermons, or in the offering up of prayers: in all these religious services, matter and opportunity are afforded to her of seeing visions.

It is at this point that Tertullian moves on to describe the actual circumstances in which the divine revelation was given on the question of the soul.

> It may possibly have happened to us, while this sister was rapt in the spirit, that we had discoursed in some ineffable way about the soul. After the people are dismissed at the conclusion of the sacred services, she is in the regular habit of reporting to us [*renuntiare nobis*] whatever things she may have seen in vision (for all her communications are examined with the

24. Tertullian, *Anim.* 9 (ANF 3:188–89). I am indebted to the detailed analysis of this passage by Tabernee, "To Pardon or Not to Pardon?," 380.

most scrupulous care, in order that the truth may be probed). "Among other things," she said, "there has been shown to me a soul in bodily form."

Setting aside Tertullian's argument about the soul and the content of the woman's vision, I want to draw attention to various details in Tertullian's description of what commonly happened in his worshiping assembly. Of special interest is the description of the divine service itself, which provides the setting and inspiration for the woman's ecstatic visions. The service consists in the reading of the Scriptures, psalmody, preaching, and prayer. We should also remember in passing that there is no evidence of purpose-built church buildings from this early period in Christian history, suggesting that Christian congregations were still small enough to gather in domestic settings. It has been calculated that the average Carthaginian congregation in Tertullian's time consisted of not more than about seventy members, including children, assembled in a house-church.[25] Yet even in this domestic setting, and notwithstanding the ecstatic raptures experienced in and among the prescribed liturgical actions, there is no lack of formality in the proceedings as Tertullian describes them. For at the completion of the solemn celebration, after the congregation is dismissed, there follows what Tertullian relates as customary practice: the prophetess reports "to us" what she has seen in her visions; the contents are carefully "set down in proper order," and are subsequently "tested."

Who is this "us"—*nobis*—to whom the prophetess regularly reports her oracles after the liturgy, and who undertake some kind of (supposedly) theological evaluation of her revelations? Scholars vary in their interpretation on this point.[26] For some, it refers to a "pro-Montanist" group that stayed behind after the "catholic" service. Others believe it refers to a board of spiritual elders, appointed and approved by the congregation for the task. Yet others argue that *nobis* here is best read as a literary plural, and therefore as a reflexive reference to Tertullian himself.

Support for this third possibility is found in three factors. First, Tertullian was probably unique in his literary and theological prowess. As Tabernee points out,

> That Tertullian should have the role of recording, arranging, safeguarding, and, perhaps, circulating the utterances of Carthage's contemporary prophets is not surprising. Recent

25. Hopkins, "Christian Number and Its Implications," 185–226; also Tabernee, "To Pardon or Not to Pardon?," 380–81.

26. See Tabernee, "To Pardon or Not to Pardon?," 380.

studies on literacy among early Christians have confirmed how rare Tertullian's literary skills were.[27]

Second, Tertullian's writings elsewhere contain numerous examples of oracles he attributes to the Paraclete, communicated via mainly women prophets, and which he alone preserved in writing.[28] Not all of these come from Tertullian's alleged "Montanist" period, and therefore are best understood as examples of prophetic utterances or extraordinary revelations that were made by "catholic" charismatics in the course of regular Sunday worship. These were recorded by Tertullian as part of a vetting process in which he, either alone or with others, evaluated their content, and which, if approved, were then assimilated as divinely given teaching in the catholic congregations amenable to Tertullian's influence and to the ascetic charisms and rigorous disciplines of the New Prophecy movement.

How did Tertullian go about weighing and testing the validity of the oracles communicated by the prophets? How do you distinguish between the Holy Spirit and an evil spirit? In his treatise on monogamy, Tertullian states that an evil spirit betrays himself by the heterodoxy of his teaching.[29] He perverts the faith and perverts good morals. By contrast, the Holy Spirit testifies to the same Christ in whom we place our faith, glorifies him and brings to mind what he taught, witnesses to the whole design of God's creation, and confirms any new discipline by integrity of teaching.

In other passages, we are given a sense of similar criteria by which Tertullian judged alleged oracles. Prominence is given to the rule of faith, which he basically summarizes in terms of a brief Trinitarian creed, "which is altogether one, alone immovable and irreformable." If novelty is admitted, it is only in the area of discipline and correction. For it is the office of the Paraclete to direct doctrine, reveal the Scriptures, reform understanding, and advance us toward better things.[30] That said, however, Tertullian knows that matters of discipline are not without doctrinal implication. Take, for example, the question of whether to grant forgiveness in cases of apostasy, adultery, or murder; or whether it is licit for a Christian to remarry after his or her spouse's death; or even the question of a coming earthly reign of Christ. Confirmed in his views by the oracles of the New Prophecy, Tertullian regarded his belief and teaching on such matters as binding and non-negotiable. If there were bishops or worldly Christians who believed or

27. Tabernee, "To Pardon or Not to Pardon?," 380.

28. See, e.g., Tertullian, *Virg.* 1.7; 17.3; *Marc.* 1.29.4; 3.24.3–4; *Prax.* 8.5; *Anim.* 58.8; *Ieiun.* 13.5; *De pud.* 21.7.

29. Tertullian, *De mon.* 2 (ACW 13:71).

30. Tertullian, *Virg.* 1, in Dunn, *Tertullian,* 143.

practiced otherwise, they had God to answer to. As for Tertullian and his circle, they cited the authority of the Paraclete and the trajectory of apostolic tradition. In this respect, we may detect Tertullian's ecclesiology heading in a distinctly Donatist direction. Indeed, just as Tertullian regarded martyrdom to be the highest and purest form of spiritual vitality, so the later Donatists of North Africa claimed to be the true heirs of the martyrs. Among their greatest heroes we must count Perpetua and Felicity, contemporaries of Tertullian, members of the New Prophecy movement, and celebrated saints of the Carthaginian catholic community. The stories in which their memory was enshrined "depict a charismatic Christianity in which prophecy was respected and revelations in dreams trumped the authority of the clergy."[31]

LESSONS FOR TODAY

Not surprisingly, modern assessments of the integrity and usefulness of Tertullian's pneumatology, ecclesiology, and ascetic theology vary greatly. Up until recently, it was assumed that Tertullian broke communion with the catholic Church in Carthage and lived out his days among schismatic Montanists. As he admits in his work against Praxeas, "we on our part subsequently withdrew from the carnally-minded on our acknowledgement and maintenance of the Paraclete."[32] But since the 1995 work of Australian scholar David Rankin, this view has come under question, and it is now more widely accepted that it was likely Tertullian "remained within the catholic church, despite (or because of) his allegiance to the New Prophecy."[33] Assessments of Montanism have undergone similar revision. Ronald Knox once decried the movement as a form of "naked fanaticism,"[34] while William Le Saint claimed that "Montanism warped Tertullian's judgement and ruined his life."[35] But recent assessments have argued that in North Africa at least "the New Prophecy had no characteristics of a schism. There was no rival hierarchy as there was later with Novatianism and Donatism."[36] Nor did the New Prophecy judge all catholic bishops to be carnal and worldly. There were still some, thought Tertullian, who were truly spiritual.[37]

31. Tilley, "North Africa," 388.
32. Tertullian, *Prax.* 1 (ANF 3:598).
33. Osborn, *Tertullian*, 176. See Rankin, *Tertullian and the Church*.
34. Quoted by Doherty, "Competing for the Crown," 2.
35. Tertullian, *Treatises on Marriage and Remarraige*, 69.
36. Osborn, *Tertullian*, 177.
37. Tertullian, *Ieiun.* 16 (ANF 4:113).

Given the continuing phenomenon over the centuries of appeals to the authority of the Holy Spirit for this or that revisionist doctrine or reforming enterprise, not to mention the two-pronged exhortations in the New Testament to test the spirits on the one hand, and to listen to the Spirit on the other,[38] it seems important to draw some practical lessons from this episode in the Church's story for our own time. For a start we need to refer to a feature in Tertullian's anthropology that sets the scene for his spiritual enthusiasm. His openness to the New Prophecy was not just the result of a conflict with Praxeas or the Bishop of Rome, but was consistent with his conviction that ecstatic rapture represents a superior form of epistemic consciousness and transparency of the human person to God. And so when Peter was with Jesus on the Mount of Transfiguration, and babbled something about erecting three tents, he was in fact in a rapture given by the Holy Spirit, and so possessed of a higher state of knowing than his fellow disciples. As Luke reports, "he knew not what he was saying" (Luke 9:33). What does this "he knew not" mean, Tertullian asks. "Was his ignorance the result of simple error? Or was it on the principle which we maintain in the cause of the New Prophecy, namely, that rapture or ecstasy is a concomitant of grace?"[39] Josef Pieper once explored this phenomenon in a tradition running from Plato to Aquinas, according to which our profoundest insight into reality and receptivity to God are experienced in a "loss of rational sovereignty" known as *theia mania*, or divine madness.[40] Is this what Saint Paul meant when he spoke enigmatically of having been caught up to paradise and there given visions and revelations from the Lord and taught inexpressible things not permitted to tell (2 Cor 12:1–6)?

But then biblical scholars tend to agree that Paul, in spite of his personal ecstasies, advocated a controlled, non-ecstatic exercise of charismatic gifts. Just as he sets prophecy above glossolalia, and five intelligible words above ten thousand words in tongues, so he insists that the spirit of a prophet is subject to the will of a prophet, and the exercise of ecstatic gifts subject to the principles of good order and ecclesial edification (1 Cor 14:1–40).

---

38. "Do not put out the Spirit's fire. Do not treat prophecies with contempt. Test everything. Hold on to what is good. Avoid every kind of evil" (1 Thess 5:19–22); "He who has an ear, let him listen to what the Spirit says to the churches" (Rev 2:7, 11, 17, 29; 3:6, 13, 22); "Dear friends, do not believe every spirit, but test the spirits to see whether they are from God, because many false prophets have gone out into the world" (1 John 4:1); cf. "But the Paraclete, the Holy Spirit, whom the Father will send in my name, will teach you all things" (John 14:26); "I have much more to say to you, more than you can now bear. But when he, the Spirit of truth comes, he will lead you into all truth" (John 16:13). Biblical references in this chapter are from the NIV.

39. Tertullian, *Contra Marcion* IV.22 (ANF 3:383).

40. See Pieper, *Divine Madness*.

And indeed, as we have seen, Tertullian's appropriation of the oracles of the New Prophecy was similarly subject to certain theological checks and balances. Even when he invokes the special revelations given by the Paraclete in his own time, Tertullian nevertheless argues from Scripture to demonstrate the congruence of the new revelation with the teaching and example of Christ, the Apostles, and the whole economy of God in creation and history. He admits nothing that, in his view, contradicts the Church's universal rule of faith.

Then again, many of Tertullian's opponents argued from Scripture as well. He faced the same problem Irenaeus had wrestled with fifty years earlier in the latter's writings against Marcion and the Gnostics: the rule of faith derives from Scripture, yet the rule determines that nothing contrary to itself be recognized as Scripture.[41] Tertullian's appeal to the Paraclete's special revelations functions in a way parallel to Irenaeus's appeal to episcopal succession: both are attempts to break the hermeneutical circle by proposing an interpretative authority, a divinely-given living magisterium as it were, distinct from, yet alongside and inextricably dependent on, Scripture and the rule of faith.[42]

Judging by later standards, there are not a few elements in Tertullian's doctrine, as there were in early North African Christianity generally, that are legalistic, literalistic, and even perverse.[43] These would include the way he virtually equates marriage and fornication, whose difference he locates only on a nominal plane. Intrinsically they are the same, since both involve the excitation and satisfaction of passionate lust.[44] Such a position was not uncommon in Christian ascetic communities, and later played a role in Jerome's arguments against Jovinian.[45] While we do find a laudable encomium on Christian marriage in Tertullian's works, the overall sense he gives is that, in the current age of the Holy Spirit, marriage is at best a concession for the carnally minded. Given a context in which the Parousia was felt to be dramatically imminent, and in which Marcionite Christians

41. Osborn, *Tertullian*, 115.

42. On the development of tighter episcopal regulation over and against more "charismatic" forms of authority such as "the prophet, the teacher and the charismatic martyr and confessor," Stuart George Hall writes: "This process reaches its climax in Cyprian, who, in the face of widespread lapse during persecution, and the divisions in the churches over the outcome, argued that the universal episcopate was the sole authority by which individuals and groups could be judged." Hall, "Institutions in the Pre-Constantinian *Ecclesia*," 419.

43. See Tilley, "North Africa," 395–96.

44. See, for example, Tertullian, *De exhortatione castitatis* 9 (ACW 13:56–57).

45. See Hunter, *Marriage, Celibacy, and Heresy in Ancient Christianity*.

were opposing a God of pure love against a God of justice, not to mention the all-too-worldly interests of the Christian majority, Tertullian's anxiety to ensure that the Church's holiness was an "empirical holiness" is entirely understandable.[46] "Above all," Osborn argues, "Tertullian wanted to live and help others live a Christian life in a complex world."[47] And in a Church "whose corporate mediocrity (*mediocritas nostra*) repelled him."[48]

Perhaps the most noticeable difference between Tertullian's appeal to the Paraclete and many modern calls to be open to the Spirit, especially those that tout toleration and inclusivity in terms akin to political liberalism, is that for Tertullian it served to tighten Christian doctrine and practice, not loosen it. Far from invoking the Spirit in support of a more accommodating theological or pastoral position, Tertullian calls on him to shut down all laxity. The Spirit adds nothing to the substance of the gospel, nor subtracts from it. He rather strengthens what has already been given in its definitive finality in the eschatological man, Jesus Christ.[49]

In closing, we could say that for Tertullian, it really boils down to Christ or nothing. We might be justified in characterizing his charismatic morality as "a warped and exaggerated asceticism," but he believed that what the Paraclete had only recently affirmed was nevertheless entirely Scriptural and traditional. The present, persecuted Church of the Spirit was for him the final, most powerful stage of God's action in history, the dramatic and apocalyptic actualization of a virginal perfection anticipated bodily in Christ and the nascent apostolic Church. This explains why prophets and martyrs rank higher than bishops and presbyters in Tertullian's hierarchy of authority and effectual power. Purgative divine judgement is near, and even now does its painful work. God is not just if he does not purify and punish. Yet his severity is a corollary of his goodness. For his love is a holy, purifying love that will not tolerate the corruption of the good he has accomplished in creating and redeeming the world.[50] Ethics therefore, which the African understood as sanctification, are never just adjunct to some more fundamental option, but rather lie "at the heart of the Christian mystery."[51] We may only wish that Tertullian had dwelt a little more on the

---

46. Osborn, *Tertullian*, 179.

47. Osborn, *Tertullian*, 225.

48. Osborn, *Tertullian*, 225.

49. "Away with all attempts to produce a mottled Christianity of Stoic, Platonic, and dialectic composition! We want no curious disputation after enjoying the gospel! With our faith, we desire no further belief. For this is a palmary faith, that there is nothing which we ought to believe besides." Tertullian, *Praescr.* 7 (ANF 3:246).

50. See Osborn, *Tertullian*, 209–24.

51. Osborn, *Tertullian*, 225.

characteristic prayer of all martyrs, first prayed by Jesus on the cross and then by Stephen, the Church's first martyr. For Irenaeus, it was the intercession whose words summed up the ultimate purpose of the cross, and revealed the abiding inner logic of God's ways with sinful humanity: "Father, forgive them, for they know not what they do" (Luke 23:34; Acts 7:60)[52]

BIBLIOGRAPHY

Doherty, Bernard. "Competing for the Crown: Tertullian, Montanism, and 'Voluntary Martyrdom' Revisited." *Phronema* 36 (2021) 1–32.

Dunn, Geoffrey D., ed. and trans. *Tertullian*. London: Routledge, 2004.

Evans, Ernest, ed. and trans. *Tertullian: Adversus Marcionem*. Vol. 1. Oxford: Clarendon, 1972.

Hall, Stuart George. "Institutions in the Pre-Constantinian *Ecclesia*." In *The Cambridge History of Christianity*. Vol. 1, *Origins to Constantine*, edited by Margaret M. Mitchell and Frances M. Young, 415–33. New York: Cambridge University Press, 2006.

Hopkins, Keith. "Christian Number and Its Implications." *Journal of Early Christian Studies* 6 (1998) 185–226.

Hunter, David G. *Marriage, Celibacy, and Heresy in Ancient Christianity: The Jovinianist Controversy*. Oxford: Oxford University Press, 2007.

Kelly, J. N. D. *Early Christian Doctrines*. 5th rev. ed. London: Adam and Charles Black, 1977.

Litfin, Bryan M. "Tertullian on the Trinity." *Perichoresis* 17 (2019) 81–98.

Madigan, K., and C. Osiek., eds. *Ordained Women in the Early Church: A Documentary History*. Baltimore: Johns Hopkins University Press, 2005.

McGowan, Andrew. "Tertullian and the 'Heretical' Origins of the 'Orthodox' Trinity." *Journal of Early Christian Studies* 14 (2006) 437–57.

Mitchell, Margaret M., and Frances M. Young, eds. *Cambridge History of Christianity*. Vol. 1, *Origins to Constantine*. Cambridge: Cambridge University Press, 2006.

Osborn, Eric. *Tertullian: First Theologian of the West*. Cambridge: Cambridge University Press, 1997.

Pieper, Josef. *Divine Madness: Plato's Case against Secular Humanism*. Translated by Lothar Krauth. San Francisco: Ignatius, 1995.

Prestige, G. L. *God in Patristic Thought*. London: SPCK, 1964.

Rankin, David. *Tertullian and the Church*. Cambridge: Cambridge University Press, 1995.

Roberts, Alexander, and James Donaldson, eds. *The Ante-Nicene Father*. Vol. 3. Grand Rapids: Eerdmans, 1978.

———. *The Ante-Nicene Fathers*. Vol. 4. Grand Rapids: Eerdmans, 1979.

Stevenson, J., ed. *A New Eusebius: Documents Illustrating the History of the Church to AD 337*. Rev. ed. London: SPCK, 1987.

Studer, Basil. *Trinity and Incarnation: The Faith of the Early Church*. Collegeville, MN: Liturgical, 1993.

---

52. See Irenaeus *AH* 3.16.9; 3.18.5. Also, Osborn, *Tertullian*, 225.

Tabernee, William. "To Pardon or Not to Pardon? North African Montanism and the Forgiveness of Sins." *Studia Patristica* 36 (2001) 375–86.

Tertullian. *Treatises on Marriage and Remarriage.* Translated by William P. Le Saint. Ancient Christian Writers 13. Westminster, MD: Newman, 1951.

———. *Treatises on Penance.* Translated by William P. Le Saint. Ancient Christian Writers 28. New York: Newman, 1959.

Tilley, Maureen A. "North Africa." In *Cambridge History of Christianity.* Vol. 1, *Origins to Constantine,* edited by Margaret M. Mitchell and Frances M. Young, 381–96. Cambridge: Cambridge University Press, 2006.

———. Review of *Montanism: Gender, Authority, and the New Prophecy,* by Christine Trevett. *Theological Studies* 58 (1997) 726–28.

Trevett, Christine. "Asia Minor and Achaea." In *Cambridge History of Christianity.* Vol. 1, *Origins to Constantine,* edited by Margaret M. Mitchell and Frances M. Young, 314–30. Cambridge: Cambridge University Press, 2006.

6

PROPHECY AND ONEIROLOGY IN THE EARLY LATIN PATRISTIC CORPUS

Rev. Joseph Hamilton

A HALLMARK OF SOTERIOLOGICAL pneumatology is the privileged, supernatural revelation by the Holy Spirit of hidden things or future events, by means of prophecy, visions, or dreams. Such phenomena are defined in Christian theology apophatically as private revelations,[1] as opposed to the public Revelation instituted by Christ, which the traditional Churches teach ended with the death of the last apostle.[2] In early Christianity, as Anitra Bingham Kolenkow observes, these forms of discernment were considered superior even to that of exorcism, a *charismata*, and that "from the Gospel of John to Basil of Caesarea one may note the emphasis on divinity coming from the Holy Spirit or paraclete."[3] Oneiric phenomena are clearly attested to in the Gospels and in the book of Acts. They frequently appear in early Christian literature; *Shepherd of Hermas* and *Ascension of Isaiah* being two texts that immediately spring to mind.[4] A little later the acts of the Christian martyrs will be replete with visions and dream sequences.

---

1. Congregation for the Doctrine of the Faith, *Norms.*

2. *Catechism of the Catholic Church*, sec. 66–67. Henceforth *CCC.*

3. Temporini, *Aufstieg und Niedergang*, 1499n70.

4. The secondary literature, however, is by no means extensive. Essential contributions include those from Amat, *Songes et visions*; Barcellona, "Sogni E Visioni"; Siniscalco, "Sognatori E Visionari."

This chapter will investigate select accounts of oneiric phenomena from the early Christian literary corpus that, while not exhaustive, is sufficient to demonstrate their importance and the belief in such manifestations of the Holy Spirit's power. Beginning at the turn of the third century, we will briefly examine Tertullian and his contemporary the martyr Perpetua, before leaping ahead some fifty years to investigate the oneirology of the bishop, martyr and seer, St. Cyprian. After the death of Cyprian reports of the *charismata pneumatika* in the West begin to disappear, an occurrence also in the East and commented upon by Origen.[5]

It is incumbent upon the theologian of early Christianity not only to report, but also to reflect. Accordingly, the oneiric phenomena presented in this chapter are viewed through the hermeneutic suggested by Aquinas, as to why the Holy Spirit favors some souls with these extraordinary charisms, and what their *telos* may be. Before examining the patristic data, therefore, a brief review of the *status quaestionis* is warranted.

THE CATHOLIC PERSPECTIVE

The existence of the more extraordinary charisms, while enjoying wide acceptance in evangelical ecclesial communities, has received a rather mixed reception within the Roman Catholic Church. Catholicism, being the corporate memory of Christianity, is still sensitized by the memory of Montanism, and having resolved the problem of such rival *loci auctoritarum* by the end of third century, little appetite exists to reopen the debate on the authority of charismatic prophets vs. bishops.

The genesis of the charismatic gifts can be traced to the descent of the Holy Spirit at Pentecost, and the greatest thinkers of the pre-Nicene period attest to their enduring and ongoing presence in the life of the first Christian communities.[6] From the outset, however, the same gifts that built up the early Church have courted controversies that persist to the present day. A relatively recent example serves to illustrate the difficulties.

During the discussion on the draft of *De Ecclesiae* in the second session of the Second Vatican Council, a dispute emerged between the Cardinal Archbishop of Palermo, Ernesto Ruffini, and the Cardinal Archbishop of Mechelen (Brussels), Leo Suenens, on the nature of the charismatic gifts.[7] +Ruffini held that the charismatic gifts listed by Saint Paul in 1 *Cor* 12–14 were granted only to the primitive church. In support, he cited St. John

---

5. Origen, *Contra Celsum*, 7, 8, 401–2.

6. Grasso, "I Carismi nella Chiesa Antica," 671–77.

7. Second Vatican Council, *Acta Synodalia*, II/2, 360; II/3, 175–78.

Chrysostom and St. Gregory the Great.[8] Chrysostom used the image of a gardener, who, when his plants are tender, attends to them with care of every kind so as to help them resist anything that might cause them harm. So too, in the time of the early Church, God granted signs, wonders, and charisms while she was fragile and growing, but as soon as roots had been put down these assistances were withdrawn. He finished with the words that the gifts today were "*rarissima et prorsus singularia.*" In a sense +Ruffini represented the cessationist position, where there is little room for a contemporary dynamic pneumatology.

+Suenens, citing only Paul, held that the gifts were the patrimony of the Church throughout all ages even to the present day, and concluded by hoping that the Council document would open up "the faith of all in the charisms of the Spirit." His position prevailed, as stated in *Lumen Gentium* (12).[9]

However, the ensuing spread of the charismatic renewal in the Catholic Church advanced in large part by +Suenens, did not bring about a great renewal of the gifts in the life of the everyday Church. In many instances, while charismatic prayer groups are tolerated by priests and bishops, the *charismata pneumatika* are themselves often regarded with scepticism, and sometimes with scorn. For all the efforts after the Second Vatican Council to make the movement respectable, for all the talk of the Holy Spirit, there remains in the Catholic Church a visceral distrust of pneumatological enthusiasm and the gifts that Aquinas calls the *gratiae gratis datae*. Even the ministry of exorcism, boasting untouchable biblical pedigree, is viewed with suspicion, to such an extent that some bishops, ignoring the Scriptures, Church Fathers, and not to mention the magisterium of Pope Francis, refuse to appoint a diocesan exorcist.[10] The interest of the Magisterium in the question of the charismata and perhaps, somewhat unsurprisingly, their relationship to the "hierarchical gifts" continues unabated, evidenced by the promulgation of the Apostolic Letter, *Iuvenescit Ecclesia* on Pentecost 2016.

8. John Chrysostom, *In Inscrip. Actuum Apostolorum*, 2, 2 (PG 51, 81); Gregory the Great, *In Evangelia Homiliae*, 29, 4 (PL 76, 215).

9. "It is not only through the sacraments and the ministries of the Church that the Holy Spirit sanctifies and leads the people of God and enriches it with virtues, but, 'allotting his gifts to everyone according as He wills, He distributes special graces among the faithful of every rank. By these gifts He makes them fit and ready to undertake the various tasks and offices which contribute toward the renewal and building up of the Church, according to the words of the Apostle: 'The manifestation of the Spirit is given to everyone for profit.' These charisms, whether they be the more outstanding or the more simple and widely diffused, are to be received with thanksgiving and consolation for they are perfectly suited to and useful for the needs of the Church."

10. "Non esitare a fare riferimento a coloro che, nella diocesi, sono incaricati di questo delicato e necessario ministero, vale a dire gli esorcisti." Francis, *Discorso*, sec. 2.

Such contemporary ecclesiological considerations, however, fall outside the purview of the present work.

More pertinent is the question: what was, what is the purpose *per se* of the *charismata pneumatika*? Why the need for oracles of assurance, admonition and election? Why the need for prophetic visions of the future? Once again, exorcism serves as a useful example. It was considered by Tertullian, Cyprian, Cornelius, and Firmillian to be part of the *charismata pneumatika*. Tertullian provides the textual proof of this, placing the casting out of demons beside private revelations and miraculous healings, *quod calcas deos nationum, quod daemonia expellis, quod medicinas facis, quod reuelationes petis.*[11] The *telos* of exorcism is obvious, the liberation of the afflicted. But in the case of charismatic oneiric phenomena, is there an overall purpose?

To find an answer we must move forward from antiquity to the time of the Angelic Doctor. William Newton's insightful investigation into the current situation of the Catholic Charismatic Renewal makes the observation: "For Aquinas, the distinctive mark of a charismatic grace is its ordering to the justification, not of the recipient, but of another, principally through evangelization."[12] But the *Doctor Angelicus* adds a second reason: the charisms are granted for the edification of the faithful, to strengthen them in times of persecution. And so, an uncomfortable question hangs in the air: could it be the Pentecostal Churches and the Renewal have misjudged the reason for what they have seen as the "New Pentecost"?[13] Could it be that the apparent reappearance of the gifts never heralded corporate reunion of the sundered Christian confessions, but rather were a warning against the coming mass apostasy of the Christian West, and the rise of neo-paganism? This overarching question is one that must be addressed by scholars of pneumatology at the dawn of the Third Millennium.

TERTULLIAN

The first extant source in the Latin tradition, comes to us in the account of the Scillitan Martyrs.[14] Andrzej Wypustek reads in the admonition of the

---

11. Tertullian, *De Spectaculis*, 29. All of the references for Tertullian going forward correspond to the *Opera Omnia* published in Vol. 1 and Vol. 2 of the Corpus Christianorum Series Latina (CCSL I and II). Similarly, all of those for Cyprian can be found in CCSL III.

12. Newton, "Catholic Charismatic Renewal," 32.

13. As proposed by Ramsey and Suenens, *Future of the Christian Church*.

14. *Passio sanctorum Scillitanorum*, 8: "*nolite huius dementiae esse participes.*"

proconsul Saturninus a trace of the ecstasies that accompanied Montanist prophesy,[15] a position which might be supported by the apparent enthusiasm of the martyrs-to-be for death. We must wait for Tertullian, however, to unearth concrete evidence of the prophetic charism in the daily life of Church at Carthage. Writing perhaps between AD 196 and 220, Quintus Septimius Florens Tertullianus was a rhetorical genius, suffered fools little, and dispensed invective with aplomb.[16] The corpus he has bequeathed us is rich in pneumatology, expounding a theological vocabulary that will shape the future of trinitarian reflection in the West,[17] but furnishes little in terms of personal experiential phenomena of the Holy Spirit. What he does say, however, grants us a glimpse of the life of the Church at Carthage, a life that is profoundly pneumatological. The primary exposition of his pneumatological thought emerges in *De Baptismo* written at the turn of the third century,[18] the oldest extant text on Christian baptism. While the Holy Spirit permeates the entire text, nestled at the end is an instruction to the newly baptised. As they emerge from the saving font, Tertullian instructs them to open their hands in prayer before their mother the Church, and to ask for the higher gifts, i.e., the *charismata* including, presumably that of prophecy.[19] A remarkable consonance occurs in the *passio Perpetuae* where Perpetua informs us as she is baptized she does indeed do so, raising the tantalizing prospect that Tertullian's baptismal manual played a part in the formation of the young martyr.

PROPHECY IN TERTULLIAN

It is, therefore, just a little disappointing that the account of prophecy provided by Tertullian from his own community seems to be rather tame, lacking the mantic antics and pythonic prophesying reported by the heresiologists of the fourth century. Claims of an official Montanist mission at Carthage have been credibly dismissed by Antonio Quacqaurelli. However one significant instance of prophecy is reported by Tertullian. Tertullian recounts the evidence of a "sister" in his Church in Carthage, specifically

15. Wypustek, "Magic," 277.

16. The authoritative work on our subject remains Barnes, *Tertullian*.

17. Phoebadius of Agen draws at times almost word for word on *Adversus Praxean* in his *Liber contra Arianos*.

18. Barnes, *Tertullian*, 55; Tertullian, *De Baptismo*, 8, 2–3.

19. Tertullian, *De Baptismo*, 20: "*petite de patre, petite de domino peculia gratiae distributiones charismatum subiacere.*"

with reference to the prophetic gifts.[20] During the Sunday Eucharist she would experience "ecstatic visions," which is clearly in line with Tertullian's experience of the prophetic charism. During these raptures she would speak to both the angels and to Christ, she would receive both auditory and visual communications and would discern the contents of peoples' hearts. To those in need she might prescribe a Scripture verse, or a psalm, or various prayers. Tertullian's interest in the recounting of these phenomena is in her reports of the appearance of the soul. More interesting for our purposes is that the woman in question remembers the content of her prophesies and that these are then examined by the members of the Church after the Mass. Tertullian does not discuss the context of the oracles. All in all, the prophesying in the church in Carthage sounds more akin to a meeting of the Charismatic Renewal or a Pentecostal prayer service than the reports of Montanism we receive courtesy of Eusebius.[21] This is consistent with demonstrable lack of interest in doctrinal innovation that Tertullian demonstrates throughout the surviving corpus. The principal attraction was the rigour of its system of discipline and as is evident from the above, the presence in his own Church of a regular charismatic ministry.

Applying the hermeneutic of Aquinas, how might we interpret the manifestation of this particular pneumatic charism at the primitive Church in Carthage? Propagation of the faith certainly fits, but the parish ministry reported by Tertullian suggests one also of spiritual healing. The context, too, is important. Many of the converts to Christianity at that time would have come from the local cult, that of Ba'al and Tanit. While the gory requirements of the religion of the Phoenicians have been well documented,[22] the associated psychological impact on families can only be speculated upon. This new faith, that cherished life from conception to natural death would also have recognized the wounds incurred upon individuals and families by the horrors of child sacrifice. The ministry in Tertullian's community may, in that sense, find parallels to many faith communities in contemporary Christianity.

---

20. Tertullian, *De Anima*, 10.

21. Eusebius, *Ecclesiastical History*, V, 16, 9: ὡς καὶ ἑτέρας τινὰς δύο γυναῖκας ἐπεγεῖραι καὶ τοῦ νόθου πνεύματος πληρῶσαι, ὡς καὶ λαλεῖν ἐκφρόνως καὶ ἀκαίρως καὶ ἀλλοτριοτρόπως. While from a Catholic perspective Montanism remains problematic, contemporary secondary literature has moved towards a rehabilitation, if not a celebration of the Cataphyrgians.

22. Doak and López-Ruiz, *Oxford Handbook of the Phoenician and Punic Mediterranean*; Rives, "Tertullian on Child Sacrifice," 316; Smith et al., "Age Estimations."

THE PASSIO PERPETUAE

Just a few years into the literary career of Tertullian, wider Carthaginian society was swept up, *et factus est populus immensus*,[23] by the dramatic arrest of a group of catechumens, one of whom, Perpetua, was from a prominent local family.[24] Her eponymous companion, Felicity, is often characterized in Christian art as a slave.[25] Irrespective of the social standing of Perpetua or indeed that of Felicity, the celebration of their faith and bravery captured the imagination of, and very quickly entered into, the popular mind of the Christian tradition, as evidenced from the numerous references to their deaths in the early literature. From the mid-fourth century their names have appeared in the *depositio martyrum* in Rome and entered the Canon of the Mass, anchoring them in the liturgical life of the Christian Church. By the sixth century they had already been immortalized in art in the archiepiscopal chapel in Ravenna. In the early nineteenth century, the saints were the inspiration for a highly perfumed rose bred for Louis-Philippe, the Duke of Orleans. The devotional appeal of St. Perpetua and her companions endures to this day.

For reasons not entirely unclear, the *passio* has become one of the most discussed texts from the early Christian era, producing a plethora of secondary material, ranging from the sublime to the silly.[26] In the etic stampede to claim, contain or ordain Perpetua, a frequently overlooked aspect of the text is manifestations of the Holy Spirit's power through oneiric phenomena, experienced by both Perpetua and her companions.

Before any prophecies or visions occur, however, Perpetua self-identifies as a prophetess. As noted above, immediately after her Baptism in prison, the Holy Spirit tells Perpetua to pray only for the grace to withstand the physical suffering that is ahead. Here is the first prophetic element in the text, which also fulfils the instruction of Tertullian in his treatise on baptism, while the *et mihi Spiritus dictavit*, literally "the Holy Spirit told me," establishes Perpetua's credentials as a prophetess, credentials which will shortly be bolstered when she is asked by her fellow Christians to request a

23. Amat, *Passion*, 122.

24. Amat, *Passion*, 30–32.

25. Here, the primary text is moot. Felicity is introduced in the text as the *conserva eius* of Revocatus. The *Thesaurus Linguae Latinae* (*TLL*) 4.0.422, in the first instance suggests "slave," which corresponds to the Greek, σύνδουλοι, Amat, *Passion*, 104. However, the second translation from the TLL suggests a companion in the Christian faith, which is supported by the *Acta* where Felicity is described as *soror eius*. Amat, *Passion*, 278.

26. Wilhite, "Perpetua of History," 309–10.

vision from the Lord.[27] *Spiritus dictavit* is the first example in the *passio* of what Gertrude Gillette describes as Perpetua's being at the total disposal of the Holy Spirit.[28]

This brings us to the first of Perpetua's four visions, of which only two are prophetic, the others pertaining to a ministry of intercessory prayer. Perpetua's brother, also a catechumen, requests a prophetic vision,[29] to which Perpetua accedes,[30] and the first vision occurs. Some apposite points before discussing the vision itself. Perpetua immediately, *statim*, recounts the vision to her brother and they interpret from it that they are going to suffer.[31] Aside from the certainty of death that the vision conveys, the circumstances surrounding it merit some examination. Firstly, Perpetua receives a vision, not a dream. Her emergence from the vision is denoted by the verb construction *experta sum*, derived from *expergisci* which implies something other than waking from a natural sleep.[32] Second, she remembers the content of her vision—she is not *amens* as per the accusation sometimes levelled against Monanists. She certainly would not fall into Epiphanius's definition of Montanist visions. There is no evidence that Perpetua's visions involved either glossolalia or ecstasy—primary characteristics of Montanistic prophesying. Finally, the detail Perpetua relays upon emerging from her vision with the taste of the sweet cake still in her mouth,[33] *commanducans adhuc dulcis nescio quid*, provides a bridge between the realms of prophecy and reality, and encourages us to accept the veracity of her experience, as well as her status as prophetess.

The vision itself is replete with classical Judaeo-Christian imagery. Perpetua sees a narrow bronze ladder of *mirae magnitiudinis* that reaches from Heaven to Earth. Most scholars agree that this represents Jacob's ladder. Attached to the ladder are various sorts of weapons—swords, daggers, spikes and hooks, which classical scholarship identifies as either the instruments of the passion of the martyrs, or representing the path of suffering that

27. Amat, *Passion*, 108.

28. Gillette, "Augustine," 118.

29. Amat, *Passion*, 112: "Domina soror, iam in magna dignatione es, tanta ut postules uisionem et ostendatur tibi an passio sit an commeatus."

30. Amat, *Passion*, 112: "et ego quae me sciebam fabulari cum Domino, cuius beneficia tanta experta eram, fidenter repromisi ei dicens: Crastina die tibi renuntiabo."

31. Amat, *Passion*, 201: "passionem esse futuram."

32. *TLL* 5.2.1649.55 "non se movit nisi difficiliter, quasi de somno expertus videbitur." We encounter the same use of the same verb again in §20 after Perpetua has been assaulted by the mad heifer, she comes out of what seems to be an ecstasy—there the construction used is, "et quasi a somno expergita."

33. Amat, *Passion*, 116–18.

leads to the purification of the spiritual life. More novel, contemporary, interpretations have opted to see the instruments in other ways,[34] which, not respecting Perpetua's beliefs, can most charitably be described as original. At the foot of the ladder is Satan, taking his form as the great *draco* of Genesis and the Apocalypse, described in terms again as *mirae magnitudinis*. The dragon has a twofold purpose—both to deter/terrify—perhaps from undergoing the sufferings of martyrdom, and to attack. Rousselle sees the dragon as another phallic symbol; Augustine would differ.[35]

Saturus, ascends the ladder before her and warns Perpetua of the danger of the dragon beneath, to which Perpetua responds, *non me nocebit in nomine Iesu Christi*. While this can literally be translated as "he will not harm me in the in name of Jesus Christ," in liturgical terms the use of the Holy Name in this way represents a prayer of binding. Afterwards, almost as if he is afraid of her, the dragon slowly extends his head. In fulfilment of the prophecy of Genesis Perpetua stands on the head of the dragon, and scales the ladder of suffering to arrive in paradise.

Perpetua immediately recounts the content of the vision to her fellow Christians, and they interpret the content together, *intelleximus*.[36] Thus the vision had already been interpreted before it was set to paper. This does not detract from its prophetic value but nonetheless means that it had, in a sense, already been "processed" resulting in the consensus of the community that death is imminent—and thus we observe that the vision had a *telos*. Through the prophetic vision of Perpetua, the Spirit is preparing the martyrs-to-be for suffering and death, fulfilling Aquinas's criteria of edification.

CYPRIAN

Fifty years after the gory events of that March Day in the arena, we encounter a Carthaginian Church that has grown enormously, and where Frend observed belief in visions and dreams has begun to dramatically wane.[37] The bishop at the time, *Thascius Caecilius Cyprianus, (Cyprian)*, martyr and only non-Roman male in the Canon of the Mass, has left a veritable treasure trove of oneiric phenomena in his epistularium of which we will now examine a selection. The analysis is intentionally presented from an emic perspective, which should not be interpreted as an *apologia* for the veracity of Cyprian's visions. Etic commentary on the Church Fathers abounds in the secondary

34. Rousselle, "Dreams of Vibia Perpetua," 195.
35. Augustine, *Sermones ad Populum*, 280.
36. Amat, *Passion*, 118.
37. Frend, *Donatist Church*, 129.

literature, and is increasing, but very often fails to give sufficient weight to the lived experience of the writers.

THE SPIRIT SPEAKS THROUGH A MARTYR

Ep. 10 offers one of the more interesting, if admittedly puzzling, utterances of prophetic speech in the entire corpus. Cyprian is writing to the Confessors, a group, that although Christian, have proved something of a governance nightmare for the newly consecrated bishop. Among those being held in prison, undergoing torture, is Mappalicus, who dies as a result of his ordeal. The letter shows Cyprian at his exhortatory best, writing in beautiful Latin, rhetorically rich and replete with military imagery. §2 through §4 might nearly be described as Cyprian's own *homage* to the literary form of the *passio*: "Vidit admirans praesentium multitudo caeleste certamen dei et spiritale, proelium Christi . . . luebat sanguis qui incendium persecutionis extingueret, qui flammas et ignes gehennae glorioso cruore sopiret."[38] The events highlight the importance of the *epistularium* as a future historical source. Mappalicus appears in not only two of Cyprian's letters but also in the martyrology of Bede—using the exact wording above,[39] as well the Carthaginian calendar at the beginning of the sixth century, and the seventh-century recension of the *Martyrologium Hieronymianum*.

Matt 10:19 is one of Cyprian's most frequently referenced scriptural quotations; Christ promises to his followers that in time of persecution the Holy Spirit will place any necessary words in their mouths. In *ep.* 10, Cyprian links the Gospel pericope to the confession of the soon-to-be martyr Mappalicus. As he is being tortured a voice, Cyprian tells us, filled with the Holy Spirit roars (*prorupit*) out amidst the tortures and defiantly addresses the proconsul, "tomorrow you will see a contest!"[40] This is a very unusual account. The typical syntax for a confession of faith in the *acta* and *passiones* of the Christian Martyrs is *Christianus(a) sum*. Mappalicus, on the other hand, seems to blend a defiant confession and a prophecy. Amat has observed that Cyprian's understanding of this kind of speech is different to

38. Cyprian, *Epistles*, 10, 2.

39. Bede, *Martyrologium*, XV. Kal. Mai. "Apud Africam, natale sancti Mappalici: qui cum aliis pluribus martyrio coronatus est. Scribit beatus Cyprianus in epistola ad martyres et confessores, hoc modo: Vox plena Spiritu sancto de martyris ore prorupit, cum Mappalicus beatissimus inter cruciatus suos proconsuli diceret: 'Videbis cras agonem.'"

40. Cyprian, *Epistles*, 10, 4, 1: "vox plena spiritu sancto de martyris ore prorupuit, cum Mappalicus beatissimus inter cruciatus suos proconsuli diceret: 'uidebis cras agonem.'"

Tertullian's, *mais plutôt comme une <invasion> naturelle de l'Esprit-Saint*.[41] The martyr's voice which is full of the Holy Spirit, *plena Spiritu Sancto*, literally roars, *prorupit*, from his mouth.

Cyprian adapts *videbis cras agonem* as a paraphrase from the prophet Isaiah. This has the effect of making the oracle scriptural. While Clark notes this "inspired dictum," Robeck offers the following additional insight: he writes that Cyprian's description of the events sets Mappalicus "as little more than a mouthpiece for the words and thoughts of the Holy Spirit".[42] Mappalicus's reported use of the future tense with "*cras*" followed by his martyrdom the day after, grants to the oracle the mark of authenticity through its fulfilment. So, in this sense, the oracle is one of assurance—consonant with Aquinas's observations above.

PARACLETIC APPOINTMENTS

Writing from his place of hiding in February of 251, Cyprian announces in *ep.* 39 the appointment of a confessor, in this instance Celerinus, to the office of lector. Pains are taken to emphasis his spiritual pedigree—he is the grandson of the martyr Celerina and he had two uncles who were both martyrs. This young man had also endured nineteen days in prison, was held in irons, and possibly tortured. He is, as Cyprian says, *tanta domini dignatione venientem*,[43] implying the action of the Holy Spirit operating and sustaining him through the various trials he had suffered. Small wonder that Cyprian should seek to prevail upon him to join the ranks of the Carthaginian clergy. From a political point of view, a confessor of this quality on Cyprian's "side" would greatly strengthen his position as bishop in the face of ongoing governance challenges. Celerinus, Cyprian reports, was initially hesitant but, in an echo of *Hermas*, received a vision in which the Church herself appeared to him:

> Qui cum consentire dubitaret, ecclesiae ipsius admonitu et hortatu in uisione per noctem conpulsus est ne negaret nobis suadentibus. Cui plus licuit et coegit, quia nec fas fuerat nec decebat sine honore ecclesiastico esse quem sic dominus honorauit caelestis gloriae dignitate.[44]

41. Amat, *Songes et visions*, 105.
42. Robeck, *Prophecy in Carthage*, 169.
43. Cyprian, *Epistles*, 39, 4, 1.
44. Cyprian, *Epistles*, 39, 1, 2.

Cyprian makes clear that the recipient of this vision is not the bishop. It is also the only occasion in the corpus where the recipient is a confessor. It provides three additional noteworthy insights. Others are still receiving visions, so while the phenomenon may be in decline, the importance of those visions still counts for something. However, the visionary is in physical proximity to Cyprian which suggests a degree of charismatic dependence on the person of the bishop. Finally, this single report of a vision to a confessor, one who is part of Cyprian's court, reinforces the role of the bishop as the nexus of the *charismata pneumatika*. In other words, visions are for all, but only once they have been interpreted by the bishop. Once again, this vision fulfils Aquinas's criteria that the *charismata* are directed towards evangelization.

LITURGICAL INTERVENTION

Ep. 63 is an extraordinary letter, notable for several reasons. It is the first extant Latin source that treats the liturgical preparation of the Eucharistic chalice at length. Cyprian has matured. He is now firmly established as prophet-bishop. The confidence demonstrated in the epistle at hand offers us an example of him in his role as Metropolitan dealing with a suffragan. The recipient, Caecilius of Biltha, is also clearly a bishop, and Cyprian presumes that the letter, and the ruling contained within it, will be circulated widely within the North African episcopal college.[45] The occasion for composition of the letter was an aberration that had arisen in the preparation of the Eucharistic chalice. Instead of wine, *quod Iesus Christus docuit et fecit*, a particular group had been offering only water, rather than wine mixed with water. From the perspective of sacramental theology this invalidates the Sacrifice. Some reasons are alluded to as excuses for the practice, such as the danger of receiving the Eucharistic wine in the morning, *ne per saporem uini redoleat sanguinem Christi*,[46] which might place Christians in danger of being identified as having been to Mass.[47] Cyprian has little truck with this argument,[48] seeing in it the danger of weakening the resolve of the brethren in the face of persecution.

45. Caecilius was a bishop in *Africa Proconsularis*. This treatise was often passed down under the title *De Sacramento Calicis Domini*. Two useful contributions on this epistle come from Kazcmarek, "Tipologia eucaristica," 260–63, and Willis, "St. Cyprian and the Mixed Chalice," 110–15.

46. Cyprian, *Epistles*, 63, 15.

47. The recognition of this danger supports a dating of *Ep.* 63 as post-Decian persecution.

48. Nor does d'Alès, "pitoyable excuse en matière si sainte." d'Alès, *Théologie de Saint Cyprien*, 255.

Inside the boundaries of his own jurisdiction a bishop is the moderator of the liturgy, and it is both his duty and within his power to regulate the norms surrounding the celebration of the Eucharist.[49] Outside of that jurisdiction and in the middle of the third century, the ability of a metropolitan bishop to intervene in the affairs of another diocese is by no means clear.[50] Hence, in the absence of a canonical precedent, Cyprian's decision to interfere in a liturgical matter would need the backing of some form of authority. Furthermore, Cyprian is not naturally pugnacious—he makes clear in other letters that he has minimal zeal for interfering in the affairs of other bishops.[51] Some external force compelled and gave Cyprian the confidence to make this intervention in the life of the wider African Church, outside of what modern parlance might call his "comfort zone," and which Brent calls Cyprian's *imperium*. That impetus is revealed by Cyprian to be an admonition from the Holy Spirit.[52]

The secondary sources are anything but of one mind on the question. Harnack is dismissive, complimenting the structure of the letter, but accusing Cyprian of not trusting the strength of his own arguments and thus resorting to the claim of a specific private revelation to press his point, all the while feigning humility so as to shield himself from the criticism of playing the dictator bishop.[53] Bardy is more circumspect simply noting that while Cyprian appears to be quite balanced, he accepts without protest a divine inspiration instructing him to intervene against human interference in the preparation of the chalice.[54] Claudio Anselmetto sees in this epistle the blending of episcopal authority and the prophetic charism, demonstrating Cyprian to be subject to no other power than that from above.[55]

---

49. *Codex Iuris Canonici*, can. 392: "Ecclesiae universae unitatem cum tueri debeat, Episcopus disciplinam cunctae Ecclesiae communem promovere et ideo observantiam omnium legum ecclesiasticarum urgere tenetur. Advigilet ne abusus in ecclesiasticam disciplinam irrepant, praesertim circa ministerium verbi, celebrationem sacramentorum et sacramentalium, cultum Dei et Sanctorum, necnon bonorum administrationem."

50. The hierarchical episcopacy was evolving quickly, however. Cyprian's adversary, Stephen, was the first occupant of the See of Peter to use the prestige of Rome as a premise for widespread interference in the affairs of other local Churches. Cyprian's appeals in Epistles 65 and 67 stand as testimony (and perhaps enable) this.

51. See Cyprian, *Epistles*, 74, 26: "nemini praescribentes aut praeiudicantes quominus unusquisque episcoporum quod putat faciat, habens arbitrii sui liberam potestatem." And *Epistles*, 72, 2: "Qua in re nec nos uim cuiquam facimus aut legem damus, quando habeat in ecclesiae administratione uoluntatis suae arbitrium liberum unusquisque praepositus, rationem actus sui domino redditurus."

52. Cyprian, *Epistles*, 63, 1, 2.

53. Harnack, "Cyprian als Enthusiast," 187.

54. Bardy, "St. Cyprien," in *Dictionnaire de spiritualité*, coll. 2661–69.

55. Anselmetto, "Rivelazione Privata," 287.

It would of course be naïve *not* to consider the opinion that Cyprian is using a private revelation as a pretext for the letter, and indeed the opening tone does read as rather defensive.[56] The fact remains, however, that Cyprian had sufficient fires to fight within his diocese without needing to open fronts elsewhere. Contrary to his usual disposition, he chose to intervene and felt sufficiently confident to do so. As very recent history shows, liturgical disputes are entered into at peril at the best of times, let alone in a decade of disaster and crisis. Something, or rather Someone impelled Cyprian to do so. Amat reads oneirological plausibility in the "*admonitos autem nos scias ut in calice offerendo dominica traditio servetur*"[57] and believes that Cyprian thought it necessary for him to act upon the inspiration he had received.

Briefly reviewing the argument, Cyprian begins with the *typos* of Noah, before moving to the figure of Melchizedek. This reference is the first in Latin literature that identifies the sacrifice of Melchizedek with the bread and wine consecrated in the Eucharist.[58] More important for our purposes is Cyprian's description of the Spirit, *quod autem Melchisedech typum Christi portaret declarat in psalmis Spiritus Sanctus ex persona patris ad filium dicens: ante luciferum genui te.*[59] Cyprian uses the authority of the Spirit, speaking in the person of the Father to the Son, to reinforce Melchizedek as *typos* of Christ, with the bread (and more importantly the wine) as *typos* for the eucharistic species. The Holy Spirit *praemonstrat*,[60] a *typos* of the sacrifice of the Lord, making mention through Solomon of the sacrificial bread and wine, and of the apostles:

> Et misit suos servos, conuocans cum excelsa praedicatione ad craterem dicens: qui est insipiens declinet ad me. Et egentibus sensu dixit: uenite, edite de meis panibus et bibite uinum quod miscui uobis.[61]

Cyprian also writes that Solomon had prophesied, through the agency of the Holy Spirit, that the chalice of the Lord would be composed of wine, mixed with water. At (7,1) before introducing the *typos* from Isaiah 63.2, *Spiritus Sanctus de Domini passione testatur dicens* identifying the Holy Spirit as the speaker. At *ep.* 11, 2, the Spirit *faciens mentionem* of the Lord's chalice, says "your chalice which intoxicates" thus reinforcing the necessity for the

---

56. Cyprian, *Epistles*, 63, 2.
57. Cf. Anselmetto, "Rivelazione Privata," 312.
58. Cyprian, *Epistles*, 63, 4.
59. Cyprian, *Epistles*, 63, 4.
60. *TLL* 10.2.724–25: "antequam aliud quiddam monstretur vel fiat."
61. Cyprian, *Epistles*, 63, 5.

chalice to contain wine, not water. We therefore observe that the action of the Holy Spirit is used no less four times by Cyprian in the construction of his argument. At the risk of *apologia*, and if we were to take Cyprian's side for a moment, could it be that Cyprian is obliquely suggesting that he has received a private revelation from the Spirit directing him to use the Scripture verses above to emphasise the Spirit's soteriological action? Amat makes an interesting observation that the impersonal use of *admonitos autem nos* is suggestive that the visionary, in this instance Cyprian, is an instrument.

Nor has the prominent role of the Holy Spirit in this epistle escaped the notice of scholars seeking evidence of His identity in the Cyprianic corpus. Hughes has observed that the letter at hand is the one text of the Cyprianic corpus that meets his definition of the Spirit speaking prosopologically. He sees in *hoc idem spiritus sanctus de domini passione testatur* a "dialogical passage which can plausibly be interpreted in a theodramatic setting, when combined with a verb (*testatur*) implying some degree of personal agency."[62]

Cyprian is not so rigid as to realise that sometimes, *si quis de antecessoribus nostris vel ignoranter vel simpliciter non hoc obseruauit et tenuit quod nos dominus facere exemplo et magisterio suo docuit.* Clergy, after all, are generally human. However, from the promulgation of this letter onwards, there can be no further amnesty. Referring to the authority of the revelation received, the current college of bishops *qui nunc a domino admoniti et instructi sumus*, must take steps to correct liturgical practice. Furthermore, Cyprian has been instructed *et de hoc quoque ad collegas nostros litteras dirigamus.*[63] D'Alès noted a hundred years ago that Cyprian both begins and ends this letter with the appeal to a private revelation,[64] writing in the *conclusio* of the epistle "*Domino monente corrigere*". Harnack comments that at this stage of Cyprian's episcopacy,

> the two great powers—the greatest that religion offered—lay linked in Cyprian's hand: the power of the Office and the power of the Spirit. Who could withstand such powers; they surely subdued every insubordination! However, the attempt to unite the two in a bishop, as Cyprian did, had few, or even no successors in the Church.[65]

---

62. Hughes, *Trinitarian Testimony*, 197–98.

63. Cyprian, *Epistles*, 63, 17.

64. d'Alès, *Théologie de Saint Cyprien*, 77.

65. Harnack, "Cyprian als Enthusiast," 185.

BACKLASH

Without wishing to impute irony to the above quote from one of the greatest patristic scholars of the last century, it became rapidly clear, *pace* Harnack, that Cyprian had *not* subdued all insubordination. Cyprian's meteoric rise through the ranks of the clergy was less than universally well received, particularly amongst those who had been passed over for the position of bishop. Six years into his episcopacy,[66] it can be adduced that after persecution and plague the already disgruntled (and perhaps the newly disillusioned) were bound to be displeased with Cyprian, and his admittedly somewhat autocratic style of government. After all, Cyprian's stylus had whipped the order of virgins, castigated those who feared death, and transferred ecclesial power from the confessors and martyrs reinvesting it in the person of the bishop. In the accomplishment of the latter, dreams and visions had played no small part. We have already noted that by the mid-third century, the veneration granted to the visions and dreams of martyrs had begun to markedly decrease at Carthage. *Ep.* 66 renders in clear focus the conflict between the ordinarily charismatic (and growing) Church of the masses, and the extraordinarily charismatic (but shrinking) pneumatic Church of the martyrs. In his analysis, Harnack sees in this epistle the consummate conjunction of Cyprian's enthusiasm and episcopacy, reading its contents as written by one who believes, by virtue of office, that he has an exclusive relationship with Christ.[67] Cyprian, the prophet, the visionary, has emerged ironically as the bishop of bishops, but in a pneumatic sense.

The letter thus brings us to a crucial moment in the exercise of Cyprian's authority as bishop. The original letter in the correspondence from Florentius Puppianus is not extant, but as Cyprian methodically answers the accusations a reasonably accurate picture of the complaints emerges. The charges are manifestly grave, and Cyprian is clearly stung. The predictable niceties of the Latin language which he usually employs are dispensed with. Puppianus is addressed simply as *te frater* without the customary *carissime*, and *ep.* 66 is the only letter in the corpus where Cyprian does *not* sign off with his usual modification of the Ciceronian formula, *te opto carrisime frater bene valeas*. Rather, and most atypical of Cyprian is the sarcastic invective, *Puppianus solus integer, inuiolatus, sanctus, pudicus, qui nobis miscere se noluit, in paradiso atque in regno caelorum solus habitabit.*[68] What accusations could prompt such an uncharacteristic lapse in charity from Cyprian?

---

66. Cyprian, *Epistles*, 66, 5, 1: "iam sex annis."
67. Harnack, "Cyprian als Enthusiast," 186.
68. Cyprian, *Epistles*, 66, 7.

For starters, Puppianus raises the question of the validity of Cyprian's episcopal consecration—well trodden ground, and Cyprian's lack of humility—which elicits an amusing and not very humble riposte. But what cuts much closer to the bone is the accusation that the Church in Carthage has been divided because of Cyprian, and the implication that the dreams and visions by which Cyprian has governed are *somnia ridicula et visiones ineptas*. Harnack viewed this particular turn of phrase as evidence that the broader Carthaginian community, the institutional Church, had grown weary of bishops who simultaneously desired to be prophets. Furthermore, he adds, in the backlash against Montanism, Carthaginians had not only come to doubt the value of visions and dreams, but would ultimately come to consider them as being diabolical.[69]

Cyprian's tone suggests that he was incandescent upon receipt of the letter. Perhaps what raised his ire the most was that Puppianus was a confessor.[70] This grants him a charismatic status. One detects a note of genuine distress in Puppianus and the pain he must feel at the schism within a Church for which he personally had physically suffered, *scripsi quoque quod ecclesia nunc propter me portionem sui in disperse habeat*.[71] Cyprian, on the other hand, has yet to suffer physically for the Church. In Cyprian's defence, his epistles do demonstrate a profound compassion for suffering members of his flock. Is Puppianus part of the charismatic caucus? Might he be seeking readmission to communion with Cyprian?[72] If that were the case, he has done so while aggressively criticizing the bishop on points that are clearly sensitive. Rarely a prudent course of action.

Cyprian's response is, as Anselmetto observes,[73] strongly polemical and apologetic. Cyprian defends the sacrality of his episcopacy as being anointed by God, not man. Consequently, the private revelations he receives take on a fundamental importance. The visions are seen as a personal expression of his episcopal ministry.[74] More specifically, Cyprian responds in three ways.

First, he addresses the criticism of his dreams and visions. The incredulity Puppianus manifests towards the *oneira* with which Cyprian is favored has more to do with personal rebellion against the bishop, *sed utique illis qui malunt contra sacerdotes credere quam sacerdoti*.[75] Cyprian

---

69. Harnack, "Cyprian als Enthusiast," 136.

70. See Harnack's observation in "Cyprian als Enthusiast," 184n13.

71. Cyprian, *Epistles*, 66, 8, 1.

72. Cyprian, *Epistles*, 66, 9, 2.

73. Anselmetto, "Rivelazione Privata," 308.

74. Anselmetto, "Rivelazione Privata," 308.

75. Cyprian, *Epistles*, 66, 10, 2.

compares himself to Joseph,[76] *ecce somniator ille venit, nunc ergo venite occidamus illum,* and implies that Puppianus and his other critics will be forced to concede the veracity of Cyprian's visions once they are proven true. The figure of Joseph is employed elsewhere as a *typos* of Christ in *De zelo et livore,*[77] but also, Edwina Murphy observes, as a precursor to Cyprian's own experience of opposition to his visions.[78]

The second is to invoke the particular favor of God that the bishop enjoys which has been revealed to Cyprian in a vision, alongside a threat also vouchsafed by vision, *itaque qui Christo non credit sacerdotem facienti postea credere incipiet sacerdotem vindicanti.* Clarke quips in his notes to this particular paragraph, "few prelates can ever have had such confidence in their own inspiration or in the complete wrongheadedness of a schismatic confessor who opposed them."[79]

Third, and perhaps most extraordinary is the conclusion to Cyprian's list of requirements for (hypothetical) communion to be restored between he and Puppianus. Cyprian will personally ask "his" Lord for a vision, to determine whether God will grant permission for the *pax* to be granted to Puppianus. Cyprian writes, *et prius Dominum meum consulam an tibi pacem dari et te ad communicationem ecclesiae suae admitti sua ostensione et admonitione permittat.* Cyprian does not use *"Dominus noster".* He speaks of an entirely exclusive relationship between God and bishop. Such privileged and especial communication enables Cyprian to request a sign, supporting Anselmetto's hypothesis that claiming control of the prophetic charism was an objective of his episcopacy.[80] The parallel between Cyprian and Perpetua is marked. Cyprian's statement is reminiscent of Perpetua directly asking the Lord for a vision to determine whether or not she and her companions will survive the process initiated against them fifty years before. But Cyprian has now arrogated that charismatic authority to the person of the bishop.

THE END OF CYPRIAN'S EPISCOPACY

Ep. 69–75 record the last great crisis of Cyprian's episcopacy, the Baptism controversy, itself marked by a notable lack of oneiric phenomena. As geopolitical events overtake him and the persecution of Valerian begins, however, the phenomena resume. Cyprian soon finds himself exiled. On

76. See Gen 37:18–30.

77. Cyprian, *De Zelo,* 5.

78. Murphy, "Imitating the Devil," 85.

79. Cyprian, *Letters,* 332.

80. Anselmetto, "Rivelazione Privata," 300.

the first day of their banishment,[81] having just arrived in Carubis, the place of exile, Cyprian reports to Pontius who has travelled with him, that on that first day *before* falling asleep, *nondum somni quiete sopito*, he had received a vision. Cyprian was not asleep, and therefore the revelation cannot be described as a dream. Pontius, in fact, informs us that the motivation behind the vision was a desire on the part of God for Cyprian to be certain of his martyrdom.

> Admirabilem visitationem Dei non praeteribo, qua antistitem suum sic in exilio esse voluit de secutura passione securum, ut inminentis martyrii pleniore fiducia non exulem tantummodo Curubis sed et futurum martyrem possideret.[82]

On to the vision. A young man of unusual stature leads Cyprian to the praetorium, *iuvenis ultra modum hominis enormis*. There are clear parallels to *Ep.*11 as we have discussed above, and also to the vision of the dying bishop in *De Mortalitate*, as well as to the vision of Perpetua prior to her combat with the Egyptian.[83] In the vision Cyprian is led before the proconsul who begins to write on a tablet. The legal process does not follow the usual form. Cyprian is not asked any questions, but the young man, presumably Christ, indicates to Cyprian by means of a hand gesture that he will be executed by beheading, *manu enim expansa et complanata ad spathae modum ictum solitae*.[84] Cyprian, understanding the impending sentence, asks (in the vision) for a stay of execution of one day to allow him time to set his affairs in order. He repeats his entreaty, and the proconsul writes something down on his tablet. Cyprian realizes that the request has been granted. The young man seems to confirm this by twisting and untwisting his fingers. Cyprian, for his part, is elated by the reprieve, but confesses to great anxiety and fear as he is not entirely sure how to interpret the vision,

> Ego, quamvis non esset lecta sententia, etsi de gaudio dilationis adceptae laeto admodum corde resipisco, metu tamen inpetrationis incertae sic tremebam, ut reliquiae formidinis cor exsultans adhuc toto pavore pulsarent.[85]

---

81. Cyprian appeared before the proconsul on August 30, 257. The day of the vision would have taken place on September 14. Given his status, it is not unreasonable to assume Cyprian may have been granted some days to prepare for the journey. This makes the reported timings not implausible.

82. Pontius et al., *Vita Cypriani*, 12, 2.

83. Amat, *Passion*, 134–36.

84. Pontius et al., *Vita Cypriani*, 12, 5.

85. Pontius et al., *Vita Cypriani*, 12, 5.

Instead, the definitive interpretation is provided posthumously by Pontius. What could be clearer, he rhetorically asks? Cyprian had been granted an *ostensio*. Everything foretold in the vision was subsequently fulfilled, Pontius writes, thus establishing Cyprian as a true prophet. The delay Cyprian requested was for a day. Remarkably, though, as the historical circumstance bears out, the period of one day in the vision was to signify a year in the "real world." To be explicit, Cyprian received the martyr's crown exactly one year after having received the vision on September 14, 257. The oneiric phenomena that accompany these final days of Cyprian's life fall clearly within the second part of Aquinas's definition; the edification of the faithful. In this instance, just as Perpetua before him, Cyprian was being prepared to give the ultimate witness to his beliefs.

CONCLUSION

While doctrinal considerations as to the nature of the Holy Spirit enter most clearly into theological focus in the wake of the Arian crisis of the fourth century, that is not to say that the pre-Nicenes had no concept of the Holy Spirit, nor were they Binitarian. Rather, they had a strong sense of the Spirit living and working through them, through both the ordinary and sometimes the extraordinary *charismata*, particularly that of prophecy. By examining reports of these oneiric phenomena from an emic perspective, it is possible to analyse the phenomena on their own merits, liberated from etic constructs such as ethnicity, or gender, or socio-economic considerations. Consequently, the accounts of thinkers such as Tertullian, and Cyprian, as well as figures such as Perpetua, can be evaluated on their own merits by scholars approaching from a background of faith or of none. Little comment in the secondary literature exists as to the purpose of these phenomena. Overlaying the hypothesis of Aquinas as to the purpose of the charismatic gifts reveals that these manifestations sit comfortably within the modalities of classical theology and ecclesiology.

BIBLIOGRAPHY

Aginnensis, Phoebadius. *Liber Contra Arianos*. Turnhout: Brepols, 2010.
Amat, Jacqueline. *Passion de Perpétue et de Félicité: Suivi des Actes*. SC 417. Paris: Cerf, 1996.
———. *Songes et Visions: L'au-Delà Dans La Littérature Latine Tardive*. Paris: Etudes augustininiennes, 1985.
Anselmetto, Claudio. "Rivelazione Privata e Tradizione Nell'epistolario Di Cipriano." *Augustinianum* 30 (1990) 279–312.

Augustine of Hippo, St. *Sermones ad Populum*. Turnhout: Brepols, 2018.

Barcellona, F. Scorza. "Sogni E Visioni Nella Letteratura Martirologica Africana Posteriore al III Secolo." *Augustinianum* 29 (1989) 193–212.

Barnes, Timothy David. *Tertullian: A Historical and Literary Study*. Oxford: Oxford University Press, 1985.

Bastiaensen, A. A. R. *Atti E Passioni Dei Martiri*. Scrittori Greci E Latini. 2nd ed. Milano: Mondadori [per la] Fondazione Lorenzo Valla, 1990.

Bede, the Venerable. *Martyrologium: textus quem Beda Venerabilis composuit atque Anonymus Lugdunensis et Florus Lugdunensis retractaverunt auxeruntque.* Turnhout: Brepols, 2016.

Catechism of the Catholic Church. Rev. ed. London: Chapman, Burns and Oates, 1999.

Codex Iuris Canonici. Vatican City: Libreria Editrice Vaticana, 1983.

Congregation for the Doctrine of the Faith. *Norms Regarding the Manner of Proceeding in the Discernment of Presumed Apparitions or Revelations*. https://www.vatican.va/roman_curia/congregations/cfaith/documents/rc_con_cfaith_doc_19780225_norme-apparizioni_en.html.

Cyprian. *Lettere*. Edited by Carlo del'Osso. Scrittori Cristiani dell'Africa Romana 5. 2 vols. Roma: Città nuova, 2006.

———. *The Letters of St. Cyprian of Carthage*. Translated by G. W. Clarke. Ancient Christian Writers 43. New York: Newman, 1984.

———. *Opuscoli*. 2 vols. Scrittori Cristiani dell'Africa Romana 6. Roma: Città nuova, 2009.

———. *Sancti Cypriani Episcopi de Habitu Virginum*. CCSL IIIF. Turnhout: Brepols, 2016.

———. *Sancti Cypriani Episcopi Opera*. Edited by Manlio Simonetti and Claudio Moreschini. Corpus Christianorum. Series Latina 3a. Turnhout: Brepols, 1976.

d'Alès, Adhémar. *La Théologie de Saint Cyprien*. 2nd ed. Paris: Beauchesne, 1922.

Diercks, G. F., and George W. Clarke. *Sancti Cypriani Episcopi Epistularium-Prolegomena*. CCSL 3. Turnhout: Brepols, 1999.

Doak, Brian R., and Carolina López-Ruiz, eds. *The Oxford Handbook of the Phoenician and Punic Mediterranean*. New York: Oxford University Press, 2019.

Eusebius. *The Ecclesiastical History*. Translated by Kirsopp Lake et al. Cambridge: Harvard University Press, 1949.

Francis. *Discorso del Santo Padre Francesco ai Partecipanti al XXVIII Corso sul Foro Interno Organizzato dalla Penitenzieria Apostolica*. https://www.vatican.va/content/francesco/it/speeches/2017/march/documents/papa-francesco_20170317_corso-foro-interno.html.

Frend, W. H. C. *The Donatist Church: A Movement of Protest in Roman North Africa*. Oxford: Clarendon, 1971.

Gillette, G. "Augustine and the Significance of Perpetua's Words: 'And I Was a Man.'" *Augustinian Studies* 32 (2001) 115–25.

Gramaglia, Pier Angelo, and Tertullianus. *Il Battesimo*. Roma: Paoline, 1979.

Grasso, Domenico. "I Carismi nella Chiesa Antica." *Augustinianum* 20 (1980) 671–86.

Harnack, Adolf von. "Cyprian Als Enthusiast." *Zeitschrift für die Neutestamentliche Wissenschaft und die Kunde der älteren Kirche* 3 (1902) 177–91.

Hughes, Kyle R. *The Trinitarian Testimony of the Spirit: Prosopological Exegesis and the Development of Pre-Nicene Pneumatology*. Supplements to Vigiliae Christianae 147. Boston: Brill, 2018.

Istituto dell'Enciclopedia italiana Treccani. *Enciclopedia Dei Papi*. Roma: Istituto della Enciclopedia Italiana, 2000.

Kazcmarek, T. "Tipologia eucaristica di Noè nella lettera 63 di S. Cipriano." *Studia Patristica* 21 (1989) 260–63.

Murphy, Edwina. "Imitating the Devil: Cyprian on Jealousy and Envy." *Scrinium* 14 (2018) 75–91.

Musurillo, Herbert. *The Acts of the Martyrs*. Vol. 1, *The Acts of the Pagan Martyrs*. Oxford: Oxford University Press, 2000.

———. *The Acts of the Martyrs*. Vol. 2, *The Acts of the Christian Martyrs*. Oxford: Oxford University Press, 2000.

Newton, William. "The Catholic Charismatic Renewal through the Eyes of St. Thomas Aquinas." *Downside Review* 137 (2019) 31–46.

Novatianus, and G. F. Diercks. *Novatiani Opera Quae Supersunt*. CCSL 4. Turnhout: Brepols, 1972.

Origen. *Contra Celsum*. Translated by Henry Chadwick. Cambridge: Cambridge University Press, 1980.

Passio Sanctorum Scillitanorum. Library of Latin Texts. Series A. Turnhout: Brepols, 2010.

Patrologia Latina. Edited by J.–P. Migne. 217 vols. Paris, 1844–64.

Patrologia Graeca. Edited by J.–P. Migne. 162 vols. Paris, 1857–86.

Pontius et al. *Vita Di Cipriano*. Edited by Manlio Simonetti. Collana Di Testi Patristici. Roma: Città nuova, 1977.

Quacquarelli, Antonio. "L'antimonarchianesimo di Tertulliano e il suo Presunto Montanismo." *Vetera Christianorum* 10 (1973) 5–45.

Ramsey, Michael, and Léon Joseph Suenens. *The Future of the Christian Church*. London: SCM, 1971.

Robeck, Cecil M. *Prophecy in Carthage: Perpetua, Tertullian, and Cyprian*. Cleveland: Pilgrim, 1992.

Rives, J. B. "Tertullian on Child Sacrifice." *Museum helveticum* 51 (1994) 54–63.

Rousselle, Robert. "The Dreams of Vibia Perpetua: Analysis of a Female Christian Martyr." *Journal of Psychohistory* 14 (1987) 193–206.

Second Vatican Council. *Acta synodalia Sacrosancti Concilii Oecumenici Vaticani II*. Vatican City: Typis polyglottis Vaticanis, 1970–78.

Siniscalco, Paolo. "Sognatori e Visionari, Veggenti e Profeti dall'antichità ai Tempi Odierni." *Augustinianum* 30 (1990) 127–43.

Smith, Patricia, et al. "Age Estimations Attest to Infant Sacrifice at the Carthage Tophet." *Antiquity* 87 (2013) 191–207.

Temporini, Hildegard, et al., eds. *Aufstieg Und Niedergang Der Römischen Welt (Anrw) / Rise and Decline of the Roman World: Geschichte Und Kultur Roms Im Spiegel Der Neueren Forschung. Religion (Vorkonstantinisches Christentum: Verhalatnis Zu Römischem Staat Und Heidnischer Religion, Fortsetzung)*. Berlin: de Gruyter, 2016.

Tertullian. *Quinti Septimi Florentis Tertulliani Opera Pars 1—Opera Catholica-Adversus Marcionem*. CCSL 1. Turnhout: Brepols, 1954.

———. *Quinti Septimi Florentis Tertulliani Opera Pars 2—Opera Montanistica*. CCSL 2. Turnhout: Brepols, 1954.

Thesaurus Linguae Latinae. https://tll.degruyter.com.

Viller, Marcel. *Dictionnaire de spiritualité: ascétique et mystique, doctrine et histoire*. Paris: Beauchesne, 1937.

Wilhite, David E. "Perpetua of History in Recent Questions." *Journal of Early Christian Studies* 25 (2017) 307–19.

Willis, Geoffrey G. "St. Cyprian and the Mixed Chalice." *Downside Review* 339 (1982) 110–15.

Wypustek, Andrzej. "Magic, Montanism, Perpetua, and the Severan Persecution." *Vigiliae Christianae* 51 (1997) 276–97.

7

THE SPIRIT AS DOVE IN PATRISTIC INTERPRETATIONS OF THE CANTICLE OF CANTICLES

Kevin A. Wagner

THE REPRESENTATION OF THE Holy Spirit as a dove is ancient and scriptural. A beautiful image that has the power to excite the imagination, the dove is an important catechetical tool that could benefit from a revival, in order that it may better convey the reality of the Holy Spirit. The dove appears frequently in the *Canticle of Canticles* and this image proved to be a popular topic for patristic interpreters of this text. In this chapter we will draw on the commentaries and homilies of Origen and Gregory of Nyssa on the *Canticle* in order to add color and texture to our modern understanding of this ancient image of the Third Person of the Trinity. Ultimately, our hope is that patristic theologizing on the image can aid our catechesis today.

The dove appears regularly throughout the Hebrew Scriptures. We find it first mentioned explicitly in Genesis 8, where Noah sends a dove to seek out dry land in the midst of the floodwaters.[1] Most commonly, however, we find the dove employed as a metaphor, especially in the Psalms,[2] Prophets,[3]

---

1. Gen 8:8–12. Dixon provides an excellent account of the arguments for and against reading Gen 1:2 as an allusion to the dove and as an inspiration for the Markan account of the dove in Mark 1:10. Dixon, "Descending Spirit and Descending Gods," 761–64.

2. Pss 55:6; 68:13; 74:19. It appears also in the introductory statement of Ps 56.

3. Isa 38:14; 59:11; 60:8; Ezek 7:16; Hos 7:11; 11:11; Nah 2:7.

the Song of Songs (henceforth the *Canticle*),[4] and non-canonical 4 Ezra.[5] As we move to the New Testament, the dove appears in each Gospel account of Jesus' baptism by John,[6] and then only once more in the warning of Jesus to His disciples to be "innocent as doves" (Matt 10:16).[7] This extensive deployment of the dove as a metaphor in the Hebrew Scriptures hints at a depth to this image that goes beyond its simple identification with the Holy Spirit who descended "like or as a dove" on Jesus at his baptism by John. Indeed, both the authors of the Scriptures and their early interpreters, drawing on contemporary scientific observations of the dove, took the dove to be a multifaceted symbol. Not only was the dove renowned for its supposed innocence, chastity and modesty, but it was lauded for its beauty and speed. Important too, was its presumed preference for abiding in hidden places in solitude. We shall see too that the use of the dove in Jewish worship rituals added to the symbolic value of the animal.

In this chapter, we will examine some of ways that Origen and Gregory of Nyssa interpret passages of the *Canticle* that refer to the dove, in order to show the depth of the image of the dove for the early fathers. The two fathers both wrote extensively on the *Canticle*: three of ten books of Origen's *Commentary on the Song of Songs* and two homilies on the *Canticle* have survived, and from Gregory of Nyssa we have a series of fifteen homilies on the *Canticle*. It would be too grand a task to detail more than a few relevant insights from these works, so we will focus our attention on one principal theme from each writer. In the case of Origen, we will unpack his use of the image of the dove to construct a beautiful catechesis on the necessity of the Holy Spirit for the interpretation of Scripture and for assimilation to the Word. From Gregory, we will show how the eyes that are doves are those

---

4. Song 1:15; 2:14; 4:1; 5:2, 12; 6:9.

5. 4 Ezra 2:15; 5:26. Stone makes the claim that 4 Ezra, a text believed to have been written in the late first-century AD, offers some type of allegorical interpretation of the *Canticle*, "conceivably of an eschatological cast, in which the love is redemption or the Redeemer." Of particular importance here, we note that he describes "the source of the imagery in *4 Ezra* 5:26 as 'an allegorical interpretation of Song 2:14 and 5:2,'" passages which make mention of the dove. Stone, "Interpretation of Song of Songs in 4 Ezra," 229.

6. Matt 3:16; Mark 1:10; Luke 3:22; John 1:32. Dixon argues, *contra* the mainstream view of Hebraic inspiration, that Mark drew inspiration from Homeric literature in choosing to depict the Spirit as a bird. His argument, while fascinating, seems to open the door to an adoptionist Christology as he contends that "the syntax of Mark's Gospel suggests that Mark, at least, intended to convey that the Spirit descended 'into Jesus'" rather than "upon" Him (as Mark 1:10 is commonly translated). Dixon, "Descending Spirit and Descending Gods," 765–69, 771–72.

7. Biblical references in this chapter are from the RSV.

that have contemplated the Spirit and have become that on which they have gazed, the beauty of the bridegroom.[8]

Before analyzing the primary texts themselves, a few words are necessary regarding the patristic reception of the *Canticle* in order to show how the works of Origen and Gregory fit within the tradition. Having done this, we will briefly address some textual issues regarding the word translated "dove" or "turtledove" in the *Canticle* and the works of Origen and Gregory.

PATRISTIC RECEPTION OF THE CANTICLE OF CANTICLES

Any serious reader of the *Canticle* must ask why this series of erotic songs was originally included in the Jewish canon of Scripture. One argument for its inclusion that deserves consideration is that of Gerson Cohen, who proffered the view that it was included in order to present a positive view of the covenantal or nuptial relationship between Israel (who was notoriously unfaithful to God) and her spouse.[9] On this view, the *Canticle's* original meaning was not to be taken literally as an erotic exchange between human lovers, but rather, it was to be understood figuratively or allegorically; that is, as a "dialogue of the mutual longing and desire that Israel and God express for each other."[10] Regardless of the original reasons for its inclusion in the canon, the traditional practice of reading the *Canticle* figuratively or allegorically justified its continued place in the canon. We note that traditional Jewish interpretations of the *Canticle* came to fall into two categories; those that related the text to the Torah (the midrashic tradition), and those that linked the text "to abstract ideas" (the allegorical tradition).[11]

While there is some debate as to the precise relationship between Jewish and Christian interpretations of the *Canticle* (that is, which came first, and who inspired whom), there is strong reason to believe that Origen simply learnt his allegorizing of the *Canticle* from the Jewish traditions.[12] The consequences of Origen's Jewish borrowings for the reception of the *Canticle* by the Christian church cannot be understated. While Hippolytus of Rome's commentary on the *Canticle* is the first we know of, Origen's interpretation was far more influential on later commentators.[13] Indeed, it

8. Gregory of Nyssa, *Cant. Hom.* 4 (Norris, 117).

9. Stern, "Ancient Jewish Interpretation of the Song," 91–92.

10. Stern, "Ancient Jewish Interpretation of the Song," 91.

11. Stern, "Ancient Jewish Interpretation of the Song," 88.

12. Stern, "Ancient Jewish Interpretation of the Song," 88.

13. For a recent English translation of Hippolytus' *Commentary*, see Smith, *Mystery of Anointing*.

has been said that his *Commentary* inspired all pre-modern commentaries on the book.[14] Of prominence among patristic commentaries on the text are those of Athanasius, Gregory of Nyssa, Theodore of Mopsuestia, Theodoret of Cyrus, Ambrose of Milan, Gregory the Great, Apponius, Maximus the Confessor, and the Venerable Bede.[15]

Common among these commentaries is the fact that the authors see the relationship between the protagonists of the *Canticle* as a metaphor for other relationships, such as those "between a bride and a bridegroom, between God and Israel as God's chosen people, between God and the individual soul, between Christ and the individual soul, or between Christ and the Church."[16] In the case of Origen, the groom of the Song may be identified with the Word of God, while the bride could be seen as "either the individual soul or the church."[17] For Gregory, the groom usually represents God and the bride the individual soul who seeks to ascend "towards an incorporeal and spiritual and undefiled marriage with God."[18] As we shall see, however, Gregory does not hesitate to mix his metaphors if it assists in his interpretation of the text.

TEXTUAL ISSUES

Within the Masoretic text of the *Canticle*, we find two different Hebrew words that are translated variously in English bibles as "dove" or "turtledove." The rarer of the two is *tôr* (turtledove) which appears only in Song 2:12 and is translated as τρυγόνος in the LXX.[19] While this tends to be translated as "turtledove" in modern English translations, "turtle" and "dove" are common alternatives. On the other hand, the Hebrew word *yônâ*—which is used in Song 1:15; 2:14; 4:1; 5:2,12; 6:9—is usually translated simply as "dove." We note that in each of these verses of the *Canticle*, the LXX translates *yônâ* as

---

14. O'Keefe, "Origen," 9.

15. O'Keefe, "Origen," 9; Lawson, "Introduction," in Origen, *Song of Songs*, 6.

16. Wright, *Proverbs, Ecclesiastes, Song of Solomon*, xlvi. O'Keefe describes it as "a figural (non-literal) tale narrating the desire of the soul and the church for intimacy with God. It is not a poetic narrative celebrating sexual love between a bride and a bridegroom." O'Keefe, "Origen," 1.

17. Origen, *Cant. Hom.* Prol. (Lawson, 21).

18. Gregory of Nyssa, *Cant. Hom.* 1 (Norris, 15).

19. We note that the Masoretic text of Song 1:10 uses the word *battôrîm* (from *tôr* meaning circlet, plait, turn of hair, succession, order), which the LXX translates as τρυγόνες (turtledoves). It would seem the translators of the Septuagint mistook the two homonyms.

περιστερά, and in modern English translations of the LXX this tends to be rendered as "dove."

We note that typically Origen does not distinguish between the dove and turtledove, but in at least one place he does draw a distinction. In his Second Homily on the *Canticle* he writes:

> The dove [*columba*] denotes the Holy Spirit. But when the great and more hidden mysteries are in question, and the things that many people cannot grasp, then the Holy Spirit is represented under the appellation of a turtle-dove [*turturis*]—of the bird, that is to say, that always dwells on mountain ridges and in the tops of trees. But in the valleys, in the things that all men understand, He figures as a dove [*columba*].[20]

This distinction in relation to the Holy Spirit is not evident in Gregory's *Homilies* on the *Canticle*. In his *Homilies* the two Greek words περιστερά and τρυγόνος are used extensively; περιστερά fifty times and τρυγόνος fourteen times. Interestingly, Gregory only uses τρυγόνος when quoting or explaining Song 1:10 and 2:12, the only places τρυγόνος appears in the LXX translation of the *Canticle*.

ORIGEN

Origen is a polarizing figure who attracted great admirers and severe critics in his own lifetime and in the centuries after his death. Crouzel and Prinzivalli note that there were six discernible moments of anti-Origen conflict, beginning with opposition to Origen during his own lifetime.[21] Perhaps inspired more by ecclesial politics than concern for doctrinal purity, the Origenist controversy of AD 400 spearheaded by Alexandrian patriarch Theophilus led to the first major destruction of texts from the Origenian corpus.[22] More significantly, the condemnation of Origen at two councils in

---

20. Origen, *Cant. Hom.* 2 (Lawson, 303). Here we have inserted Rufinus's Latin. We see that in his references to *Song* 1:15 and 2:14 that Rufinus consistently translates περιστερά as *columba* and τρυγόνος as *turtur*. See Origen, *Commentaire sur le Cantique des Cantiques*, 494, 678.

21. Crouzel and Prinzivalli, "Origenism."

22. "Socrates, Sozomen, and Palladius . . . lead their readers to assume that theology was not central to the debate, and the little of it that appears was served up by the bishop of Alexandria as a guise to further his ecclesiastical politics." Indeed, these three historians were clearly hostile to Theophilus and sided with "the theological opinions espoused by the suspected Origenists." Clark, *Origenist Controversy*, 44.

Constantinople (AD 543 and 553)[23] resulted in the systematic destruction of his work.[24] De Lubac describes the senseless destruction of his work: "Nearly all of Origen's work perished. Thus, out of his vast correspondence . . . only two letters and a few fragments remain. Of his exegetical works— although his principles of exegesis had not at all been questioned—we have in the original only scarcely one-twentieth left today."[25]

Origen's commentary on the *Canticles* did not escape unscathed. Originally composed in Greek, the text comprised ten books. Today we are left with just three books (preceded by a long prologue) in Latin, thanks to the work of Rufinus, a late fourth-century admirer of Origen's work.[26] Fortuitously, we also possess two homilies on the *Canticle*, translated by Jerome, which provide further insight into Origen's reading of the *Canticle*.

The Dove in Origen's *Commentary on the Song of Songs*

In Book IV of the *De Principiis*, Origen sets out his doctrine on the triadic nature of Scripture and links it to his anthropology. For Origen, the body of the Scriptures contains "common and literal interpretation" and is accessible to the somatic reader.[27] The soul of Scripture, which is probably not the moral sense, is of value to the psychic reader; that is, the one who has begun to make a little progress in the spiritual life and is "moving toward perfection."[28] Finally, the spiritual law of the Scriptures, which is accessible to the pneumatic or spiritual person, deals with "the mysteries of the Christian faith, such as the nature of the Son, his incarnation, the true nature of the world, and our place in it."[29]

23. The council in 543 was a local one, while the council in 553 was ecumenical. Lubac, *History and Spirit*, 43n150, 44.

24. O'Keefe, "Origen," 2. Matis, *Song of Songs*, 25.

25. Lubac, *History and Spirit*, 44.

26. O'Keefe, "Origen," 2. O'Keefe curiously states that Origen's commentary "now endures as four books in the Latin of Rufinus," a statement which is contradicted by Lawson, the translator of Origen's commentary and homilies on the *Canticle*; "The Latin translation by Rufinus offers the long prologue to the *Commentary* and the first three books of the same." One can only presume that O'Keefe counts the Prologue as one of the books. Lawson, "Introduction," 4. See also Matis, *Song of Songs*, 25.

27. O'Keefe, "Scriptural Interpretation," 194. See also Origen, *De Principiis* IV.2.4 (Butterworth, 364).

28. O'Keefe, "Scriptural Interpretation," 194. See also Origen, *De Principiis* IV.2.4 (Butterworth, 364).

29. O'Keefe, "Scriptural Interpretation," 194. See also Origen, *De Principiis* IV.2.4 (Butterworth, 364).

These three stages in the spiritual life correspond to the three branches of divine philosophy:[30] ethics or morals; physics or the study of the natural; and epoptics or the inspective.[31] These branches fortuitously correspond to Proverbs, Ecclesiastes, and the Song of Songs. The Book of Proverbs trains one in "discernment and behaviour"; that is, ethics.[32] Ecclesiastes goes further, instructing one in physics, which is the ability to distinguish "the causes and natures of things" and to "recognize the vanity of vanities that he must forsake, and the lasting and eternal things that he ought to pursue."[33] To cap off one's formation, one is to read the *Canticle*, which deals with "dogmatic and mystical matters," to help one advance "to the contemplation of the Godhead with pure and spiritual love."[34]

In his writings on the *Canticle*, Origen comments on Song 1:15 (1:14 Vulg.), "'Behold, thou art fair, My neighbour; behold, thou art fair. Thine eyes are doves.'" Here Origen directly associates the dove with the Holy Spirit. He writes, "Her eyes, moreover, are compared to doves, surely because she understands the Divine Scriptures now, not after the letter, but after the spirit, and perceives in them spiritual mysteries; for the dove is the emblem of the Holy Spirit."[35] For Origen, the inspiration of the Holy Spirit is the key for opening up the spiritual sense of the Scriptures. This spiritual sense enables one to understand both the Law and the Gospel rightly. In his second homily on the *Canticles* he writes,

> If you understand the Law spiritually, your eyes are those of a
> dove; so too if you understand the Gospel as the Gospel means

---

30. Origen "divided philosophy into ethics, physics, epoptics, and logic (the Stoic tripartition plus *epoptica*), identifying the crowning of philosophy with epoptics, i.e., theology (*de divinis et caelestibus*)—a term already used by Clement and the Eleusinian mysteries. Theology is part and parcel of philosophy and cannot be studied without philosophical foundations (*Cant. Com.* prol. 3.1–3)." Ramelli, "Origen and the Platonic Tradition," 2. "Epoptics is the branch of philosophy that investigates 'the divine and heavenly things' (*epoptica de divinis et caelestibus*), that is, theology." Ramelli, "Divine," 167–88. Here we note that Ramelli uses the term *eptopics* when *enoptics* is a common alternative. Cf. Origen, *Cant. Com.* Prol. 3 (Lawson, 40).

31. Origen, *Cant. Com.* Prol. 3 (Lawson, 40). Logic is "mingled and interwoven" in these other disciplines. It "deals with the meanings and proper significances and their opposites, the classes and kinds of words and expressions, and gives information as to the form of each and every saying."

32. Origen, *Cant. Com.* Prol. 3 (Lawson, 43–44).

33. Origen, *Cant. Com.* Prol. 3 (Lawson, 43–44).

34. Origen, *Cant. Com.* Prol. 3 (Lawson, 43–44). For excerpts from patristic commentaries on these three scriptural books, see Wright, *Proverbs, Ecclesiastes, Song of Solomon*.

35. Origen, *Cant.Com.* 3.1 (Lawson, 170).

itself to be understood and preached, seeing Jesus as healing all manner of sickness and infirmity not only at the time when those things happened in the flesh, but also at the present day, and realizing that He not only came down then to men, but comes down and is present here today; for, Behold, I am with you all days, even to the consummation of the world.[36]

For Origen then, the spiritual sense is not simply the allegorical, anagogical, or moral meaning of the text (adopting the mediaeval language), but rather, that sense which incarnates the Word for us today. Awareness of this should spark our interest anew in Origen's exegetical work. There is much talk of the need to make the Christian faith relevant for today, but what Origen promises to those who are gifted dove's eyes is an ability to "perceive and know how great is the splendour of the Word."[37] Such perception and knowledge is uniquely relevant, as the Word is God.

Origen takes this metaphor of the dove further, drawing both on Ps 68:12–13[38] and the capacity of the dove for flight to show that such perception leads one to wisdom:

> To understand the Law and the Prophets in a spiritual sense is, therefore, to have the eyes of a dove. So her eyes are called doves here; but in the Psalms a soul of this sort longs to be given the wings of a dove, that she may be able to fly in the understanding of spiritual mysteries, and to rest in the courts of wisdom.[39]

Later in his commentary, Origen draws on the dove motif once again to unpack what he means by wisdom. Commenting on Song 2:12b—"the voice of the turtledove is heard in our land" (RSV)—Origen equates the "voice of the turtle-dove" with "that wisdom which the steward of the Word speaks among the perfect, the deep wisdom of God which is hidden in mystery."[40] Origen makes this connection on the basis of his understanding of the turtle-dove's dwelling places. According to Origen, the turtle-dove "spends

36. Origen, *Cant. Hom.* 2 (Lawson, 290).

37. Origen, *Cant. Com.* 3.2 (Lawson, 172).

38. "The women at home divide the spoil, though they stay among the sheepfolds—the wings of a dove covered with silver, its pinions with green gold" (Ps 68:13–14 RSV).

39. Origen, *Cant. Com.* 3.1 (Lawson, 170). See also Origen, *Cant. Com.* 3[4].14 (Lawson, 240). "And, did He not perceive her to be able to receive the Holy Spirit, who descended on Jesus at the Jordan in the form of a dove, He would not say to her, 'My dove.' For she had conceived the love of the Word of God and was desiring to come to Him by a swift flight, saying: '*Who will give me wings like a dove, and I will fly and be at rest?* I will fly with my affection, I will fly with my spiritual perceptions and rest, when I have understood *the treasures of His wisdom and knowledge*.'"

40. Origen, *Cant. Com.* 3[4].14 (Lawson, 241).

its life in the more hidden and remote localities, away from crowds; it loves either mountainous wastes, or the secret parts of the forests, is always found far from the multitude, and is a stranger to crowds."[41]

It is important to take note that Origen's account of the flight to the mysterious courts of wisdom, achieved through conformity to the Holy Spirit, is no mere rhetorical wordplay. Indeed, Origen has a profound awareness of the spiritual life. Origen allows for the fact that this springtime of intimacy in the heavenly courts may only come after a "winter of the soul," an experience anyone who has sought to live a spiritual life can appreciate.[42] This winter is a genuine struggle for the soul during which "[s]he gets no flowers of zest from the Divine Scriptures then, nor do the secrets of the deeper wisdom and the hidden mysteries sound as by the turtle-dove's voice."[43]

We will wrap up this exposé on Origen with a brief account of his interpretation of the Jewish practice of sacrificing doves at the purification ritual for newborns (Lev 12:6,8). Commenting on Song 1:15 (Vulg. 1:14), Origen gives a Christological interpretation of the eyes of the bride that are doves. He argues that as Christ is the Head, then it seems to him "by no means absurd . . . to take the eyes of those who understand spiritually according to the inward man and have a spiritual judgement, as meaning the Holy Spirit."[44] Going further, Origen suggests that the sacrifice of the Passover lamb—which is a type of the sacrifice of Christ—is an action of the head for the purification of *all people*. Following the same logic, Origen then postulates that the sacrifice of doves at infancy is perhaps a figure for the action of the Holy Spirit, who purifies *the individual* as he or she enters into the world, giving the recipient spiritual judgement and insight.[45] We will return to this point in the final section of this chapter.

GREGORY OF NYSSA

Gregory of Nyssa has been lauded by Jean Daniélou as "the great master of Christian mystical theology."[46] His reading of Scripture reflects this as he seeks to move beyond the "material historical symbols to higher divine

---

41. Origen, *Cant. Com.* 3[4].14 (Lawson, 241).

42. Origen, *Cant. Com.* 3[4].15 (Lawson, 247).

43. Origen, *Cant. Com.* 3[4].15 (Lawson, 248).

44. Origen, *Cant. Com.* 3.1 (Lawson, 170).

45. Origen, *Cant. Com.* 3.1 (Lawson, 171).

46. McGuckin, "St. Gregory of Nyssa," 26.

truths";[47] that is, from the "perceptible to [the] intelligible, from [the] literal to [the] spiritual, from [the] particular to [the] universal," or more succinctly, from *historia* to *theoria*.[48] Doing thus, he undertakes to lead his readers to discover

> the need for a repentant purification of the mind, then a growing awareness of the profundity of the spiritual message contained in a given story (*theoria*), and then a dawning realization that its ultimate significance far exceeds the human capacity—a darkness of the intellect which is, paradoxically, a much closer drawing-near to the essential mystery of the Ungraspable God.[49]

It would take us too far from our present task to delve much further into Gregory's notion of spiritual ascent and the attainment of perfection, but it is worth noting that both the *Homilies* on the *Canticle* and his *Life of Moses*— though commentating on vastly different scriptural texts—are consistent in their exposition of the soul's ascent to God.[50]

Gregory wrote and delivered his series of *Homilies on the Song of Songs* (*In Canticum canticorum*) in response to a request by the wealthy young benefactress, Olympia. While the precise dating of these homilies is uncertain, we can safely date them to the last five years of his life, sometime between AD 390 and 395.[51] The series comprises fifteen homilies, introduced by a short preface that serves as an *apologia* for his prolific use of allegory in the homilies that follow. This *apologia* is directed against "some church leaders" who are unwilling to go beyond the letter of the Scriptures in their exegesis.[52] To counter these leaders, Gregory argues that certain passages, if taken according to the letter alone, "do not furnish us with models of the good life"[53] and that other passages (in both the Old and New Covenants) use figurative language which cannot be adequately interpreted by appeal to

---

47. McGuckin, "St. Gregory of Nyssa," 26.

48. Norris, "Introduction," xlvii.

49. McGuckin, "St. Gregory of Nyssa," 26.

50. Perhaps the best, and most succinct, summary of Gregory's understanding of spiritual ascent and perfection comes from his work *On Perfection*: "Changing in everything for the better, let him [the Christian] exchange 'glory for glory,' in becoming greater through daily increase, ever perfecting himself, and never arriving too quickly at the limit of perfection. For this is true perfection: never to stop growing towards what is better and never placing any limit on perfection." Gregory of Nyssa, *On Perf.* (Callahan, 122).

51. Norris, "Introduction," xxi–xxiii.

52. Gregory of Nyssa, *Cant. Pref.* (Norris, 3).

53. Gregory of Nyssa, *Cant. Pref.* (Norris, 5).

the letter alone.[54] On the basis of these two arguments, and considering the language of the *Canticle*, it should be no surprise to find that Gregory will allegorize extensively in his homilies on the *Canticle*.

The Dove in Gregory's *Homilies on the Song of Songs*

Here we will focus our attention on Gregory's interpretation of those passages in the *Canticle* that equate the eyes with the dove (1:15; 4:1; 5:11). Before we do so, a few remarks on ancient theories of vision, perception, and the eyes are necessary in order to appreciate more fully Gregory's efforts to establish the literal sense (the *historia*) of the *Canticle*.[55]

In his fourth homily on the *Canticle*, Gregory draws on the experts who believe that "the eye activates its vision by receiving the impressions of the images given off by visible bodies."[56] This understanding of the nature of vision was not uncommon in antiquity and late antiquity. Thibodeau divides ancient theories of vision into four categories: (1) extramissionist (the eye emits a substance towards the object seen); (2) intromissionist (the object emits a substance perceived by the eye); (3) a combination of extra- and intro-missionist elements (both the eye and object emit a substance that facilitates perception by the eye); and (4) theories that incorporated an "activated medium" such as air or water.[57] It is not straightforward to categorize Gregory's theory within this fourfold schema.

Wessel explains Gregory's understanding of sensory perception through the sense organs generally:

> Apprehension through these organs came about, Gregory said, when the mind or *nous* fixed its attention upon objects outside of the body and then inscribed images of these objects or phenomena upon itself. For this inscription to take place, the body, which was imagined as being innately receptive to the

54. Gregory declares that failure to apply "subtle and discerning inquiry" to these passages using figurative language is akin to serving "unprepared grain on the table for human beings to eat." Gregory of Nyssa, *Cant. Pref.* (Norris, 11).

55. An examination of the various uses of the technical term *historia* in Gregory's work may be found in Mateo-Seco and Maspero, *Brill Dictionary of Gregory of Nyssa*, 390–96. We note that Gregory's writings are replete with references to medicine, which is perhaps a little unexpected, given he appears not to have studied this discipline formally. Keenan notes that medical allusions in Gregory's writings concern areas as diverse as "anatomy, physiology, pathology, therapeutics, clinical medicine, and surgery." Keenan, "St. Gregory of Nyssa," 150.

56. Gregory of Nyssa, *Cant. Hom.* 4 (Norris, 117).

57. Thibodeau, "Ancient Optics," 199–204.

objects of its perception, was made to contain a certain wax-like form which, being neither too moist nor too solid, enabled it to receive such images and then to perceive them.[58]

Applied to visual perception specifically, Gregory's theory of the sense organs shows at least that the perceived object had to impress itself somehow on the wax-like body of the viewer. Once perceived and impressed upon the body, it could be apprehended by the mind.[59] Given Gregory's observation that visible bodies "give off" images, it seems his theory may be classified as intromissionist. This conclusion must, however, be tempered by the fact that, for Gregory, the mind (nous) is the faculty or power (dynamis) that "passes through each of the organs of sense and lays hold of existing things [τῶν ὄντων]."[60] We must, therefore, reserve judgement as to whether the nous constitutes a substance emitted from the eye that strikes the viewed object or activates the air between the viewer and object.[61]

Song 1:15b reads, "Behold, you are beautiful: your eyes are doves." In his interpretation of this verse, Gregory uses his theory of vision to expound a beautiful account of the transformative power of sight. As we have seen, Gregory believes that the eye acts as a receptor of images emitted by material objects.[62] Thus, Gregory concludes, "people receive in themselves the likeness of whatever they gaze upon intently."[63] Perhaps unsurprisingly, Gregory applies a spiritual interpretation to this medical explanation of vision as he opines that the one who has eyes shaped like doves gazes not on "flesh and blood," but rather, on that which is spiritual.[64] Indeed, for Gregory, the good choices one makes regarding his or her "gaze" lead to

---

58. Wessel continues, "What precisely the nature of this wax-like substance was, or where it was located, Gregory does not say. That it was connected somehow to the function of the cerebral membrane, which was identified as the encasement for the brain and as the foundation for the sense organs, is a distinct possibility. Because the membrane was said to be covered with a moist substance known as 'vapors,' it may have been the location for the wax-like substance into which the sensory images were impressed." Wessel, "Reception of Greek Science," 27–28.

59. Wessel, "Reception of Greek Science," 30.

60. "αὐτὸς ὁ ἐγκείμενος νοῦς, ὁ δι' ἑκάστον τῶν αἰσθητηρίων διεξιὼν, καὶ τῶν ὄντων ἐπιδρασσόμενος." Gregory of Nyssa, De opificio hominis 6 (PG 44.140). Translation mine.

61. Gregory's assertion that the mind draws images to itself leads Wessel to suggest that Gregory may have been influenced by the psychic pneuma theories of Galen and the Stoics. Wessel, "Reception of Greek Science," 29–30.

62. Gregory of Nyssa, Cant. Hom. 4 (Norris, 117).

63. Gregory of Nyssa, Cant. Hom. 4 (Norris, 117).

64. Gregory of Nyssa, Cant. Hom. 4 (Norris, 117).

the purification of the vision of the soul and the shaping of one's life "in conformity with the grace of the Holy Spirit, for the Holy Spirit is a dove."[65]

Developing further his theory of vision and its relationship to the soul and the spiritual life, Gregory likens the eye to a mirror. Expounding on Song 4:1a—"Your eyes are doves"—Gregory declares:

> since the images of all visible things, when they make contact with a pure pupil <of the eye>, bring about vision, it is necessary that one assume the form of that toward which one looks, receiving through the eye, in the fashion of a mirror, the form of the visible thing.[66]

This analogy of the mirror is further applied to the soul in the fifteenth of Gregory's homilies on the *Canticle* as he seeks to explain Song 6:3, "I am for my kinsman, and my kinsman is for me." Here Gregory describes the soul as a "life-endued and choice-endowed mirror."[67] Unlike a conventional mirror then, the soul plays a role in how it receives the form of that on which the person gazes. The soul can thus declare, "[s]ince I focus upon the face of my kinsman with my entire being, the entire beauty of his form is seen in me."[68]

The dynamics of love that enable the bride to image the bridegroom's beautiful form in her soul are explicated in Gregory's exegesis of Song 2:13c—"Arise! Come! My close one, my beauty, my dove." With rhetorical flourish, Gregory notes the precise ordering of this phrase, which details the movement of the bride towards her lover: "She hears the command. She is empowered by the Word. She rises up. She moves forward. She is brought close. She becomes a beauty. She is named dove."[69] The very possibility that the bride could come to image the bridegroom is only possible, Gregory contends, if the soul of the bride—like a mirror—receives "the impression of a lovely form" by drawing near to the archetypal Beauty.[70] Having done so, the bride "makes known the presence of the Holy Spirit."[71] We see then, that

---

65. Gregory of Nyssa, *Cant. Hom.* 7 (Norris, 229–31).

66. Gregory of Nyssa, *Cant. Hom.* 7 (Norris, 229–31).

67. τὸ προαιρετικόν τε καὶ ἔμψυχον κάτοπτρον. Gregory of Nyssa, *Cant. Hom.* 15 (Norris, 466–67).

68. Gregory of Nyssa, *Cant. Hom.* 15 (Norris, 467). See also, *Cant. Hom.* 3 (Norris, 101).

69. ἀκούει τοῦ προστάγματος, ἐνδυναμοῦται τῷ λόγῳ, ἐγείρεται, προέρχεται, πλησιάζει, καλὴ γίνεται, περιστερὰ ὀνομάζεται. Gregory of Nyssa, *Cant. Hom.* 5 (Norris, 162–63).

70. Gregory of Nyssa, *Cant. Hom.* 5 (Norris, 163).

71. Gregory of Nyssa, *Cant. Hom.* 5 (Norris, 163). Echoes of this analogy may be found in Gregory of Nyssa, *De opificio hominis* 12.9 (PG 44.161). Here the analogy is applied to the mind (*nous*) rather than the soul.

the bride whose "eyes are doves" is the soul that has received the Holy Spirit by the process of purification and mortification and has fixed its gaze on the archetypal Beauty; that is, "the beauty of the bridegroom."[72]

Before finalizing our reflection on Gregory, I would like to offer his analysis of Song 5:11c–12 as an interesting development on his teaching on "dove-eyes." Here we find Gregory preferring to identify the bridegroom with the bishop, rather than with God. This preference allows Gregory to draw from these verses a teaching on the means by which bishops may become "adapted to the golden Head."[73] Adaption to Christ is achieved in three stages: washing in water; washing in milk; and sitting by full pools of water.

In v. 11c the bridegroom's eyes are described "as doves by pools of water." The eyes, Gregory opines, are the seeing organs of the body and—given their high position in the body—may be seen as analogous to the overseers of the church, who are to be as innocent as doves in order to "supervise, oversee, and inspect in purity."[74] This innocence is to be attained through the washing one's eyes with water drawn from the pools; water that represent the virtues, which all flow from "a single wellspring."[75]

Gregory now turns to explain v. 12—"Washed in milk, sitting by pools of waters"—and he does so by drawing on his earlier discussion of the imaging power of mirrors. He declares that, unlike water and all other liquids, milk does not reflect any image or likeness. Consequently, bishops whose eyes are washed in milk

> do not mistakenly image anything unreal and counterfeit and empty that is contrary to what truly is but look upon what *is* in the full and proper sense of that word. They do not take in the deceitful sights and fantasies of the present life. For this reason, the perfect soul judges that it is the bath in milk that most surely purifies the eyes.[76]

---

72. Gregory of Nyssa, *Cant. Hom.* 4 (Norris, 117). Similarly, in *On Virginity*, Gregory writes, "For, just as the eye cleansed from rheum sees objects shining brightly in the distance in the air, so also the soul through incorruptibility acquires the power to perceive the Light. The goal of true virginity and zeal for incorruptibility is the ability to see God, for the chief and first and only beautiful and good and pure is the God of all, and no one is so blind in mind as not to perceive that even by himself." Gregory of Nyssa, *Virg.* 11 (Callahan, 42).

73. Gregory of Nyssa, *Cant. Hom.* 13 (Norris, 419).

74. Gregory of Nyssa, *Cant. Hom.* 13 (Norris, 417).

75. Gregory of Nyssa, *Cant. Hom.* 13 (Norris, 417).

76. Gregory of Nyssa, *Cant. Hom.* 13 (Norris, 417–19).

Bathed in milk, the bishop becomes pure like a dove, "inerrant and undeceived like milk."[77]

The final stage of becoming adapted to Christ the head is achieved "by persistence and assiduity," as the bishop takes his seat "by the pools of divine waters" and gazes on them; that is, on the divine teachings (the Scriptures).[78] Gregory's interpretation of the scriptural text here is grounded in the pastoral realities of his age. He recognizes that many bishops do not gaze on the Word as they should and so he finished his homily proper with these strong words of encouragement to ground oneself in the Word:

> The Word wants the seers and watchers to be people who set the surety of the divine teachings before them like the brow of an encompassing wall but conceal by a humility like an enclosing eyelid the purity and radiance of their way of life, lest the beam of self-conceit, falling upon the pure pupil of the eye, become an obstacle to sight.[79]

INSIGHTS FOR CATECHESIS TODAY

Having explored the image of the dove in the works of Origen and Gregory on the *Canticle*, we are now well placed to determine how their insights might enrich our understanding of this somewhat common motif. We have seen that Origen has showed himself to be more grounded in the literal meaning of the dove than the Nyssan. Origen, as we have seen, noted the observable characteristics of the dove and used these to draw out the spiritual meaning of the text. Gregory, on the other hand, perhaps assuming his audience was well aware of the supposed innocence, purity, and loftiness of the dove, moved quickly to identify the dove with the Spirit and grounded much of his exegesis on this.[80]

Our study of Origen has shown that those who have "dove-eyes" are able to look at the world in an en-spirited or in-spired way. In particular, they are able to read and understand the Scriptures in the way the author (and by this we mean the divine author) intended. This correct reading of

---

77. Gregory of Nyssa, *Cant. Hom.* 13 (Norris, 419).

78. τὰ θεῖα μαθήματα. Gregory of Nyssa, *Cant. Hom.* 13 (Norris, 419). Lampe notes that for Origen, in his *Contra Celsum*, this phrase refers to Scripture. Lampe, *Patristic Greek Lexicon*, s.v. "μάθημα."

79. Gregory of Nyssa, *Cant. Hom.* 13 (Norris, 419).

80. Edwards neatly summarizes the different approaches of the two; "for Origen the truth is inscribed in the text, whereas for Gregory the text is rather an illustration or index of the truth." Edwards, "Origen and Gregory of Nyssa," 91.

the Word enables the reader to "fly from earthly and corporeal places to celestial ones" and to penetrate "the deep wisdom of God which is hidden in mystery."[81] Such a way of reading the Word is dynamic and appealing as it recognizes the reader as an active participant in the drama of salvation. Furthermore, as Origen shows, the Holy Spirit fills the reader with power, sanctifies her, and fills her with His gifts so that she is made fit to play her part in this encounter with the Word.

If we are to learn from Origen's insights into the imagery of the dove, then we would do well to examine our catechetical programs to see that they present a lively view of the dove as the one who inspires. In the first instance, such programs ought to include adequate catechesis on scriptural inspiration that is informed by an orthodox theology of inspiration. One could do worse than to base this on the 2014 text from the Pontifical Biblical Commission (PBC), *The Inspiration and Truth of Sacred Scripture*. Here, for instance, we find a clear affirmation that the Scriptures are the Word of God; that is, that they come from God and thus can "speak of God in an adequate and reliable way."[82] In an age when the Scriptures are often viewed as archaic, historically unreliable, and devoid of divine origin, this declaration from the PBC confirms the simple and beautiful truth that God really speaks to us through his Scriptures.

Our catechetical programs must also recognize that readers need to be inspired in order to plumb the depths of the scriptural text. The aforementioned PBC document asserts that "the Spirit in which the [scriptural] books were written . . . should be the Spirit in which we listen to them."[83] On Origen's view, this is akin to reading the Scriptures with dove-eyes. Of course, one must guard against purely spiritual readings of the text for the spiritual sense is founded on the literal.[84] As Origen taught, not all readers of the Scriptures are adequately prepared to read the Scriptures in a spiritual way. Aware of this, catechists ought to be wary of how the Scriptures are taught. For example, are we introducing those we teach to the right texts at the right stage of their development? Are we adopting a cookie-cutter approach to teaching the Scriptures, oblivious to the different stages of faith development in our students? In Origen's terms, do we give milk to the spiritually infant and strong meat to the mature?[85] We could ask many other questions of this nature, but perhaps one of the more important

---

81. Origen, *Cant. Com.* 3.14 (Lawson, 240–41).

82. PBC, *Inspiration and Truth* 3 (Esposito and Gregg, xx).

83. PBC, *Inspiration and Truth* 53 (Esposito and Gregg, 55).

84. Benedict XVI, *Verbum Domini*, 37.

85. Origen, *Cant. Hom.* Prol. (Lawson, 22).

ones relates to the literal sense of the Scriptures, a sense Origen believed was accessible even to the somatic reader. How can we help those we teach to understand the literal sense when they are two thousand or more years removed from the *Sitz im Leben* of the scriptural text? And furthermore, how can the Scriptures be taught to those who are separate from the community in which the text was written?[86]

The dove does not merely inspire the reading of Scripture. Reading the Scriptures is not a simple intellectual exercise, the success of which is measured by how well we can speak or write about the Word. If we really believe that the Word is living and active (Heb 4:12), then we must also accept that the Word is able to transform our lives. Such transformation demands reception of the Word in such a way that it becomes meaningful to us. This does not mean, of course, that we are to adapt the Word to "fit" our weak human nature. Rather, we must allow ourselves to be adapted to the Word. The Holy Spirit makes this possible. In his reflection on the sacrifice of doves for newborns, Origen asserts that the Spirit provides spiritual judgement and insight. Reception of the free and generous gift of the Spirit at baptism and confirmation inspires the recipient such that he or she is able to discern what God is saying through his Word, making it possible for transformation to occur.

Naturally, one's ability to hear and respond to the Word can improve or worsen depending on choices made. Origen teaches that there is a dynamic relationship between the reading of the Word and living the spiritual life. Hearing the wisdom of God in the Word can draw the hearer more profoundly into the wisdom of God. Furthermore, partaking in the sacramental life, performing the corporal and spiritual works of mercy, and growing in love, opens one to receiving "flowers of zest from the Divine Scriptures" and drawing closer to the heavenly courts.[87] With this in mind, we are called to ensure our catechesis strongly affirms that the dove's gentle cooing calls us to intimacy with the deep and hidden mystery of God.[88]

Gregory, while clearly reliant on Origen's *Commentary*, draws different lessons for his reader to Origen. The Nyssan co-opts the image of "dove-eyes" for explaining the spiritual ascent. He stresses the need for purification and mortification, and this teaching is always relevant. Even more pertinent, I would suggest, is his explanation of the role the eye plays in shaping or

---

86. We note that these questions and others like them are (or ought to be) ever present in the minds of those of us tasked with teaching the Scriptures to an increasingly secular cohort of students.

87. Origen, *Cant. Com.* 3[4].15 (Lawson, 248).

88. It would seem that such catechesis should be accompanied by formation that extols the beauty and desirability of wisdom.

forming one's inner life. While the science he bases his conclusions on is clearly archaic, the lessons he teaches are eternally true. In an age driven by the image, Gregory reminds us of the importance of diverting one's gaze from the corporeal and transitory to the divine and eternal.

Space dictates that we cannot possibly account for all the instances where the image veils the essence of things (think pornography, the consumer culture, social media and mainstream media, and so on). We can, however, pose some questions to assist the development of our catechesis on the dove. Do we, for instance, realize that the Spirit given in the sacraments empowers us to choose what we gaze on? That is, despite the fatalistic mentality of many who deem that we are slaves to our biology and upbringing, do we believe that the Spirit can really help us to choose the good and to grow in virtue? Furthermore, do we accept that the dove can purify our sight such that we are able to see what truly is? Finally, echoing the teaching of Origen, do we believe that the Spirit can not only help us to read Scripture, but that it can teach us the humility to read it rightly?

I would like to finish with one final insight from Gregory that strikes me as crucial for today. Gregory co-opts the image of the eyes of a dove to demonstrate the importance of *eros* for bringing the lover into the embrace of the beloved. In order to acquire the eyes of a dove, the bride needs to listen for the voice of the bridegroom as he seeks to woo her. Drawn by that which she cannot yet perceive with her senses, she is empowered to rise, move forward, and draw close to her beloved. Only then when she moves close is her soul able to reflect that on which she gazes, the beauty of the eternal and divine bridegroom, Beauty itself. *Eros* therefore leads to *agape*, and the creature is conformed to the image of the creator. In a word, the lover is deified.

In an age in which *eros* is the only form of love known to many, Gregory's mapping of the dynamics of love between the bridegroom and his bride offer a divine elixir that promises true happiness. The cooing of the dove calls the creature to an intimacy beyond anything imaginable. Seen in this light, the reception of the dove at baptism and again in confirmation is a gift of eternal and inestimable value. Origen and Gregory teach us that the Spirit, who descended like a dove on Jesus at his baptism and again on the disciples on the first Pentecost, transforms those who welcome it. Their teaching is ever old and ever new; it is an invitation to focus our gaze of the Lord such that we may hear him truly, see him clearly, and become like him.

BIBLIOGRAPHY

Benedict XVI. *Verbum Domini*. https://www.vatican.va/content/benedict-xvi/en/apost_exhortations/documents/hf_ben-xvi_exh_20100930_verbum-domini.html.

Clark, Elizabeth A. *The Origenist Controversy: The Cultural Construction of an Early Christian Debate*. Princeton: Princeton University Press, 1992.

Crouzel, H., and E. Prinzivalli. "Origenism." In *Encyclopedia of Ancient Christianity*, edited by Angelo Di Berardino, 2:983–83. Downers Grove, IL: InterVarsity, 2014.

Dixon, Edward P. "Descending Spirit and Descending Gods: A 'Greek' Interpretation of the Spirit's 'Descent as a Dove' in Mark 1:10." *Journal of Biblical Literature* 128 (4) (2009) 759–80.

Edwards, Mark. "Origen and Gregory of Nyssa on the Song of Songs." In *Exploring Gregory of Nyssa: Philosophical, Theological, and Historical Studies*, edited by Anna Marmadoro and Neil B. McLynn, 75–92. Oxford: Oxford University Press, 2018.

Gregory of Nyssa. "De opificio hominis." In *Patrologia Graeca*, edited by J.-P. Migne, 44:124–256. Paris: Migne, 1863.

———. *Homilies on the Song of Songs*. Translated by Richard A. Norris Jr. Atlanta: Society of Biblical Literature, 2012.

———. "On Perfection." In Gregory of Nyssa, *Ascetical Works*, translated by Virginia Woods Callahan, 91–122. Washington, DC: The Catholic University of America Press, 1999.

Ierodiakonou. Katerina. "On Galen's Theory of Vision." *Bulletin of the Institute of Classical Studies. Supplement* 114 (2014) 235–47.

Keenan, Mary Emily. "St. Gregory of Nyssa and the Medical Profession." *Bulletin of the History of Medicine* 15 (1944) 150–61.

Lampe, G. W. H. *A Patristic Greek Lexicon*. Oxford: Clarendon, 1961.

Lubac, Henri de. *History and Spirit: The Understanding of Scripture according to Origen*. Translated by Anne Englund Nash and Juvenal Merriell. San Francisco: Ignatius, 2007.

Mateo-Seco, Lucas F., and Giulio Maspero. *The Brill Dictionary of Gregory of Nyssa*. Leiden: Brill, 2010.

Matis, Hannah W. *The Song of Songs in the Early Middle Ages*. Boston: Brill, 2019.

McGuckin, John Anthony. "St. Gregory of Nyssa: Bishop, Philosopher, Exegete, Theologian." In *Exploring Gregory of Nyssa: Philosophical, Theological, and Historical Studies*, edited by Anna Marmadoro and Neil B. McLynn, 7–28. Oxford: Oxford University Press, 2018.

Norris, Richard A., Jr. "Introduction." In *Homilies on the Song of Songs*, translated by Richard A. Norris Jr., xiii–liv. Atlanta: Society of Biblical Literature, 2012.

O'Keefe, John J. "Origen (c. 185–c. 253): *Commentary on the Song of Songs*." In *Christian Spirituality: The Classics*, edited by Arthur Holder, 1–12. London: Routledge, 2009.

———. "Scriptural Interpretation." In *The SCM Press A-Z of Origen*, edited by John A. McGuckin, 193–97. London: SCM, 2006.

Origen. *Commentaire sur le Cantique des Cantiques, tome II (Livres III–IV)*. Edited by Luc Brésard et al. Paris: Cerf, 1993.

———. *On First Principles*. Translated by G. W. Butterworth. Notre Dame: Ave Maria, 2013.

————. *On First Principles: A Reader's Edition.* Translated by John Behr. Oxford: Oxford University Press, 2019.

————. *The Song of Songs: Commentary and Homilies.* Translated by R. P. Lawson. New York: Newman, 1956.

Pontifical Biblical Commission. *The Inspiration and Truth of Sacred Scripture.* Translated by Thomas Esposito and Stephen Gregg. Collegeville, MN: Liturgical, 2014.

Ramelli, Ilaria. "The Divine as Inaccessible Object of Knowledge in Ancient Platonism: A Common Philosophical Pattern across Religious Traditions." *Journal of the History of Ideas* 75 (2014) 167–88.

————. "Origen and the Platonic Tradition." *Religions* 8 (2017). doi:10.3390/rel8020021.

Smith, Yancy. *The Mystery of Anointing: Hippolytus' Commentary on the Song of Songs in Social and Critical Contexts: Texts, Translations, and Comprehensive Study.* Piscataway, NJ: Gorgias, 2015.

Stern, David. "Ancient Jewish Interpretation of the Song of Songs in a Comparative Context." In *Jewish Biblical Interpretation and Cultural Exchange,* edited by Natalie B. Dohrmann and David Stern, 87–107. Philadelphia: University of Pennsylvania Press, 2013.

Stone, Michael. "The Interpretation of Song of Songs in 4 Ezra." *Journal for the Study of Judaism in the Persian, Hellenistic, and Roman Period* 38 (2007) 226–33.

Thibodeau, Philip. "Ancient Optics: Theories and Problems of Vision." In *A Companion to Science, Technology, and Medicine in Ancient Greece and Rome,* edited by Georgia L. Irby, 198–214. Hoboken, NJ: Wiley and Sons, 2016.

Trigg, Joseph W. *Origen.* London: Routledge, 2005.

Wessel, Susan. "The Reception of Greek Science in Gregory of Nyssa's 'De Hominis Opificio.'" *Vigiliae Christianae* 63 (2009) 24–46.

Wright, J. Robert, ed. *Proverbs, Ecclesiastes, Song of Solomon.* Downers Grove, IL: IVP Academic, 2014.

8

GOD'S PRESENCE IN HISTORY

The Work of Christ and the Spirit in St. Gregory of Nazianzus' Fifth Theological Oration *and* Oration *38* On the Nativity

Mario Baghos

FAITH IN GOD AS Trinity undoubtedly conditioned the view of history of the fourth century Cappadocian Father, St. Gregory of Nazianzus. In fact, the saint interpreted history through the lens of what we can call—to borrow a term from postmodernism—a metanarrative, a totalizing or all-encompassing interpretive framework, which has existential import.[1] This metanarrative involved both God and the human story, especially the revelation of God as Father, Son, and Holy Spirit to the people of Israel, the Church and the world. Gregory especially gave emphasis to what we could call the christological (pertaining to Christ) and pneumatological (pertaining to the Spirit) aspects of this metanarrative.

---

1. Stephens and McCallum, *Retelling Stories, Framing Culture*, 6. Postmodernism has been characterized by an "incredulity towards meta-narratives." Lyotard, *Post-Modern Condition*, xxiv. Nevertheless, I have chosen to positively appropriate this concept and interpret it from a Christian perspective. In my application of it to Gregory's writings, I acknowledge that the saint never used this concept; rather, I believe it is amenable to Gregory's vision of history and can be usefully employed as a hermeneutic as such.

This chapter elicits and constructs an existential metanarrative of history based on Gregory's orations. It demonstrates that Gregory contributed a view of history that is not only holistic, but by focusing on history as guided by the Holy Spirit, along with the gradual disclosure of the trinitarian God and having Jesus Christ as its source and final goal, gives order and meaning to what in some historical trends has been viewed as either meaningless or chaotic flux or as a series of endless, divisive power struggles.[2] In other words, this chapter is interdisciplinary, incorporating aspects from secular historiography, existential philosophy, postmodernism and patristic theology and interpreting these for the lens of the Christian experience. This interdisciplinarity is useful in order to demonstrate that an existential metanarrative of history can be found in Gregory's orations.

Although neither the secular historiographical method nor one based on patristic interpretation can claim exclusivity, my goal is to demonstrate that the theological interpretation of history[3] elicited from the works of Gregory is just as valid as any secular approach, revealing aspects that have been obscured by the sceptic and even nihilistic outcomes of some trends in contemporary history writing, especially in light of "death" of the theological metanarrative espoused by Keith Jenkins in the late twentieth century.[4] This chapter begins with an analysis of chapters twenty-five and twenty-six of Gregory's *Fifth Theological Oration* (*Oration* 31) in order to elicit the characteristics of the theological metanarrative which unfolds within the historical continuum or the "age," and is marked by God's gradual self-disclosure as three persons: Father, Son, and Holy Spirit. It will especially hone in on the work of the Spirit, the third person of the blessed Trinity, in history, in this section. It will then interpret these features within the framework of chapters 10–13 of his *Oration* 38, where the historical metanarrative in *Oration* 31 can be framed within the cosmic work of the Son of God, who both initiates the age with his creation of the world(s) and will return to consummate it as promised (that is, at the second coming). It will conclude by asserting that, for Gregory, the gradual disclosure of God's trinitarian life, guided by the Holy Spirit and framed by and localized in the person and work of Jesus Christ, constitutes the cornerstone of his

---

2. For an interpretation of history as chaotic flux, see Carr, *What Is History?*, 156. For more on history as comprised as a series of power struggles—and the dangers inherent in this heuristic—see Murray, *Madness of Crowds*, 53, 51–63; Peterson, *12 Rules for Life*, 305–7.

3. It must be stated from the outset that Gregory never attempted historiography *per se*.

4. Jenkins, *Re-thinking History*, 71–72. Jenkins's analysis has its antecedents in Friedrich Nietzsche's "death of God" theory in the nineteenth century.

metanarrative of history. To this end, the conclusion will attempt to reiterate the significant contribution that the saint's metanarrative can make to contemporary historiography.

SOME CHARACTERISTICS OF GREGORY'S METANARRATIVE IN THE *FIFTH THEOLOGICAL ORATION*

Following from the above, at the beginning of the twenty-fifth chapter of his *Fifth Theological Oration*, Gregory affirmed that "there have been two transformations of life manifested out of the entire age (τοῦ παντὸς αἰῶνος)."[5] In his *Hexaemeron*, St. Basil of Caesarea, a contemporary and friend of Gregory, identified the one day of creation (ἡμέρα μία) mentioned in the Septuagint translation of Genesis 1:5 with the recapitulation of all history from the beginning of creation to that which paradoxically lies beyond it—i.e., the eschatological "eighth day"—a summary that he analogously referred to as the αἰῶν or age.[6] It is clear that Gregory was here attempting a similar all-encompassing approach to history with his statement τοῦ παντὸς αἰῶνος (*tou pantos aiōnos*), which literally refers to "the entire age" but can be understood as "history in its entirety," if history is to be understood as framed by the cosmos as mentioned above. We have seen that this macro or universal approach is a characteristic of the metanarrative insofar as it attempts to give a comprehensive account of the historical drama and the persons, events or sub-narratives that it includes.

Gregory then went on to clarify that the two life-changing transformations "are called two 'covenants,' and, so famous was the business involved, two 'earthquakes,'"[7] before affirming that: The first [covenant or shaking] was the transition from idols to the Law; the second, from Law to

5. Gregory of Nazianzus, *Fifth Theological Oration* (Oration 31): *On the Holy Spirit* 25, in *St. Gregory of Nazianzus: On God and Christ*, 136 (PG 36, 160D). Unless otherwise stated, all quotations from the *Fifth Theological Oration*, referenced throughout as *Oration 31*, will be taken from this translation and will include the chapter and page numbers. The *Patrologia Graeca* will be referenced only when I have included the Greek text or have translated it myself.

6. Basil of Caesarea, *Hexaemeron* 2.8, in *Exegetic Homilies*, 33–36 (PG 29, 48B–52B). For Basil, the ἡμέρα μία represented both the origin and climax of creation, thereby recapitulating within itself all of history from beginning to end as metaphorically illustrated by the creation narrative of Genesis, as well as paradoxically including the transcendent "eighth day" symbolizing the eschaton. For a detailed analysis of this recapitulation of history, as well as the relationship between ἡμέρα μία, the αἰῶν or "age" and the "eighth day," see Baghos, "Recapitulation of History," 151–68.

7. Gregory of Nazianzus, *Oration* 31.25, 136.

the Gospel. The Gospel also tells of the third "earthquake," the change from this present state of things to what lies unmoved, unshaken, beyond.[8] The first covenant is that which was inaugurated by God's disclosure of the Law to the prophet Moses, and the second by the revelation of God in the person of Jesus Christ.[9] The first is enshrined in the Old Testament, the second in the New. Notice that in his clarification of these covenantal transformations—which are not without experiential relevance insofar as they impact upon the worship and belief of the people of God, however interpreted—Gregory was not interested in episodical events; just those events/experiences that have resulted in a transformation of life. Transformation, however, involves a process of becoming.

In this case, "becoming" can be interpreted as an existential movement away from idols—which is paganism—into the Law—which is Judaism—and finally from the Law to the Christian Gospel. But our present state is also conditioned by movement and becoming insofar as we anticipate a final transition into that which is unshaken and unmoved—i.e., the eschatological state. The historical process of becoming, therefore, contains *logos* within its *telos*, manifesting a rational orientation as it unfolds towards its final purpose. We will return to this eschatological dimension towards the end of the article. Suffice it say for the moment that the eschaton, according to Gregory, will be inaugurated by a third and final earthquake, an event which, if taken at face value, would seem to lend itself to an apocalyptic interpretation—a sudden and chaotic disruption of the historical continuum. Gregory avoided this with reference to the two "earthquakes" or covenants that have already taken place: An identical feature occurs in both covenants. The feature? They were not suddenly changed, even at the first moment the changes were put in hand. We need to know why. It was so that we should be persuaded, not forced.[10] Far from resulting in chaos or confusion, for Gregory the earthquakes were positive metaphors serving to reinforce God's gradual transfiguration of the historical process for our sakes through the covenants. The earthquakes signify both a rupture with an existing state and a tangible change in composition that is precisely

---

8. Gregory of Nazianzus, *Oration* 31.25, 136.

9. Although earthquakes feature often in the Scriptures, in his exposition of the gradual stages of revelation Georges Florovsky included a translation of the above text within which he bracketed a possible antecedent for St. Gregory's use of this theme, having cited Haggai 2:7: "I will shake (συσσείσω-LXX) heaven and earth, sea and land, and all nations, and the treasure of all nations will come hither." Florovsky, *Eastern Fathers of the Fourth Century*, 127.

10. Gregory of Nazianzus, *Oration* 31.25, 136.

analogous to μετάνοια, an "earth-shattering" change of mind.[11] This nuance is emphatically expressed by humanity's transition from idols to the Law, and from the Law to the Gospel. Gregory then gave the reasons why the transition from one covenant to another occurred gradually rather than suddenly, affirming that the covenants are an outcome of God's pedagogical concern.

If God applied force, then our internal resolve would be unspontaneous and thus impermanent. Instead, God preferred that "the issue should be ours"[12]—that we respond to his call freely and without coercion.[13] Moreover, God acts like a doctor or schoolmaster in removing from us certain unnecessary burdens. Gregory declared:

> The first change cut away idols but allowed sacrifices to remain; the second stripped away sacrifices but did not forbid circumcision. Then, when people had been reconciled to the withdrawal, they agreed to let go what had been left them as a concession. Under the first covenant that concession was sacrifice, and they became Jews instead of Gentiles; under the second, circumcision—and they became Christians instead of Jews, brought round gradually, bit by bit, to the Gospel. Paul shall convince you here. He progressed from circumcising and keeping ceremonial cleansings to the point of declaring, "But if I, brethren, preach circumcision, why am I still being persecuted? [Gal 5:11]" His earlier conduct was an accommodation to circumstance; his later conduct belonged to the full truth.[14]

The gradual changing of the mind of God's people represented by the covenantal earthquakes was thus concretely manifested in the successive concessions made by God; concessions which were necessary in order to wean humanity from idolatry and the Law and for their change in disposition to be sincere and willing. And these concessions can be viewed as somehow exemplified on a personal level in the evolution of St. Paul's disposition towards circumcision, a ritual that, if undertaken, necessitates the observance of the entire Law. The verse from Galatians 5:11 above is preceded by a brief argument against the need for circumcision, a practice

---

11. Lampe, *Patristic Greek Lexicon*, 855.

12. Gregory of Nazianzus, *Oration* 31.25, 136.

13. In other words, the worries expressed by contemporary scholars such as Carr that a theological metanarrative would entail an effacement of humanity's role in the historical continuum are not justified. St. Gregory's belief in a divinely guided history was no less a human history, but a truly synergetic one.

14. Gregory of Nazianzus, *Oration* 31.25, 136–37.

that the Apostle would have in fact advocated before his conversion to the Gospel, but certainly not thereafter.[15]

His remarks are thus to be interpreted as a rhetorical response to false allegations of adherence to circumcision and hence the Law; a response cleverly quoted by Gregory in his attempt to demonstrate the dramatic change in attitude by the Apostle to the Gentiles. This change can be interpreted as a "metanoic" transformation associated with the second covenantal earthquake from the Law to the Gospel, illustrating the existential significance of the dramatic movement from one covenant to the next, a movement summed up in St. Paul's personal experience of becoming.

So far, we have seen that Gregory described these covenantal earthquakes as having marked two important existential changes through omissions or negations relating to ritualistic practices. In the beginning of chapter twenty-six, however, he went on to illustrate their most positive dimension, affirming that the "growth towards perfection"[16] facilitated by them occurred through additions—additions which the saint believed took place with reference to the doctrine or revelation of God as it unfolded in the historical interim between the Old and New covenants. Here, God's revelation is associated with existential growth culminating in perfection:

> In this way, the old covenant made clear proclamation of the Father, a less definite one of the Son. The new covenant made the Son manifest and gave us a glimpse of the Spirit's Godhead. At the present time, the Spirit resides amongst us, giving us a clearer manifestation of himself than before. It was dangerous for the Son to be preached openly when the Godhead of the Father was still unacknowledged. It was dangerous, too, for the Holy Spirit to be made (and here I use a rather rash expression) an extra burden, when the Son had not yet been received.[17]

15. Bruce, *Epistle of Paul to the Galatians*, 236–37.

16. Gregory of Nazianzus, *Oration* 31.26, 137. This "growth towards perfection" can be understood as tantamount to deification or *theosis* as articulated by the Eastern patristic tradition. According to Norman Russell, the saint placed a great emphasis on an imitation of Christ to be understood not as adherence to an external model, but as an internal reshaping through the sacraments and the philosophical life that allows human beings "to transcend their earthly limitations, with the result that they are transformed." Among Gregory's favorite expressions to describe this transformation is the word *theosis*, the frequency of which is recorded by Russell as part of his attempt to illustrate that, for the saint, deification had already occurred with the incarnation, and all that remained was "the believer's appropriation of this by accepting baptism and struggling to live the moral life." Russell, *Doctrine of Deification*, 214–15, 225.

17. Gregory of Nazianzus, *Oration* 31.26, 137.

It is thus made clear that, for the saint, the two covenants had a dual effect—to gradually strip away false beliefs and practices and to manifest the truth concerning God as Trinity. The first covenant, established through the Mosaic Law, discredited idolatry and "made clear proclamation of God as Father," and the new or second covenant "made the Son manifest and gave us a glimpse of the Spirit's Godhead." Gregory stated that, in revealing himself as Father, Son, and Holy Spirit, God pedagogically considered humanity's ability to cope with this self-disclosure. Indeed, God's self-disclosure can result in another type of μετάνοια or "change of mind" on behalf of the people to whom he discloses himself; for it is only when the Father was acknowledged by those to whom he chose to reveal himself that the Son was subsequently revealed, and likewise with the Spirit, who was only acknowledged once the Son had been fully received.

As with the gradual concessions that he permitted regarding ritualistic practices, God reveals himself in stages, lest humans endanger themselves (presumably through incredulity or misinterpretation), jeopardizing what is within their powers to grasp, as happens, according to Gregory, "to those encumbered with a diet too strong for them or who gaze at sunlight with eyes too feeble for it."[18] That God did finally reveal his true existence as three persons, and that this was not only received on a conceptual basis but lived experientially, was attested to by the saint in a way that places the emphasis squarely on the inspiration of the Holy Spirit:[19]

> No, God meant it to be by piecemeal additions, "ascents" as David called them, by progress and advance from glory to glory, that the light of the Trinity should shine upon more illustrious souls. This was, I believe, the motive for the Spirit's making his home in the disciples in gradual stages proportionate to their capacity to receive him—at the outset of the gospel when he performs miracles, after the Passion when he is breathed into

18. Gregory of Nazianzus, *Oration* 31.26, 137.

19. Kilian McDonnell designated God's gradual self-disclosure as a progressive revelation. He based this assertion on an ostensible remark by St. Gregory in chapter 26 of his *Fifth Theological Oration* that there occurred a "progress of the doctrine of God." McDonnell, *Other Hand of God*, 143. However, any word resembling the notion of dogma or doctrine is missing from the original text (see PG 36, 161C). Behr is correct when he asserted that the saint "is not advancing a theory of the 'development of doctrine.' There are no new doctrinal facts to be introduced in addition to the gospel, at some subsequent historical stage. Rather, there is an increasing comprehension of the truths that it contains, as the contemplative theologian advances in maturity of understanding." Behr, *Formation of Christian Theology*, 368. In other words, the "faith that was once and for all entrusted to the saints" (Jude 1:3) undergoes no inherent change; what changes is our understanding in accordance with the "growth towards perfection," which I mentioned above.

the disciples, after the Ascension when he appears in fiery tongues. He was gradually revealed by Jesus also, as you too can substantiate by a more careful reading. "I will ask the Father," he says, "and he will send you another Comforter, the Spirit of Truth" [John 14:16–17]—intending that the Spirit should not appear to be a rival God and spokesman of another power. Later he says: "He will send him in my name" [John 14:26]—leaving out "I will ask" but retaining "He will send." Later on he says: "I shall send" [15:26]—indicating the Son's own rank; and later: "He will come" [16:7]—indicating the Spirit's power.[20]

Thus, for Gregory, the entire historical process—the metanarrational "entire age"—advanced on a conceptually distinguishable macro and micro level.[21] On a macro level, it moved from one covenantal earthquake to another: from the revelation of the Father with a glimpse of the Son, to the revelation of the Son with a glimpse of the Spirit. This movement is associated with a dual process of becoming insofar as God pedagogically weans humanity from false practices and beliefs to a gradual acquiescence of his true existence as three persons—as Father, Son, and Holy Spirit. Indeed, Jesus unveils the Spirit's Godhead in stages proportionate to his disciples' acceptance of him as the Son of God: moving from a request to the Father to send him, to an "objective" affirmation of his being sent by the Father in the Son's name, culminating in a dual promise that he himself will send the Spirit and that the Spirit will in fact come.

It is therefore clear that this stripping away of falsities "through omissions" and revelation of the truth "through additions" is an existential process, but that this process of becoming occurs in a much more profound manner was articulated by Gregory when he affirmed that, on a micro level, the progress of the revelation of God was reflected by the Apostles themselves, within whom the Spirit dwelt permanently "in gradual stages proportionate to their capacity to receive him." These gradual stages were analogous to the Son's earthly ministry and unfolded through the Apostolic witness of Christ's earliest miracles to his breathing the Spirit on them after his resurrection and, finally, to the Spirit's alighting in flames upon their heads at Pentecost. For Gregory, this Apostolic experience of the Spirit radiantly manifests "growth towards perfection," what has been described in the Greek tradition as divinization or *theosis*.[22] That this growth is not yet complete but awaits its consummation at the eschaton—the final term

20. Gregory of Nazianzus, *Oration* 31.26, 137–38.

21. Gregory of Nazianzus, *Oration* 31.25, 136.

22. For more on St. Gregory's perception of *theosis*, see Tollefsen, "Theosis according to Gregory," 257–70.

of the historical process—was illustrated by Gregory in his *Oration* 38, a text which not only provides a glimpse into the saint's eschatology, but also contributes the proper framework for interpreting the characteristics of his metanarrative, insofar as it is framed by and anchored in Jesus Christ.

FRAMING THE *FIFTH THEOLOGICAL ORATION* WITHIN *ORATION* 38

Putting forward a two-stage theory of the creation of the spiritual and material realms inspired by Platonic cosmology in his *Oration* 38.10, Gregory expounded upon the creation of the human being as a sort of recapitulation of this process, a blending or mixing of the intelligible and material realms in a single "second world" (δεύτερον κόσμον),[23] what we can call a microcosm (μικρός κόσμος).[24] Both the creation of the spiritual and material realms (with the former preceding the latter) and their mystical synthesis in the human being were undertaken, affirmed the Nazianzen in chapter eleven, by the Demiurge Logos (δημιουργοῦ Λόγου),[25] who is the Son of God the Father. Gregory went on to affirm that the human being contains something of the divine in its spiritual-earthly constitution and, while educated in the here and now, "is transferred elsewhere, and to complete the mystery, deified through inclination towards God."[26]

Relating this process to himself, Gregory implied that the light and truth he experienced in the here and now were bearing him towards what we can describe as a definite end or *telos*, which he went on to explicate as an experience of "the radiance of God, which is worthy of the one who has bound me (to flesh) and will release me and hereafter will bind me in a higher manner."[27] This is an allusion to the final resurrection of the body at the eschaton or the last things by "the one who has bound" human nature together—i.e., the Demiurge Logos, Jesus Christ—and can be related to Gregory's affirmation above that the eschaton will be precipitated

---

23. Gregory of Nazianzus, *Oration 38: On the Nativity* 10, in *Festal Orations: Saint Gregory of Nazianzus*, 67 (PG 36, 321B). Unless otherwise stated, all references to *Oration* 38 will be from this translation and will include the chapter and page numbers. The *Patrologia Graeca* will be referenced only when I have included the Greek text or have translated it myself.

24. Tracing the antecedents of the microcosm as it appears in the thought of St. Maximus the Confessor, Lars Thunberg identified St. Gregory's use of the term in *Oration* 28.22 (PG 36, 57A). See Thunberg, *Microcosm and Mediator*, 135.

25. Gregory of Nazianzus, *Oration* 38.11, 68. PG 36, 321C.

26. Gregory of Nazianzus, *Oration* 38.11, 68–69.

27. Gregory of Nazianzus, *Oration* 38.11, 69.

by a third earthquake that has yet to take place but which will mark "the change from this present state of things to what lies unmoved, unshaken, beyond."[28] In other words, the universal *telos* of the historical process or advancement of the age finds its concrete realization in the human persons who are resurrected on the last day; a representation of the final stage of the historical process of becoming in a process guided by the Holy Spirit since, as we saw above, the Spirit's power now resides in the Church and, it is implied, guides it towards the eschaton.

Gregory seems to perceive the "entire age" as having been inaugurated with the creation of the world by God the Logos before moving in a sort of continuum from the first covenantal earthquake to the second— which is the present state within which we anticipate the third and final earthquake that will translate the cosmos into an unshaken, unmoved mode of being.[29] Indeed, the saint stipulated that the Demiurge Logos both initiates the historical process with the creation of the cosmos (i.e., the spiritual and material realms) and implied that—in a manner consistent with the eschatological teaching of the early Church—the same Demiurge Logos, Jesus Christ, will return to "bind him in a higher manner," that is, to transfigure both the saint and, by extension, the entire created cosmos at the eschaton, the third and final earthquake. We stated in our first section that the *telos* of history—the end to which it is geared—is also its *logos*, and that from a Christian perspective this *logos* or reason is to be identified with none other than the Word of God incarnate, Jesus Christ. This we have now confirmed was in fact Gregory's position. However, if Christ, as Gregory affirmed, stands at the beginning and end of the "entire age" as both creator and consummator, then he indeed simultaneously constitutes the *logos* and the *telos* of the historical process insofar as it begins and ends with him.[30] This is in fact made explicit by the saint in the first chapter of this *Oration*, where, after extolling the birth of Christ, he asked rhetorically: "Who would not worship the one 'from the beginning' [1 John 1:1]? Who would not glorify 'the Last'? [Rev 1:17; 2:8]"[31]

Contrary, therefore, to the reductionist presentation of the early Church as establishing, and henceforth being solely preoccupied with, a linear conception of history tracing its origins to the creation of the world

28. Gregory of Nazianzus, *Oration* 31.25, 136.

29. A mode of being that transcends history as we have come to know and experience it.

30. See Revelation 22:13, where the Lord says: "I am the Alpha and the Omega, the first and the last, the beginning and the end." Biblical references in this chapter are from the NRSV.

31. Gregory of Nazianzus, *Oration* 38.1, 61.

based on a literal interpretation of the Old Testament book of Genesis (*Anno Mundi*) or, alternately, to the birth of Jesus (*Anno Domini*), here we see a cycle that begins and ends with Christ. However, even this cyclical projection might be insufficient, because although it has Christ as its first and last point of reference, it does not account for his presence in the interim, let alone for the gradual disclosure of the Father, Son (or, the incarnate Logos), and the Holy Spirit in the historical continuum, a disclosure which initiated that process of movement and becoming illustrated above. *Oration* 38 seems to allude to some of the above-mentioned characteristics of the *Fifth Theological Oration*, while bringing out varying nuances and giving a more comprehensive depiction of Gregory's theological metanarrative. Indeed, if we were to conflate the *Fifth Theological Oration*, where Gregory speaks of the gradual disclosure of God as three persons and especially of the Spirit's full manifestation and presence in the Church, and *Oration* 38 which speaks of history framed and marked by the person of God the Son, we see that both Christ and the Spirit (and, by implication, the Father), while forever transcendent, permeate by grace the entire historical continuum from alpha to omega.

After situating the Son—the Demiurge Logos—on either end of the historical spectrum in chapter eleven, Gregory moved to an allegorical interpretation of the paradisal experience of the first human being and the fall in chapter twelve. Describing the paradisal vegetation as "divine thoughts,"[32] the saint asserted that the first human (Adam) was called to cultivate these through contemplation, with the ordinance—delineated in pedagogical terms—to abstain from contemplating the tree of knowledge. The tree could only be possessed at the right time in Adam's spiritual development or maturation, "just as adult food is not useful for those who are still tender and in need of milk."[33] Indeed, there is a parallel here with the self-disclosure of God's existence as Father, Son and Holy Spirit, mediated to post-lapsarian humans in gradual stages (corresponding to the transition from the idols to the Law, and the Law to the Gospel mentioned above) out of a pedagogical concern for their welfare.

As the exposition unfolds, it mentions the roles of the devil and Eve who, in their persuasion of Adam, made him forget the commandment given so that he "yielded to the bitter taste" of the fruit.[34] The saint then made

32. Gregory of Nazianzus, *Oration* 38.12, 69.
33. Gregory of Nazianzus, *Oration* 38.12, 69.
34. Gregory of Nazianzus, *Oration* 38.12, 70.

it clear that, despite this tragic failure of "becoming," even the banishment from paradise had a positive dimension,[35] affirming:

> And at once he came to be banished from the tree of life and from paradise and from God because of the evil. . . . He gained a certain advantage from this; death is also the cutting off of sin, that evil might not be immortal, so the punishment becomes love for humankind. For thus, I am persuaded, God punishes.[36]

Here, the punishment for the transgression or sin (where sin is commensurable with evil) of the first human is not death. Instead, death became advantageous to humans insofar as it curtails the perpetuation of evil. For Gregory, the first human was punished with a love for humankind, which he clarified a little further down in the passage as "the transfer of worship from Creator to creatures"[37]—in other words, idolatry, "the last and first of all evils."[38]

Concluding his discussion on the fall and the problem of evil mentioned above, Gregory continued with a two-stage divine pedagogy of history that seems to fit into the metanarrational scheme articulated at length in the second section of this chapter. Chapter thirteen of his *Oration* 38 begins with the following exposition:

> The human being was first educated in many ways corresponding to the many sins that sprouted from the root of evil for different reasons and at different times; by word, law, prophets, benefits, threats, blows, floods, conflagrations, wars, victories, defeats; signs from heaven, signs from the air, from earth, from sea; unexpected changes in men, cities, nations; by all this God sought zealously to wipe out evil. At the end a stronger remedy was necessary for more dreadful diseases: murders of each other, adulteries, false oaths, lusts for men, and the last and first of all evils, idolatry and the transfer of worship from Creator to creatures. Since these things required a greater help, they also obtained something greater. It was the Word of God himself, the one who is before the ages, the invisible, the ungraspable, the incorporeal, the Principle from the Principle, the light from the light, the source of life and immortality, the imprint of the

---

35. This is symbolized by the transition from the contemplation of divine thoughts to thoughtlessness through hasty consumption (and thence from life to death).

36. Gregory of Nazianzus, *Oration* 38.12, 70.

37. Gregory of Nazianzus, *Oration* 38.13, 70.

38. Gregory of Nazianzus, *Oration* 38.13, 70.

archetypal beauty, the undistorted image, the definition and explanation of his Father.[39]

This exposition puts forward a scheme that was common among the saint's peers, most notably St. Basil.[40] In this scheme, sufferings or punishments, mentioned above as issuing forth from the "punitive" love of humankind or creatures, resulted in the sprouting of many sins that were addressed by God in different historical epochs according to the various circumstances and manifested especially in the Old Testament. The list of remedies for this evil—alternating between positive and negative (i.e., word, law, prophets, benefits *vis-à-vis* threats, blows, floods, conflagrations, etc.)—were not contextualized by Gregory. Instead, he only briefly referred to them in an attempt to convey that they constituted the means by which God sought to rid the world of evil. Most importantly, Gregory prefigured the entire discussion by affirming that this process was nevertheless educational or pedagogical; a process which, on account of our vehement obstinacy, "required a greater help"—i.e., the Word or Logos of God himself, who, by way of inference, we can assert taught us the precepts of virtue and truth directly and without hindrance.

Applying in a very basic way the principle of intertextuality with reference to these Gregorian texts, we observe an explicit thematic correlation between chapters eleven, twelve, and especially chapter thirteen of *Oration* 38, and Gregory's discussion in chapter twenty-five of his *Fifth Theological Oration* of history as an existential movement from one covenantal earthquake to another: from the idols to the Law punctuated by the revelation of the Father, and from the Law to the Gospel marked by the incarnation of the Son. Although in that oration the saint expounded upon the characteristics of what we have called his metanarrative—his view of those significant events that mark the "entire age" or history in its entirety—we were not given an insight into their precipitating factors, or, more specifically, into why it is that God acts pedagogically in history in such a way (something which both orations maintain). In *Oration* 38.12–13 we observe that for Gregory, humanity was punished after the fall with a love of creatures and idolatry. Therefore, there is an implicit connection between the first characteristic of the metanarrative articulated in chapter twenty-five of the *Fifth Theological Oration*—the transition from the idols to the Law—and idolatry as the summit of all post-lapsarian evils mentioned in *Oration* 38.13. In this chapter of the *Oration* the Law numbers among

39. Gregory of Nazianzus, *Oration* 38.13, 70–71.

40. Basil of Caesarea, *Homily Explaining That God Is Not the Cause of Evil* 5, in *Saint Basil the Great: On the Human Condition*, 71.

many inter-related responses by God, including his prophets, his word, etc., all of which were implemented in order to curtail the evils that have their root in idolatry.

And the parallels do not end there. We saw with reference to the *Fifth Theological Oration* 25–6 that the transition from the idols to the Law had a dual effect: God was gradually disclosing his trinitarian existence, as Father, Son and Holy Spirit, and leading his people away from idolatry. When interpreted via the lens of *Oration* 38.13, we observe that this process was part of a more complex endeavor to wipe out the evil that sprouted from idolatry. The same can be said about the transition from the Law to the Gospel mentioned in the *Fifth Theological Oration*. Interpreting this transition through the prism of *Oration* 38.13, we see that as these evils—"murders of each other, adulteries, false oaths [etc.]"—continued to persist under the Law, a greater remedy was needed; the incarnation of the Son and Word of God, the fountainhead of the Gospel, who points towards the Holy Spirit before the latter's full disclosure within the holy Apostles at Pentecost. Indeed, next to Christ, it is precisely these Spirit-bearing Apostles that can be described, in this context, as the first-fruits of our "growth towards perfection."[41]

The cornerstone of Gregory's existential metanarrative is, therefore, God's trinitarian disclosure localized, if you will, in the person of the Son, who comes from the Father and points towards/sends the Spirit. According to both his *Fifth Theological Oration* and *Oration* 38, history can be viewed as the domain within which God attempts to curtail evil in various ways until it finally becomes necessary that the Word or Logos of God—the "imprint," "undistorted image," and "explanation" of God the Father—enter into history by assuming humanity as Jesus Christ. Having briefly articulated the relationship of the Son and Logos to the Father in chapter thirteen of *Oration* 38—what we can call a pre-incarnational christology (on the level of "theology")—Gregory continued with an explication of the mystery of the incarnation[42] (on the level of "economy"):[43]

41. In 1 Corinthians 15:20 St. Paul called the resurrected Lord "the first-fruits of those who have fallen asleep."

42. Indeed, this seems to constitute a more robust exposition of the paradoxical nature of the incarnation that the saint already outlined in chapter 2. Gregory of Nazianzus, *Oration* 38.2, 62. PG 36, 313AC.

43. There is a conceptual distinction in the Cappadocians, employed consistently by Gregory in his corpus, between θεολογία and οἰκονομία. The former pertains to the contemplation of God as he reveals himself to his creation, and the latter, related to the first, concerns God's relationship with the created order. For more information, see Beeley, *Gregory of Nazianzus*, 194–95. Hence, insofar as it relates to the Logos' assumption of humanity as Jesus Christ, incarnational christology represents the summit of God's "economic" relationship with his creation.

> He [the Word] approaches his own image and bears flesh because
> of my flesh and mingles himself with a rational soul because of
> my soul, purifying like by like. And in all things he becomes a
> human, except sin. He was conceived by the Virgin, who was
> purified beforehand in both soul and flesh by the Spirit, for it
> was necessary that procreation be honored and that virginity be
> honored more. He comes forth, God with what he assumed, one
> from two opposites, flesh and spirit, the one deifying and the
> other deified. O the new mixture! O the paradoxical blending!
> He who is comes into being, and the uncreated is created, and
> the uncontained is contained, through the intervention of the
> rational soul, which mediates between the divinity and the
> coarseness of the flesh. The one who enriches becomes poor;
> he is made poor in my flesh, that I may be enriched through his
> divinity. The full one empties himself; for he empties himself
> of his own glory for a short time, that I may participate in
> his fullness. What is the wealth of his goodness? What is the
> mystery concerning me? I participated in the [divine] image
> and I did not keep it; he participates in my flesh both to save
> the image and to make the flesh immortal. He shares with us a
> second communion, much more paradoxical than the first; then
> he gave us a share in what is superior, now he shares in what is
> inferior.[44]

In a profound reflection upon the mystery of the convergence of divinity
and humanity in Christ's person, Gregory declared that, in his assumption
of a body and a rational soul, the pre-existent Logos became in all things
his own image, i.e., a real human being, with the exception of sin. Affirming
the virgin birth, he expressed wonder at the creation of the uncreated and
the circumscription of the uncircumscribable—at the ineffable reality of the
God-man and the deification of the human flesh that he assumed. But all of
this was done, the saint continued, for the sake of humanity that had gone
astray through evil, and so the greatest expression of God's pedagogical
concern for his creation is manifested in the Word's incarnation as Christ
Jesus, which Gregory related to himself.

By emptying "himself of his own glory" the incarnation of the Word
of God has existential implications for both the saint and for humanity in
its entirety; a humanity which is recapitulated into the God-man.[45] The

---

44. Gregory of Nazianzus, *Oration* 38.13, 71.

45. Gregory here depicts himself as representative of the entire human race that
is recapitulated into Christ in the incarnation. For more information on the deifying
effects of the incarnation for humanity in the thought of the saint, see Wesche, "Union
of God and Man," 83–98.

intimate reciprocity between Christ and Gregory is then interpreted on a broader scale when the saint affirmed that with his incarnation Jesus has shared with us—that is, humanity in general—a second communion, the first being that which was effected with the creation of the worlds; "then he gave us a share in what is superior, now he shares in what is inferior."[46]

The kenotic outpouring of the Word represents both the nadir of God's interaction with us and the zenith of the process of our deification in him; a process we saw above was expressed by the characteristics of Gregory's metanarrative, from idolatry to the Law with its full disclosure of the Father, and from the Law to the Gospel in the revelation of the Son.[47] At the end of that section, we hinted that the process of *theosis*—discussed with reference to the manifestation of the Holy Spirit, and the Apostles' experience of him, at Pentecost—begins in the here and now but will not be consummated until the eschaton, the third and final "earthquake." Exploring the subject of the eschaton, we noticed that in *Oration* 38.11, Gregory states that the same Demiurge Logos who created the worlds will one day return to transfigure them permanently and "bind him in a higher manner"—a reference to the general resurrection. From this we deduced Gregory's belief that Jesus, the Word of God incarnate, frames either end of the historical continuum as "the Alpha and the Omega, the first and the last, the beginning and the end" (Rev 22:13). However, in light of his discussion on the incarnation in chapter thirteen above, it is clear that for Gregory history both orbits around and is permeated by Christ—and by implication God the Trinity— at its "center." God the Trinity is therefore not only the *logos* and *telos* of the historical process of movement and becoming; God is also its axis, around which history in its entirety is ordered and made whole.[48]

---

46. Gregory delineated this first communion with reference to the creation of both the spiritual and material realms and of the human being as their microcosm. Gregory of Nazianzus, *Oration* 38.10–11, 67–68.

47. McDonnell attempted to emphasize the Spirit's role in Gregory's exposition of God's gradual self-disclosure through the covenants. However, on more than one occasion he refers to Jesus' ascension as his "departure," after which the deity of both the Son and the Spirit is received in a manner proportionate to the believer's capacity. His language is misleading, especially in light of our lengthy reflection on the fact that Christ, as the *logos* and *telos* of the historical continuum (or, the alpha and omega of all that is), permeates history in its entirety—meaning that, although he has "departed" in the sense that he no longer physically among us, he nevertheless remains spiritually or mystically present in all things. McDonnell, *Other Hand of God*, 143–44.

48. Standing at the beginning, the end, and at an indefinite "middle" of the historical continuum, Jesus represents what in traditional societies is known as the *axis mundi* or "centre of the world." For more on this concept, see Eliade, *Sacred and the Profane*, 35–37.

CONCLUSION

It is my conviction that this existential metanarrative of history, comprising themes elicited from Gregory's orations—some of which are paradigmatic across the plethora of patristic literature—can be of service to contemporary historiography by offering alternative, theological insights into the flux of history. This flux has the potential of becoming indecipherable and even chaotic outside of some positive interpretive tool, abandoning us to sceptic and nihilistic views that appear in much of today's historical writing. Assessing the "entire age" or history in its entirety in chapter twenty-five of his *Fifth Theological Oration* through the lens of *Oration* 38, it is clear that Gregory articulated a view of history which is both richly nuanced and existentially significant. It was Gregory's conviction that the trinitarian God has deigned to reveal himself, a revelation which he described symbolically as taking the form of two great earthquakes; ruptures in belief and practice that effectuated, firstly, the transition or movement of God's people from the worship of pagan idols to adherence to the Mosaic Law, and secondly, the transition from the Law to the Christian Gospel.

This weaning process was accompanied by a positive revelation of God's true existence as Father, Son, and Holy Spirit, a revelation that finds its existential locus in the incarnation of the Son. For Gregory, Jesus Christ frames either end of the historical spectrum as the Demiurge Logos who has fashioned the cosmos and, subsequently, the human being as a microcosm. It is this same Demiurge Logos who will return to permanently refashion all things at the eschaton. As such, Jesus represents both the *logos* and *telos* of the historical process. But far from depicting a linear view of history with Christ at either end, the saint deliberately pinpointed the convergence of divinity and humanity in Christ's person at the incarnation, the significance of which (as both a remedy to evil and as opening up the potential for deification) places Christ metaphorically at the centre of the historical process. As the axis around which all of history turns, finds meaning and is sanctified, Christ permeates the entire historical continuum, securing the possibility of our deification, which, we saw briefly (with reference to the Apostles) is worked out concretely in the Holy Spirit. Infusing the historical continuum with a sense of existential—and in fact a deifying—meaning and purpose, it is clear that for Gregory the key to experiencing, understanding, and writing history can be found in the encounter with him who holds "the keys of Death and Hades" (Rev 1:18), the life-giving Demiurge Logos of God, Jesus Christ, and, by extension, the manifestation and experience of God as Trinity.

BIBLIOGRAPHY

Baghos, Mario. "The Recapitulation of History and the 'Eighth Day': Aspects of St. Basil the Great's Eschatological Vision." In *Cappadocian Legacy: A Critical Appraisal*, edited by Doru Costache and Philip Kariatlis, 151–68. Sydney: St. Andrew's Orthodox, 2013.

Beeley, Christopher A. *Gregory of Nazianzus on the Trinity and Knowledge of God*. Oxford: Oxford University Press, 2008.

Behr, John. *Formation of Christian Theology*. Vol. 2, *The Nicene Faith (Part 2)*. Crestwood, NY: St. Vladimir's Seminary Press, 2004.

Bruce, F. F. *The Epistle of Paul to the Galatians: A Commentary on the Greek Text*. Exeter: Paternoster, 1982.

Carr, E. H. *What Is History?* Edited by R. W. Davies. Victoria: Penguin, 2008.

Eliade, Mircea. *The Sacred and the Profane: The Nature of Religion*. Translated by W. R. Trask. New York: Harcourt Brace Jovanovich, 1959.

Florovsky, Georges. *The Eastern Fathers of the Fourth Century*. Edited by R. S. Haugh. Translated by C. Edmunds. Vaduz: Büchervertriebsanstalt, 1987.

Harrison, Nonna Verna, trans. *Festal Orations: Saint Gregory of Nazianzus*. Crestwood, NY: St. Vladimir's Seminary Press, 2008.

———. *St. Basil the Great: On the Human Condition*. Crestwood, NY: St. Vladimir's Seminary Press, 2005.

Jenkins, Keith. *Re-thinking History*. New York: Routledge, 2007.

Lampe, G. W. H. *A Patristic Greek Lexicon*. Oxford: Clarendon, 1961.

Lyotard, Jean-François. *The Post-Modern Condition: A Report on Knowledge*. Translated by Geoff Bennington and Brian Massumi. Minneapolis: University of Minnesota Press, 1984.

McDonnell, Kilian. *The Other Hand of God: The Holy Spirit as the Universal Touch and Goal*. Collegeville, MN: Liturgical, 2003.

Murray, Douglas. *The Madness of Crowds: Gender, Race, and Identity*. London: Bloomsbury Continuum, 2020.

Patrologia Graeca. Edited by J.-P. Migne. 162 vols. Paris, 1857–86.

Peterson, Jordan B. *12 Rules for Life: An Antidote to Chaos*. Toronto: Random House Canada, 2018.

Russell, Normal. *The Doctrine of Deification in the Greek Patristic Tradition*. New York: Oxford University Press, 2004.

Stephens, John, and Robyn McCallum. *Retelling Stories, Framing Culture: Traditional Story and Metanarratives in Children's Literature*. New York: Routledge, 1998.

Thunberg, Lars. *Microcosm and Mediator: The Theological Anthropology of Maximus the Confessor*. 2nd ed. Chicago: Open Court, 1995.

Tollefsen, Torstein Theodor. "Theosis according to Gregory." In *Gregory of Nazianzus: Images and Reflections*, edited by Jostein Bortnes and Tomas Hägg, 257–70. Copenhagen: Museum Tusculanum, 2006.

Way, Agnes Clare, trans. *St. Basil, Exegetic Homilies*. The Fathers of the Church Series 46. Washington DC: The Catholic University of America Press, 2003.

Wesche, Kenneth Paul. "The Union of God and Man in Jesus Christ in the Thought of Gregory of Nazianzus." *St. Vladimir's Theological Quarterly* 28 (1984) 83–98.

Williams, Frederick, trans. *St. Gregory of Nazianzus: On God and Christ: The Five Theological Orations and the Two Letters to Cledonius.* Crestwood, NY: St. Vladimir's Seminary Press, 2002.

9

CHRISTIAN TRANSFORMATION

Bonaventure's Appraisal of the Holy Spirit's Work in Francis of Assisi

Benjamin Luke Johnson, OFMCap

THIS CHAPTER BRINGS TO light some important insights from Saint Bonaventure of Bagnoregio's thought on Christian mystical experience that may offer a certain corrective to contemporary approaches to spirituality. I contend that his appreciation of the affective dimension of the person avoids both a Pelagian approach and a passive one to the reception of the Holy Spirit's grace. Why would this medieval thinker's vision be helpful for spirituality today? The answer, to this question that I wish to advance, at least partly, centers on the role of the "virtues" of poverty and humility.[1] These form part of the Holy Spirit's work that shapes the soul for the gift of divine charity.[2] The insights that I draw from the Seraphic Doctor's thought, most especially his *Itinerarium mentis in Deum* (*The Soul's Journey into*

1. The idea of poverty and humility as Christian "virtues" within the Franciscan tradition will be outlined further in this chapter. For a detailed overview of this Franciscan nuance in Bonaventure, see Johnson, *Soul in Ascent.*

2. Unless specifically outlined, I am referring generally to the work of the Holy Spirit as a "gift"/"grace," rather than looking specifically at Bonaventure's thought on the sevenfold gifts of the Holy Spirit.

God), present the Christian journey in the reality of the total gratuity of divine grace and the possibility for a full affective response to this gift.[3]

According to Bonaventure, it is through the Holy Spirit that the human capacity for love is brought to its perfection, the love of the crucified Christ. *The Soul's Journey* reflects upon the life of Saint Francis of Assisi, and yet this work is not biographical. Rather, Bonaventure uses the transformation of the *Poverello* to present universal principles for Christian mystical experience. The transformation of Francis, as portrayed by Bonaventure, offers us a clear example of how the Holy Spirit achieves the divine shaping of the person through the affective capacity of their soul. For our contemporary times, this approach offers a strong account of the absolute gratuity of the grace of the Holy Spirit while, at the same time, valuing greatly the affective response required of the person.

I propose that an essential part of the work of the Holy Spirit is to aid the Christian in the recognition of their poverty, both moral and ontological.[4] The Bonaventurian vision of the role of poverty offers a certain antidote to contemporary tendencies in spirituality, including, but not limited to, *nouvelle* forms of Pelagianism, sentimentalism, and materialism. Indeed, today in our market culture "spirituality" may be conceived of as more of a "self-help" type consumer product.[5] Bonaventure's thought from *The Soul's Journey* offers us pertinent insights into the Christian journey led by the Holy Spirit that avoids the superficiality of vainglorious man. This chapter thus seeks to outline intuitions from Bonaventure's depiction of the Christian journey that convey the true way in which the Holy Spirit works in the life of the soul.

THE TRINITY AND THE CREATED ORDER: AN OVERVIEW OF BONAVENTURIAN THOUGHT

Bonaventure's development of the Dionysian understanding of the good's self-diffusiveness holds particular importance within his trinitarian

3. While *The Soul's Journey* does not directly expound a pneumatology, it does outline the practical implications for the Christian who seeks Christ sincerely—what is essentially the work of the Holy Spirit.

4. Ontological poverty, in the Bonaventurian sense, occurs in the person's recognition of their creatureliness and thus total dependence upon God, their First Principle. See Johnson, *Soul in Ascent*, 30n100.

5. Johnson, "Mysticism in Vogue," 12–18. In this article I examined how contemporary forms of mysticism run counter to both Old and New Testament forms of mysticism. And to offer an example from Christian times that authentically remains in harmony with the biblical tradition I outlined the poverty and humility of Saint Francis of Assisi.

theology. The Father, as the fontal source of everything, speaks a perfect Word. The Holy Spirit proceeds from the Father and the Son, manifesting both their oneness in love and the fruitfulness of the divine will. The goodness and fruitfulness in the created order thus has special reference to the Holy Spirit in Bonaventurian thought.[6]

The trinitarian interpersonal relations of love also reveal the shape of divine charity in the created order. Charity in the divine order comes about through the trinitarian Persons' one essence as the supreme good, and because this goodness is diffusive, there is the most intimate union between them. Therefore, love requires the possibility of the most intimate union, and the most intimate and indivisible union of love is, namely, that between the Father, Son, and Holy Spirit. Interestingly, this perfection of union between the trinitarian Persons allows Bonaventure to claim that God is an "uncreated hierarchy;"[7] hierarchy in the sense that the divine *ordo* is perfect *unity* and *trinity*.[8] This divine order is reflected in the order of God's creation, and thus the advent of sin marks a dis-*order*.

Therefore, in the restoration of the created order, in Bonaventure's thought, the Incarnation and the cross not only reveal the healing prepared but also, from this full revelation of divine love, manifest the destiny of humanity. Bonaventure develops here the Dionysian thought of the good's self-diffusiveness, with Augustine's model of love represented by Richard of Saint Victor, to show that the Incarnation marks the completion of creation and the restoration of order.[9] In this way the Son remains the exemplar of all creation while the Holy Spirit works to bring the created order to its perfection in Christ.

Here, we find Bonaventure's twofold purpose for the Incarnation. First, when the Word of God becomes man, this serves the fulfillment of humanity. Wayne Hellmann states that, for Bonaventure, the Incarnation "is the consummation of all God's works" whereby "the last is joined to the first."[10] The joining of the last to the first in Bonaventurian thought signifies that there is the completion of the circle. Furthermore, the whole universe finds its completion in this perfecting of the human person through Christ's

6. The following sources provide comprehensive analyses of Bonaventure's Trinitarian theology, Goff, *Caritas in Primo*; Hayes, *Hidden Center*; Hellmann, *Divine and Created Order*.

7. Bonaventure, *Commentaria in quatuor libros sententiarum*, Vol. II, d. 9, prologue (Q. II, 238), in *Opera Omnia*. "Prima autem definitio, quae est hierarchiae increatae, exprimit ipsam quantum ad trinitatem et unitatem . . . in quo signatur quod in trinitate et unitate consistit omnimoda et summa perfectio."

8. Wrisley-Shelby, "Part V," 217–18.

9. Cullen, *Bonaventure*, 118.

10. Hellmann, *Divine and Created Order*, 74–75.

Incarnation.[11] The Incarnation of Christ leads all humanity (and thus creation as well) back to the Father by the grace of the Holy Spirit.

The second purpose of the Incarnation Bonaventure locates within this completing and perfecting act of the Word, which is the *reparatio* of humanity.[12] Humankind is redeemed through the completion of the circle, that is, as part of the *reductio* of creation to the Father. At the hypostatic union of the Word, Christ joins humanity to its first principle. According to Hellmann, although in the writings of Bonaventure there is significant attention given to the concept of the Incarnation as perfective of humanity and creation, the Seraphic Doctor does assert that the explicit reason for it is the redemption of humanity.[13] For our study of the nature of the Holy Spirit's work, this analysis demonstrates that grace serves the transformation of the human soul for perfection in Christ. This transformative grace both redeems humanity and, through the recapitulation of all reality in Christ, also participates in perfecting the whole created order.

Indeed, what is completed by Christ is brought to fruition in the soul through the grace of the Holy Spirit who establishes and strengthens true bonds of love. The Holy Spirit conforms the Christian to the Trinity, and thus man participates in the *reductio* of the created order to its divine origin established by Christ. The soul, made in the image of God, through the twofold dynamic of the intellect and the will, is by nature open to God and *capax Dei*.[14] For Bonaventure, the will has a certain primacy, even surpassing the reach of reason, precisely because this faculty forms the manner by which God draws the person to Himself.[15] When we consider the effects of grace upon the soul, we can comprehend that for the Seraphic Doctor, the human person, made in the image of God, is also graced to become a *likeness* of the triune God.

It seems that Bonaventure appreciates a certain distinction here, assigning likeness of God to the operation of grace.[16] The soul naturally

11. For one of the clearest examples of this theme in Bonaventure's Christology, see Bonaventure, *Breviloquium*, IV (Monti, 131–68). Hellmann also articulates this thread in the Seraphic Doctor's thought, see Hellmann, *Divine and Created Order*, 76.

12. One can see throughout the *Breviloquium* a certain fondness of Bonaventure for referring to Christ as our "restoring principle." For the Seraphic Doctor, *reparatio* refers to the ongoing work of the grace of Christ that will find fulfillment at the end of time, where in the incarnate Word all creation and history will come to its perfection.

13. Hellmann, *Divine and Created Order*, 76.

14. Bonaventure, *Breviloquium*, VII, 7, 2 (Monti, 292–93).

15. Youmans, *"Haec Visio Rapit,"* 119; Rocco, *L'antropologia di San Bonaventura*, 10.

16. Bonaventure, *II Sent.*, d.16, a. 2, q. 3, resp. (Q. II, 405). "Similitudo vero principalius consistit in unione animae ad Deum quae quidem est per gratiam." Christopher Cullen examines this distinction to outline and clarify the Bonaventurian

possesses the image of God (memory, intellect, will) to which supernatural grace then perfects these natural capacities.[17] The gift of the Holy Spirit influences the soul to desire sanctifying grace that orders it towards its supernatural end. Bonaventure thus understands that the conferral of grace is most appropriate in the moment that best elicits the person's desire for and cooperation with it.

MAN'S AFFECTIVE CAPACITY ACCORDING TO BONAVENTURE

This glimpse into Bonaventure's system is very much in harmony with his presentation of the structure of love. It is the affective capacity of the person that enables the subject and object to move closer together. This possibility for union is key to human interpersonal relationships but takes on a special significance for Bonaventure in relation to the soul and God. The loving search of the person, even though impoverished after the Fall, finds in this quest for God the greatest possible fulfillment because of the nature of man's affective potency.

Marianne Schlosser articulates succinctly Bonaventure's thought on the dynamic of the soul's affective love with God, stating:

> While knowledge of something good does not automatically "make them good," love for something good means that man becomes good. The longed-for good, that is, the loved person, affects the whole soul and begins to "transform it." Therefore, the *affectus* has the greatest meaning in the relationship with God: because the human being, whose search turns towards God, grasps God with a greater immediacy; he becomes "a spirit with God," because he loves like him.[18]

The role of the affections in Christian transformation are key to Bonaventurian thought. In fact, I would argue that the soul's affective capacity holds vital importance on account of its place in the person's bodily experience of love in the created order. Here, the affections not only give the soul access to images and symbols but also aid her attraction to the good and repulsion against evil. In this way the *affectus* can take the person to

---

teaching on the existence of nature before the advent of grace; Cullen, "Bonaventure on Nature before Grace," 173.

17. Cullen, "Bonaventure on Nature before Grace," 173.

18. Schlosser, "Affectio," 152; my translation.

the height of Christian wisdom when the soul is graced by the Holy Spirit. Thus, for the Seraphic Doctor, the affections are much more than merely the emotional dimension of the person. Indeed, it is through one's affect that a renewed harmony of the soul and the body is brought about.

Therefore, on the part of the person, it is only through burning affections that there can be an intimate union. This union remains the gift of the Holy Spirit that orders the person to the likeness of God, opening their natural desire for God to the horizon of the glorified state of eternal union. We perceive here that in Bonaventurian thought there is an intricate tension between the reality of the totally gratuitous gift of grace and the utmost importance of the Christian soul desiring after this grace with all their heart.

THE CHRISTIAN LIFE IN THE SOUL'S JOURNEY INTO GOD

At its heart, *The Soul's Journey*, composed in 1259, theologizes Francis's Christian mystical experience. At this time, Bonaventure, recently appointed Minister General of the Order of Lesser Brothers in 1257 by the Pope, was weighed down by the difficulties of his office. From his late teens to his earlier Franciscan life, he had pursued academic interests at the University of Paris. It is on Mount La Verna, where Francis had received the marks of Christ's Passion in 1224, that Bonaventure seeks divine inspiration through prayer to understand the way to attain true and lasting peace. He wants to know the road to attain the peace of body and soul that the poor man Francis had in the face of sadness, sin, and suffering.[19]

In *The Soul's Journey*, we recognize that the mystical-bodily experience of Francis complements Bonaventure's scholastic theological inquiry and vice-versa.[20] Scholastic inquiry alone does not suffice for the Christian seeking deep and profound peace. In the text he advises the reader:

> If you wish to know how these things come about,
> ask grace not instruction,
> desire not understanding,
> the groaning of prayer not diligent reading,
> the Spouse not the teacher,
> God not man,
> darkness not clarity,

---

19. Nothing specific is known about the problems that may have faced the recently appointed Minister General of the Lesser Brothers, yet this outlook of Bonaventure reveals that in this service he had suffered a lack of peace.

20. Davies, *Weight of Love*, 12–15.

not light but the fire
that totally inflames and carries us into God
by ecstatic unctions and burning affections.[21]

This quote, one of the text's most famous references, outlines the spiritual significance of the Christian journey. Union with God is possible through an *affective* response to the Spouse in ardent prayer.[22] For Bonaventure, the soul must be sensitive to one's desires so that they may become inflamed and be carried totally into God. This sensitivity arises from the soul's cooperation with the work of grace, which disposes her to journey further along the path of lasting peace.

The idea of true peace may sound somewhat superficial to the modern ear, yet for Bonaventure, to attain it, he states that, "there is no other path but through the burning love of the Crucified."[23] The contemplation of the Passion that stirs the affections of the soul to love Christ most sincerely arises from the Holy Spirit pouring into the heart divine love. We can say then that the love of Christ that is gifted to the soul by the Holy Spirit, reorders it (hierarchizes it anew) and makes it a daughter of God, spouse of Christ, and Temple of the Holy Spirit.[24] One can perceive here the highly relational nature of the soul's affective response to the infusion of divine charity.

In a sermon on Francis, Bonaventure concisely outlines what he proposes in *The Soul's Journey*, connecting the presence of the gifts of the Holy Spirit to the bodily signs of Christ's cross in the poor man of Assisi. He states:

> The seven gifts of the Holy Spirit are given to us that we may do good works with zeal. Christ's cross is the sign of God's boundless grace because from the cross, that is, from Christ's sufferings, flow all the gifts of grace. So, once again, we should expect to find the sign of the Son of man, the cross of Christ, on Saint Francis who was filled with the gifts of the Holy Spirit.[25]

---

21. Bonaventure, *Soul's Journey into God*, VII, 6 (Cousins, 115). I have retained the layout of this work as it appears in this English edition, due to the arguments put forward by the translator Ewert Cousins. He states that he was seeking to recapture the original poetical and symbolic structure of the text. And, I agree that in this way the nuances of Bonaventure's style read well.

22. Perez-Soba, *Amore*, 78–79.

23. Bonaventure, *Soul's Journey into God*, prologue, 3 (Cousins, 54). "Via autem non est nisi per ardentissimum amorem Crucifixi."

24. Bonaventure, *Soul's Journey into God*, IV, 8 (Cousins, 93).

25. "The Evening Sermon on. Saint Francis, 1262," in Armstrong et al., *Francis of Assisi*, 2:729.

Indeed, one envisages that for Bonaventure, Francis manifests most beautifully each person's potential for divine transformation through the gifts of the Holy Spirit. The soul filled with the Holy Spirit's gifts will manifest Christ bodily. The crucified body of Christ reveals the shape of perfect love, and its contemplation will therefore, through the grace of the Holy Spirit, influence the Christian to manifest this gift bodily. Bonaventure advocates that the gifts of the Holy Spirit that filled the soul of Francis also signed his body. This reality affirms the intimate link between the experience of divine charity and the role of the body in the participation of this love. For the Seraphic Doctor, the Holy Spirit works to incarnate divine love in the Christian, the experience of which orders their life in relationship to the trinitarian communion and with other members of the Body of Christ.

The figure of Francis remains intimately linked to the image of the suffering Christ, who is the source of all graces and who returns the soul to the Father. The work of the Holy Spirit always serves this trinitarian purpose, as Bonaventure states in the *Breviloquium*,

> Therefore, the "grace which makes pleasing" makes the soul the temple of God, the bride of Christ, and the daughter of the eternal Father. And since this cannot occur except through a supremely gracious condescension of the part of God, it could not be caused by some naturally implanted habit, but only by a free gift divinely infused.[26]

Grace is therefore not itself the Holy Spirit, but something created and gifted to the soul. Grace is not identical with charity for the Seraphic Doctor, rather, it "refers to that assistance that God gives us for the actual acquisition of merit. This gift is called 'the grace that makes pleasing,' without which no one may acquire merit, advance in good, or attain eternal salvation."[27] This grace aids growth in divine charity that then brings about the affective union of the Christian with their beloved. All gifts and graces serve the inflaming of the soul in charity, enabling the person to journey into the depths of crucified love. It is precisely in the depths of this divine charity that the soul is transformed to love in a cruciform manner. The soul, infused with the gifts of the Holy Spirit, will, through her experience in the created order, be able to make sense of her bodily existence only in reference to the suffering and glorified body of Christ.

Bonaventure, in the sixth chapter of *The Soul's Journey into God*, urges the Christian to contemplate the divine order of charity through the self-diffusive goodness of God. He states:

26. Bonaventure, *Breviloquium*, V, 1, 5 (Monti, 172).
27. Bonaventure, *Breviloquium*, V, 2, 2 (Monti, 174).

If, therefore, you can behold with your mind's eye
the purity of goodness,
which is the pure act
of a principle loving in charity
with a love
that is both free and due and a mixture of both,
which is the fullest diffusion
by way of nature and will,
which is a diffusion by way of the Word,
in which all things are said,
and by way of the Gift, in which other gifts are given,
then you can see
that through the highest communicability of the good,
there must be
a Trinity of the Father and the Son and the Holy Spirit.[28]

At this sixth stage of journeying into unitive love, the Christian, having reached this height, is invited to contemplate the very nature of love itself. God, as pure act, *loves charitably*. Charity, as love, is both free and necessary in God due to His nature and will.

The charity gifted to the person then re-*orders* them to the One who is love. Original sin had made the person "bent over" (*incurvatus*),[29] but the work of grace restores him to uprightness through the re-hierarchization of his soul. Here, Bonaventure sees a beautiful orderliness returned to the soul. He outlines that this re-formation of the soul's six powers corresponds to the six stages of the soul's journey into God, revealing not only his love of numerical symmetry but also the beauty in the congruence between the divine and created orders.[30] Importantly, Bonaventure presents the powers of the soul, like the stages of ascent into God, in a hierarchical manner, with the highest power being the "summit of the mind or the spark of synderesis."[31] This journey to the heights of wisdom necessitates the purification and perfection of the spark of synderesis, wherein the will is ordered to supernatural beatitude. Therefore, the sixth stage of the soul's journey comprises the fulfillment of its innate desire for the good, and through the reformative work of grace the soul is drawn into union through the fire of divine charity.

28. Bonaventure, *Soul's Journey into God*, VI, 2 (Cousins, 104).

29. Bonaventure, *Soul's Journey into God*, I, 7 (Cousins, 62).

30. For a detailed analysis into this overarching theme in Bonaventure's writings, see Hellmann, *Divine and Created Order*.

31. Bonaventure, *Soul's Journey into God*, I, 6 (Cousins, 62). I have retained the specific word *synderesis*, which Cousins had translated to "conscience."

The journey of growing in grace through the Holy Spirit reforms the person, because what belongs to the person by nature, though deformed by sin, is not only recovered but further ordered toward eternal glory. The grace of the Holy Spirit that establishes loving union with God also re-establishes a renewed harmony between the person's body and spirit. The soul, with its spark of synderesis,[32] grows in ardent desire for the good, recognizing through grace that the highest good is divine union within the trinitarian communion. The graced affective capacity of the person urges their will to unite them ever more intimately with the source of love.

For Bonaventure, the *affectus* impressed with the divine image tends the person to the Highest Good. Indeed, God's impression on the soul's affective dimension, through synderesis, is for the guiding towards perfect love. This capacity for divine union through love is transformative of the person, shaping them into the likeness of perfect love. And thus, the affective dimension, in this sense, reigns supreme in the heights of the loving mystical encounter with God because within this capacity the unitive work of the Holy Spirit is achieved. Indeed, for Bonaventure, mystical experience is more than a meeting of God but actually unites the person to Him by drawing the soul *into* Him.[33] Through the gift of divine charity the soul experiences divine life as it journeys further into an affective union of love. The inflamed affections draw the person to the object of their love (divine communion) by the grace and charity of the Holy Spirit. This inflaming of the soul is restorative for the Christian because grace *hierarchizes* the soul, likening it to the triune God.[34]

We can understand that, in the Seraphic Doctor's thought, the grace of the Holy Spirit works in an acutely orderly fashion as this serves union. In reference to our capacity to perform meritorious acts, he states that grace can be understood in three different senses. Generally, it is the free assistance from God without which a creature could do nothing; but more particularly grace is preparatory for the reception of the gift of the Holy Spirit (*gratia gratis data*). Finally, in the proper sense, grace is that which makes the soul pleasing (*gratia gratum faciens*).[35] The gift of the Holy Spirit, through which the Christian may acquire merit for salvation, requires an

---

32. For Bonaventure, synderesis, at its most fundamental level, is any capacity that incites one to the good. Conscience properly commands while synderesis stimulates one to goodness or provokes them to escape evil. See Pasquale, "Synderesis," 789–97; Bonaventure, *II Sent.* d. 39, a. 2, q. 1 (Q II, 908–11).

33. Herein lies the significance of the title of Bonaventure's mystical work, that conveys a journey not only "to" God, but also "up" and "into" God.

34. Wrisley-Shelby, "Part V," 219.

35. Bonaventure, *Breviloquium*, V, 2, 1–2 (Monti, 173–74).

initiation by a gratuitously given grace. The "assisting helps" from God aid the soul's preparation for the reception of, and growth in, the "grace that makes pleasing," which occurs only through God's condescension.[36]

The question remains as to how one can then grow in this grace that makes the soul pleasing to God and without which the soul can do nothing meritorious. Bonaventure first asserts that to God alone belongs the infusion of this grace, but, in reference to its increase, this belongs to the grace itself and our subsequent proper use of it within the created order.[37] This totally gratuitous grace that is gifted to the soul also becomes possessed by the person for their transformation through a free-willed cooperation with the Holy Spirit. The soul is made pleasing through the exercise of the gift of the Spirit in which the person incorporates the divine love in the concrete reality of their life. In this way, Bonaventure states that the Christian not only merits an increase in this grace (*de digno*) but has an absolute right (*de condigno*) to its perfecting in heaven.[38] The Christian who lovingly cooperates with the grace of the Holy Spirit draws into harmony their daily experience with eternal glory and gives them a real participation in Christ's return of all things to the Father.

From this examination, one can see that the Seraphic Doctor asserts the total gratuity of grace and, at the same time, demonstrates how this grace functions within the loving cooperation of the Christian person. The soul, which by taking possession of this "grace that makes pleasing," must cooperate affectively with it through a recognition that this gift is always given solely through the condescension on the part of God. The condescension of God enables the soul, through the "grace that makes pleasing," to journey into God since the Holy Spirit imparts the unitive power of divine love. This special gift of grace, beyond the capacity and merit of the person, therefore, can take the person beyond themselves and into the generous dynamic of divine charity—the trinitarian communion.

GRACE AND THE JOURNEY OF CHRISTIAN TRANSFORMATION

For the Christian, the fruit of the work of the Holy Spirit is the hierarchization of the soul, in light of Christ incarnate. The created grace gifted to the Christian serves to make them as like as possible to the Trinity, which enables and fosters their participation in the divine life. For Bonaventure, the soul

36. Bonaventure, *Breviloquium*, V, 2, 3 (Monti, 175–76).
37. Bonaventure, *Breviloquium*, V, 2, 4 (Monti, 177).
38. Bonaventure, *Breviloquium*, V, 2, 5 (Monti, 177–78).

filled with the gifts of the Holy Spirit finds in Christ the only satisfactory answer to its existence. In the Seraphic Doctor's theological-mystical vision one perceives that, at the Incarnation, it is not so much that Christ became like us, but that we all became like Him. Therefore, the whole Christian journey to holiness centers on the incarnate and suffering Christ, in whom is the perfection of all reality.

Interestingly, Bonaventure does not praise the man Francis in *The Soul's Journey*, but rather he lauds the work of grace achieved in him by the Holy Spirit.[39] The Seraphic Doctor states that the soul, through grace, is enlightened "to gaze in admiration upon its Spouse," and that:

> When this is achieved, our spirit is made hierarchical in order to mount upward, according to its conformity to the heavenly Jerusalem which no man enters unless it first descend into his heart through grace, as John saw in the Apocalypse. It descends into our heart when our spirit has been made hierarchical—that is, purified, illumined and perfected—through the reformation of the image, through the theological virtues, through the delights of the spiritual senses and through mystical ecstasies. Our soul is also marked with nine levels when within it the following are arranged in orderly fashion: announcing, declaring, leading, ordering, strengthening, commanding, receiving, revealing, and anointing. These correspond level by level to the nine choirs of angels.[40]

One can perceive from this text that the experience of Francis, the hierarchical man, provides the template for the work of the Holy Spirit. Indeed, grace, having a decisively dispositive character here, draws the person further into divine communion. For Bonaventure, the character impressed upon the soul at Baptism by the Holy Spirit cannot account for any subjective holiness of the person but acts essentially as the foundation for that person's assimilation into God.[41]

Therefore, the increase in grace through further sacramental participation serves to consummate the soul in divine charity, provided that the Christian cooperates with its dispositive work—essentially the healing of venial sin and the tendency toward it. Bonaventure would say himself that

---

39. In this same text, one recognizes a more practical application of the operation of grace in light of the theory outlined in the *Breviloquium*.

40. Bonaventure, *Soul's Journey into God*, IV, 4 (Cousins, 90).

41. Connolly, "Sacramental Character," 138. For general overviews of the teaching on sacramental character with reference to the medieval period, see Granados, *Introduction to Sacramental Theology*, 263–94; Leeming, *Principles of Sacramental Theology*, 129–40.

this work of the Holy Spirit *hierarchizes* the soul so that the person becomes ordered to the reception of divine charity. The Holy Spirit works a sacred reordering of the person, leading them through the material world to God. This movement depicted in *The Soul's Journey* also portrays the function of the sacramental principle in Bonaventure's thought. The Seraphic Doctor understands the fittingness of how the Holy Spirit hierarchizes the soul through material elements since it was through the material world that humanity fell away from God and became disordered.[42]

Indeed, from the example of Francis' life, we find his soul inflamed by the gift of charity through a radical identification with the poor and humble crucified Christ, his Spouse. Francis' poverty sought to protect and nurture the bond of love established in him by the Holy Spirit. In this way, Bonaventure articulates a certain universal experience of the gifts of the Holy Spirit, wherein they form the Christian to love in the highest manner—to burn with the affective love of the poor and humble Christ. At the same time, the effects of grace are particular to each Christian because their embodiment of Christ's virtues occurs within the concrete reality of their experience within the created order. This point is further demonstrated by the logic Bonaventure employs in attributing the six stages of the journey to the six wings of the Seraph, where the soul begins in the sense world, then passes through it aided by grace, which transforms the soul within the perfection of loving union with its First Principle, the Trinity.[43] This journey accords with a universal logic of grace that plays out most intimately in individual hearts by shaping their desires to become like Christ in the reality of their own experiences.

Bonaventure's depiction of the Christian's *itinerating* reveals his conception of how our experience of love may be drawn into its divine exemplar. This love can never be static, as the lover continues to go forth from, and return to, themselves for greater union with an-*other*. Hence, when the soul passes over into God and rests, Christ crucified remains always present to it as the shape of perfect love. In this way Bonaventure presents Christ as the One who manifests the exaltation of the human body in virtuous relationship with the divine and created orders. Livio Melina highlights that in the Bonaventurian understanding of the Christian's movement from action to contemplation there must be a real exercising of

---

42. Bonaventure, *Breviloquium*, VI, 1, 3 (Monti, 212). "verum etiam aliquid haberet de sensibilibus signis, ut, sicut haec sensibilia fuerunt animae occasio labendi, ita essent ei occasio resurgendi."

43. Bonaventure lists the six stages as follows: sense, imagination, reason, understanding, intelligence, and the spark of *synderesis*. Bonaventure, *Soul's Journey into God*, I, 6 (Cousins, 62).

Christ's virtues, not a static imitation of them.[44] Melina understands that the Seraphic Doctor's great contribution is a Christocentric presentation of the virtues, in which the heart of Christ is to be lived in the concrete reality of daily life in all times and places. The Bonaventurian approach to living virtuously requires the personal embodiment of the heart of Christ, to whom all desires need to be ordered. The moral life forms the means that moves the person, through action, to mystical union with God since the grace of the Holy Spirit transforms the heart of the Christian to burn with the very love that burned in the crucified Christ's heart.

Indeed, to articulate this movement, Bonaventure, in *The Soul's Journey*, intentionally turns his focus to the figure of Francis. In this text he does not seek to highlight specific historical details that depict this saint to be *like* Christ through a mere outward impersonation of His words and actions. Rather, the focus rests in the depiction of how Christ manifests Himself in the particular and varied life of this man from Assisi.[45] In this way Bonaventure presents what he understands to be universal in the journey of transformation by the grace of the Holy Spirit. The key to the Christian life, for Seraphic Doctor, remains an authentic identification with Christ crucified who manifests how the path to perfect love is by way of poverty and humility.

The Holy Spirit offers the Christian life a dynamic embodiment of Christ's virtues that need to bear fruit in our concrete experience; that truly *hierarchizes* our souls in likeness of the Trinity. Hierarchy and order in the created world, for the Seraphic Doctor, manifest beauty, which he relates to the Holy Spirit. Indeed, in reference to the threefold powers of the soul (memory, understanding, and will), the will relates to the third Person of the Trinity since it deals with the "order of living" which leads to the goodness of the Holy Spirit.[46] Interestingly, Bonaventure outlines this appraisal of the soul's "natural" relationship to the Holy Spirit at the end of chapter three of *The Soul's Journey*, before charting the soul's reformation by the gifts of grace in chapter four. Here one perceives the Bonaventurian perspective of how grace works in cooperation with human nature. The soul's hierarchization, by way of grace, orders the will toward eternal beatitude, to which the human person has some natural attraction.[47] Here, we have one of the key Bonaventurian principles, namely the importance of natural human desire

---

44. Melina, *Sharing in Christ's Virtues*, 132.

45. Falque and Solignac, "Penser en Fransciscain," 297–325.

46. Bonaventure, *Soul's Journey into God*, III, 6 (Cousins, 84–85).

47. For a detailed discussion of this point, see Cullen, "Bonaventure on Nature before Grace," 174–75.

in light of man's relation to God. The affective capacity of humanity provides for the possibility of their transcendence through the work of grace.

Bonaventure's vision of Christian transformation thus remains characterized by the practical and mystical bodily life of the *Poverello*, most especially by the way the incarnate Christ makes sense of the whole reality of each person, including their corporeality.[48] For the Seraphic Doctor, Francis offers a distinctive example of transformation into Christ (*cruciformitas*), wherein the gifts of the Holy Spirit inflame the love of the heart to the point that one may conform themselves totally to the suffering Christ.

The work of the Holy Spirit elicits the soul's cooperation and spurs its desire for the highest good. The Seraphic Doctor, in his biography of Francis, articulates how the latter's bodily life on earth prefigured the life to come:

> When this blessed man [Francis]
> traveled away from this world,
> his sacred spirit,
> as it entered his home of eternity,
> was glorified by a full draught from the fountain of life
> and left certain signs of future glory
> imprinted on his body,
> so that his most holy flesh,
> which had been crucified along with its passions
> and transformed into a new creature,
> might bear the image of Christ's passion
> by a singular privilege
> and prefigure the resurrection
> by this unprecedented miracle.[49]

For Bonaventure, the Christian not only participates spiritually in Christ's supreme act of love but their inflamed affections draw their body into a real experience of His charity by the grace of the Holy Spirit. Being disposed to the gift of divine love shapes the person into the likeness of the crucified Christ (*cruciformitas*). The work of the Holy Spirit in the soul of the Christian strengthens them in divine goodness, so that their Christian acts of virtue may lead towards an embodiment of crucified love. In this way, the person has the capacity to manifest bodily Christ's passion like the

---

48. Laure Solignac reminds us that Bonaventure takes symbolic theology further along the Christian path than Pseudo-Dionysius. For Solignac, the Seraphic Doctor always holds Christ's Incarnation at the centre, so that He is our model of all reality including our own flesh. Solignac, "De la théologie symbolique," 425.

49. Bonaventure, *Legenda Maior*, XV, 1 (Cousins, 321–22).

stigmatized Francis bearing the marks outwardly of a heart totally inflamed by divine charity.

POVERTY: THE ROAD TO DIVINE LOVE

At this point we can now examine more closely Bonaventure's thought on the role and place of humility and poverty for Christian transformation. Since our daily experiences and affective life, while essential, can only take us so far on the journey into God, the grace of the Holy Spirit opens up our reality to see our ontological and moral poverty. Here, the person comes to understand their ultimate dependence on God with a profound sense of gratitude for the divine condescension in the gift of grace. For Bonaventure, the practice of these virtues of Christ fosters a deeper participation in the unitive divine love as they render the perfection of all human desire.

There is a convergence of poverty as a virtue, exemplified in the life of Christ incarnate, and the poverty of the creature on account of sin. Timothy Johnson states that, in this way, poverty for Bonaventure, "is a comprehensive theological category comprising the poverty of being and the poverty of sin."[50] Johnson argues that Bonaventure understands both are part of humanity's dependence on God. The importance of poverty rests in the recognition of how God acts and the realization of the Christian's total dependence upon God.

The virtue of poverty in regard to mystical union involves much more than a rejection of material goods. For union with God, the virtue of poverty involves a quietening of human intellectual speculation. In the final stage of *The Soul's Journey*, Bonaventure states that the "mind reaches that point where it contemplates in the First and Supreme Principle and in the *mediator of God and men*, Jesus Christ, those things whose likeness can in no way be found in creatures and which surpass all penetration by the human intellect."[51] Some scholars have stated that Bonaventure incorporates the Pseudo-Dionysian notion of *apophasis*.[52] However, Balthasar, more correctly I believe, demonstrates that Bonaventure takes this Dionysian idea further than simply a transcending from the intellect into the eternal. He states that the passing over into "ecstatic rapture" is part of a nuptial experience. To characterize Bonaventure's use of the Dionysian apophasis model as nuptial, Balthasar emphasizes the role of the loving bridegroom. The bridegroom is the source of the unitive love in which people are not only

---

50. Johnson, *Soul in Ascent*, 46.

51. Bonaventure, *Soul's Journey into God*, VII, 1 (Cousins, 111).

52. See, for example, Delio, *Crucified Love*, 99.

carried above themselves but rather, through union with the bridegroom, enters into God and is lost within Him.[53] The Holy Spirit graces their souls with a burning love for the crucified Christ, and this experience takes them out of themselves and unites them to Christ and thus to the Father. As such, this love is utterly transformative for the Christian.

The stripping away of all things in Franciscan poverty is the *via negativa* that leads the soul into ecstasy which is given by God as grace. And as Balthasar states, this "fundamental experience," according to Bonaventure, is ultimately "nothing other than the human realization of the objective revelation."[54] Bonaventure cannot be accused of mere spiritual sentimentality. In fact, for him, poverty serves as the very antidote to any romanticization of mystical experience. The graced road of poverty divests us of the power to make a god in our image. The Christian who contemplates the historical events of Jesus Christ, especially the Incarnation and Crucifixion, becomes illumined affectively and intellectually.[55] To contemplate Christ allows the Holy Spirit to re-*hierarchize* one's soul through desire for divine charity.

The completion of the journey, in which one passes over from the activities of the self into God, occurs through the doorway of Christ crucified. The historical events of the life, death, and resurrection of Christ have consequences for all of history. The imitation of Christ crucified in the life of Francis is nothing sentimental but a real participation in Christ's personhood and therefore in the divine life itself. *The Soul's Journey* reminds the contemporary Christian that the Holy Spirit strengthens the person to live the very virtues of Jesus Christ in their own concrete reality. The virtue of poverty is thus a vehicle out of oneself into the crucified Christ and thereby into the Father. The Christian, who participates through poverty in the divine condescension at the Incarnation and Crucifixion, can then join with Christ in the *reductio ad Patrem*. In this way, the Holy Spirit makes virtuous the recognition of our ontological and moral poverty, which strengthens us against sin and transforms our hearts in burning love for the Crucified.

CONCLUSION

Bonaventure presents the work of the Holy Spirit as gifting the soul grace that perfects, vivifies, and unites the person to the Trinity. The soul is

53. Balthasar, *Glory of the Lord*, 2:269–70.

54. Balthasar, *Glory of the Lord*, 2:270–71.

55. Bonaventure highlights these points in both *The Soul's Journey* and *The Tree of Life*. Johnson argues in relation specifically to *The Tree of Life* that the response of the soul, who contemplates the mysteries of the life of the Word made flesh, is a result of the devout desire to be in complete union with Christ. Johnson, *Soul in Ascent*, 45–46.

hierarchized so as to participate in the heavenly hierarchies. Grace thus maintains a Trinitarian framework that orders the soul in greater likeness of the perfect communion. The Seraphic Doctor's theological-mystical insight has much to offer our contemporary world, most especially his emphasis on the place of the affections in divine union. We are reminded by him that transformation in Christ, by the working of the Holy Spirit, requires the acceptance of our poverty (ontological and moral), which opens our hearts. The thought contained in *The Soul's Journey* challenges any contemporary audience that may tend to minimize the reality of sin, especially personal sin, with the realization that the virtue of poverty aids the attainment of true peace. In this way, we can say that the Holy Spirit makes us poor so that we may be drawn into true riches. For one to receive and give love requires poverty, and its associated vulnerability, which disposes the human heart further to the work of grace. The Seraphic Doctor offers us a model of transformation in Christ, founded on the example of the *Poverello*, who exemplified cooperation with the work of the Holy Spirit through the embracing of poverty.

Let us leave the final words to the Saint from Bagnoregio, wherein he connects the theological virtues from the Holy Spirit with their Trinitarian operation for the mind's journey:

> Filled with all these intellectual illuminations,
> our mind like the house of God
> is inhabited by divine Wisdom;
> it is made
> a daughter of God, his spouse and friend;
> it is made
> a member of Christ the Head, his sister and coheir;
> it is made
> a temple of the Holy Spirit,
> grounded on faith, built up by hope
> and dedicated to God
> by holiness of mind and body.
> All of this is accomplished
> by a most sincere love of Christ
> which *is poured forth in our hearts*
> *by the Holy Spirit*
> *who has been given to us.*[56]

---

56. Bonaventure, *Soul's Journey into God*, IV, 8 (Cousins, 93).

BIBLIOGRAPHY

Armstrong, Regis, et al., eds. *Francis of Assisi: Early Documents*. Vol. 2, *The Founder*. New York: New City, 2000.

Balthasar, Hans Urs von. *The Glory of the Lord: A Theological Aesthetics*. Vol. 2, *Clerical Styles*. Translated by A. Louth et al. San Francisco: Ignatius, 1984.

Benson, Joshua. "The Christology of the *Breviloquium*." In *A Companion to Bonaventure*, edited by Jay M. Hammond et al., 247–88. London: Brill, 2014.

Beschin, Giuseppe. "Amore." In *Dizionario Bonaventuriano*, edited by Ernesto Caroli, 157–71. Padua: Editrici Francescane, 2008.

Bonaventure. *Bonaventure: The Soul's Journey into God, The Tree of Life, The Life of Saint Francis*. Translated by Ewert H. Cousins. The Classics of Western Spirituality. New York: Paulist, 1978.

———. *Breviloquium*. Translated by Dominic Monti. St. Bonaventure, NY: Franciscan Institute, 2005.

———. *Doctoris Seraphici S. Bonaventurae Opera Omnia*. Edited by Studio et Cura PP. Collegii a S. Bonaventura. 10 vols. Quaracchi: Collegium S. Bonaventurae, 1882–1902.

Bougerol, Jacques Guy. *Introduction to the Works of Bonaventure*. Paterson, NJ: St. Anthony Guild, 1964.

Connolly, Graham. "Sacramental Character in the Teachings of Saint Bonaventure." *Collectanea Franciscana* 33 (1963) 129–58.

Cousins, Ewert H. *Bonaventure and the Coincidence of Opposites*. Chicago: Franciscan Herald, 1978.

Cullen, Christopher. *Bonaventure*. Oxford: Oxford University Press, 2006.

———. "Bonaventure on Nature before Grace." *American Catholic Philosophical Quarterly* 85 (2011) 161–76.

Davies, Robert. *The Weight of Love: Affect, Ecstasy, and Union in the Theology of Bonaventure*. New York: Fordham University Press, 2017.

Delio, Ilia. *Crucified Love: Bonaventure's Mysticism of the Crucified Christ*. Quincy, IL: Franciscan, 1998.

Dreyer, Elizabeth. "A Condescending God: Bonaventure's Theology of the Cross." In *The Cross in Christian Tradition*, edited by Elizabeth Dreyer, 192–210. New York: Paulist, 2000.

Gilson, Etienne. *The Philosophy of St. Bonaventure*. Translated by Illtyd Trethowan and Frank. J. Sheed. Paterson, NJ: St. Anthony Guild, 1965.

Goff, Jared. *Caritas in Primo*. Bedford, MA: Academy of the Immaculate, 2015.

Hayes, Zachary. "Bonaventure's Trinitarian Theology." In *A Companion to Bonaventure*, edited by Jay Hammond, et al., 189–245. Leiden: Brill, 2014.

———. *The Hidden Center: Spirituality and Speculative Christology in St. Bonaventure*. New York: Paulist, 1981.

Hellmann, J. A. Wayne. *Divine and Created Order in Bonaventure's Theology*. Edited and translated by Jay M. Hammond. St. Bonaventure, NY: Franciscan Institute, 2001.

Falque, Emmanuel, and Laure Solignac. "Penser en Fransciscain." *Études franciscaines, nouvelle série* 7 (2014) 297–325.

Granados, José. *Introduction to Sacramental Theology*. Translated by Michael J. Miller. Washington, DC: Catholic University of America, 2021.

Johnson, Benjamin L. "Mysticism in Vogue." *Franciscan Connections* 68 (2018) 12–18.

Johnson, Timothy J. *The Soul in Ascent: Bonaventure on Poverty, Prayer, and Union with God*. Quincy, IL: Franciscan, 2000.

LaNave, Gregory. *Through Holiness to Wisdom: The Nature of Theology according to St. Bonaventure*. Rome: Istituto Storico dei Cappuccini, 2005.

Leeming, Bernard. *Principles of Sacramental Theology*. London: Longmans, 1960.

Melina, Livio. *Sharing in Christ's Virtues: For a Renewal of Moral Theology in Light of "Veritatis Splendor."* Translated by William E. May. Washington, DC: The Catholic University of America Press, 2001.

Pasquale, Gianluigi. "*Synderesis.*" In *Dizionario Bonaventuriano*, edited by Ernesto Caroli, 789–97. Padua: Editrici Francescane, 2008.

Perez-Soba, Juan José. *Amore: Introduzione a un mistero*. Sienna: Cantagalli, 2012.

Rocco, Giuseppe. *L'antropologia di San Bonaventura*. Vicenza: Editrice Veneta, 2009.

Schlosser, Marianne. "*Affectio.*" In *Dizionario Bonaventuriano*, edited by Ernesto Caroli, 150–56. Padua: Editrici Francescane, 2008.

Solignac, Laure. "De la théologie symbolique comme bon usage du sensible chez saint Bonaventure." *Revue des sciences philosophiques et théologiques* 95 (2011/2012) 413–28.

Wrisley-Shelby, Katherine. "Part V: On the Grace of the Holy Spirit." In *Bonaventure Revisited: Companion to the* Breviloquium, edited by Dominic Monti and Katherine Wrisley-Shelby, 215–43. St. Bonaventure, NY: Franciscan Institute, 2017.

Youmans, Nicholas. "*Haec Visio Rapit*: Mystic Love and the Erotic in Bonaventure's *Sunday Sermons*." In *Franciscans and Preaching*, edited by Timothy J. Johnson, 115–43. Leiden: Brill, 2012.

10

AQUINAS, HIS INTERPRETERS, AND SPIRIT CHRISTOLOGY

Matthew Levering

DOMINIC LEGGE HAS RECENTLY argued that Thomas Aquinas offers "a rich Spirit-Christology."[1] But what is Spirit Christology? Although the phrase has been given various meanings, Myk Habets has defined Spirit Christology along lines that are broadly representative of the viewpoint of its practitioners: "Jesus is unique, largely due to his relationship to the Father in or by the Holy Spirit of God."[2] A Spirit Christology conceives of Jesus Christ not primarily in light of the Word but primarily in light of the Holy Spirit.

Habets argues that Spirit Christology was present in many second-century Fathers, although, at the time, it tended toward adoptionism. According to Habets, Justin Martyr led the movement toward a Logos Christology, which then gradually became dominant in large part due to Irenaeus and Origen. By the fourth century, Spirit Christology had been largely suppressed by Logos Christology, even if Athanasius and the Cappadocians, in emphasizing the Spirit's anointing of Christ, pushed back somewhat.[3] Habets affirms the truth of the dogmatic teaching of the Council

---

1. Legge, "Incarnate *De Spiritu Sancto*," 175.

2. Habets, *Anointed Son*, 54.

3. Habets comments with regard to Athanasius, "While not a Docetist his adherence to a Logos Christology meant that he could not *adequately* account for the humanity of Jesus Christ. . . . Logos Christology is not a sufficiently comprehensive model for accounting adequately for the full divinity and full humanity of Jesus Christ" (Habets, *Anointed Son*, 72–73).

of Chalcedon, but he also blames it for failing to "leave sufficient space for the equally important Spirit Christology of the Bible and the early church."[4]

For Habets, the solution today is to seek to develop a Spirit Christology that complements rather than replaces Logos Christology. In his view, such a Spirit Christology can be articulated by affirming that "the giving of the Holy Spirit by the Father constitutes the basis of both Jesus's mission in the world and his filiological relation to the Father."[5] By contrast, I hold that the basis of Jesus' "filiological relation to the Father" is simply the Son's eternal generation by the Father. Yet, I agree that the Son's coming forth from the Father and the Son's corresponding mission as Jesus Christ are never without the procession of the Spirit and the corresponding mission of the Spirit. Habets expands upon his position by saying, "Jesus is related to God as Son because of his relation to the Holy Spirit as the anointed One."[6] Again, this way of articulating a Spirit Christology seems exaggerated. I think it makes more sense to say that Jesus is related to God as Son because he *is* the eternal Son, due to the grace of the hypostatic union. Habets's further claim that "Jesus is not only divine because of the possession of a divine nature but because God relates to him as Son through the eternal Spirit" also seems to me to miss the mark.[7] Jesus is divine because he is the incarnate Word.

In what follows, therefore, I hope to show how a Spirit Christology can fulfill the goals of Habets without falling into exaggeration. I will be arguing that the Thomistic Spirit Christology advocated by Dominic Legge is, in fact, the solution. But to get to this solution, I will first examine a detour taken by the Jesuit theologian Francisco Suárez (1548–1617) that had a notable impact upon Christology for more than four centuries. This detour was rooted in what I call the mysticism of the Word—that is, in the insistence, characteristic of the Church Fathers, that the Word had an extraordinary impact upon the human nature of the Word. Suárez and the many theologians who followed him credited the hypostatic union as such, rather than the grace of the Holy Spirit, with the sanctification of Christ's human nature.

Indebted to Legge, I will argue that this position mistakenly downplays the role of the Holy Spirit. I propose that the path forward is to advance a form of Spirit Christology without sacrificing the insights of the mysticism of Word. This can be done by emphasizing that the Word is always the Word that breathes forth Love—so that the mission of the Word is never without

---

4. Habets, *Anointed Son*, 79.

5. Habets, *Anointed Son*, 221.

6. Habets, *Anointed Son*, 222.

7. Habets, *Anointed Son*, 261.

the mission of the Holy Spirit. In what follows, I will make this argument by comparatively expositing the positions of two Dominicans: Réginald Garrigou-Lagrange, who advocates for the position flowing from Suárez, and Dominic Legge, whose solution constitutes the core of my chapter.

FROM FRANCISCO SUÁREZ TO RÉGINALD GARRIGOU-LAGRANGE: A MYSTICISM OF THE DIVINE WORD

Directing attention to the influence of Suárez's understanding of a "hypostatic order," Andrew Hofer and Jonah Teller have pointed out that for almost all Dominican theologians since Suárez (as well as almost all of his fellow Jesuits), the grace of the hypostatic union of the Word was enough to sanctify perfectly the humanity of Christ.[8] Hofer and Teller exemplify this by reference to Réginald Garrigou-Lagrange's *Christ the Savior: A Commentary on the Third Part of St. Thomas' Theological Summa.*

Let me focus directly upon Garrigou-Lagrange's text. Commenting upon *Summa Theologiae* III, question 7, he begins by reflecting on "Christ's Substantial Grace of Union as the Source of His Sanctification."[9] What he calls the "substantial grace of union" is simply the gift of the hypostatic union, the union of the two natures in the Person of the Word. Why, in his view, is this union the source of Christ's sanctification?

The answer has its roots in the insight that since Christ's human nature did not merit union with the divine nature in the Person of the Word, the hypostatic union was a radical grace.[10] For Garrigou-Lagrange, then, it

8. See Hofer and Teller, "Reordering Thomistic Josephology," 77–99.

9. Garrigou-Lagrange, *Christ the Savior*, 248.

10. Thus, Thomas Joseph White, OP, comments that the hypostatic union is not only utterly unique, but also "is a mystery without pure analogy in the order of sanctifying grace. For Christ cannot be understood adequately even by comparison with saints or holy persons who possess by grace a most perfect degree of human union with God. Such union is real: sanctifying grace does permit moral cooperation with God and the indwelling presence of God in the soul of the human person. It does not, however, constitute a substantial or hypostatic union, as if by grace a human being might 'become' a subsistent divine person. Consequently, there is no perfect analogy either in the order of nature or in the order of grace for the hypostatic union" (White, *Incarnate Lord*, 84). On the grace of union, see also Garrigues, "'Natural Grace' of Christ in St. Thomas," 103–9. Garrigues traces the development of Aquinas's theology of the grace of union from his *Commentary on the Sentences* through the *Summa Theologiae*, showing that in his early work Aquinas "saw the grace of union as disposing Christ's human nature to its assumption by the Word" (Garrigues, "Natural Grace," 106). Indeed, Aquinas states that "everything that befits . . . the human nature united to God is grace of union, whether it be on the part of the body or of the soul" (*In III Sent.*, d. 13, q. 3, a. 1, as cited in Garrigues, "Natural Grace," 106). I suspect that the position of the Thomistic

makes sense that this grace of the hypostatic union overflows upon Christ's humanity so as to sanctify it.

Garrigou-Lagrange notes that some differences emerge at this juncture within the theological tradition. John Duns Scotus held that Christ's human nature was "radically sanctified by the grace of union" but was not formally sanctified by the grace of union.[11] In response, Dominican and Jesuit theologians argued that the grace of union both radically *and* formally sanctified Christ's human nature. Garrigou-Lagrange lists these thinkers, beginning with the Dominicans and then adding the Jesuits (although it was Suárez who first promoted this view): "John of St. Thomas, Godoy, Soto, Salmanticenses, Gonet, Billuat, and more recent Thomists, as also Suarez, de Lugo, Valentia, Vasquez, Franzelin, Billot, Hurter, and Pesch."[12] Garrigou-Lagrange argues that the Dominican and Jesuit position has the status of a theological certitude. In his view, it makes sense that the "substantial and uncreated union of the Word with the human nature" had the profound and immediate effect of sanctifying in every respect the human nature of Christ.[13]

What does the distinction between "radically" and "formally" mean here? Garrigou-Lagrange explains that insofar as the hypostatic union (or the grace of the hypostatic union) "radically" sanctifies Christ's human nature, then it is the union in the Person of the Word that causes habitual grace in Christ's human nature. But if the hypostatic union "formally" sanctifies Christ's human nature, then the Word's Incarnation suffices to sanctify Christ's human nature perfectly; there is no need for habitual grace.

To defend this claim regarding the grace of union's *formal* sanctification of Christ's human nature, Garrigou-Lagrange cites a set of patristic texts that invoke what I have described above as the mysticism of the divine Word. The Fathers are in awe of the union of the human and divine natures in the Word. Garrigou-Lagrange cites Cyril of Alexandria to the effect that the holy anointing of Christ came about due to the Word becoming flesh. Similarly, Gregory of Nazianzus comments that Christ's divine nature, due to the Incarnation of the Word, serves as the holy unction of anointing that sanctifies Christ's human nature. The point is that the incarnate Word must be holy, simply because Christ is the divine Word. If being the human nature of the Word would not make a human nature absolutely holy, then

---

commentators from Suárez onward was significantly impacted by the *Commentary on the Sentences.*

11. Garrigou-Lagrange, *Christ the Savior*, 249.

12. Garrigou-Lagrange, *Christ the Savior*, 249.

13. Garrigou-Lagrange, *Christ the Savior*, 249.

nothing would! Garrigou-Lagrange adds citations from John of Damascus and Augustine, both to the effect that the divinity of Christ sanctifies the humanity of Christ; the Word sanctifies his own human nature.[14]

Garrigou-Lagrange argues that the position he finds in the Church Fathers is also held by Thomas Aquinas. In Garrigou-Lagrange's view, it is clear that Aquinas affirms that the grace of union—the Incarnation of the Word—accomplishes the sanctification of the human nature. He directs attention to *Summa Theologiae* III, q. 6, a. 6, where Aquinas states that "the habitual grace pertaining to the spiritual holiness of the man is an effect following the union, according to John i. 14 . . . by which we are given to understand that because this Man (as a result of the union) is the Only-begotten of the Father, He is full of grace and truth."[15] Aquinas prefaces this statement with a definition of the grace of union as "the personal being that is given gratis from above to the human nature in the Person of the Word, and is the term of the assumption."[16] From the "personal being" of human nature in the Word flows the effect of absolute holiness (Christ's "habitual grace"). Again, since the human nature is the divine Word's human nature, that human nature is absolutely holy. Garrigou-Lagrange sums up: Christ's holiness follows directly from "the union of his soul with the Word."[17]

Aquinas makes the same point in question 22 of the *tertia pars*, on Christ's priesthood—at least in the edition employed by Garrigou-Lagrange. In III, q. 22, a. 2, ad. 3 (a text not contained in later critical editions), Aquinas states that Christ's humanity during his Passion "acquired . . . the actual holiness of a victim, from the charity which it had from the beginning, and from the grace of union sanctifying it absolutely."[18] The fact that this passage is not in most editions of the *Summa* is important, but Garrigou-Lagrange also cites a similar text from the *Compendium Theologiae*: "There is another conjunction of man with God that is brought about, not only by affection or inhabitation, but also by the unity of *hypostasis* or person. . . . [T]his is the singular grace of the man Christ, that He is united to God in unity

---

14. The citation from Cyril comes from his *Commentary on John*, Book IV, ch. 29; the citation from Gregory comes from his Oration 30, no. 31; the citation from John of Damascus comes from *On the Orthodox Faith*, Book III, ch. 3; and the two citations from Augustine come from his *Commentary on John*, Tractate 108, no. 5 and his *De Trinitate*, Book XV, ch. 26.

15. Aquinas, *Summa Theologiae*, III, q. 6, a. 6, cited (in part) in Garrigou-Lagrange, *Christ the Savior*, 251.

16. Aquinas, *Summa Theologiae* III, q. 6, a. 6, cited in Garrigou-Lagrange, *Christ the Savior*, 251.

17. Garrigou-Lagrange, *Christ the Savior*, 251.

18. Garrigou-Lagrange, *Christ the Savior*, 251.

of person. . . . [T]his grace also makes Him supremely pleasing to God."[19] Here Aquinas goes on to say that the grace of union is what grounds God's praise of Jesus at his baptism, "This is my beloved Son, with whom I am well pleased" (Matt 3:17). Garrigou-Lagrange also cites III, q. 24, a. 1, where Aquinas observes that Christ was predestined in his human nature to be the incarnate Word, "according to the grace of union." Garrigou-Lagrange argues that for Aquinas, "Christ, as man, was predestined primarily and principally for natural and divine sonship, or for the grace of union, and secondarily and consequently for habitual grace and glory, as the effects of the grace of union."[20]

I think Garrigou-Lagrange is correct that Aquinas has a strong mysticism (to use my term) of the Word in its effects upon the human nature of Christ. It seems reasonable that the grace of union can hardly do other than immediately, from the very outset of the union, make Christ's human nature holy.

Garrigou-Lagrange moves from the Fathers and Aquinas to his own constructive theological proof that Christ's "substantial sanctity" does not require sanctifying or habitual grace but only requires the grace of union.[21] He argues that Christ certainly has sanctifying or habitual grace, but only as "accidental sanctity," that is to say, not as something *requisite* for the holiness of the incarnate Word.[22] In Garrigou-Lagrange's constructive proof, he begins by observing that four things are required for "formal sanctity": that a person be united with God, that a person be in some sense a beloved "son" and heir of God, that a person be fully ordered to supernatural good works, and that a person contain the "principle of life" rather than being captive to sin and death.[23] In Christ, these four things would be present whether or not Christ had habitual grace, since they are all present due to the grace of union. Garrigou-Lagrange remarks, "Christ possesses these four conditions in a much higher degree [than we possess them] by reason of His substantial and increate grace of union, even independently of habitual grace."[24]

Garrigou-Lagrange's argument here is simple. The grace of union substantially unites the human nature of Christ with the divine nature, whereas habitual grace is only a participation in God. The grace of union

19. Aquinas, *Light of Faith*, no. 214 (p. 256), cited in Garrigou-Lagrange, *Christ the Savior*, 251–52.

20. Garrigou-Lagrange, *Christ the Savior*, 252.

21. Garrigou-Lagrange, *Christ the Savior*, 257.

22. Garrigou-Lagrange, *Christ the Savior*, 257.

23. See Garrigou-Lagrange, *Christ the Savior*, 252–53.

24. Garrigou-Lagrange, *Christ the Savior*, 253.

makes Christ to be the natural Son of God, not merely an adopted son. The grace of union enables Christ to be the agent of theandric actions. Lastly, the grace of union ensures absolute impeccability. Garrigou-Lagrange concludes that, even prior to the positing of habitual grace, it is true that "to be the natural Son of God means the maximum of sanctity."[25] The divine holiness formally causes the sanctification of the human nature of Christ. As Garrigou-Lagrange puts it, "what formally sanctifies Christ's human nature is precisely the divine nature that is included in the personality of the Word."[26]

Note that Garrigou-Lagrange does not deny that Christ has perfect habitual grace. On the contrary, he leaves a place for the grace of the Holy Spirit in Christ. In his view, habitual grace serves to make supernatural acts connatural to Christ's human faculties. Christ's habitual grace is therefore not superfluous, even though it is "accidental" in contrast to the "substantial" sanctity caused by the grace of union. Garrigou-Lagrange quotes Isaiah 11 as evidence that Christ's humanity does indeed possess the gifts of the Holy Spirit.[27] Likewise, Scripture makes clear that Christ has all the "virtues that presuppose habitual grace, such as charity, humility, and the other virtues."[28]

25. Garrigou-Lagrange, *Christ the Savior*, 254.

26. Garrigou-Lagrange, *Christ the Savior*, 256. In emphasizing habitual grace, Karl Rahner goes to the opposite extreme, as Thomas Joseph White, OP, has shown in his *The Incarnate Lord*, ch. 1. Rahner affirms Chalcedon, but, as White observes, "Rahner locates the ontological union of God and man in Christ in the same place where Nestorianism typically locates it: uniquely in the spiritual operations of the man Jesus, particularly as they are conformed by divine indwelling to the mystery of God in himself. Just in this way, then, he makes the basis for the hypostatic union a union of 'mere' moral cooperation between the man Jesus Christ and God (something found analogously in saints or in human persons made holy by grace).... On Rahner's model, the 'grace of union' has been in effect reduced solely to a union of 'habitual grace'" (White, *Incarnate Lord*, 76–77). See also White's discussion of the grace of union and Christ's habitual grace according to Alexander of Hales, who favored the view that "habitual grace is given to the human nature of Christ as a necessary precondition or disposition in view of the hypostatic union," whereas for Aquinas "God can unite a human nature to himself hypostatically *immediately* and not through the medium of created grace. More to the point, this is the only way he can do so, because habitual grace is only a property of a human soul (however crucial that property may be!). The grace of union . . . pertains to the whole substance of the human nature of Christ, insofar as it is united to the Word hypostatically" (88–89). White concludes, "It is not the case that an intensive degree of habitual grace prepares the humanity of Christ adequately for its union with the Word. Rather, habitual grace flows forth from the hypostatic union as a result of that union, and not as its precondition" (90).

27. See Garrigou-Lagrange, *Christ the Savior*, 259.

28. Garrigou-Lagrange, *Christ the Savior*, 260.

Garrigou-Lagrange is also well aware that the Church Fathers affirm the presence of the grace of the Holy Spirit in Christ. Having shown that the Fathers attribute the sanctity of Christ's human nature to its anointing by the Word, Garrigou-Lagrange quotes John Chrysostom, Cyril of Alexandria, and Augustine to the effect that the Holy Spirit has poured out his grace upon Christ. Garrigou-Lagrange also quotes Bernard of Clairvaux, who connects the holiness of Christ's human nature both to the Spirit and to the Word. Garrigou-Lagrange grants that the Fathers and Bernard do not distinguish as "clearly between the increate grace of union and created habitual grace as the Scholastics do and especially as St. Thomas does."[29]

When Garrigou-Lagrange discusses Christ's habitual grace (i.e., the grace of the Holy Spirit), he emphasizes that its cause is ultimately the hypostatic union. As he says in a line of reasoning drawn from Aquinas, "The nearer any recipient is to an inflowing cause, the more does it partake of its influence. But Christ's soul is most closely associated with the Word of God, the Author of grace. . . . Therefore Christ's soul receives the maximum influx of grace from God."[30] Garrigou-Lagrange adds that the Virgin Mary's exalted degree of grace comes, too, from her unique closeness to the incarnate Word.

Again, for Garrigou-Lagrange habitual grace—the grace of the Holy Spirit—is not redundant in Christ even if his substantial sanctity is the result of the grace of union. The grace of union constitutes Christ's holy personal being, but the grace of union does not give Christ the ability to act connaturally in supernatural ways. Garrigou-Lagrange holds that in order for "Christ's soul [to] be inclined intrinsically and permanently to vital supernatural acts, it had to have habitual grace" elevating the soul's essence and powers.[31] Admittedly, however, although habitual grace was necessary for Christ in this sense, Garrigou-Lagrange thinks that in another sense "Christ, in virtue of the grace of union, and with a transient help, could have elicited supernatural and even meritorious acts."[32] But Christ could not have done this connaturally without habitual grace. Thus, Garrigou-Lagrange and Suárez, along with many others, agree that "habitual grace was required in Christ's soul for the completion and perfection of His sanctity," even though habitual grace was not *strictly required* for Christ to be able to undertake supernatural, meritorious acts.[33]

29. Garrigou-Lagrange, *Christ the Savior*, 261.

30. Garrigou-Lagrange, *Christ the Savior*, 261.

31. Garrigou-Lagrange, *Christ the Savior*, 262.

32. Garrigou-Lagrange, *Christ the Savior*, 262.

33. Garrigou-Lagrange, *Christ the Savior*, 263. As Garrigou-Lagrange goes on to

I resonate with the accentuation of the Word that continually comes through in the patristic, medieval, and post-Tridentine testimony to Christ. This mysticism of the Word highlights the wondrous character of what it must mean to be the Word incarnate. I agree with Aquinas and with Garrigou-Lagrange that "the nearer any recipient is to an inflowing cause, the more does it partake of its influence."[34] Surely the union with the divine nature in the Person of the Word is not nothing with regard to sanctifying the humanity of Christ! Cyril of Alexandria highlights the Word's action upon the Word's humanity when he draws the following analogy: "if it is true that fire has converse with materials which in their own natures are not hot, and yet renders them hot since it so abundantly introduces to them the inherent energy of its own power, then surely in an even greater degree the Word who is God can introduce the life-giving power and energy of his own self into his very own flesh."[35] Garrigou-Lagrange is attempting to say something equivalent to this in his attribution of Christ's "substantial sanctity" to the grace of union.

At the same time—as Garrigou-Lagrange recognizes—Cyril appreciates the role of the Holy Spirit in Christ's humanity. Cyril remarks, "the Son came, or rather was made man, in order to reconstitute our condition within himself. . . . This was why he himself became the first one to be born of the Holy Spirit . . . so that he could trace a path for grace to come to us. He wanted us to have this intellectual regeneration and spiritual assimilation to himself, who is the true and natural Son."[36] Cyril's theology of the incarnate Word brings together Word and Spirit. No one has a deeper appreciation of the Word's significance than Cyril, who recognizes that the Word is none other than Jesus Christ, insofar as "the same one [Christ] is

---

say, "For Christ's soul to act supernaturally by the love of charity, it was at least the normal requisite for His soul to have habitual grace. It would have been something absolutely abnormal for Christ not to have this habitual grace" (264). Aquinas puts the matter more strongly: "To Christ, inasmuch as He is the natural Son of God, is due an eternal inheritance, which is the uncreated beatitude through the uncreated act of knowledge and love of God, i.e., the same whereby the Father knows and loves Himself. Now the soul was not capable of this act, on account of the difference of natures. Hence it behooved it to attain to God by a created act of fruition which could not be without grace" (Aquinas, *Summa Theologiae*, III, q. 7, a. 1, ad. 2).

34. Aquinas, *Summa Theologiae*, III, q. 7, a. 1. As Garrigou-Lagrange puts it in *Our Saviour and His Love for Us*, 105: "Through its personal union with the Word, the soul of Jesus has an innate, substantial, uncreated sanctity which is in consequence absolutely perfect."

35. Cyril of Alexandria, *On the Unity of Christ*, 132–33.

36. Cyril of Alexandria, *On the Unity of Christ*, 62.

at once God and man."[37] The union of the two natures takes place in the Person of the Word, as Aquinas and Garrigou-Lagrange (both adherents of Cyrillian Christology) affirm strongly. In the Incarnation, Cyril states, "the divine nature of the Word supported the limitations of the manhood," and "after the union (I mean with the flesh) even if anyone calls him Only Begotten, or God from God, this does not mean he is thought of as being separated from the flesh or indeed the manhood."[38] In the Word, the divine nature and the human nature "came together in a mysterious and incomprehensible union without confusion or change," and to speak of Christ is to speak of the Word, who was born and has died on a Cross.[39]

Yet Cyril equally insists that, according to the flesh, the Word was "born of the Holy Spirit."[40] For Cyril as for Garrigou-Lagrange, the Holy Spirit "is through him [the Word Jesus Christ] and in him, through whom he himself dwells in the saints"; and the Holy Spirit is "the Spirit of Christ and the mind of Christ."[41] Filled with the Spirit, Christ is able to "supply the Spirit" to those who believe in him.[42] Cyril emphasizes that Christ "is the supplier of the Spirit, 'for from his [Christ's] fullness we have all received,' as John [1:16] says, and he [Christ] himself is the one who says to us, 'Receive the Holy Spirit' [John 20:22]."[43]

AQUINAS'S TRINITARIAN CHRISTOLOGY

While I respect Garrigou-Lagrange's mysticism of the Word—which flows from a post-Tridentine tradition that has patristic and medieval foundations—I do not agree with Garrigou-Lagrange's position. Instead, as indicated above, I think the solution involves appreciating that the Word is not merely any Word, but a Word that breathes forth Love. The mission of the Spirit is inseparable from the mission of the Son. As we will see, this

---

37. Cyril of Alexandria, *On the Unity of Christ*, 77.

38. Cyril of Alexandria, *On the Unity of Christ*, 78–79.

39. Cyril of Alexandria, *On the Unity of Christ*, 77; cf. 92.

40. Cyril of Alexandria, *On the Unity of Christ*, 62.

41. Cyril of Alexandria, *Commentary on John*, 2:197, 260.

42. Cyril of Alexandria, *Commentary on John*, 2:208. Cyril adds, "His Holy Spirit is what unites us to Christ our Savior" (210). Building upon Christ's parable of the vine and branches, Cyril states, "Christ is presented as a vine and we are joined to him like branches, enriched, as it were, by his grace and drinking in through the Spirit the power for bearing spiritual fruit" (212).

43. Cyril of Alexandria, *Commentary on John*, 2:220.

point greatly assists theological reflection about the relationship of Christ's grace of union and Christ's habitual grace.[44]

No one has shown this better than Dominic Legge in his *The Trinitarian Christology of St. Thomas Aquinas*, and so my purpose in this section is to appreciatively bring forward his work. Early in *The Trinitarian Christology of St. Thomas Aquinas*, Legge devotes a good bit of attention to describing Aquinas's theology of the "missions" of the Son and Spirit. Habitual grace is the created effect of the invisible mission or personal presence of the Holy Spirit. Christ receives the fullness of the Spirit's invisible mission as an immediate corollary of the hypostatic union; as the Word incarnate, he is filled with the Spirit.

When he turns to the impact of the grace of union upon the human nature of Christ, Legge begins with a question. He asks, "Why is it important to underline this invisible mission of the Holy Spirit to Christ? Is it not enough to say that Christ is the Word of God in person, and therefore, as the God-man and in virtue of the hypostatic union, that he is both personally holy and capable of saving the world through what he does and suffers?"[45] This question reminds us how absolutely extraordinary it is for a human nature to be the human nature of the *Word*. Given that this is so, why not focus on the Word's impact on the humanity of Christ and assume that this impact must be an elevating and sanctifying one? Why bring the Spirit in as *necessary* for elevating and sanctifying the Word's human nature?

As we saw, for Garrigou-Lagrange it is in fact the case that Christ in his humanity possessed the fullness of the invisible mission of the Spirit from the instant of his conception, so that Christ possessed habitual grace, the infused virtues, the gifts of the Holy Spirit, and so on in the most perfect way possible. But Garrigou-Lagrange thinks this was not strictly necessary for the elevation and sanctification of Christ's humanity. As noted above, he holds that the sanctification of Christ is caused also (as "substantial sanctity") by the grace of union.

Whereas Garrigou-Lagrange contends that Aquinas himself holds this viewpoint, Legge maintains that Aquinas does not hold it—a position bolstered by the fact that Legge employs a better edition of the *Summa*, since, as noted above, Garrigou-Lagrange's edition has Aquinas assenting to the viewpoint.

---

44. As White maintains in a somewhat different context (discussing the human knowledge of Christ), "In a rightly ordered Christology . . . we should not be obliged to choose between an ontology of the hypostatic union and an anthropological theology that focuses upon the human actions of Christ" (White, *Incarnate Lord*, 67).

45. Legge, *Trinitarian Christology*, 133.

Legge first explores Aquinas's teaching that Christ possessed habitual grace. In III, q. 7, a. 1, on whether Christ possessed habitual grace, Aquinas offers three objections to his own perspective. The objections argue (1) that Christ did not possess habitual grace, a created participation in God, because Christ was God; (2) that Christ, as the incarnate Word, could accomplish all the things made possible by grace without possessing "any further grace beyond union with the Word" (i.e., beyond the grace of union);[46] and (3) that Christ's human nature, as an instrument of his Godhead,[47] does not need infused virtues in order to perform supernatural acts. As Legge points out, the second and third objections express Garrigou-Lagrange's emphasis that Christ does not *need* anything beyond the grace of union.

Aquinas responds by insisting in the *sed contra* that, according to the prophetic (Christological) text of Isaiah 11:2, Christ does possess the Holy Spirit. Garrigou-Lagrange would agree with this, of course. Aquinas argues, however, that it is *necessary* that Christ possess habitual grace (the grace of the Holy Spirit). He gives three reasons in his *respondeo*, two of which are reasons of fittingness but strong ones nevertheless. The three reasons are the union of Christ's human soul with Christ's divinity (in the Word), which makes it fitting that Christ receive divine grace in his soul due to his closeness to God; the need for Christ to receive grace in his soul in order to perform supernatural acts of knowing and loving; and the fittingness of Christ's having grace that can be shared with all other humans. Recall that Garrigou-Lagrange granted all these points while still arguing that the "substantial sanctity" that was absolutely necessary for Christ's humanity comes from the grace of union, and that God could accomplish everything else in other ways. Citing Aquinas's reply to the first objection, however, Legge argues that for Aquinas, "To hold that the hypostatic union elevates or divinizes Christ's humanity irrespective of habitual grace lets a kind of monophysitism enter through the back door. If the union to the divine nature were itself to transform or divinize Christ's human nature as such, the result would be just the sort of confusion . . . anathematized by Chalcedon."[48] The union of the two natures in the Person of the Word cannot cause a change in the human nature as such. For the human nature to be sanctified or divinized, this must be accomplished in the way that properly pertains to a rational creature: namely, through the created participation in God that

---

46. Aquinas, *Summa Theologiae*, III, q. 7, a. 1, obj. 2.

47. For further discussion of the point that "the human nature of Jesus (his body and soul) is an instrument of his person, in an analogical and unique sense of the term," see White, *Incarnate Lord*, 113–16.

48. Legge, *Trinitarian Christology*, 134.

is habitual grace, attributable to the invisible mission of the Holy Spirit in the creature.

Aquinas's reply to the objection highlighted by Legge reads, "Christ is the true God in Divine Person and Nature. Yet because together with unity of person there remains distinction of natures . . . the soul of Christ is not essentially Divine. Hence it behooves it to be Divine by participation, which is by grace."[49] The point that Aquinas is making here is that the union with the divine nature in the Person of the Word—the grace of union—does not supernaturalize (elevate or supernaturally sanctify) the human nature. It remains just a human nature, as befits the grace of union which unites the two natures without conflating or changing them. To be supernaturalized or sanctified, the human nature requires participation in God by way of habitual grace, which is the path by which any human nature is supernaturalized or sanctified. Habitual grace differs completely from the grace of union, insofar as habitual grace accomplishes something quite different—not union, but sanctification. Legge states, "Saying this does not diminish the infinite dignity of Christ's person, nor the surpassing uniqueness of the hypostatic union, nor its central importance, but rather acknowledges that such a union calls for that nature to be elevated *as a human nature*, according to the way in which such a nature can participate in the divine life."[50]

Legge augments his point by reference to Aquinas's biblical exegesis. He quotes a rich passage from Aquinas's commentary on John 3:34–35,[51] where the evangelist (or perhaps John the Baptist) proclaims, "For he whom God has sent utters the words of God, for it is not by measure that he gives the Spirit; the Father loves the Son, and has given all things into his hand."[52] Discussing this text in its Parisian Vulgate version, Aquinas comments that "the ability to proclaim divine truth is present in Christ in the highest degree, because he does not receive the Spirit in a partial way; and so he says, 'for God does not bestow the Spirit in fractions' [John 3:34]."[53] To other humans the Holy Spirit's gifts are given partially, but these gifts are given fully to Christ. Of course, as the Word, Christ possesses the Spirit in absolute fullness, since the Spirit proceeds from the Father and the Son. Even as man, however, "Christ has the Spirit beyond measure."[54] This leads

49. Aquinas, *Summa Theologiae*, III, q. 7, a. 1, ad. 1.

50. Legge, *Trinitarian Christology*, 134–35.

51. Aquinas, *Commentary on the Gospel of John*, §544, 201.

52. Aquinas, *Commentary on the Gospel of John*, Lecture 6.

53. Aquinas, *Commentary on the Gospel of John*, §541, 199.

54. Aquinas, *Commentary on the Gospel of John*, §543, 200.

Aquinas into a discussion of the diverse kinds of grace in Christ: the grace of union, habitual grace, and the grace of headship—each of which Christ receives in absolute fullness.

Legge directs our attention to what Aquinas says next. Aquinas writes, "The grace of union, which is not habitual grace, but a certain gratuitous gift, is given to Christ in order that in his human nature he be the true Son of God, not by participation, but by nature, insofar as the human nature of Christ is united to the Son of God in person."[55] This is called a "grace" because the human nature does not merit it; it is sheer gift. But it is *not* called a grace in the sense of sanctifying or elevating a human nature by participation in God. Christ receives the *latter* kind of "grace" at the instant of his conception, and it is called habitual grace.

Aquinas grants that habitual grace, as a created gift, is finite—and so the question arises as to how it can be without measure. In Aquinas's view, the answer is found on the side of the Giver: "when its [the created nature's] total natural capacity is filled, it is not given to it by measure, because even though there is a measure on the part of the one receiving, there is none of the part of the one giving, who is prepared to give all."[56] God gave Christ literally everything that could be given as habitual grace; the only limit was what the created nature could receive.

Yet, Aquinas provides another reason for Christ's habitual grace being without measure that may seem to support Garrigou-Lagrange's position. Aquinas says the following: "if someone has a fountain which could produce an infinite amount of water, he would be said to have water in an infinite way and without measure. Thus, the soul of Christ has infinite grace and grace without measure from the fact that he has united to himself the Word, which is the infinite and unfailing source."[57] This may seem to imply that the human nature of Christ is joined to the divine nature in the Word and thus enjoys, due to the presence of the Word, the "substantial sanctity" about which Garrigou-Lagrange speaks. In fact, Legge says, what it instead implies is that Christ's humanity, precisely as the Word's humanity, receives the Spirit in full, by which Christ's humanity is sanctified and elevated absolutely. After all, habitual grace is what sanctification and elevation are in a human nature; as Legge puts it, "Christ's humanity is a true humanity, which implies a participated divinization proportioned to that humanity— namely, habitual grace."[58]

---

55. Aquinas, *Commentary on the Gospel of John*, §544, 201.

56. Aquinas, *Commentary on the Gospel of John*, §544, 201.

57. Aquinas, *Commentary on the Gospel of John*, §544, 202.

58. Legge, *Trinitarian Theology*, 135.

Had it been any other way, then Christ would have received sanctity in his human nature along lines that do not befit a human nature. This is why Legge raises the specter of monophysitism. He imagines what would be the case if Christ's human nature were divinized by union with the Word through a "substantial sanctity" that is not the participation in God (habitual grace) proper to a divinized human nature. This situation would entail that Christ's human nature in fact became a *tertium quid*. Making this point strongly, as Legge does, does not mean that there is no relation between the Incarnation (the grace of union) and the supernaturalizing and sanctifying of Christ's human nature (habitual grace). On the contrary, I hope it will already be clear that for Legge, as for Aquinas, there is a profound relation between the two.

Legge admits that the relation between the grace of union and habitual grace can be a bit difficult to pinpoint in III, q. 7, a. 1.[59] This is because of an ambiguity in the *respondeo*. At the outset of this *respondeo*, Aquinas remarks that he will defend the claim that "it is necessary to suppose habitual grace in Christ."[60] Such a necessity is what Legge holds must be so. But the first reason that Aquinas gives for this necessity, in a passage I have already partially quoted above, ends with fittingness rather than necessity. Aquinas explains that the necessity is due to "the union of His soul with the Word of God. For the nearer any recipient is to an inflowing cause, the more does it partake of its influence. Now the influx of grace is from God. . . . And hence it was most fitting that His soul should receive the influx of Divine grace."[61] If it is simply "most fitting" but not strictly necessary, then this conclusion accords with the position of Garrigou-Lagrange on the relation of the grace of union and habitual grace.

As we saw, Garrigou-Lagrange and many others assumed that Aquinas here confirms their position.[62] Legge traces the basic idea back to Scotus, for whom the human nature's dependence on the Word (through the grace of union) does not imply any other relation. For Scotus, it is possible that the human nature of the Word might not have received habitual grace at all.[63] Although Scotus does think that Christ has preeminent sanctifying

---

59. Legge, *Trinitarian Theology*, 135.

60. Aquinas, *Summa Theologiae*, III, q. 7, a. 1.

61. Aquinas, *Summa Theologiae*, III, q. 7, a. 1.

62. For twentieth-century Thomists holding this position, Legge directs attention to Margelidon, *Études thomistes*, 11–47.

63. Legge cites John Duns Scotus, *Ordinatio III Sent.* d. 13, q. 4. He also directs attention to Cross, *Metaphysics of the Incarnation*, 140–41, 318–24; Cross, *Duns Scotus*, 122–24; Rohof, *Sainteté substantielle*.

and elevating gifts of grace, he denies that they follow necessarily from the hypostatic union.

Cardinal Cajetan and other sixteenth-century Dominican Thomists argued against Scotus's position. Domingo Bañez held that Christ's human nature, as hypostatically united to the divine nature, necessarily receives habitual grace. These Thomists emphasized that Christ's Person is the divine Word, and so his Person is wondrously holy; but his human nature is distinct from his Person and requires habitual grace for it to be supernaturalized. By contrast, arguing on the basis of the unity of Christ, Suárez and others insisted that Christ in his human nature must already and necessarily be holy solely on the basis of the grace of union. As we have seen, for Suárez Christ's habitual grace was fully present but was not *necessary* for the holiness of Christ's human nature. This is the view of Garrigou-Lagrange.

In a footnote, Legge observes that Aquinas, in his *Commentary on the Sentences*, rejects the view that the divinity of the incarnate Word could formally sanctify the human nature of Christ, as though the divine Word could in some way act as a "form" of the human nature, or as if the grace of the Holy Spirit were not necessary for this sanctification.[64] But commentators were led in the opposite direction not only by III, q. 7, a. 1's apparent reference to the fittingness (rather than necessity) of habitual grace in Christ, but also by III, q. 22, a. 2, ad. 3's spurious text (not at the time recognized as spurious) which, as we saw, describes "the grace of union sanctifying it [Christ's humanity] absolutely."[65]

How does Legge respond to the *respondeo*'s reference to habitual grace's fittingness? Legge suggests that rather than seizing upon the use of the phrase "most fitting," we need to keep in view Aquinas's consistent way of framing the matter. Namely, Aquinas consistently affirms the dignity and holiness of Christ's one divine Person (the Word), affirms Christ's perfection of soul, and affirms that this perfection and all Christ's human perfections come from participation in God by habitual grace. Absent this threefold framework, what is true of Christ's (divine) Person will be applied without proper qualification to what is true of Christ's human nature, and the result will be monophysite. In addition, Legge draws attention to the scriptural

64. See Legge, *Trinitarian Christology*, 134n15, citing Aquinas, *III Sent.*, d. 13, q. 1, a. 1; and see also Legge's discussion of this on 141. Legge directs attention in this regard to Torrell, *Encyclopédie*, 996. Legge underlines that for Aquinas, "if the Word's divinity were added to the human nature as a form, Christ would no longer be human. Rather, Christ is made 'formally holy' by the same grace by which he justifies others, namely, his fullness of habitual grace" (Legge, *Trinitarian Christology*, 141).

65. Legge points out that Yves Congar, OP, appears to assume that Aquinas holds the position attributed to him by Garrigou-Lagrange and many others. Legge, *Trinitarian Christology*, 143n46 (see Congar, *Parole et le Souffle*, 139–51).

emphasis on Christ's anointing by the Holy Spirit, and thus to the centrality of the invisible mission of the Spirit to the humanity of the Word.

Legge recognizes that a recent Thomist as historically and textually informed as Jean-Pierre Torrell takes as his own position the view that Christ's habitual grace does not *necessarily* follow from the grace of union.[66] In his *Encyclopédie* Jésus le Christ chez saint Thomas *d'Aquin*, Torrell holds (against Garrigou-Lagrange) that the grace of union cannot be the source of the holiness of Christ's human nature, but he also holds that there is no necessary relation between the Incarnation of the Word and the sanctifying mission of the Spirit in Christ. Torrell is moved to adopt this position on the grounds of q. 7, a. 1's reference to fittingness.

Legge deems Torrell's position to be the strongest alternative to his own. Legge observes, "Aquinas repeatedly seems to speak of habitual grace as necessarily consequent to the union (for example, he compares it to the light that proceeds from the presence of the sun, to the heat that is a natural property proceeding from the presence of fire, and even says that it is 'derived from the union of the Word itself')."[67] In Torrell's view, as Legge says, these texts must be read in light of q. 7, a. 1's reference to fittingness, with the result that there can be no strict necessity that the mission of the Word in Christ be paired with the mission of the Spirit. Of course, Torrell holds that God does give Christ habitual grace, which is needed for performing the supernaturalized actions that Christ undertakes for our salvation. Torrell's point is simply (in Legge's words) that "Christ's habitual grace remains a causally distinct gift to his humanity that does not *necessarily* follow from the union of Christ's humanity with the Word."[68]

In response, Legge's solution is to appeal to Aquinas's doctrine of the Trinitarian missions. There is an intrinsic connection (and order) between the mission of the Word and the mission of the Spirit. Thus, there is an intrinsic connection and order between the grace of union and habitual grace in Christ. In I, q. 43, a. 3, Aquinas remarks (indebted to Book 3 of Augustine's *De Trinitate*) that sanctifying grace is the invisible mission of the Holy Spirit; and in q. 43, a. 5 he makes clear that the invisible mission of the Spirit presupposes the invisible mission of the Son: "one mission cannot be without the other."[69]

66. Legge, *Trinitarian Christology*, 143.

67. Legge, *Trinitarian Christology*, 143, citing Aquinas, *Summa Theologiae*, III, q. 7, a. 13, ad. 2; and III, q. 34, a. 1.

68. Legge, *Trinitarian Christology*, 144–45.

69. Aquinas, *Summa Theologiae*, I, q. 43, a. 5, ad. 3.

The text upon which Legge focuses is even more explicit. In III, q. 7, a. 13, on whether Christ's habitual grace followed after the union, Aquinas answers in the affirmative along lines that require the intrinsic relation of the missions of the Word and Spirit. Aquinas states, "Now the mission of the Son is prior, in the order of nature, to the mission of the Holy Spirit, even as in the order of nature the Holy Spirit proceeds from the Son. . . . Hence the personal union, according to which the mission of the Son took place, is prior in the order of nature to habitual grace, according to which the mission of the Holy Spirit takes place."[70] The latter—habitual grace—follows the grace of union, says Aquinas, "as light follows the sun."[71] The co-implication of the missions, in their ordering to each other, means that habitual grace is just as necessary in Christ's humanity as it is necessary that the mission of the Holy Spirit will be present in a rational creature wherever the mission of the Word is present. Legge comments that the ultimate ground for this relation is the Trinity itself. He states, "The most fundamental relation between these distinct graces [the grace of union and habitual grace] is the ordering of their primordial principles, which are not only the missions but the eternal processions themselves, since the missions include the divine processions and 'extend' them into time."[72]

In other words, there can be no doubt that the visible mission of the Word in the Incarnation (the grace of union) is intrinsically and necessarily related to an invisible mission of the Spirit (habitual grace) in Christ's humanity, since as Aquinas puts it, "the Son is the Word, not any sort of word, but one Who breathes forth Love."[73] Aquinas adds: "one mission cannot be separated from another," because one Person cannot be "separated from the other."[74] Of course, the intrinsic relation between the missions of the Word and Spirit involves no differentiation in time: "the grace of union . . . precedes the habitual grace of Christ, not in order of time, but by nature and in thought."[75] At the very instant of the conception of the incarnate Word, the incarnate Word is filled superabundantly with the Spirit. Aquinas makes the same point in q. 2, a. 12, where he remarks, "these two kinds of grace are said to be natural to Christ, inasmuch as He had them from His nativity, since from the beginning of His conception the human nature was united to the Divine Person, and His soul was filled

70. Aquinas, *Summa Theologiae*, III, q. 7, a. 13.

71. Aquinas, *Summa Theologiae*, III, q. 7, a. 13.

72. Legge, *Trinitarian Christology*, 148.

73. Aquinas, *Summa Theologiae*, I, q. 43, a. 5, ad. 2.

74. Aquinas, *Summa Theologiae*, I, q. 43, a. 5, ad. 3.

75. Aquinas, *Summa Theologiae*, III, q. 7, a. 13.

with the gift of grace."[76] Legge draws the conclusion: "the eternal Word is eternally with the Holy Spirit that he breathes forth. Aquinas maintains only an order of nature between the missions, the same order as that between the divine processions and the divine persons themselves."[77] Given that the Son is sent in the grace of union, the Holy Spirit is necessarily sent in habitual grace to the humanity of Christ.[78] Just as the Word eternally and necessarily breathes forth Love (the Holy Spirit) in the Trinity, so also in the Trinitarian missions—which extend the Trinitarian processions in time—"the Son's visible mission intrinsically implies the Word breathing forth the Spirit to that same humanity."[79]

A question arises, however: has this position made the grace of the Holy Spirit in Christ's humanity not "grace" at all, but a mere necessary emanation triggered by the Incarnation of the Word? Legge is sensitive to this question, and he denies that his explanation (or Aquinas's) entails that the Spirit's mission to Christ's humanity is necessary in any negative sense. Instead, what is at play is the Trinity's free decision regarding the plan of salvation. Assuming the existence of the grace of union, there will

76. Aquinas, *Summa Theologiae*, III, q. 2, a. 12.

77. Legge, *Trinitarian Christology*, 148. Legge remarks, "For Aquinas, the divine persons come into the world as they are in themselves—which is to say, necessarily in relation to and interpenetrated by the other divine persons. The idea that a person could be sent into the world but might somehow fail to disclose and make present his eternal procession, or might somehow be severed from the other persons, would be self-contradictory for Aquinas" (150). Again, Legge hammers home the point: "The Son's visible mission does not only disclose his relation to the Father (the Son who is sent by the Father is manifested to be *from* the Father), but it also includes his relation to the Holy Spirit: to be the Father's Word means both to be from the Father, and to be the Word that breathes forth Love. The humanity in which there is a visible mission of the Son must therefore also receive an invisible mission of the Holy Spirit" (151).

78. Legge observes further, "Note . . . that the created objects of these two missions in Christ's human nature are distinct: the visible mission of the Son is accomplished in the assumption of a human nature; its created effect is Christ's human nature itself insofar as it is united to the Word" (Legge, *Trinitarian Christology*, 147).

79. Legge, *Trinitarian Christology*, 149. Legge adds, "In eternity *and* in time, the Word proceeds from the Father, breathing forth Love" (149). On the same page, he confirms this point with a marvelous passage, attributed by Aquinas to Athanasius, from *Contra errores Graecorum* II, c. 1: "Christ himself as God the Son sent the Spirit from above, and as man below he received the Spirit; from himself to himself, therefore, the Spirit dwells in his humanity from his divinity." Yet another summation along these lines by Legge deserves to be quoted for its clarity and insight: "When the Word is personally united to the human nature of Christ, that Word breathes forth or bursts Love—that is, the Word bestows the Holy Spirit on that human nature in the gift of habitual grace, which blossoms in wisdom and love, so that Christ knows and loves God perfectly in that nature and according to a properly human mode" (Legge, *Trinitarian Christology*, 152).

also necessarily be habitual grace; but both are grounded in the Trinity's freedom with regard to creation. The Trinitarian Persons are free in relation to creatures, but they are not free in relation to each other, including in the relations to the Father and Spirit enjoyed by the incarnate Word. Legge quotes an instructive passage from Aquinas's *Contra errores Graecorum* (I, 13): "in the name 'Christ' is understood the Holy Spirit by reason of concomitance, because wherever Christ is, there also is the Spirit of Christ, just as wherever the Father is, there also is the Son."[80] To this passage, Legge appends a final summation of the key argument for why habitual grace necessarily follows upon the grace of union. Legge states, "Christ's human nature is hypostatically united to the Son alone, but it is simultaneously filled with the presence of the Holy Spirit because the Son and Spirit are never apart."[81]

Aquinas makes two other arguments in q. 7, a. 13 that demonstrate the necessity—not simply the fittingness—of habitual grace in the incarnate Word. The first is that wherever God is present (and God is preeminently present in the incarnate Word), God is present as the cause of sanctifying grace. Drawing upon Aquinas's *Commentary on the Sentences*, Legge underlines that the divine presence here signifies not solely the presence of the Word but also the presence of the Spirit and the Father. The second argument is that the Word became incarnate in order to act for our salvation, and such human actions require infused habits whose cause is habitual grace. As the human nature of a Person (the Word), the human nature of Christ receives habitual grace, so that Christ can act as man for our salvation.

Legge ends his discussion by observing that both the grace of union and habitual grace are created effects that are caused by the three Persons acting as one. Yet the term of the union is the Word, and the charity produced by habitual grace "terminates in and conforms the soul to the Holy Spirit himself," who proceeds distinctly as Love in the Trinity.[82] It follows that the distinction between divine essence and divine Persons is no impediment to the above arguments, but serves them. Legge also notes that his position does not minimize or relativize the significance of the Incarnation of the

---

80. Quoted in Legge, *Trinitarian Christology*, 152.

81. Legge, *Trinitarian Christology*, 152–53.

82. Legge, *Trinitarian Christology*, 158. Thus, Legge remarks, "the important thing is not to distinguish different actions belonging to different divine persons, but to distinguish the divine persons within the one divine action" (158). Legge directs attention here to no. 1775 (ch. 17, lect. 5) of Aquinas's *Commentary on the Gospel of John*, and to the discussion of this passage in Marshall, "What Does the Spirit Have to Do?," 69.

Word, as might be feared by proponents of the position taken by Garrigou-Lagrange. Legge maintains, "the hypostatic union is always first and in a class by itself (since Christ *is* the divine Son)," whereas the Holy Spirit does not become incarnate. Christ's habitual grace, while unique in degree, is not so radically unique as is the Incarnation. Thus, the centrality and impact of the grace of union is not relativized by observing that a crucial part of its impact has to do with the Spirit breathed forth by the Word.

The impact of the Word upon his humanity comes about by the Word's breathing forth of the Spirit upon his humanity, not by a sanctification of his humanity that bypasses the Spirit. While Christ's humanity cannot be said to be "owed" grace (since no rational creature, even the humanity of the Word, is owed grace)—and in this sense habitual grace is fitting rather than necessary—Christ's habitual grace nevertheless flows necessarily from the grace of union. In *this* sense, as Aquinas says, "habitual grace . . . is a certain effect of Filiation in the soul of Christ."[83]

It should be clear that Legge's argument that the co-implication of the Trinitarian missions solves the problem of interpreting Aquinas on the relationship of Christ's habitual grace to the grace of union is a powerful one. Particularly notable, in my view, is Legge's demonstration that this position—namely that the grace of union is not what sanctifies or supernaturalizes the human nature of Christ, since habitual grace (the mission of the Spirit) necessarily flows from the grace of union (the mission of the Son)—does not downplay the extraordinary impact of the union of the two natures in the Word. The impact of the Word is not minimized, but rather is rightly understood, since the Word is a Word that breathes forth Love. The Trinitarian processions are the ground of the Trinitarian missions in the economy of salvation.

CONCLUSION

As we have seen, Christ's sanctification does not come about because of the dignity of the hypostatic union—that is, of his human nature's union with the divine nature. It comes about instead because the Word who becomes incarnate is a Word who breathes forth Love. The mission of the Word is inseparable from the mission of the Holy Spirit, just as the generation of the Word in the Trinity is inseparable from the procession of the Holy Spirit.[84] The Incarnation of the Word brings with it, at the very instant of the Incarnation, the superabundant outpouring of the grace of the Holy Spirit

83. Aquinas, *Summa Theologiae*, III, q. 23, a. 4, ad. 2.
84. This point is emphasized by Weinandy, *Trinity*.

in the Word's human nature. Word and Spirit are inseparable in the mystery of the Incarnation.

Through reference to the work of Myk Habets, I indicated at the outset of this chapter that according to many contemporary Spirit Christologies, a "Logos Christology" needs to be complemented and balanced by a "Spirit Christology." In my view, attention to Spirit Christology is indeed highly salutary, so as to avoid a one-sided focus on the Word. This is so despite the value of mystical appreciation of the Word's Incarnation. But the division of Christology into "Logos Christology" and "Spirit Christology" should not mask the more profound truth identified by Legge. A true Christology of the Word will be, at the very same time, a Spirit Christology, because the Word—as the Word who breathes forth Love—is never present without the Spirit.

BIBLIOGRAPHY

Aquinas, Thomas. *Commentary on the Gospel of John: Chapters 1–5*. Edited by Daniel Keating and Matthew Levering. Translated by Fabian Larcher and James Weisheipl. Washington, DC: The Catholic University of America Press, 2010.

———. *Light of Faith: The Compendium of Theology*. Manchester, NH: Sophia Institute Press, 1993.

———. *Summa Theologiae*. Translated by the Fathers of the English Dominican Province. Westminster, MD: Christian Classics, 1981.

Congar, Yves. *La Parole et le Souffle*. Paris: Desclée, 1984.

Cross, Richard. *Duns Scotus*. Oxford: Oxford University Press, 1999.

———. *The Metaphysics of the Incarnation*. Oxford: Oxford University Press, 2002.

Cyril of Alexandria. *Commentary on John*. Vol. 2. Edited by Joel C. Elowsky. Translated by David R. Maxwell. Downers Grove, IL: IVP Academic, 2015.

———. *On the Unity of Christ*. Translated by John Anthony McGuckin. Crestwood, NY: St. Vladimir's Seminary Press, 1995.

Duns Scotus, John. *Ordinatio*. *Opera Omnia*. Vol. 9. Vatican City: Typis Vaticanis, 2006.

Garrigues, Jean-Miguel. "The 'Natural Grace' of Christ in St. Thomas." In *Surnaturel: A Controversy at the Heart of Twentieth-Century Thomistic Thought*, edited by Serge-Thomas Bonino, translated by Robert Williams, 103–15. Ave Maria, FL: Sapientia, 2009.

Garrigou-Lagrange, Réginald. *Christ the Savior: A Commentary on the Third Part of St. Thomas' Theological Summa*. Translated by Bede Rose. St. Louis: Herder, 1957.

———. *Our Saviour and His Love for Us*. Translated by A. Bouchard. Aeterna, 2016.

Habets, Myk. *The Anointed Son: A Trinitarian Spirit Christology*. Eugene, OR: Pickwick, 2010.

Hofer, Andrew, and Jonah Teller. "Reordering Thomistic Josephology: Sanctifying Grace in Christ, Saint Joseph, and Us." *Nova et Vetera* 20 (2022) 77–99.

Legge, Dominic. "Incarnate *De Spiritu Sancto*: Aquinas on the Holy Spirit and Christ's Conception." *Thomist* 84 (2020) 173–205.

———. *The Trinitarian Christology of St. Thomas Aquinas*. Oxford: Oxford University Press, 2017.

Margelidon, Philippe-Marie. Études *thomistes sur la théologie de la redemption. De la grace à la resurrection du Christ.* Perpignan: Artège, 2010.

Marshall, Bruce D. "What Does the Spirit Have to Do?" In *Reading John with St. Thomas Aquinas: Theological Exegesis and Speculative Theology,* edited by Michael Dauphinais and Matthew Levering, 62–77. Washington, DC: The Catholic University of America Press, 2005.

Rohof, Jan. *La sainteté substantielle du Christ dans la théologie scolastique. Histoire du problème.* Fribourg: Suisse Éditions St-Paul, 1952.

Torrell, Jean-Pierre. *Encyclopédie Jésus le Christ chez saint Thomas d'Aquin.* Paris: Cerf, 2008.

Weinandy, Thomas. *The Trinity: Eternity and Time.* Ave Maria, FL: Sapientia, 2022.

White, Thomas Joseph. *The Incarnate Lord: A Thomistic Study in Christology.* Washington, DC: The Catholic University of America Press, 2015.

11

ST. THOMAS AQUINAS ON THE PRIMACY OF THE DIVINE TEACHER IN THE PERSON OF THE HOLY SPIRIT

Some Pedagogical Implications

Pamela van Oploo

St. Thomas Aquinas understands education as involving three interactive levels of causality: God is the principal and primary cause of all teaching and learning and is also its final end; the student is the principal secondary agent; and the human teacher is an instrumental secondary agent.[1] However, there is little discussion of divine causality in the literature. Most attention is on secondary causation, while the first and ultimate cause is often overlooked. This gives rise to an incomplete account of education leading to the possibility of false pedagogies. In this work I will address this deficiency by focusing on the unique pedagogy of the Holy Spirit in the teaching and learning process.

For Aquinas, the Holy Spirit has a key role to play in the process of teaching and learning. To understand Aquinas' thinking, I will first examine

---

1. Aquinas, *Summa Theologica* (hereafter, ST) I, q. 105, a. 3; I, q. 105, a. 4, c; Aquinas, *Summa Contra Gentiles, Book Two*, c. 75; Aquinas, *On Creation*, q. 3, a. 7; ST I, q. 116, a. 1, c.

why he posits God as our Primary Teacher. I will then briefly explore the distinct pedagogies of the Father and the Son to delineate the pedagogy of the Holy Spirit more clearly. The analysis of the pedagogy of the Holy Spirit will then allow a final discussion of some fundamental pedagogical implications.

GOD AND EDUCATION

Aquinas believes that God alone is our primary teacher, "the teacher of all truth,"[2] who teaches interiorly and principally,[3] being the principal efficient cause of all learning and teaching.[4] By contrast, human teachers act as instrumental secondary agents, teaching under God as part of His governance of creatures[5] in fulfillment of His provident plan.[6] Thomas explicitly lists teaching as one of two activities by which we share in the divine governance, the other being the procreation of offspring. Teaching ensures the education of such offspring.[7] For Thomas "to teach is nothing else than to cause knowledge in another in some way."[8] He regards human learning as an operation that involves an interior change from a potential knower to an actual knower, either through self-discovery or via the reception of knowledge from another.[9]

Aquinas states that our entire perfection as humans lies in knowing God[10] and that we reach this end principally through education.[11] He says, "the final perfection toward which man is ordained consists in the perfect knowledge of God, which, indeed, man can reach only if God, who knows Himself perfectly, undertakes to teach him."[12] Trinitarian teaching involves engaging both the intellect and the will; the intellect hears and love learns.[13] The response to this teaching should be the acquiring of virtue "for

2. Aquinas, *Literal Exposition of Job*, c. 13.

3. Aquinas, *Teacher, the Mind*, q. 11, a. 1, c.

4. Aquinas, ST I, q. 105, a. 3.

5. Aquinas, ST I, q. 105, a. 4, c; Aquinas, *Summa Contra Gentiles, Book Two*, c. 75.

6. Aquinas, *On Creation*, q. 3, a. 7; ST I, q. 116, a. 1, c.

7. Aquinas, ST supp., q. 41, a. 1.

8. Aquinas, *Teacher*, q. 11, a. 1.

9. Aquinas, *Commentary on Aristotle's "Posterior Analytics,"* 1.1.

10. Aquinas, *Commentary on the Gospel of John, Chapters 13–21*, #1777.

11. Aquinas, *Commentary on the Gospel of John, Chapters 1–5*, #826.

12. Aquinas, *Disputed Questions on Truth*, vol. 2, q. 14, a. 10.

13. Aquinas, *Commentary on the Gospel of John, Chapters 13–21*, #1916, #1958–59, #2090, #2102; Boland, *St. Thomas Aquinas*, 98.

nature intends not only the begetting of offspring, but also its education and development until it reach the perfect state of man as man, and that is the state of virtue."[14] By virtue, Thomas means both intellectual and moral, natural and supernatural.[15] Such an education enables a union with one's divine teacher, for God will ever work to develop our character and make us holy as the sun is always lighting up the air.[16]

The ultimate purpose of education is to obtain union with God where we cognitively assimilate this Supreme being, so becoming wise,[17] for human maturation lies in returning to the source of our origin, the divine mind.[18] Thomistic education has an eschatological end brought about by our cooperation with the interior teacher, the Holy Spirit, who forms our mind to the degree that we are united with that same Spirit.[19]

GOD THE PRIMARY TEACHER

The claim that God is our principal Teacher permeates Aquinas' writings. What we can achieve follows from what we have the potential to do. God creates us and sustains us by His all-powerful Word and provides us with our rational capacity, hence Aquinas regards Him as our primary teacher. For Thomas the power of God's divine Word holds the created order in being, if His Word were withdrawn from things, then they would cease to be.[20] In this respect Aquinas judges the creative act to be continuous.[21] This has a flow on effect when it comes to human teaching. Aquinas states that art, (including the art of the teacher) presupposes nature and that nature presupposes God. Why? Because the operation of art cannot be accomplished without the operation of nature and God operates in the operation of nature therefore everything nature does God has a hand in so to speak.[22] This is why Thomas

---

14. Aquinas, ST Supp., q. 41, a. 1; Aquinas, *Commentary on the Gospel of John, Chapters 13–21*, #1766.

15. Aquinas, *Summa Contra Gentiles, Book Three, Part 2*, c. 97; Aquinas, *Disputed Questions on Truth*, vol. 3, q. 27–29; Boland, "Truth, Knowledge and Communication," 289.

16. Aquinas, ST II–II, q. 4, a. 4, ad. 3.

17. Williams, "Argument to Bliss," 506; Ozolins, "Aquinas," 10.

18. Aquinas, *Commentary on the Gospel of John, Chapters 13–21*, #1738; see also Aquinas, *Commentary on the Gospel of John, Chapters 1–5*, #641; Aquinas, *Summa Contra Gentiles, Book One*, c. 1.

19. Aquinas, ST I–II, q. 68, a. 4, ad. 3; Williams, "Argument to Bliss," 511.

20. Aquinas, *Commentary on the Gospel of John, Chapters 1–5*, #135.

21. Aquinas, *Commentary on the Gospel of John, Chapters 1–5*, #739; ST I, q. 45.

22. Aquinas, *On Creation*, q. 3, a. 7; see also Aquinas, *Summa Contra Gentiles, Book Three, Part 1*, c. 67.

holds that humans only teach in a secondary sense and because he sees that the human teacher's craft is imperfect (limited) and thus needs to flow from a perfect source of knowledge and understanding. Aquinas holds that, "that which is by nature prior to all other things and sets them all in motion, must be more perfect than all the rest."[23]

With intellectual learning, we are especially in need of God's help.[24] Our intellect is a secondary principle by which we obtain truth. It is dependent upon a first principle; God moves our intellect to understand things and gives us the power to understand them.[25] In his *Commentary on Boethius' "De Trinitate,"* Aquinas writes,

> Just as the bodily eye is related to seeing bodies, so the intellect is related to perceiving intelligible truth ... but the bodily eye cannot see bodies without the additional illumination of the corporeal sun. Therefore, neither can the human intellect see the truth without being illumined by the light of the invisible Sun, who is God.[26]

In his work entitled *On Spiritual Creatures*, Aquinas explores this at great depth. He says firstly that if something belongs to a thing in a partial way it must be in something else in a complete way. We are rational animals, composed of a rational soul and a body. He posits therefore that there must be something higher than our soul whose whole nature is intellect from which the intellectuality of our soul is derived and on which it depends for its act of understanding.[27] Secondly, he notes that for anything moveable there must exist something immoveable on which it depends. Now when we come to understand something we do so by discursive reasoning, which involves a movement from being a potential knower to an actual knower. Aquinas states therefore that above the human soul there must be an intellect "whose power of understanding is fixed and at rest without discursive thinking of this sort."[28] Thirdly, because absolutely speaking act is prior to potency. Aquinas holds that initially while we have the potential to know things in an intellectual manner, we come into this world devoid of rational knowledge. He further states that we will never attain the truth of all intelligible things that can be known in this life. Hence, he concludes that

---

23. Aquinas, *Compendium of Theology*, c. 20.

24. Aquinas, ST I–II, q. 109, a. 1, c; Aquinas, *Commentary on the Gospel of John, Chapters 1–5*, #100.

25. Aquinas, ST I, q. 105, a. 5, ad. 2.

26. Aquinas, *Faith, Reason, and Theology*, q. 1, a. 1.

27. Aquinas, *On Spiritual Creatures*, a. 10.

28. Aquinas, *On Spiritual Creatures*, a. 10.

there must be an intellect greater than ours that "always exists in act and is wholly perfect in its understanding of truth" on which human knowledge is ultimately reliant.[29]

It is to God that we owe our natural intellectual light,[30] "the light of reason divinely implanted within us, by which God speaks within us."[31] Our intellect is not of this world since it is not of our bodily or sensible nature. Rather our intellectual nature is "enlightened by an intellectual and spiritual light."[32] Aquinas goes on to say that we do not come into the world according to our bodily nature but rather according to our intellectual nature which comes from God and thus is sourced external from the world.[33] Aquinas relates that it "is immediately received from the first principle of life, whence it is called the life of wisdom."[34]

Thomas claims that just as we have within us a natural principle of health to which a doctor may supply aid "so in the learner there is a natural principle of knowledge, namely the agent intellect," by which we abstract the intelligibility of things from the sensible world that surrounds us.[35] He holds that the agent intellect is a power of our soul, akin to an intellectual light which is in us by participation from God. Aquinas states that God

> teaches from within in that He pours forth this kind of light into our souls; and over and above this kind of natural light, out of His goodness, He generously grants other lights, such as the light of faith and the light of prophecy, [both of which involve the agency of the Holy Spirit].[36]

There is only one "primary light which flows into all minds,"[37] "through the light of the agent intellect, which makes things intelligible,"[38] it being a natural illuminative power. Thomas says that the special characteristic of the agent intellect is that it is a power participating in the higher substance that is God. Like Aristotle, he considers the agent intellect to be "a kind of constant state, like light,"[39] the very light of God permanently sealed upon

29. Aquinas, *On Spiritual Creatures*, a. 10; ST I, q. 79, a. 4, c; ST I, q. 12, a. 11, ad. 3.

30. Aquinas, ST I, q. 117, a. 1, ad. 1.

31. Aquinas, *Teacher*, q. 11, a. 1, ad. 13.

32. Aquinas, *Commentary on the Gospel of John, Chapters 1–5*, #129.

33. Aquinas, *Commentary on the Gospel of John, Chapters 1–5*, #129.

34. Aquinas, *Commentary on the Gospel of John, Chapters 1–5*, #771.

35. Aquinas, *On the Uniqueness of the Intellect*, c. 5.

36. Aquinas, *Questions on the Soul*, l. 5, c; see also Boland, *St. Thomas Aquinas*, 61.

37. Aquinas, *On Spiritual Creatures*, a. 10, reply 13.

38. Aquinas, *On Spiritual Creatures*, a. 10, reply 8.

39. Aquinas, *Questions on the Soul*, l. 5, c.

us. Aquinas is careful not to say that the agent intellect is God Himself. Rather, God is related to our souls as an active universal principle, while the agent intellect is an active particular principle structured towards our essential intellective operations.[40]

Thomas says "though by ourselves, without the divine activity, we are insufficient to think of anything, a new light need not be communicated to us in all our knowledge."[41] We know and judge things through the likeness of God's truth implanted in us under whose power we are able to discern intelligible reality much like the way in a scientific demonstration secondary principles are certain only because of primary principles.[42] Our ability to see self-evident principles is evoked in this light immediately upon initial sense experience.[43] Aquinas holds that these universal conceptions serve as universal principles by which we "judge about other things, and in which we foreknow these others."[44] Hence these supply the foundational basis of all future learning and teaching.[45]

In like manner, the outward action of a teacher can have no effect upon us without the inward principle of knowledge that is the agent intellect.[46] As its source is divine Thomas holds that God alone is "teacher" in the fullest sense of the word.[47] Aquinas says that Jesus as the wisdom of God teaches everyone. "Thus the disciples called Him Lord . . . and Teacher. . . . And with good reason. For He is the Lord, who alone creates and restores. . . . And he is the only Teacher who teaches from within: 'You have one master, the Christ' (Mt 23:10)."[48]

God is the source of truth as He is Truth itself,[49] who establishes all truth and who equips humans both to know such truth and to desire it in fulfillment of their human nature.[50] Aquinas justifies his stance here by

40. Aquinas, *Questions on the Soul*, l. 5, c.

41. Aquinas, *Faith, Reason, and Theology*, q. 1, a. 1, ad. 1.

42. Aquinas, *Compendium of Theology*, c. 129.

43. Shannon, "Aquinas on the Teacher's Art," 383; see Aquinas, *Summa Contra Gentiles, Book Three, Part 1*, c. 47; Aquinas, *Teacher, the Mind*, q. 10, a. 6, ad. 6.

44. Aquinas, *Teacher, the Mind*, q. 10, a. 6, c.

45. Aquinas, *Literal Exposition of Job*, c. 38.

46. Aquinas, *Summa Contra Gentiles, Book Two*, c. 75; Aquinas, *Aquinas Catechism*, 154.

47. Aquinas, *Commentary on the Gospel of John, Chapters 13–21*, #1775, #2201.

48. Aquinas, *Commentary on the Gospel of John, Chapters 13–21*, #1775; see also ST I, q. 43, a. 5.

49. Aquinas, *Commentary on the Gospel of John, Chapters 1–5*, #33, #534.

50. Aquinas, ST I–II q. 109, a. 2, ad. 3; Aquinas, *Summa Contra Gentiles, Book Two*, c. 75; Aquinas, *Summa Contra Gentiles, Book One*, c. 62.

claiming that because the teacher and learner understand the same thing there must needs be the same illuminating principle for each, else this would be impossible.[51] This principle is the Triune divine teacher.

Thomas tells us that "we acquire knowledge in three ways: by way of discovery, by way of revelation, or by way of instruction (*disciplina*). In discovery, we learn from the things we are investigating. . . . [I]n revelation, we learn directly from God. When we learn from a *disciplina*, however, we learn from a teacher."[52] For Aquinas, all three Persons of the Godhead are teachers[53] because all three Persons comprehend the divine essence[54] and make this essence known to us. However, each Person's pedagogy is distinct. The teaching of the Father is by way of revelation and discovery in nature, while the teaching of Christ and the Holy Spirit is by way of instruction through which God's truth and love perfect us.

THE PEDAGOGY OF GOD THE FATHER

God the Father by way of appropriation, as principle not from a principle, is our most preeminent teacher but we discern His pedagogy primarily through His Son. The Father's primary subject as teacher is Christ Himself.[55] Sacred Scripture mediates this teaching, helping us to participate in Christ.[56] Aquinas relates: As in creatures there exists a first and a secondary principle, so also in the divine Persons, in Whom there is no before or after, is formed the principle not from a principle, who is the Father; and the principle from a principle, who is the Son.[57] God the Father is a "first" principle by reason of His not being from another who is known "both by paternity and by common spiration, as regards the Persons proceeding from Himself."[58] The God-man Christ Jesus is the Father's great artwork and His perfect witness. Aquinas states, "now His office is to bear witness"[59] because in Jesus Christ

51. Aquinas, *On the Uniqueness of the Intellect*, c. 5.

52. Aquinas, *Commentary on the Gospel of John, Chapters 6–12*, #1040.

53. Aquinas, *Commentary on the Gospel of John, Chapters 13–21*, #2103.

54. Aquinas, *Commentary on the Gospel of John, Chapters 1–5*, #219.

55. Aquinas, *Commentary on the Gospel of John, Chapters 13–21*, #1874; Sherwin, "Christ the Teacher," 175.

56. Levering, *Participatory Biblical Exegesis*, 63.

57. Aquinas, ST I, q. 33, a. 4, c.

58. Aquinas, ST I, q. 33, a. 4, c.

59. Aquinas, *Commentary on the Gospel of John, Chapters 1–5*, #116.

"the very essence of the Father is received by generation, and He Himself is the Word."[60]

God's creation comes from His Word.[61] Burrell, citing Aquinas, says of this that the word spoken to create is anchored "in the Word proceeding within divinity, as its eternal pattern."[62] Aquinas states, "therefore all things made by God must have pre-existed in the Word of God, before existing in their own nature."[63] Thomas holds that things are knowable to us because of their God-given substantial forms, which we have the capacity to take into our intellects in an immaterial way. These forms determine things to be what they are and come from the divine intellect.[64] Creation then is a principle of our learning under God.[65] That God was in the world giving *esse* to the world means that God manifests Himself and His teaching through the world.[66] Elsewhere, in the *De Vertitate*, Aquinas calls sensible forms "a kind of sealing of the divine knowledge in things"[67] and in the *Sentences*, he speaks of the vocation of creation, in that we first learn through the created order.[68] This claim is repeated in his *Commentary on the Gospel of St. John*.[69] Thus, it is that the Father teaches us through His creatures.

The Father's book of nature is completed by His book of revelation, which according to Thomas represents a distinctly new method in the processes of teaching and learning.[70] With the teaching of revelation comes an education rooted in historical concrete events and personal dialogue with the Godhead.[71] Aquinas states that the ultimate aim of creation is that the light of Christ might be manifested in it, the Logos through whom all

---

60. Aquinas, *Commentary on the Gospel of John, Chapters 1-5*, #534.

61. Aquinas, *Commentary on the Gospel of John, Chapters 1-5*, #26; Burrell, "Creation," 121.

62. Burrell, "Creation," 121; see also Aquinas, *Commentary on the Gospel of John, Chapters 1-5*, #750; ST I, q. 34, a. 3, c; ST I, q. 45, a. 6, ad. 2.

63. Aquinas, *Summa Contra Gentiles, Book Four*, c. 13.

64. Aquinas, ST I, q. 16, a. 2, c; ST I, q. 47, a. 1; Aquinas, *Commentary on the Gospel of John, Chapters 13-21*, #817.

65. Aquinas, *Academic Sermons*, 102; Boland, "St. Thomas's Sermon," 467.

66. Aquinas, *Commentary on the Gospel of John, Chapters 1-5*, #133.

67. Boland, *St. Thomas Aquinas*, 140.

68. Aquinas, I *Sentences* 41, 2 ad. 3.

69. Aquinas, *Commentary on the Gospel of John, Chapters 1-5*, #649; Boland, *St. Thomas Aquinas*, 140.

70. Aquinas, *Commentary on the Gospel of John, Chapters 1-5*, #618.

71. Hibbs, *Dialectic and Narrative in Aquinas*, 34.

things were made.[72] We read the Scriptures as sacred teaching[73] in order
to come to know and learn from the divine Teacher so as to bring about "a
deifying participation in God the Teacher."[74]

Revelation has both a sacramental and pedagogical character but one
must first recognize this Teacher by faith before His teaching in Scripture
can be understood.[75] This requires us to heed the prompting of the Holy
Spirit[76] in imitation of the sacred hagiographers themselves who were
inspired by the Holy Spirit in the provision of their paternal precepts.[77]
God's public revelation is ordered and reflects a pedagogical structure that
is well suited to humans, that of an "increasing disclosure on God's part."[78]
This long initiation into the mystery of God is a part of the divine pedagogy[79]
and a reflection of the fact that humans learn gradually.[80] Revelation thus
displays a trajectory of perfection driven by the virtues leading to life.[81]
When Thomas speaks of life here he means it in a threefold sense: the "life
of grace," which makes possible the "life of justice" that consists in moral
action, which is than consummated in the "life of glory."[82] Hence he calls
Revelation the most useful of all teaching.[83]

Most especially, God the Father teaches by giving us the light of
his Son.[84] The Word is firstly the exemplar by which the Father created
the world,[85] then this Word becomes the exemplar by which the world is
redeemed.[86] Aquinas says that the Son of God is "light,"[87] because no one
can arrive at knowledge of the Father except through the door that is His

72. Aquinas, *Commentary on the Gospel of John, Chapters 1–5*, #136; Burrell,
"Creation," 126.

73. Aquinas, *Commentary on the Gospel of John, Chapters 1–5*, #209.

74. Levering, *Participatory Biblical Exegesis*, 64.

75. Levering, *Participatory Biblical Exegesis*, 65.

76. Aquinas, *Aquinas Catechism*, 73.

77. Aquinas, *Selected Writings*, 8.

78. Velde, "Natural Reason," 134.

79. Aquinas, ST I–II, q. 106, a. 3, c; ST I, q. 107, a. 1–3.

80. Boland, "Truth, Knowledge, and Communication," 298.

81. Aquinas, *Selected Writings*, 6.

82. Aquinas, *Selected Writings*, 7; Levering, *Participatory Biblical Exegesis*, 74–75.

83. Aquinas, *Selected Writings*, 7.

84. Aquinas, *Commentary on the Gospel of John, Chapters 1–5*, #95.

85. Aquinas, *On the Power of God*, q. 2, a. 1.

86. Aquinas, *Commentary on the Gospel of John, Chapters 13–21*, #1781; Sherwin,
"Christ the Teacher," 175; Bonino, "Role of the Apostles," 329–30.

87. Aquinas, *Commentary on the Gospel of John, Chapters 1–5*, #118.

Son.[88] Aquinas goes on to say that the Father comes in three ways; through a knowledge of the truth, through the affection of love, and through imitative action that the disciple must hear and learn.[89] This is a Trinitarian pedagogy. One needs to have the Father's intelligible testimony which is inwardly inspired in the heart to recognize the one He has sent.[90]

THE PEDAGOGY OF THE SON

Thomas says that Christ Jesus, as the wisdom of God, is the supreme pedagogue who teaches everyone.[91] He makes known everything that can be known in that things are understood through their substantial forms and all created forms exist through the Word. Aquinas states that the Word is the art full of living forms, who is not only light in Himself but makes known all things, as all intelligibility comes through Him.[92] Hence it is that Aquinas relates that Christ "is the Truth and teaches all truth."[93] Boland says that Thomas sees Jesus' primary task as serving truth, and in carrying out this task He shows Himself the most excellent of teachers.[94]

Christ is the principle *par excellence* of the life of wisdom because, through His divinity He is wisdom itself (the Word)[95] but also in His humanity the Word-made-flesh "becomes a wisdom attainable by us."[96] Christ incarnates truth, His human intellect from the moment of conception knew every truth,[97] because His human nature was united to divinity[98] hence it is that Christ becomes the witness of truth itself.[99] This Word is expressive of all that God is and all that God does with regard to creatures

---

88. Aquinas, *Commentary on the Gospel of John, Chapters 13–21*, #1887.

89. Aquinas, *Commentary on the Gospel of John, Chapters 6–12*, #946.

90. Aquinas, *Commentary on the Gospel of John, Chapters 1–5*, #820.

91. Aquinas, *Commentary on the Gospel of John, Chapters 13–21*, #1775; see also Aquinas, *Commentary on the Gospel of John, Chapters 6–12*, #845.

92. Aquinas, *Commentary on the Gospel of John, Chapters 1–5*, #118.

93. Aquinas, *Commentary on the Gospel of John, Chapters 13–21*, #1870; Aquinas, *Commentary on the Gospel of John, Chapters 1–5*, #27; Burrell, "Creation," 120; Lamb, "Eternity and Time," 132.

94. Boland, "Truth, Knowledge, and Communication," 302; Aquinas, ST III, q. 40, a. 1, c.; Aquinas, ST III, q. 42, a. 4, c.

95. Aquinas, *Commentary on the Gospel of John, Chapters 1–5*, #34.

96. Sherwin, "Christ the Teacher," 175; see also Aquinas, *Commentary on the Gospel of John, Chapters 1–5*, #188.

97. Aquinas, *Commentary on the Gospel of John, Chapters 13–21*, # 2201.

98. Aquinas, *Commentary on the Gospel of John, Chapters 1–5*, # 188.

99. Bonino, "Role of the Apostles," 320.

because God understands Himself and everything else through His essence by a single act.[100] "God alone is a perfect agent, His act of self-knowledge is the Second Person of the Blessed Trinity, God's Word."[101]

In terms of his pedagogy, Christ teaches by way of discipleship and shows Himself the supreme pedagogue[102] who not only teaches us on the natural level, but also on the level of grace and faith.[103] To be a student, a "discipulus," is to enter into a discipline under a master.[104] Thomas holds that the ultimate discipline is to reach the perfection of our human nature, its proper telos or end.[105] To learn the doctrine is "disciplina." Jesus truly showed us how to live; if we respond to this teaching, revelation becomes redemptive and revelation is then understood "as a relation of teach-learn."[106]

Thomas sees Jesus as the supremely skilled teacher, the one who knows how to pose the right questions and to give the best illustrations of His teaching, particularly through the divine pedagogy of His parables and sacramental system. Thomas thinks this should be imitated in all human teaching.[107] He claims that the teaching of Christ is always joined to some appropriate visible action, "so that what is invisible can be made known through the visible."[108] Hence it is that God uses historical events, people, physical things, and words as part of His pedagogy of revelation.[109]

Above all else, Christ shows Himself the supreme teacher by the love He has for His disciples and by His divine power to teach not only externally, as a human teacher does but also interiorly in the soul.[110] The word of Christ is not the same as the words of a human teacher. A human word "is first in potency before it is in act. But the Word of God is always in act," hence its

---

100. Aquinas, *Commentary on the Gospel of John, Chapters 1–5*, # 27: Burrell, "Creation," 120; Lamb, "Eternity and Time," 132.

101. Mayer, *Philosophy of Teaching*, 139.

102. Aquinas, *Commentary on the Gospel of John, Chapters 1–5*, #221.

103. Aquinas, *Commentary on the Gospel of John, Chapters 1–5*, #96, #525, #530; Boland, "Thomas Aquinas," 49; Davies, "Aquinas on Teaching and Learning," 647.

104. Boland, *St. Thomas Aquinas*, 95.

105. Aquinas, *Disputed Questions on Truth*, vol. 2, q. 14, a. 10.

106. Moran, "Revelation as Teaching-Learning," 278; Levering, *Participatory Biblical Exegesis*, 73.

107. Aquinas, *Commentary on the Gospel of John, Chapters 1–5*, #276; Boland, "Thomas Aquinas," 58.

108. Aquinas, *Commentary on the Gospel of John, Chapters 1–5*, #699.

109. Hibbs, *Dialectic and Narrative in Aquinas*, 34.

110. Aquinas, *Commentary on the Gospel of John, Chapters 1–5*, #422, #428; Boland, "Thomas Aquinas, Catholic Education," 61.

almighty power.[111] Christ uses a questioning pedagogy to teach His disciples because He wants them to reflect and meditate on the words of God, so stirring their understanding.[112] In this He shows Himself as the master of the Socratic style.[113]

Thomas uses the Last Supper discourse to show us that, for Christ, learning and the contemplation of truth needs to occur in tranquility.[114] He relates that reasoning involves a motion from potency to act, with understanding being a journeying to rest.[115] We have a natural desire to seek the causes of observable effects.[116] Once we begin to wonder about something our intellects do not rest until we have obtained the truth about it in some measure. When we understand a thing our mind then rests happy and satisfied with the knowledge it possesses.[117] Therefore Thomas claims that "understanding is best compared to quiet rest."[118] Our minds are able to reflect, to come to knowledge of truth and so be at rest.

Christ's teaching itself becomes the common ground of His friendship with the apostles and enables them to become teachers of the whole world in union with God's Holy Spirit, providing through the Church a living continuum and witness of the life of Christ on earth and so of His teaching.[119] In like manner to the Father's pedagogy, the Son's teaching is meant to lead us to the Father[120] "because this way is not separated from its destination but united to it."[121] However, this will not happen without the action of God's Holy Spirit within us.

111. Aquinas, *Commentary on the Gospel of John, Chapters 1–5*, #26.

112. Aquinas, *Commentary on the Gospel of John, Chapters 13–21*, #1773, # 2617.

113. Aquinas, *Commentary on the Gospel of John, Chapters 6–12*, #850, #1518, #1752–54, #1773; Boland, "Truth, Knowledge, and Communication," 302.

114. Sherwin, "Christ the Teacher," 187.

115. Aquinas, ST I, q. 79, a. 8, c; Williams, "Argument to Bliss," 510.

116. Aquinas, *Commentary on the Metaphysics of Aristotle*, bk. 1, l. 1, #1.

117. Aquinas, *Commentary on the Gospel of John, Chapters 1–5*, #281; Aquinas, *Commentary on the Gospel of John, Chapters 13–21*, #1770.

118. Aquinas, *Commentary on Aristotle's De Anima*, bk. 1, l. 8, #125.

119. Aquinas, *Commentary on the Gospel of John, Chapters 1–5*, #281; Aquinas, *Commentary on the Gospel of John, Chapters 6–12*, #864; Boland, *St. Thomas Aquinas*, 98.

120. Aquinas, *Commentary on the Gospel of John, Chapters 13–21*, #1871.

121. Aquinas, *Commentary on the Gospel of John, Chapters 13–21*, #1868.

THE PEDAGOGY OF THE HOLY SPIRIT

Thomas tells us that the mission of the Holy Spirit and His teaching "is to make us sharers in the divine wisdom and knowers of the truth."[122] Our intellect can be strengthened not only by the light of faith but also by the gifts of the Holy Spirit.[123] We have an obediential potency that enables us to be moved by supernatural grace in a non-violent manner[124] following the promptings of the Holy Spirit.[125] By this potency we obey God and are able to receive from Him whatever He has willed, including His teaching.[126]

Aquinas tells us that the Holy Spirit's gifts of knowledge (*scientia*), understanding (*intellectus*), and wisdom (*sapientia*) bring the theological virtues of faith, hope, and charity to perfection in us.[127] All the gifts of the Holy Spirit are ordered to the perfection of the theological virtues.[128] We are intended to participate in God's own mode of knowledge, which is by way of simple insight, and for this we need the gifts of the Holy Spirit to be operative in us.[129] By these gifts we are placed in direct contact with God as First Truth. They operate as principles in acquiring truth, facilitating even natural learning in that they guard our minds from error and provide us with a "harmonious view of reality through an integration of supernatural and natural truths."[130] Hence students endowed with the light of faith and the gifts of the Holy Spirit are more able to seek the truth in any discipline.

Aquinas claims that Christ teaches us through the simultaneous action of the Holy Spirit as we cannot learn the Father's teaching without the inward inspiration of the Holy Spirit.[131] Boland, paraphrasing Thomas, states "love proceeds from the truth because the Spirit is sent by the Son, but love also leads to knowledge of the truth, because the Spirit teaches the truth about

---

122. Aquinas, *Commentary on the Gospel of John, Chapters 13–21*, #1958; see also Aquinas, *Commentary on the Gospel of John, Chapters 6–12*, #1628.

123. Aquinas, ST I, q. 12, a. 13, c.

124. Jenkins, *Knowledge and Faith in Thomas Aquinas*, 141, 143.

125. Aquinas, *Commentary on the Gospel of John, Chapters 13–21*, #1916.

126. Aquinas, *Disputed Questions on Truth*, vol. 3, q. 29, a. 3 ad. 3.

127. Aquinas, ST II–II, q. 8; q. 9; q. 45. These align with Aristotle's three intellective virtues of *episteme, nous* and *Sophia* see Boland, "Thomas Aquinas," 55.

128. Aquinas, ST II–II, q. 9, a. 1, ad. 3.

129. Aquinas, ST II–II, q. 45, a. 1, ad. 2; ST II–II, q. 9, a. 1, ad. 1; Williams, "Argument to Bliss," 510.

130. Gulley, *Educational Philosophy*, 63.

131. "The Spirit makes us know all things by inspiring us from within, by directing us and lifting us up to spiritual things." See Aquinas, *Commentary on the Gospel of John, Chapters 13–21*, #1959; see also #1756.

the Son."[132] The work of Christ and the Holy Spirit are concurrent as there is only one integral teaching coming from the Father, through the Word, in union with the Holy Spirit.[133] While the Son's teaching leads to the Father, the Spirit's teaching leads to the Son.[134] Even Christ's exterior teaching through words and actions is only understandable to us through the action of the Holy Spirit;[135] "the Son, since He is the Word, gives teaching to us; but the Holy Spirit enables us to grasp it. . . . [T]he Son Himself, speaking by means of His human nature, is not successful unless He works from within by the Holy Spirit."[136] Aquinas claims that in order to be like Him we need to be spiritually regenerated by having His Spirit.[137]

The Holy Spirit helps us to assimilate the teaching of Christ.[138] Bonino likens this twofold action of the Word and the Spirit in our knowing to the two elements needed in the acquisition of knowledge in general: the "exterior communication of an objective teaching and the interior action of subjectively assimilating this teaching."[139] According to Thomas this divine aid is especially needed in the supernatural order of knowledge because our intellects are not directly proportional to the truths Christ wishes to teach,[140] in that "the words of Christ are so profound and so above human understanding that we can understand no more of them than what He reveals."[141] Hence Aquinas states, "as long as God's help and the interior Preacher are not there, the words of the preacher have no effect."[142] Put theologically, the supernatural virtues are what Aquinas calls rudimentary inclinations that turn us towards the divine but these can only become

132. Boland, *St. Thomas Aquinas*, 98; Aquinas, *Commentary on the Gospel of John, Chapters 13–21*, #1916.

133. Bonino, "Role of the Apostles," 329; Lamb, "Eternity and Time," 128; Aquinas, *Commentary on the Gospel of John, Chapters 1–5*, #23–67.

134. Aquinas, *Commentary on the Gospel of John, Chapters 13–21*, #1958.

135. Sherwin, "Christ the Teacher," 188; Bonino, "Role of the Apostles," 328.

136. Aquinas, *Commentary on the Gospel of John, Chapters 13–21*, #1958.

137. "Now there is a reason why spiritual generation comes from the Spirit. It is necessary that the one generated be generated in the likeness of the one generating; but we are regenerated as sons of God, in the likeness of His True Son. Therefore, it is necessary that our spiritual regeneration come about through that by which we are made like the true Son, and this comes about by having His Spirit." See Aquinas, *Commentary on the Gospel of John, Chapters 1–5*, #442.

138. "The Spirit in a hidden way aids our ability to know." Aquinas, *Commentary on the Gospel of John, Chapters 13–21*, #1960.

139. Bonino, "Role of the Apostles," 328–29.

140. Bonino, "Role of the Apostles," 329.

141. Aquinas, *Commentary on the Gospel of John, Chapters 13–21*, #1816.

142. Aquinas, *Commentary on the Gospel of John, Chapters 13–21*, #2582.

steady dispositions through the promptings of the Holy Spirit and through the actualization of His gifts.[143]

According to Aquinas when we "taste" truth (that is, contemplate it), it is the work of the Holy Spirit.[144] "Since the Holy Spirit is from the Truth, it is appropriate that the Spirit teach the truth, and make those He teaches like the one who sent Him."[145] Aquinas teaches that "unless the Spirit is present to the heart of the listener, the words of the teacher will be useless: the breath of the Almighty makes Him understand (Job 32:8)."[146] The entirety of God's teaching must be taken up interiorly. God's teaching is connected to love and friendship, which is assigned to the work of the Holy Spirit within us.[147] These qualities of the Holy Spirit are present in the spiritual man.[148] "The Spirit teaches because he makes us share in the wisdom of the Son and He brings things to our remembrance because, being love, He incites us."[149]

Aquinas sees the Holy Spirit's role as twofold. First, there is a preliminary sanctification through sanctifying grace which enables an initial understanding of Christ by way of the virtue of faith.[150] Second, this enables a fuller reception of the Spirit which only comes to the loving and obedient disciple.[151] As the Holy Spirit is love, He is given to those who love and to those who are obedient to God.[152] Thomas states,

> No one can love God unless he has the Holy Spirit: because we do not act before we receive God's grace, rather the grace comes first. . . . [W]e should say therefore, that the apostles first received the Holy Spirit so that they could love God and obey His commands. But it was necessary that they make good use, by their love and obedience, of this first gift of the Holy Spirit in order to receive the spirit more fully.[153]

---

143. Jenkins, *Knowledge and Faith*, 157.

144. Aquinas, ST II–II, q. 45, a. 1, c; ST II–II, q. 45, a. 2, c; Boland, "Truth, Knowledge, and Communication," 301.

145. Aquinas, *Commentary on the Gospel of John, Chapters 13–21*, #2102.

146. Aquinas, *Commentary on the Gospel of John, Chapters 13–21*, #1958.

147. Boland, *St. Thomas Aquinas*, 99.

148. Aquinas, *Commentary on the Gospel of John, Chapters 1–5*, #456.

149. Aquinas, *Commentary on the Gospel of John, Chapters 13–21*, #1960.

150. Aquinas, *Commentary on the Gospel of John, Chapters 13–21*, #1762–65, #2203; Sherwin, "Christ the Teacher," 189; Bonino, "Role of the Apostles," 333.

151. Aquinas, *Commentary on the Gospel of John, Chapters 13–21*, #1908.

152. Aquinas, *Commentary on the Gospel of John, Chapters 13–21*, #1908.

153. Aquinas, *Commentary on the Gospel of John, Chapters 13–21*, #1909.

The Holy Spirit then enlightens the disciples' intellect through instruction and teaching.[154] He ensures their moral development by purifying their hearts.[155] This moral development occurs through friendship with the Holy Spirit.[156]

The Spirit's teaching role flows from His procession from the Father and the Son,[157]

> The Holy Spirit leads to the knowledge of the truth, because He proceeds from the Truth. . . . [I]n us, love of the truth arises when we have conceived and considered truth. So also in God, Love proceeds from conceived Truth, which is the Son. And just as Love proceeds from the Truth, so love leads to knowledge of the truth . . . [because] it is love that impels one to reveal one's secrets.[158]

Hence Aquinas calls the Holy Spirit the most excellent of gifts because He is the Spirit of truth who gives of His gifts.[159]

The Gifts of the Holy Spirit

The gifts of the Holy Spirit have a special significance in human education, ordering us to supernatural happiness along with the supernatural virtues, perfecting one in matters concerning the good life.[160] We cannot be completely educated without the operation of these gifts within us. The gifts enable us to live the law of freedom, where we are spontaneously and personally moved towards good acts by God.[161] Aquinas claims "that the gifts are the origins or foundations (*principia*) of the intellectual and moral

---

154. Aquinas, *Commentary on the Gospel of John, Chapters 13–21*, #195; see also #2099, #2103, #2152.

155. Bonino, "Role of the Apostles," 329.

156. Aquinas, *Commentary on the Gospel of John, Chapters 13–21*, #1959, #1916; Bonino, "Role of the Apostles," 331.

157. Sherwin, "Christ the Teacher," 189.

158. Aquinas, *Commentary on the Gospel of John, Chapters 13–21*, #1916.

159. Aquinas, *Commentary on the Gospel of John, Chapters 13–21*, #1916.

160. Aquinas, ST I–II q. 68, q. 4, ad. 1; Williams, "Argument to Bliss," 512; Pinckaers, *Sources of Christian Ethics*, 180.

161. Aquinas, ST I–II, q. 68, a. 1, c; ST I–II, q. 68, a. 2, c; Pinckaers, *Sources of Christian Ethics*, 185.

virtues."[162] It is in this sense too that Aquinas considers the Holy Spirit as the origin of any truth that is spoken by us, be it natural or supernatural.[163]

The gifts of the Holy Spirit are categorized as "*habitus*,"[164] which could be translated as habits or as dispositions.[165] These gifts dispose us to be moved by God in a divine manner, preparing us for divine inspiration.[166] Thomas writes, "spiritual water has an eternal cause, that is, the Holy Spirit, who is the unfailing fountain of life."[167] The gifts provide a wonderful enhancement to human cognition. Faith of itself is blind and dark, in that one accepts God's revelation based on His authority.[168] It is the task of the intellectual gifts to enrich our faith "by a penetration and judgement of the supernatural truths proposed by faith."[169] In so doing the gifts mitigate against faith's intrinsic limitation, which is that it accepts truth unseen and uncomprehended. Thus, the gifts provide students with a check list to weigh what they learn against ultimate Truth, enabling them to form an integrated view of reality. Here each truth is assessed with reference to every other truth, forming and ordering one's intellect under First Truth.[170]

The end point of the gifts and the virtues are the fruits of the Holy Spirit.[171] They are not "*habitus*" but "some kind of actualization or manifestation of the virtues and gifts."[172] Thomas uses the terms "*actus*" and "*operatio*" when speaking of the fruits.[173] When replete with the fruits of the Holy Spirit, one not only witnesses to God naturally but also spiritually, "inasmuch as God is glorified among men by their good works."[174]

162. Pinsent, "Aquinas and the Second Person," 51.

163. Boland, *St. Thomas Aquinas*, 29.

164. Aquinas, ST I–II, q. 68, a. 3, c.

165. Pinsent, "Aquinas and the Second Person," 51.

166. Aquinas, ST I–II, q. 68, a. 1, c; Jenkins, *Knowledge and Faith*, 157; Williams, "Argument to Bliss," 512.

167. Aquinas, *Commentary on the Gospel of John, Chapters 1–5*, #586.

168. Aquinas, *Disputed Questions on Truth*, vol. 2, q. 14, a. 1.

169. Gulley, *Educational Philosophy*, 66.

170. Aquinas, *Commentary on the Gospel of John, Chapters 1–5*, #34.

171. Aquinas, ST I–II, q. 11, a. 3, c.

172. Pinsent, "Aquinas and the Second Person," 56.

173. Aquinas, ST II–II, q. 28, a. 4, c.

174. Aquinas, *Commentary on the Gospel of John, Chapters 1–5*, #116.

PEDAGOGICAL IMPLICATIONS OF THE HOLY SPIRIT'S TEACHING

What pedagogical implications follow from an appreciation of the primacy of the divine teacher in the Person of the Holy Spirit? Thomas says that God's Word is "a living Word and so in God besides the Word there is will and love . . . [and] just as the Word of God is the Son of God, so is God's love the Holy Spirit. Consequently, a man has the Holy Spirit when He loves God."[175] This is the Spirit's primary teaching function, to be the giver of life, and this not only for the individual but for the Church.[176] Aquinas states, "the soul's life is union with God, inasmuch as God is the life of the soul. . . . Now, the Holy Spirit unites us to God by love, for He is Himself God's love, which is why He gives life."[177] This is why the Catholic Church is a living entity. The more the Holy Spirit is animating the Church, the more alive it is and the more able it is to preserve the living tradition and to evangelize.

The example of the apostles demonstrates that God communicates to His creatures the dignity of secondary efficient causation.[178] Thomas holds that "where the Spirit of the Lord is, there is liberty, the reason being that He makes us love God and cease to love the world."[179] Hence teachers of the faith need to communicate the fact that freedom lies in a strong possession of God's divine Spirit.

It follows that there are tremendous benefits in opening classrooms to God's Holy Spirit. We could learn from Thomas how to do this. For Aquinas, prayer, and the teaching-learning relation are intimately interwoven. Prayer unites us with this divine guest and increases His ability to teach us.[180] We cannot know Christ through book learning, only through experience, says Thomas,[181] and such experience requires the action of the Holy Spirit within us because it is brought about through loving obedience, by our hearing the Father draw us to His Son.[182] Without seeking this union with God in prayer through the Spirit's agency, our intellects are not rightly subordinated to

---

175. Aquinas, *Aquinas Catechism*, 71.

176. Aquinas, *Aquinas Catechism*, 72.

177. Aquinas, *Aquinas Catechism*, 72.

178. Aquinas, *Commentary on the Gospel of John, Chapters 1–5*, #119; Gulley, *Educational Philosophy*, 38, 40; Sherwin, "Christ the Teacher," 184; Bonino, "Role of the Apostles," 318.

179. Aquinas, *Aquinas Catechism*, 72.

180. Aquinas, ST II–II, q. 180, a. 3, ad. 4; see Aquinas, *Aquinas Catechism*, 107.

181. Aquinas, *Commentary on the Gospel of John, Chapters 1–5*, #293.

182. Aquinas, *Commentary on the Gospel of John, Chapters 1–5*, #294: Aquinas, *Commentary on the Gospel of John, Chapters 13–21*, #2487.

First Truth, the source of all truth, and are instead subject to pride and a godless autonomy.[183] The more personally united we are to this truth, the better we integrate singular truths with ultimate truth. We learn according to what we receive from God, hence the more we open ourselves in prayer to divine illumination the stronger our intellects will be.[184] Aquinas states, "we should prepare our soul by prayer, and we do this by going to God through our desires," using the interior impulses of the Holy Spirit.[185]

There is an urgent need for moral formation in the process of education. While Thomas holds that there is objective reality which can be known, we can err in our judgement about reality because of defects in our character.[186] Aquinas says that it is the evil in man that has him love the world and not the things of the spirit.[187] Carnal vice weakens the operation of our intellect by impairing our judgement and our understanding of first principles.[188] Thomas teaches that likeness is a cause of love[189] because the more like God we are the more perfect is our love of God and hence our union with Him.[190]

A Thomistic pedagogy of education, then, will insist upon moral rectitude and the control of one's passions by reason, in order to be well taught by God's Holy Spirit and others.[191] For "if a man is to become wise he must first achieve an inner tranquility."[192] He goes on to state that happiness, our last end, cannot inhabit a violent or coercive person.[193] Here God's Holy Spirit cannot abide. Thus, we need moral as well as intellective development, which terminates in rest, in completeness of self.[194]

The more moral goodness we possess the more we absorb God's goodness and His good teaching because "whatever is received into something is received according to the condition [nature] of the recipient."[195]

183. Aquinas, *How to Study*, 21.

184. Aquinas, *Summa Contra Gentiles, Book Two*, c. 75.

185. Aquinas, *Commentary on the Gospel of John, Chapters 1–5*, #680.

186. Smith, "Come and See," 197.

187. Aquinas, *Commentary on the Gospel of John, Chapters 1–5*, #139; Smith, "Come and See," 205.

188. Aquinas, ST II–II, q. 15, a. 3, c.

189. Aquinas, ST I–II, q. 27, a. 3, c.

190. Aquinas, *Commentary on the Gospel of John, Chapters 1–5*, #753; ST II–II, q. 45, a. 2, c; Smith, "Come and See," 200.

191. Boland, "Thomas Aquinas," 51.

192. Aquinas, *Commentary on Aristotle's De Anima*, bk. 1, l. 8.

193. Aquinas, *Commentary on Aristotle's De Anima*, bk. 1, l. 8.

194. Davies, "Aquinas and the Academic Life," 341.

195. Aquinas, ST I, q. 75, a. 5, c.

Thus Aquinas stresses the role of love in the attainment of truth.[196] This ultimate concern for moral formation is for personal moral formation, not some politicized version. Aquinas would have no interest in educational pedagogies that are merely virtue signaling or involve a form of political morality that does not happen under God, because this necessarily ends in a denial of personal morality which frustrates the complete development of the human person. Our moral goodness also makes us better teachers and witnesses to God's glory.[197]

In general, we need to be open to the action of God's Spirit in the human relationship that is teaching and learning. All understanding and character development is ultimately sourced from God and happens under God's primary agency.[198] Aquinas writes that, even for the learner, the "intelligence gives being only to the extent that the divine power is in it."[199] Thus it is that the perfection of our rational powers of operation are maximized according to the measure of God's reign within us, which is brought about by the action of the Holy Spirit.[200] Our capacity to receive the Godhead is dependent on our purity of heart and charity.[201] In other words, it depends on our openness to the Spirit's internal teaching. We need to cooperate as much as possible by listening to this internal teacher who teaches wisdom by His words.[202] Boland writes,

> If the acquisition of the cardinal virtues, and the developmental understanding of the human being that it presupposes, is directly connected with teaching and learning, so the level of grace and the theological virtues must also be related to teaching and learning. For Aquinas, it becomes a question of a lifestyle that will support the acquisition and living out of this vision.[203]

CONCLUSION

The fullness of our human development is not complete without adhering to the divine interior teacher. So, a completely integral education cannot be Godless. From the beginning, the Spirit must condition it, for God is

196. Aquinas, *Commentary on the Gospel of John, Chapters 6–12*, #947.

197. Aquinas, *Commentary on the Gospel of John, Chapters 1–5*, #116.

198. Aquinas, ST I, q. 88, a. 3, ad. 1.

199. Aquinas, *On Creation*, q. 3, a. 7.

200. Aquinas, ST I, q. 105, a. 3, c; Boland, "What Happens When Minds Meet," 12.

201. Aquinas, *Commentary on the Gospel of John, Chapters 13–21*, #1855.

202. Aquinas, *Commentary on the Gospel of John, Chapters 13–21*, #1776.

203. Boland, *St. Thomas Aquinas*, 201.

the minds' ultimate *telos*. Human teaching needs to reflect the nature of God in that "it must be true and it must be whole."[204] In this way the learner will be encouraged to pursue what is most excellent in life with a discerning spirit capable of right judgement about reality. For this to occur, the teacher needs to be able to direct "the attention of the student toward the transcendent,"[205] in contrast to an approach that would either deny its existence (Existentialism) or avoid the question of the transcendent altogether (the Pragmatist approach).[206] To be open to a first or ultimate being provides a unifying element to human formation. It will not be random. When we do not know God as our Primary Teacher, we do not know ourselves for what we are truly meant to be and thus knowledge of our ultimate end cannot inform our free agency.

BIBLIOGRAPHY

Aquinas, Thomas. *The Academic Sermons: Mediaeval Continuation*. Translated by Mark-Robin Hoogland. Washington DC: The Catholic University of America Press, 2010.

———. *The Aquinas Catechism*. Translated and edited by Ralph McInerny. Manchester, NH: Sophia Institute, 2000.

———. *Commentary on Aristotle's "De Anima."* Translated by Kenelm Foster and Silvester Humphries. South Bend, IN: Dumb Ox, 1994.

———. *Commentary on the Gospel of John, Chapters 1–5*. Translated by Fabian R. Larcher and James A. Weisheiplg. Washington, DC: The Catholic University of America Press, 2010.

———. *Commentary on the Gospel of John, Chapters 6–12*. Translated by Fabian R. Larcher and James A. Weisheipl. Washington, DC: The Catholic University of America Press, 2010.

———. *Commentary on the Gospel of John, Chapters 13–21*. Translated by Fabian R. Larcher and James A. Weisheipl. Washington, DC: The Catholic University of America Press, 2010.

———. *Commentary on the "Metaphysics" of Aristotle*. Translated by John P. Rowan. Chicago: Regnery, 1962.

———. *Commentary on the "Posterior Analytics" of Aristotle*. Translated by Richard Berquist. South Bend, IN: Dumb Ox, 2007.

———. *Compendium of Theology*. Translated by Cyril Vollert. St. Louis: Herder, 1952.

———. *The Disputed Questions on Truth*. Vol. 2. Translated by James V. McGlynn. Chicago: Regnery, 1953.

———. *The Disputed Questions on Truth*. Vol. 3. Translated by Robert W. Schmidt. Chicago: Regnery, 1954.

204. Bayne, "God Is the Teacher," 265.
205. Collins, "Aristotle," 69.
206. Collins, "Aristotle," 78; Donohue, *St. Thomas Aquinas and Education*, 11.

———. *Faith, Reason, and Theology: Questions I–IV of the Commentary on Boethius' "De Trinitate."* Translated by Armand Maurer. Toronto: Pontifical Institute of Mediaeval Studies, 1987.

———. *How to Study: Being the Letter of St. Thomas Aquinas to Brother John de Modo Studenti.* Translated by Victor White. London: Aquin, 1953.

———. *The Literal Exposition of Job: A Scriptural Commentary concerning Providence.* Translated by Anthony Damico. Atlanta: Scholars, 1989.

———. *On Creation [Quaestiones Disputatae De Potentia Dei, Q. 3].* Translated by Susan C. Selner-Wright. Washington, DC: The Catholic University of America Press, 2010.

———. *On Spiritual Creatures.* Translated by Mary C. Fitzpatrick. Milwaukee, WI: Marquette University Press, 1951.

———. *On the Uniqueness of the Intellect against the Averroists.* Translated by Ralph McInerny. West Lafayette, IN: Purdue University Press, forthcoming.

———. *The Power of God.* Translated by the English Dominican Fathers. London: Burns, Oates, and Washbourne, 1932–34.

———. *Questions on the Soul.* Translated by James H. Robb. Milwaukee, WI: Marquette University Press, 1984.

———. *Scriptum Super Libros Sententiarum [Sentences].* Edited by Pierre Mandonnet and Maria Moos. Paris: Lethieulleux, 1929.

———. *Selected Writings.* Edited and translated by Ralph McInerny. London: Penguin, 1998.

———. *Summa Contra Gentiles, Book One.* Translated by Anton C. Pegis. London: University of Notre Dame Press, 2014.

———. *Summa Contra Gentiles, Book Two.* Translated by James F. Anderson. South Bend, IN: University of Notre Dame Press, 2012.

———. *Summa Contra Gentiles, Book Three, Part 1.* Translated by Vernon J. Bourke. South Bend, IN: University of Notre Dame Press, 2012.

———. *Summa Contra Gentiles, Book Three, Part 2.* Translated by Vernon J. Bourke. South Bend, IN: University of Notre Dame Press, 2009.

———. *Summa Contra Gentiles, Book Four.* Translated by Charles J. O'Neil. South Bend, IN: University of Notre Dame Press, 2013.

———. *Summa Theologiae.* Translated by the English Dominican Fathers. New York: Christian Classics, 1981.

———. *The Teacher, the Mind (Truth, Questions X, XI).* Translated by James McGlynn. Chicago: Regnery, 1962.

Bayne, Stephen. "God Is the Teacher." In *The Christian Idea of Education: Papers and Discussions*, edited by Edmund Fuller and William G. Pollard, 255–65. New Haven, CT: Yale University Press, 1957.

Boland, Vivian. *St. Thomas Aquinas.* Edited by Richard Bailey. Vol. 1. Bloomsbury Library of Educational Thought. London: Bloomsbury, 2014.

———. "St. Thomas's Sermon *Puer Iesus*: A Neglected Source for His Understanding of Teaching and Learning." *New Blackfriars* 88 (2007) 457–70.

———. "Thomas Aquinas, Catholic Education, and the Transcendental Properties of Truth, Goodness, Beauty, and Integrity." In *Education in a Catholic Perspective*, edited by Stephen McKinney and John Sullivan, 49–64. London: Routledge, 2013.

———. "Truth, Knowledge, and Communication: Thomas Aquinas on the Mystery of Teaching." *Studies in Christian Ethics* 19 (2006) 287–304.

———. "What Happens When Minds Meet: Thomas Aquinas on the Mystery of Teaching and Learning." *Doctrine and Life* 56 (2006) 3–17.

Bonino, Serge-Thomas. "The Role of the Apostles in the Communication of Revelation according to the *Lectura Super Ioannem* of St. Thomas Aquinas." In *Reading John with St. Thomas Aquinas: Theological Exegesis and Speculative Theology*, edited by Michael Dauphinais and Matthew Levering, 318–46. Washington, DC: The Catholic University of America Press, 2005.

Burrell, David. "Creation in St. Thomas Aquinas's *Super Evangelium S. Joannis Lectura*." In *Reading John with St. Thomas Aquinas Theological Exegesis and Speculative Theology*, edited by Michael Dauphinais and Matthew Levering, 115–38. Washington, DC: The Catholic University of America Press, 2005.

Catholic Truth Society. *New Testament and Psalms the CTS New Catholic Bible*. Vicenza: Catholic Truth Society, 2012.

Collins, Peter. "Aristotle and the Philosophy of Intellectual Education." *Irish Journal of Education* 24 (1990) 62–88.

Davies, Brian. "Aquinas and the Academic Life." *New Blackfriars* 83 (2002) 336–46.

———. "Aquinas on Teaching and Learning." *New Blackfriars* 95 (2014) 631–47.

Donohue, John. *St. Thomas Aquinas and Education*. New York: Random House, 1968.

Gulley, Anthony. *The Educational Philosophy of Saint Thomas Aquinas*. New York: Pageant, 1964.

Hibbs, Thomas. *Dialectic and Narrative in Aquinas: An Interpretation of the Summa Contra Gentiles*. South Bend, IN: University of Notre Dame Press, 1995.

Jenkins, John. *Knowledge and Faith in Thomas Aquinas*. Cambridge: Cambridge University Press, 1997.

Lamb, Matthew. "Eternity and Time in St. Thomas Aquinas' Lectures on St. John's Gospel." In *Reading John with St. Thomas Aquinas: Theological Exegesis and Speculative Theology*, edited by Michael Dauphinais and Matthew Levering, 127–39. Washington, DC: The Catholic University of America Press, 2005.

Levering, Matthew. *Participatory Biblical Exegesis: A Theology of Biblical Interpretation*. South Bend, IN: University of Notre Dame Press, 2008.

Mayer, Mary. *The Philosophy of Teaching of St. Thomas Aquinas*. Milwaukee, WI: Bruce, 1929.

Moran, Gabriel. "Revelation as Teaching-Learning." *Religious Education* 95 (2000) 269–83.

Ozolins, Janis. "Aquinas and His Understanding of Teaching and Learning." In *Aquinas, Education, and the East*, edited by Thomas Brian Mooney and Mark Nowacki, 9–25. Dordrecht: Springer, 2013.

Pinckaers, Servais. *The Sources of Christian Ethics*. Translated by Mary Thomas Noble. Washington, DC: The Catholic University of America Press, 1995.

Pinsent, Andrew. "Aquinas and the Second Person in the Formation of Virtues." In *Aquinas, Education, and the East*, edited by Thomas Brian Mooney and Mark Nowacki, 47–71. Dordrecht: Springer, 2013.

Shannon, G. J. "Aquinas on the Teacher's Art." *Clergy Review* 31 (1949) 375–85.

Sherwin, Michael. "Christ the Teacher in St. Thomas's Commentary on the Gospel of John." In *Reading John with St. Thomas Aquinas: Theological Exegesis and Speculative Theology*, edited by Michael Dauphinais and Matthew Levering, 173–93. Washington, DC: The Catholic University of America Press, 2005.

Smith, Janet. "Come and See." In *Reading John with St. Thomas Aquinas: Theological Exegesis and Speculative Theology*, edited by Michael Dauphinais and Matthew Levering, 194–211. Washington, DC: The Catholic University of America Press, 2005.

Velde, Rudi te. "Natural Reason in the Summa Contra Gentiles." In *Thomas Aquinas: Contemporary Philosophical Perspectives*, edited by Brian Davies, 117–40. New York: Oxford University Press, 2002.

Williams, Anna. "Argument to Bliss: The Epistemology of the Summa Theologiae." *Modern Theology* 20 (2004) 505–26.

12

THE HOLY SPIRIT IN IGNATIAN SPIRITUALITY

Robin Koning, SJ

FOR A TEXT CALLED the *Spiritual Exercises*, which lies at the heart of Ignatian spirituality and is renowned for opening countless people to spiritual renewal, it is surprising that the Holy Spirit does not feature prominently. What are we to make of this paucity of explicit references to the Spirit in the text which lies at the very heart of Ignatian spirituality?

To answer this question, I begin by exploring the historical context which rendered problematic any emphasis on the Holy Spirit at the time Ignatius was composing the *Exercises*. I proceed to an initial examination of the *Exercises*, focusing solely on overt references to the Spirit. I then look at two later texts—Ignatius' spiritual diary and two founding documents of the Society of Jesus (the Formula of the Institute and the Constitutions) which he composed. This will reveal the significant role the Spirit played in his own spiritual life and in his vision of how the Society should operate. In this light, I return to the *Exercises* themselves for a deeper examination going beyond the overt references to the Spirit. Having shown the problematic nature of one attempt to include the Holy Spirit more explicitly in the *Exercises*, I then show how they do in fact allude in significant ways to the Spirit's role.

HISTORICAL CONTEXT

The historical context in which Ignatius found himself provided good reasons for downplaying the place of the Holy Spirit in Christian life. Ever since the controversy around Joachim Fiore in the thirteenth century, Church authorities had suspected various movements of unorthodox teachings about the Holy Spirit.[1] Though they did not call themselves this, members of these movements came to be known as *Alumbrados* (Enlightened Ones), a name which "originated as a term of mockery, abuse and accusation."[2] The goal of the spiritual life for such people was abandonment to the divine will, understood as a passive reliance on God to which any activity was an obstacle, including asking God for anything, meditating on Christ's humanity, or engaging in any particular form of prayer.[3]

The *Alumbrado* problem was not simply the broader context in which Ignatius operated but had a direct impact on his life. Various people believed that the *Alumbrado* spirit tainted Ignatius' spirituality, and it was precisely these suspicions that led to his appearances before the Inquisition on a number of occasions. The issues at stake are evident from an encounter with the Dominicans in Salamanca that Ignatius recounts in his autobiography.[4] Having told the friars that in his spiritual conversations with people he would speak about virtues and vices, praising the former and criticizing the latter, Ignatius faced this response:

> You aren't learned . . . and you're speaking of virtues and vices. About this no one can speak except in one of two ways: either through learning or through the Holy Spirit. If it's not learning, then it's the Holy Spirit. *And this point: that it is of the Holy Spirit, is what we would like to know about.* (#65)

Ignatius recognized the danger of this line of questioning, doubtless because he was aware of the context of suspicion about the *Alumbrados'* emphasis on the direct inspiration of the Spirit. He replied that he would not speak further except to those who had authority to question him. So, the Dominicans reported him to the Inquisition where he was eventually vindicated with the warning that, if he wished to continue to speak about such matters, he would need to do some study (#70).

This experience at Salamanca, along with other experiences before the Inquisition in Alcala and Paris, seem to have had their impact on the *Exercises*. There Ignatius shows great restraint in his references to the Holy Spirit, as we shall now see.

---

1. Sachs, "Spirit of the Risen Lord," 22.

2. O'Leary, "Mysticism," 84.

3. O'Leary, "Mysticism," 85.

4. The version of Ignatius' autobiography used here may be found in Ignatius of Loyola, "Reminiscences." References to paragraph numbers will be in the text.

THE HOLY SPIRIT IN THE SPIRITUAL EXERCISES

There are eight explicit mentions of the Holy Spirit in the *Exercises*.[5] Six of these are in points for meditation on five different scriptural passages, four of them being direct quotations from Scripture (in italics here) while the other two are Ignatius' paraphrase:

- The Visitation: "*Elizabeth, full of the Holy Spirit, cried out*" (#263).

- The Baptism of the Lord: "*The Holy Spirit came*" (#273).

- The appearance of the Risen Jesus in the upper room: "He gives them the Holy Spirit, saying, '*Receive the Holy Spirit*'" (#304).

- The Great Commission: "*Go and teach all peoples, baptizing them in the name of the Father and of the Son and of the Holy Spirit*" (#307).

- Jesus instructing his disciples in Acts 1 to await Pentecost: "He ordered them to wait in Jerusalem for the Holy Spirit" (#312).

These Scriptural allusions were safe enough for no one could fault them without accusing the Evangelists themselves of being *Alumbrados*.

The most significant references occur in a paragraph crafted by Ignatius himself in which the Holy Spirit is mentioned not just once but twice. In the Rules *Sentire Cum Ecclesia*, i.e., Rules for Thinking or Feeling with the Church, we read:

> To maintain a right mind in all things we must always maintain that the white I see, I shall believe to be black, if the hierarchical Church so stipulates; for we believe that between Christ our Lord, the bridegroom, and the Church, His bride, there is *the same Spirit* who governs and directs us for the good of our souls because it is by that *same Spirit* and Lord of us all who gave the Ten Commandments that our holy mother Church is directed and governed. (#365; emphasis added)

Here, with great clarity, we see Ignatius undermining any possible accusation of being an *Alumbrado*, situating his references to the Spirit squarely within an ecclesial context. The Holy Spirit who "governs and directs us for the good of our souls" is the same Spirit who directs and governs the Church, who unites the Church as bride to Christ as Bridegroom, and who reveals the basis of the moral life in the ten commandments. This is significant since the *Alumbrados*, along with their emphasis on the personal,

---

5. The version of the *Spiritual Exercises* used here may be found in Ignatius of Loyola, *Spiritual Exercises*. References to paragraph numbers will be in the text.

interior movement of the Holy Spirit, manifested a dismissive attitude to the authority of the Church and to its external rituals.[6]

Thus, operating as he was in a climate of suspicion of appeals to the Holy Spirit because they often came hand-in-hand with contempt for the visible Church, in the *Exercises* Ignatius makes clear his respect for the Church and its structures while being very circumspect in his explicit references to the Holy Spirit, limiting them to direct quotes from Scripture or comments on such quotes, and two references affirming the intimate nexus between the Spirit and the Church.

THE HOLY SPIRIT IN THE SPIRITUAL DIARY

This lack of explicit reference to the Holy Spirit in the *Exercises* is all the more striking when we look at the important role the Spirit plays in Ignatius' own spiritual life. We find clear evidence of this in the notebook, known as his Spiritual Diary or Spiritual Journal, in which he noted the daily movements of different spirits within him, especially when he was praying or celebrating Mass. The only extant section of his journal covers the period of just over a year from February 2, 1544 until February 17, 1545.[7]

A number of the many mystical experiences Ignatius records in his journal involve the Holy Spirit. Sometimes these are experiences of all three persons of the Trinity with the particular part of each person clearly differentiated, as in this entry:

> After I had unvested and was praying at the altar, once more the same Being and spherical vision allowed itself to be seen: in some way I saw all three Persons as I had seen the first, viz, the Father in one part, the Son in another and the Holy Spirit

---

6. O'Leary, "Mysticism," 85. O'Leary notes further: "Much of our knowledge of the early expression of *alumbradismo* (around the 1520s) comes from an edict of faith issued by the Inquisitor General in 1525" (84–85). Thus, the edict is contemporaneous with the pilgrim Ignatius soon after his conversion. This edict condemned propositions which "expressed contempt for the cult of the saints, the worship of images, bulls, indulgences, fasting, abstinence and the commandments of the Church" (85). Far from showing contempt for these practices, Ignatius explicitly praises or esteems many of them in his Rules for Thinking with the Church: "We should praise the cult of the saints, venerating their relics and praying to the saints themselves, praising also the stations, pilgrimages, indulgences, jubilees, dispensations and the lighting of candles in churches. . . . We should praise the decrees about fasting and abstinence. . . . Finally, we should praise all the precepts of the Church" (##358–59, 361).

7. The version of the Spiritual Diary used here may be found in Ignatius of Loyola, "Spiritual Diary." It is customary to reference the diary by the date of the entries, which will be given in the text.

in another, all three coming forth or having their derivation from the Divine Essence, without leaving the spherical vision. On feeling and seeing this, new impulses and tears. (Thursday, March 6)

At other times, his experiences are associated with one or other divine person. Of relevance for our theme, some of these are of the Holy Spirit alone:

> A little later I made a colloquy with the Holy Spirit, in preparation for saying His mass; I experienced the same devotion and tears, and seemed to see or feel Him in a dense clarity or in the colour of burning flame—a way quite strange to me. (Monday, February 11)

> Throughout mass, a gentle flow of tears, very copious; the same after mass: before mass I felt the impulse to weep and felt or saw the Holy Spirit Himself; complete submission. (Saturday, March 22)

In another entry, Ignatius makes a point of specifying that he experienced movements associated with the Spirit but not the other two persons:

> I felt intense devotion and wept on feeling or seeing in some way the Holy Spirit . . . and I could neither see nor feel either of the other two Divine Persons in this way. (Monday, February 11)

As with his experiences in prayer, so too with his interlocutors, Ignatius sometimes speaks to all three persons of the Trinity and sometimes to one or other person. In this entry, he addresses each person individually, and then the Trinity:

> Later while I prepared the altar and vested, there came to me: "Eternal Father, confirm me"; "Eternal Son, confirm me"; "Eternal Holy Spirit, confirm me"; "Holy Trinity, confirm me"; "My One Sole God, confirm me." I repeated this many times with great force, devotion and tears, and very deeply did I feel it. And when I asked once, "Eternal Father, will you not confirm me?" I knew he would: so also with Son and Holy Spirit. (Monday, February 18)

While more often his interlocutors are the Father or the Son, in one entry, already noted above, he makes a colloquy with the Holy Spirit (Monday February 11).

On occasion, Ignatius also prays for the gift of the Holy Spirit:

> I prayed to Our Lady, then to the Son, and to the Father, that He
> might give me his Spirit. (Monday, February 11)

Five days later, he prays to be able to experience the movement of the Spirit:

> With this same warmth, I implored grace to reason with His
> spirit and to be moved by that spirit. (Saturday, February 16)[8]

Elsewhere Ignatius is illuminated in relation to the role of the Spirit in the
economy of salvation, alongside that of the Father and the Son:

> At this moment other lights came to me, namely, how the Son
> first sent the Apostles to preach in poverty, and afterwards, the
> Holy Spirit, giving His Spirit and the gift of tongues, confirmed
> them, and thus the Father and the Son sending the Holy Spirit,
> all Three Persons confirmed the mission. (Monday, February 11)

The Spiritual Journal also points to Ignatius' devotion to the Holy
Spirit in the number of votive Masses of the Holy Spirit that he offers. For
the period covered by the extant part of his spiritual journal, Ignatius makes
notes on his spiritual experience during some 359 Masses. For about a third
of these, he notes what Mass he is saying—whether it is the Mass of the day,
a feast day or a votive Mass. Of the seventy votive Masses, ten are Masses of
the Holy Spirit, while another twenty-nine are Masses of the Blessed Trinity.

These texts reveal in how intimate and profound a way the Holy Spirit
acted within Ignatius' spiritual life. This only serves to highlight, by way of
contrast, the paucity of references to the Spirit in the *Spiritual Exercises*.

THE HOLY SPIRIT IN THE FOUNDING DOCUMENTS OF THE SOCIETY OF JESUS

If the Holy Spirit features prominently in Ignatius' own spiritual life, so does
the Spirit feature in significant ways in his vision of how the Society of Jesus
should operate. We can see this in two key foundational documents of the
Society—the Formula of the Institute and the Constitutions.[9] While there

---

8. Surprisingly, the translators translate "spirit" here with no capital, though the
context would suggest that this could well be a reference to the Holy Spirit. William
Young (Ignatius of Loyola, "Spiritual Journal") in his translation certainly uses capitals
for both references to "spirit" here. I have not had the opportunity to ascertain whether
there is ambiguity in Ignatius' handwritten text.

9. The version of the Formula of the Institute and the Constitutions used in this
chapter will be those found in Society of Jesus, "Constitutions." References will be in the
text, with the Constitutions referred to simply by paragraph number while the Formula
will be referred to by the paragraph number preceded by "Formula." The Formula of the

are other ways in which the Spirit is alluded to in these documents, I will focus on the explicit references only as these will give us enough of a sense of how significant a role he sees the Spirit should have in the ongoing life of the Society he is founding.

In the Formula, we find three references to the Holy Spirit. Firstly, the Spirit is at work in the diversity within unity of the Society. While Jesuits are united in that they should all keep before their eyes and live according to the Society's Institute, each is to do so "according to the grace which the Holy Spirit has given to him" (Formula #1). Secondly, Ignatius holds together the work of the Holy Spirit and the Church's structure as we have already seen in the *Exercises*. The Formula states one reason for some Jesuits to make a special vow of obedience to the Pope is "for the sake of . . . surer direction of the Holy Spirit" (Formula #3). Far from ecclesial authority being opposed to the direction of the Holy Spirit, it is seen as guaranteeing the Spirit's "surer direction." Thirdly, the Spirit moves people to their vocations and offers them grace to live out their vocation. Hence candidates for the Society should "ponder long and seriously . . .whether the Holy Spirit who moves them is offering them so much grace that with his aid they have hope of bearing the weight of this vocation" (Formula #4).

In the Constitutions themselves, Ignatius mentions the role of the Holy Spirit at significant points in three different contexts. Firstly, in the Preamble to the Constitutions proper, Ignatius makes a statement of principle about the respective roles of the Holy Spirit and the written word of the Constitutions in relation to the goal of preserving, directing and carrying forward the Society: "what helps most toward this end must be, more than any exterior constitution, the interior law of charity and love which the Holy Spirit writes and imprints upon hearts" (#134).

Secondly, the Spirit will guide superiors in matters the Constitutions do not provide for, or where they do offer some guidelines which it will be up to the Superior to determine how to apply in concrete situations. Ignatius notes four such situations:

1. Should a professed member of the Society need to be dismissed, a circumstance Ignatius can hardly imagine would arise, he offers no guidelines except that "the charity and discretion of the Holy Spirit will indicate the manner which ought to be used" (#219).

Institute was a broad outline for their proposed new religious institute which Ignatius and his first companions presented to Pope Paul III for his approval, which he gave in 1540. Ten years later, Pope Julius III approved another version of the Formula, revised and expanded somewhat in light of experience. It is this revised version of the Formula to which I refer in this chapter.

2. During their formation, Jesuit scholastics "ought to be instructed about the manner of acting proper to a member of the Society, who has to associate with so great a diversity of persons throughout such varied places." Given this diversity of people and situations, the Constitutions can but offer suggestions which might "help and prepare for the effect that is to be produced by divine grace." But in reality, "all this can be taught only by the unction of the Holy Spirit [1 John 2:20, 27] and by the prudence which God our Lord communicates to those who trust in his Divine Majesty" (#414).

3. In Part VII, Chapter 2, "The Missions Received from the Superior of the Society," the Constitutions set out criteria as to places to which Jesuits might be sent and ministries in which they might be engaged in those places. In this context, Ignatius first states a general principle about the role of the Holy Spirit in all decisions a superior makes and then applies this in particular to the question of the missioning of Jesuits: "it is the supreme providence and direction of the Holy Spirit that must efficaciously bring us to make the right decision in all matters, and to send to each place those who are best fitted and suited to the people and tasks for which they are sent" (#624). In this same section, he further applies this to the question of how many Jesuits to assign to a particular place. Generally it is good to send two rather than one on his own, but the superior might send more "accordingly as the unction of the Holy Spirit inspires him or as he judges in the sight of his Divine Majesty to be better and more expedient" (#624).

4. In relation to the sorts of men who might be admitted to the Society, Ignatius sets out a series of criteria before concluding that "the measure to be observed in all things will be taught by holy unction of the Divine Wisdom [1 John 2:20, 27] to those who are charged with this matter" (#161).[10]

Thirdly, the remaining references to the Spirit in the Constitutions concern the election of the Superior General. On the day of the election, the

---

10. It is true that the Holy Spirit is not mentioned explicitly here, but rather "the Divine Wisdom." It is also the case that, elsewhere in the Constitutions, Jesus is referred to as "the Eternal Wisdom" (##705, 708) while in a number of places the referent for "Wisdom" is not evident—whether it is the Spirit, Jesus, the Father, or simply "God" (#136 ["the Most Perfect and Infinite Wisdom"], #243 ["Divine Wisdom"], #284 ["the Eternal Goodness and Wisdom"], #307 ["the Divine and Eternal Wisdom"], #711 ["the First and Supreme Wisdom"]). But in this paragraph, given the references to 1 John, one can readily understand Ignatius to mean "the Holy Spirit" since he uses these same scriptural references explicitly in relation to the unction of the Holy Spirit in #414 as noted in point 2 above.

participants in the General Congregation are to celebrate the Mass of the Holy Spirit (#697) and then to pray the *Veni Creator Spiritus* (#698). Ignatius allows the possibility of someone being chosen by popular acclamation, in which case no voting is needed "for the Holy Spirit who has moved them to such an election supplies for all procedures and arrangements" (#700). If this is not the case, the election proceeds. In this case, after all have written their votes, before they are handed in and counted, the "grace of the Holy Spirit" is invoked once more (#701).

Hence we find in the Constitutions that Ignatius speaks of the Spirit's role in a number of situations: in the initial discernment by the candidate; in the discernment of the Society as to their admission; in forming Jesuits in how to minister in disparate contexts; in how each Jesuit is to live out the Jesuit way of life; in the dismissal of Jesuits; in decisions about missioning of Jesuits and in the election of a Superior General. Moreover, Ignatius makes two general statements about the overall role of the Holy Spirit, not confined to any particular situation—that it is the Holy Spirit who must guide us in making the right decision in all matters and that the inner law of love written in our hearts by the Spirit will be more helpful than any written law. In all this, Ignatius describes the activities of the Spirit using a range of terms: giving grace; moving people; writing and imprinting in human hearts; indicating; teaching; providing; directing; bringing us to make right decisions; and inspiring.

So even by just looking at the explicit references to the Holy Spirit, we find in the Constitutions a rich understanding of the Holy Spirit's role in the life of the Society.

THE HOLY SPIRIT IN THE SPIRITUAL EXERCISES REVISITED

Our review in the previous two sections of explicit references to the Holy Spirit in Ignatius' Spiritual Diary and in the Constitutions has highlighted the important role of the Spirit both in Ignatius' own life and in the governance of the Society.[11] All of this only serves to underline, by way of contrast, the point made earlier about the lack of such explicit reference in the *Spiritual Exercises*. So, we return now to the Exercises to look at ways in which Ignatius refers to the Spirit in implicit ways. Before doing so, though,

---

11. Another area of investigation would be explicit references to the Spirit in Ignatius' letters. But given his extant correspondence contains over seven thousand letters, many of which are not readily available and have not been translated into English, such research is beyond the scope of this chapter.

we will look at one wrong turn that some commentators make in relation to the Spirit and the Exercises.

A Problematic Way of Introducing the Spirit into the Exercises

Some people have used Ignatius' concern about being associated with the *Alumbrados* to argue for a problematic adaptation of one form of prayer Ignatius proposes in the Exercises, namely the Triple Colloquy. In the Triple Colloquy, I am invited to enter into a colloquy or conversation firstly with Our Lady, asking her to join me in seeking a particular grace from her Son. I then go to Jesus and ask him in turn to join me in seeking this same grace from the Father. Finally, I go with Jesus to the Father to ask him for the same grace (##63, 147).

Some directors suggest that non-Catholics who are uncomfortable praying to Our Lady might replace her in the Triple Colloquy with the Holy Spirit, so that one prays first to the Spirit, then to Jesus and then to the Father. This is sometimes justified on the basis that the prayer is clearly meant to be trinitarian but that, because of sensitivities we have noted about the mention of the Holy Spirit at the time, Ignatius instead made Mary the first interlocutor in the Triple Colloquy.[12] As I have argued elsewhere, this proposal is problematic for a number of reasons.[13] Let me name just two for our purposes here.

Firstly, in the privacy of his Spiritual Diary, where, as we have seen, Ignatius shows no reticence in speaking of the Holy Spirit and even making a colloquy with the Spirit, we see him making a Triple Colloquy in precisely the form he gives us in the Exercises, namely going first to Mary, then to Jesus, and finally to the Father. Moreover, the grace he is seeking in this Triple Colloquy is precisely that the Father might give him the Spirit (Monday February 11).

Secondly, the suggestion that the Spirit might replace Mary in the Triple Colloquy is theologically problematic. The Triple Colloquy is structured as a prayer involving a twofold mediation. We do not simply speak to Mary and then to Jesus and then to the Father. Rather, we ask Mary to intercede for us with Jesus, and for Jesus to intercede for us before the Father. It makes no sense to ask the Spirit to obtain a grace for us from Jesus when the Spirit,

---

12. Anderson, "Reflections," 18; Chadwick, "Giving the Exercises in Ecumenical Context," 38; Huggett, "Ignatian Spirituality Hooks Protestants," 33; Veltri, *Orientations*, vol. 2, ch. 8.

13. Koning, "Revisiting," 154–59.

who is God, is quite capable of giving any grace. This would be suggesting the Spirit is subordinate to Jesus and to the Father.

Some might argue that a similar argument could be made about having Jesus as an intercessor in the Triple Colloquy. Is this not also theologically problematic, making Jesus subordinate to the Father? William Young points out that this issue was in fact raised by some early opponents of the *Spiritual Exercises*.[14] This issue is readily resolved in light of the distinction between the two natures of Jesus. Ignatius is of course speaking about Jesus in his humanity. There is ample scriptural warrant for Jesus, after his Ascension to the Father, acting as intercessor through his human nature. St. Paul speaks of Jesus as the one mediator between God and humankind (cf. 1 Tim 2:5–6), interceding for us at God's right hand (cf. Rom 8:34). Likewise St. John refers to Jesus as our advocate with the Father (cf. 1 John 2:1) while Hebrews states that the ascended Jesus "always lives to make intercession" (Heb 7:25).[15]

The early Jesuits were aware of the issue that some contemporaries saw with having Jesus as intercessor in the Triple Colloquy so that at least one of the early directories of the *Spiritual Exercises* recommends how to address this concern should it arise with a retreatant:

> As regards the second colloquy . . . where Christ is addressed as mediator to obtain from the Father the graces mentioned there, an explanation ought to be given to less well educated persons. They should be told that while it is true that in his divine nature, by which he is equal to the Father, it is Christ's role to bestow grace and not to ask for it, nevertheless in his human nature,

14. Ignatius, "Spiritual Journal," 224n26. The context of Young's comment is the entry for Thursday 28 February in which Ignatius tells of a vision of Jesus at the foot of the Trinity. Young notes: "This exceptional and delicate representation of the one Mediator between God and men 'at the foot of the Most Holy Trinity,' scandalized P. M. Baumgarten, according to Father Larrahaga. It was also a source of scandal to some of the early opponents of the Spiritual Exercises, who looked with suspicion on the role given to the Son in the Triple Colloquy of Ignatius." Three other statements in Ignatius' journal would also concern these commentators as Ignatius seems to speak of Jesus as distinct from the Trinity. In one, he asks the saints to "pray to Our Lady and her Son to be intercessors . . . before the Blessed Trinity" (Monday, February 18). Later in the same prayer, he writes, "I made the concluded confirmation of my offering to the Blessed Trinity, giving thanks with great and intense affection, first to the Divine Persons, then to Our Lady and her Son" (Monday, February 18). Then on another day we read: "On entering the Chapel, greater impulses, more tears, all directed to the Blessed Trinity, and also, at times, to Jesus; at times the two were united or almost united. . . . At night I found I was turning in devotion to the Blessed Trinity and to Jesus so that they manifested themselves to my understanding, allowing me to catch sight of them in some way. . . . The intuition or vision of the Blessed Trinity and of Jesus continued for a while" (Sunday, March 9).

15. Scriptural quotations in this chapter are from the NRSV.

by which he is less than the Father, he can ask graces from the Father, from himself in his own divine nature, and from the Holy Spirit.[16]

Implicit References to the Holy Spirit in the Exercises

There are only a handful of references to the Spirit, most of them in direct quotations from Scripture passages that Ignatius proposes for prayer. Moreover, in the Fourth Week on the Resurrection, while Ignatius has contemplations on the Resurrection narratives and the Ascension, there is nothing on Pentecost.

We turn now to implicit references to the Spirit in the Exercises. I take it as given that the action of the Spirit is presumed throughout the Exercises, even if there is little by way of explicit reference.[17] For while we have seen that two of those explicit references set the Spirit's role firmly in an ecclesial context in paragraph 365, they do so not to deny the Spirit's action in individual human souls. Rather this paragraph affirms Ignatius' belief in such action for he states there that the Spirit who directs and governs the Church is the same Spirit who "governs and directs us for the good of our souls" (#365).

We begin our review of less explicit references to the Holy Spirit by noting that, in each prayer exercise, Ignatius would have the retreatant pray for a particular grace: I am invited "to ask God for what I want and desire" (#48 and passim). Now such graces are what the tradition refers to as actual graces as distinct from sanctifying grace. But all grace is the gift of the Spirit, as the *Catechism* notes:

> Grace is first and foremost the gift of the Spirit who justifies and sanctifies us. But grace also includes the gifts that the Spirit grants us to associate us with his work, to enable us to collaborate in the salvation of others and in the growth of the Body of Christ, the Church.[18]

Hence each time we pray for particular graces in the Exercises we are praying for gifts of the Spirit.

16. Palmer, *On Giving the Spiritual Exercises*, 128. The directories were more detailed instructions for people giving the *Spiritual Exercises*.

17. As one of the early directories of the Exercises puts it, "the primary role belongs to the Holy Spirit; it is the Holy Spirit who stirs the will, draws the soul to himself, and inflames it with the sweet fire of his charity." Palmer, *On Giving the Spiritual Exercises*, 206.

18. *CCC*, sec. 2003.

One such gift is the gift of freedom, the freedom of the children of God. St. Paul affirms that it is the Spirit who gives us this freedom: "Where the Spirit of the Lord is, there is freedom" (2 Cor 3:17). We are "called to freedom," to "live in the Spirit" (Gal 5:13,16). Yet Paul also knows that we can fall back into a spirit of unfreedom, of slavery (cf. Rom 8:15). The aim of the Exercises is to claim the freedom of the Spirit in any areas of our lives where we might be enslaved—what Ignatius calls disordered or ill-ordered attachments (##1, 21). The importance of this freedom is manifest in that Ignatius would have us pray repeatedly in the Second and Third Weeks, in that form of prayer called the Triple Colloquy which he suggests when a grace is particularly important, for the gift of "the highest spiritual poverty" by which I am completely free and open to whatever God may call me to (#147).

A key text in the Exercises is, of course, the set of guidelines known as the Rules for the Discernment of Spirits. Here Ignatius speaks about spiritual consolation in these terms:

> On spiritual consolation. I use the word "consolation" when any interior movement is produced in the soul that leads her to become inflamed with the love of her Creator and Lord, and when, as a consequence, there is no created thing on the face of the earth that we can love in itself, but we love it only in the Creator of all things.
>
> Similarly, I use the word "consolation" when one sheds tears that lead to love of one's Lord, whether these arise from grief over one's sins, or over the Passion of Christ Our Lord, or over other things expressly directed towards His service and praise.
>
> Lastly, I give the name "consolation" to every increase of hope, faith and charity, to all interior happiness that calls and attracts a person towards heavenly things and to the soul's salvation, leaving the soul quiet and at peace in her Creator and Lord. (#316)

Love, hope, faith, joy, peace, increase in hope, contrition for sin, compassion for Christ in his suffering—all of these are clearly gifts of the Spirit, some of which St. Paul lists in Galatians 5, where he calls them fruits of the Spirit. Ignatius himself makes this connection between consolation and the Spirit in his own Directory on the Exercises: the director "should give a full explanation of what consolation is, going through all its aspects, viz., inner peace, spiritual joy, hope, faith, love, tears, and elevation of mind, all of which are gifts of the Holy Spirit."[19]

19. Palmer, *On Giving the Spiritual Exercises*, 8.

Furthermore, in his instructions to directors at the start of the Exercises, Ignatius emphasizes that the director should be sparing in giving the retreatant points for prayer. If the retreatant comes to his or her own insights or appropriates the passage in a more personal way, this will be "more gratifying and spiritually profitable," whether this comes by way of one's own natural powers of reasoning or from the enlightenment of divine grace," (#2) that is, that grace which is a gift of the Spirit.

The clearest allusions to the Holy Spirit come in an important contemplation at the end of the Exercises. By this point, the contemplations on scriptural scenes have taken us through the life of Christ from infancy through his public ministry to his Passion and Resurrection. We noted earlier that Ignatius does not include Pentecost amongst the scenes to be contemplated. In fact, he explicitly states that the retreatant should pray through "all the Mysteries of the Resurrection . . . up to the Ascension inclusive" (#226).[20] To be sure, amongst the Resurrection scenes, he includes the "Johannine Pentecost" in which the Risen Jesus breathes on his disciples and says, "Receive the Holy Spirit" (John 20:22). But he does not draw any particular attention to it precisely as a Pentecost; it is simply listed as the sixth of thirteen Resurrection appearances to be contemplated (#304).[21] So the final scriptural contemplation in the Exercises is of the Ascension, leaves the retreatant, with the Apostles, awaiting the coming of the promised Spirit.

What we do have after the Ascension is a concluding contemplation, the *Contemplatio*, the Contemplation to Attain Divine Love. Throughout the Exercises, an important interpretive key as to the aim of each exercise is the grace which is to be prayed for. In the *Contemplatio*, I ask for "interior knowledge of all the good I have received so that acknowledging this with

20. Likewise, at the start of the Exercises, where Ignatius briefly notes the content of the four Weeks, he speaks of the content of this Fourth Week in terms of "the Resurrection and Ascension" (#4).

21. Ignatius presents the Risen Jesus as consoler in these contemplations on the Resurrection narratives. We are invited to "observe how Christ Our Lord fulfils the office of consoler, and to draw comparisons with the way friends are accustomed to console one another" (#224). O'Leary wonders whether this displacement of the role of consoler to the Risen Christ from the Holy Spirit, to whom this office is attributed in the Church's tradition, is a further sign of Ignatius' concern about emphasizing the Holy Spirit in the Exercises (O'Leary, "Consoler and Consolation, 64–65). But he then goes on to point to what appears to me to be the simplest explanation—that there is in fact no displacement of the Spirit's office onto Christ but rather in the Resurrection scenes Christ does act as consoler. So, for the apostles in the scenes the retreatant is contemplating, consolation comes from their engagement with the Risen Christ, whereas any consolation the retreatant experiences will be from the Holy Spirit. Jesus does, after all, speak of the Holy Spirit as "another consoler" (John 14:16), implying that he himself is truly a consoler. See also 1 John 2:1.

gratitude, I may be able to love and serve His Divine Majesty in everything" (#233). As St. Paul tells us, it is the Spirit who enables us to be aware of the God's gifts: "we have received . . . the Spirit that is from God, so that we may understand the gifts bestowed on us by God" (1 Cor 2:12).

In the body of the *Contemplatio*, Ignatius elaborates four points. In the first I am invited "to bring to memory the benefits received . . . pondering with great affection how much God Our Lord has done for me, and how much He has given me of what He has" (#234). Then, beyond the gifts God has given me, I am to consider also how "it is the Lord's wish, as far as He is able, to give me Himself" (#234). God does things for me and God gives me things. But true love between friends cannot be based simply on doing things for the other and giving gifts to the other, but must involve the gift of one's own self, a genuine self-communication. So too, God gives his own self. As Jonathon Sachs puts it in commenting on this text, "the name we give to the divine gift of self as truly communicated to us is Holy Spirit."[22]

In the second point, I am to ponder God's indwelling in creation: "how God dwells in creatures—in the elements, giving being, in the plants, causing growth, in the animals, producing sensation, and in humankind, granting the gift of understanding" (#235). While again, it does not mention the Spirit explicitly, Ignatius' text "corresponds well with central biblical themes concerning the Spirit as the creative presence and action of God in the world."[23] Ignatius goes further: God "dwells also in me, giving me being, life and sensation, and causing me to understand . . . He makes a temple of me" #235). This image of humans as temples of course draws on 1 Corinthian where Paul tells us that we are God's temples, and in particular, temples of the Holy Spirit: "Do you not know that you are God's temple and that God's Spirit dwells in you?" (1 Cor 3:16; cf. 6:19).[24]

In the third point, Ignatius invites me to "consider how God works and labours on my behalf in all created things on the face of the earth, i.e., 'He behaves in the same way as a person at work,' as in the heavens, elements, plants, fruits, cattle, etc, He gives being, conserves life, grants growth and feeling, etc." (#236). This text points to God's continuing labor; creation is not seen simply as God's action at the beginning, but as God's ongoing holding of creation in being and laboring within it.[25] This image makes clear that the Spirit who indwells all creation, and particularly human beings as

22. Sachs, "Spirit of the Risen Lord," 25.

23. Sachs, "Spirit of the Risen Lord," 26.

24. For the Spirit's indwelling, though without the image of the temple, see also Rom 8:9 ("The Spirit of God dwells in you.") and 2 Tim 1:14 ("Guard the good treasure entrusted to you, with the help of the Holy Spirit living in us.").

25. Sachs, "Spirit of the Risen Lord," 30.

temples, is not just an impersonal energy or force but involves the personal agency akin to that of a laborer.[26]

In the fourth and final point of the *Contemplatio*, I am invited to "see how all that is good and every gift descends from on high; so, my limited power descends from the supreme and infinite power above, and similarly justice, goodness, pity, mercy, etc, as rays descend from the sun, and waters from a fountain" (#237). Here, too, we find allusions to classic images of the Spirit—light, flowing water, and descending from above, as the Spirit descended on Jesus at his baptism.[27]

So, the *Contemplatio* presents a number of clear allusions to the Holy Spirit; as God's gift of his very self, as indwelling, as actively laboring and as descending from above. For this reason, Chechon Chong, reflecting in detail on the Holy Spirit's role in Ignatian spirituality, can conclude that the *Contemplatio* is in fact the Pentecost of the Exercises.[28]

After we have pondered each of these four points, I am invited by Ignatius to reflect on myself and how I might respond. He suggests that, just as God has given me all he possesses and all that he is, so I ought in gratitude to offer the Divine Majesty "everything I have, and myself as well" (#234). It is here that he proposes his great prayer of self-offering, his *Suscipe*:

> Take, Lord, and receive all my liberty, my memory, my understanding, and my entire will, all that I have and possess. You gave it all to me; to you Lord I give it all back. All is yours, dispose of it entirely according to your will. Give me the grace to love you, for that is enough for me. (#234)

Another common English translation renders the last line as "give me Thy love and Thy grace."[29] As we have seen, all grace is a gift of the Spirit, while Thomas speaks of love as a personal name of the Holy Spirit.[30] And so we can understand this final prayer of self-offering at the end of the Exercises as a plea for a further outpouring of the Spirit who has been active throughout the Exercises.

26. Though Ignatius does not make this connection, we might think of Paul's description in Romans 8 of God's action in creation as it groans in labor pains, with humans possessing the first fruits of the Spirit's action (Rom 8:22–23).

27. Sachs, "Spirt of the Risen Lord," 32. We find some of these images of the Spirit in the Sequence for Pentecost Sunday, e.g., the image of rays of light descending and of the Spirit descending. The biblical image of the Spirit being poured out also has resonances with this point of the *Contemplatio* (cf. Acts 2:17, 18, 33; Rom 5:5; Titus 3:6).

28. Chong, "Pneumatología de la espiritualidad." See especially sec. 4.2.2 "Contemplation to Achieve Love: The Ignatian Pentecost?"

29. Ignatius of Loyola, *Spiritual Exercises*, translated by Louis J. Puhl, #234.

30. Aquinas, *Summa Theologiae*, I, q. 37, a. 1.

CONCLUSION

So, we have shown how, despite the paucity of significant explicit references to the Holy Spirit, the *Spiritual Exercises* do in fact offer a wealth of allusions to the Spirit and to the Spirit's action in the life of the retreatant. Thus, they do not stand in discontinuity from the later Ignatian texts we explored—Ignatius' Spiritual Diary, the Formula of the Institute and the Jesuit Constitutions—which reveal both Ignatius' personal relationship with the Holy Spirit and his understanding of the proper role the Spirit was to play in the governance of the Society. Rather, in their own way, the Exercises reveal the key role the Holy Spirit plays in Ignatian spirituality.

BIBLIOGRAPHY

Anderson, Susan. "Reflections on the Experience of Making and Giving the Exercises." *The Way Supplement* 68 (1990) 13–21.

Aquinas, Thomas. *Summa Theologica*. Translated by Fathers of the English Dominican Province. New York: Benziger Brothers, 1911–25.

Catechism of the Catholic Church. 2nd ed. Vatican City: Vatican, 1997.

Chadwick, Geoffrey. "Giving the Exercises and Training Directors in an Ecumenical Context." *The Way Supplement* 68 (1990) 35–41.

Chong, Chechon. "La pneumatología de la espiritualidad de San Ignacio." PhD diss., Universidad Pontificia Comillas (Madrid), 2000.

Huggett, Joyce. "Why Ignatian Spirituality Hooks Protestants." *The Way Supplement* 68 (1980) 22–34.

Ignatius of Loyola. "Reminiscences or Autobiography of Ignatius Loyola." In *Personal Writings*, translated by Joseph A. Munitiz and Philip Endean, 1–64. London: Penguin, 1996.

———. "The Spiritual Diary." In *Personal Writings*, translated by Joseph A. Munitiz and Philip Endean, 65–109. London: Penguin, 1996.

———. "The Spiritual Exercises." In *Personal Writings*, translated by Joseph A. Munitiz and Philip Endean, 279–360. London: Penguin, 1996.

———. *The Spiritual Exercises of Saint Ignatius: Based on Studies in the Language of the Autograph*. Edited and translated by Louis J. Puhl. Chicago: Loyola University Press, 1951.

———. "Spiritual Journal of Ignatius of Loyola: February 2, 1544 to February 27, 1545." Translated by William J. Young. *Woodstock Letters* 87 (1958) 195–267.

Koning, Robin. "Revisiting the Marian Dimension of Ignatian Spirituality." In *Mariology at the Beginning of the Third Millennium*, edited by Kevin Wagner et al., 140–62. Eugene, OR: Pickwick, 2017.

O'Leary, Brian. "Consoler and Consolation." *The Way Supplement* 99 (2000) 61–69.

———. "The Mysticism of Ignatius of Loyola." *Review of Ignatian Spirituality* 38 (2007) 77–97.

Palmer, Martin E., ed. and trans. *On Giving the Spiritual Exercises: The Early Jesuit Manuscript Directories and the Official Directory of 1599*. St. Louis: The Institute of Jesuit Sources, 1996.

Sachs, John R. "The Spirit of the Risen Lord." *The Way Supplement* 99 (2000) 22–34.

Society of Jesus. "The Constitutions of the Society of Jesus." In *The Constitutions of the Society of Jesus and Their Complementary Norms: A Complete English Translation of the Official Latin Texts*, 17–407 St. Louis: The Institute of Jesuit Sources, 1996.

————. "Formulas of the Institute of the Society of Jesus, Approved and Confirmed by Popes Paul III and Julius III." In *The Constitutions of the Society of Jesus and Their Complementary Norms: A Complete English Translation of the Official Latin Texts*, 3–14. St. Louis: The Institute of Jesuit Sources, 1996.

Veltri, John. *Orientations*. Vol 2. Guelph: Loyola House, 1998. https://orientations.jesuits.ca/or2a_bintro.html#content.

13

THE HOLY SPIRIT AND THE SACRAMENT OF CONFIRMATION

Peter Pellicaan

CONFIRMATION IS OFTEN DESCRIBED as the "sacrament in search of a theology."[1] In the introduction to the revised edition of Colman O'Neill's *Meeting Christ in the Sacraments*, Romanus Cessario states that "confirmation . . . fell into the hands of the historians of theology, who continue to debate whether it actually exists or not."[2] Almost any work of the last half century on confirmation acknowledges the lack of any agreed understanding of the sacrament.[3] One of the areas of confusion is the role of the Holy Spirit in the sacrament of confirmation. If the Holy Spirit is already imparted at baptism and the seven gifts of the Spirit are also received in baptism[4] and only strengthened in confirmation,[5] then what is the role of the Holy Spirit in confirmation?

---

1. Bausch appears to be the first to have coined this phrase, but many have used it since. See Bausch, *New Look at the Sacraments*, 92. Other examples of scholars struggling to engage with the biblical texts include Bohen, *Mystery of Confirmation*, 68, and Behrens, *Confirmation, Sacrament of Grace*, 9. Behrens is cited here as his approach is somewhat peculiar. He looks at the word "confirm" in Scripture even though it is not immediately relevant to the sacrament of confirmation as we understand it.

2. Cessario, "Introduction" xix.

3. Other examples include: Kavanagh, "Confirmation," 148; Martinez, *Signs of Freedom*, 122; Fisher, *Confirmation Then and Now*, viii; Cunningham, *Confirmation*; Martos, *Doors to the Sacred*, 201.

4. *CCC*, sec. 1241 and 1266.

5. *CCC*, sec. 1303.

Arguably one of the causes of confusion regarding confirmation is the lack of engagement with the biblical data in the development of theologies of confirmation. Whilst it is not possible to develop a theology of confirmation from Scripture within the limits of this chapter,[6] the focus here will be instead an examination of the role of the Holy Spirit in the sacrament of confirmation in light of the biblical evidence.[7] This discussion will identify the primary biblical texts relating to the sacrament of confirmation, what these texts reveal regarding the role of the Holy Spirit in confirmation, an examination of the biblical foundations for the seven gifts of the Holy Spirit, and finally what Scripture might offer in regard to the relationship between confirmation and the special graces. It is the intention of this discussion is to be "especially attentive to the content and unity of the whole Scripture," to interpret "Scripture within the living Tradition of the whole Church" and to "be attentive to the analogy of faith"[8] in order to build on the living tradition of the Church in an ecclesial exegesis[9] that is in continuity with the whole plan of revelation. As such, preference will be given to Scripture and the documents of the Church, as well as those authors who have contributed to the development of the living tradition.

CONFIRMATION IN SCRIPTURE

There are no references to the word "confirmation" in Scripture because the theological language of sacramentality and confirmation had not yet been developed. There is also a certain reluctance amongst some scholars to engage with the Scriptures in regard to confirmation. For example, Austin Milner states that the texts of the New Testament relating to confirmation are "so difficult to interpret" that he prefers to look at all the extra-biblical historical sources before he is willing to engage with Scripture.[10] Nevertheless, there are many references to the word "Spirit" and examples of the infilling of the Spirit that may in some way relate to what is now understood as confirmation. In order to adequately limit the scope

6. For a theology of confirmation from Scripture, see my doctoral dissertation, Pellicaan, "Theology of Confirmation."

7. The content of this chapter has been developed as a precis of chapter 7 of my doctoral dissertation. To see the larger context within a biblical theology of confirmation, see Pellicaan, "Theology of Confirmation," 166–95.

8. See *CCC*, sec. 112–14.

9. Vall identifies how premodern exegetes place themselves under the authority of the rule of faith, and how modern exegetical methods would benefit from being synthesized with premodern methods. See Vall, *Ecclesial Exegesis*, 3–4.

10. Milner, *Theology of Confirmation*, 11.

of this discussion, the focus will be on the biblical texts that are already identified as relating to confirmation. These are defined with reference to three of the Church's documents, *Divinae consortium naturae*, (the *Apostolic Constitution on the Sacrament of Confirmation*), the texts to be used in the conferral of confirmation as per *The Order of Confirmation*, and finally the current *Catechism of the Catholic Church*.

In these three documents there are sixty-four biblical citations, but only five of these are found in all three documents: Luke 4:12–21, Acts 1:8, Acts 2, Acts 8:15–17, and Hebrews 6:2–5. In these five biblical references the essential data for the theology of the sacrament can be found. Jesus, whom the Spirit of the Lord is upon (cf. Luke 4:12–21), promises the Holy Spirit (cf. Acts 1:8) and then sends the Holy Spirit (cf. Acts 2). The apostles are then filled with the Holy Spirit and impart the Holy Spirit through the laying on of hands (cf. Acts 8:16–17), which becomes part of Christian initiation (cf. Heb 6:2–5). With this in view, the archetypal "confirmation" event is found in Acts 2 when the apostles are filled with the Holy Spirit. Pope Paul VI affirms this when he writes that the sacrament of confirmation "in a certain way perpetuates the grace of Pentecost in the Church."[11]

The Centrality of Pentecost

The centrality of Pentecost to the sacrament of confirmation is important for developing a biblical theology of the sacrament. If confirmation perpetuates the grace of Pentecost in the Church, the question follows: what is the grace of Pentecost? To address this, it is necessary to observe Luke's account of the ascension. Here Jesus asks his apostles to stay in Jerusalem (cf. Acts 1:4) and then says to them, "you will receive power when the Holy Spirit has come upon you; and you will be my witnesses in Jerusalem, in all Judea and Samaria, and to the ends of the earth" (Acts 1:8).[12] Jesus makes clear that the grace to be given, which unbeknown to the disciples would be received at Pentecost, would be an empowerment to be Christ's witnesses. The account of Pentecost further confirms this.

> When the day of Pentecost had come, they were all together in one place. And suddenly from heaven there came a sound like the rush of a violent wind, and it filled the entire house where they were sitting. Divided tongues, as of fire, appeared among them, and a tongue rested on each of them. All of them were filled with the Holy Spirit and began to speak in other languages,

11. Paul VI, *Divinae Consortium Naturae*, ix.

12. Scriptural references will be from the NRSV unless otherwise stated.

as the Spirit gave them ability. Now there were devout Jews from every nation under heaven living in Jerusalem. And at this sound the crowd gathered and was bewildered, because each one heard them speaking in the native language of each (cf. Acts 2:1–7).

Short of reproducing the whole chapter here, Luke's account of these events also includes the proclamation of Peter to the crowd (cf. 14–41) and the effects of these events which include many new converts and the development of the early Christian community (cf. 42–47).

The day of Pentecost is significant because it is one of the great celebrations of the Jewish community inaugurated at the foot of Mt. Sinai and is at the culmination of the Feast of Weeks.[13] In the same way that the Passover provides the theological context for the institution of the Eucharist, the Pentecost celebration can be understood as providing the theological context for the infilling of the Holy Spirit.[14]

Luke's account of the Pentecost event reveals an infilling of the Holy Spirit to empower the proclamation of the gospel. The apostles are filled with the Holy Spirit and speak in other languages in order that those present can hear the gospel proclaimed in their native tongue. Peter's proclamation to the crowd results in three thousand new converts (cf. Acts 2:41). As Jesus

---

13. Pentecost is first alluded to in the book of Exodus as part of the inauguration of the Feast of Weeks, which is referred to as the Festival of Harvest and Festival of Weeks (See Exod 23:16; 34:22–23). Pentecost is the final celebration on the fiftieth day at the end of the Feast of Weeks. More detailed instructions for the Feast of Weeks can be found in Leviticus 23:15–22, Numbers 28:26–31, and Deuteronomy 16:9–12.

14. The correlations between the Pentecost event and the Theophany at Mt. Sinai in the book of Exodus are not insignificant. The wind (Acts 2:2) corresponds to the thick cloud (Exod 19:16), the fire on the heads of the disciples (Acts 2:3) corresponds to the Lord descending in fire (Exod 19:18) and the speaking in tongues (Acts 2:4) corresponds to the thunder (Exod 19:16), which literally translates as "voices." Vanderkam explains that Jewish exegetes such as Philo and others interpreted Exodus 19 as the law being communicated in seventy languages. He concludes his argument by stating that it "is reasonable to conclude that Luke, in Acts 2, chose to express the gift of the Spirit through the symbols of fiery tongues, which enabled the apostles to speak the languages of their international audience of pilgrims in conscious dependence on Jewish ways of interpreting texts in the Sinai pericopes and the developed meaning of Pentecost/weeks." Vanderkam, "Covenant and Pentecost," 252. Finally, at Mt. Sinai the law is given to Moses (Exod 20); at Pentecost, the new law, the gospel is given to the people (Acts 2:14–36). Though there is much more to be said on these correlations which are beyond the scope of this chapter, these detailed Old Testament correspondences can be recognized as an inferred type or prefiguration of Pentecost, and by reference to Pentecost, to confirmation. I explore the possible typological relationship between Pentecost in Exodus and the Pentecost event in Acts 2. See for example, Pellicaan, "Theology of Confirmation," 110–65.

promised, this power that would be received from the Holy Spirit would and did inspire the disciples to "be my witnesses" (Acts 1:8). If the grace of Pentecost is empowerment for mission, it follows that the central *telos* of confirmation and the grace received is an empowerment for mission. Here it is recognized that the term "mission" refers to both the making of disciples as well as the service to the Church for the common good (1 Cor 12:7). In this light, confirmation completes baptism because the grace received in confirmation empowers the newly confirmed to now represent the Church—to go on mission.

In light of this, how then does the Holy Spirit empower the confirmand for mission? To address this question, it is necessary to observe three other accounts in Acts where the apostles impart the Holy Spirit. Each of these examples can be recognized as a kind of "Pentecost event" that in some way is related to and mirrors the pattern of the Pentecost event in Acts 2. As such, each of these texts can further inform the theology of confirmation. These examples are found in Acts 8:14–17, 10:44–48, and 19:1–6.

Acts 8:14–17

The text of Acts 8:14–17 is as follows:

> Now when the apostles at Jerusalem heard that Samaria had accepted the word of God, they sent Peter and John to them. The two went down and prayed for them that they might receive the Holy Spirit (for as yet the Spirit had not come upon any of them; they had only been baptised in the name of the Lord Jesus). Then Peter and John laid their hands on them, and they received the Holy Spirit.

This text is commonly recognized as informing a theology of confirmation.[15] While Acts 4:31 provides an account of a situation where apostles are filled with the Spirit and proclaim the word much like in Acts 2, the text in Acts 8 is the first example whereby the apostles specifically pray that others will receive the Holy Spirit.

While in Acts 2, the apostles are filled with the Holy Spirit, in Acts 8, the apostles impart the Holy Spirit through prayer and the laying of hands. The Samaritans who receive the Spirit in this account have their own kind of "Pentecost" experience, but this time it is initiated by the apostles rather than being an unsolicited act of God. What is explicit in verse 16 is that the Samaritans have been baptized but that "the Spirit had not come upon

---

15. *CCC*, sec. 1315.

any of them." As such, the Spirit is imparted and received subsequent to conversion. As will become clear in the analysis of the other texts in Acts, Luke provides a variety of examples of the relationship between conversion and the infilling of the Holy Spirit that do not always fit the same pattern (cf. Acts 2:4, 8:16–17, 9:17, and 19:6).[16] Nonetheless, as Craig Keener points out, Luke associates the Spirit with empowerment rather than conversion.[17] While this is not explicit in Acts 8, it will become clearer as the other texts are examined. What is also interesting is that there is a difference between the Pauline texts, which generally associate the receiving of the Spirit with conversion and therefore regeneration (cf. Rom 6–8; Gal 5:16–25; Eph 1:13–14), and Luke, who, in the Acts of the Apostles, focuses on the receiving of the Spirit as empowerment, which is at times received separately from conversion. This distinction can aid in identifying what is received in baptism (regeneration) compared to what is received in confirmation (empowerment for mission).

Acts 8 also provides the first example of the laying on of hands for the impartation of the Holy Spirit. Examples are also found in Acts 9:17 and 19:6, while in Acts 2 and 10, there is no record of laying on of hands. John Oulton points out that it is difficult to assess the relationship between the Holy Spirit, baptism and the laying on of hands simply because there is no consistent picture in Acts.[18] More than a century ago, Richard B. Rackham made the claim that this laying on of hands was "the beginning of the Church's rite of confirmation."[19]

Whilst the Acts 8 texts shines little light on the effect of the infilling of the Holy Spirit, it is clear that the laying on of hands plays an important role in this instance. By application to the sacraments, and based on the *Apostolic Tradition of Hippolytus*, Godfrey Diekmann goes as far as to propose that

> laying on of hands, understood as a conferring of the Holy Spirit, constituted in early Christianity the basic liturgical rite common to all the sacraments. And further, that the post-Vatican II reforms of the sacramental rites have as a principal objective the restoration of the laying on of hands as a central liturgical rite or gesture, with a view to recovering the pneumatological signification and understanding of the sacraments.[20]

---

16. These texts all demonstrate the Spirit being imparted after conversion. The exception is 10:44, where it seems to be simultaneous.

17. Keener, *Acts*, 1524.

18. Oulton, "Holy Spirit," 236.

19. Rackham, *Acts of the Apostles*, 116–17.

20. Diekmann, "Laying on of Hands," 339.

Although such a statement may be problematic in terms of its coverage of all seven sacraments, it is certainly true of confirmation. Through the laying on of hands, the Samaritans receive the Holy Spirit but are also identified as fully-fledged members of the Christian community.

Acts 10:44–48

The next example of the apostles imparting the Holy Spirit is recorded in Acts 10:44–48.

> While Peter was still speaking, the Holy Spirit fell upon all who heard the word. The circumcised believers who had come with Peter were astounded that the gift of the Holy Spirit had been poured out even on the Gentiles, for they heard them speaking in tongues and extolling God. Then Peter said, "Can anyone withhold the water for baptizing these people who have received the Holy Spirit just as we have?" So he ordered them to be baptized in the name of Jesus Christ. Then they invited him to stay for several days.

Unlike Acts 8, there is no laying on of hands, but the gift of the Holy Spirit is evidenced by the Gentiles "speaking in tongues and extolling God." Beyond the inclusion of the Gentiles, this text is the first explicit example of the Gentiles (not just the apostles as in Acts 2) speaking in tongues. This manifestation is recognized by those present as evidence that the Gentiles had received the Holy Spirit. When Peter explains the event to the circumcised believers, he says that "the Holy Spirit fell upon them just as it had upon us at the beginning" (Acts 11:18, also cf. 10:47). Though there is no reference in the text to a violent wind or tongues of fire, Peter nonetheless makes the correlation. As previously examined, the speaking in tongues in Acts 2 enabled the apostles to preach the gospel in the native languages of those present. In this, the Holy Spirit given at Pentecost empowered the apostles to effectively engage in the mission—to make disciples. The giving of the gift of tongues to the Gentiles meant that they were no longer objects of the mission but rather "partners in mission."[21] In both the Acts 2 and Acts 10 accounts, speaking in tongues is recorded as an effect of the infilling of the Holy Spirit as an empowerment for mission.

---

21. Keener, *Acts*, 18: 10–11.

Acts 19:1–7.

The final example of the impartation of the Holy Spirit in Acts is found in Acts 19:1–7, which states:

> While Apollos was in Corinth, Paul passed through the interior regions and came to Ephesus, where he found some disciples. He said to them, "Did you receive the Holy Spirit when you became believers?" They replied, "No, we have not even heard that there is a Holy Spirit." Then he said, "Into what then were you baptized?" They answered, "Into John's baptism." Paul said, "John baptized with the baptism of repentance, telling the people to believe in the one who was to come after him, that is, in Jesus." On hearing this, they were baptized in the name of the Lord Jesus. When Paul had laid his hands on them, the Holy Spirit came upon them, and they spoke in tongues and prophesied—altogether there were about twelve of them.

A key difference in this text is the reference to prophecy as a result of being filled with the Spirit. In Acts 2:1–7, the apostles receive the Holy Spirit and speak in other tongues, in Acts 8:14–17, "they received the Holy Spirit" with no manifestations recorded. In Acts 10:44–48, they received the Holy Spirit, spoke in tongues, and extolled the Lord. In Acts 19:1–7, they received the Holy Spirit, spoke in tongues and prophesied. This explicit reference to prophecy is significant in that, like tongues, prophecy is listed by Paul as a spiritual gift in 1 Corinthians 12:10.

In these four "Pentecost events" there is a relationship between the impartation of the Holy Spirit and the gifts of the Holy Spirit. Gifts of the Holy Spirit in this case refers to those identified in the Pauline corpus, not the seven gifts of wisdom, understanding, counsel, fortitude, knowledge, piety, and fear of the Lord.[22] In three of four examples in Acts, the manifestation of Pauline spiritual gifts (tongues—and in one case prophecy) is apparent and whatever happened in the Acts 8 account was enough for the disciples to recognize that the Holy Spirit had indeed been received. This raises questions about the relationship between the sacrament of confirmation, the seven gifts of the Spirit, and the gifts of the Spirit identified in the Pauline corpus.

---

22. *CCC*, sec. 1831.

THE SEVEN GIFTS OF THE HOLY SPIRIT AND THE SPECIAL GRACES

The *Catechism* states that confirmation does "increase the gifts of the Holy Spirit."[23] Later in the *Catechism* is a section dedicated to the gifts and the fruits of the Holy Spirit which states:

> The seven gifts of the Holy Spirit are wisdom, understanding, counsel, fortitude, knowledge, piety, and fear of the Lord. They belong in their fullness to Christ, Son of David. They complete and perfect the virtues of those who receive them. They make the faithful docile in readily obeying divine inspirations.

These seven gifts have been derived from Isaiah 11:1–2, which is understood in the Christian tradition as a prophecy about Jesus. It is also interesting to note that in the text of Isaiah, there are six characteristics rather than seven. Piety is absent from the text and *might* is replaced with fortitude. The following table demonstrates the differences:

Isaiah 11:1–2	The Catechism
Wisdom	Wisdom
Understanding	Understanding
Counsel	Counsel
Might	Fortitude
Knowledge	Knowledge
Fear	Piety
—	Fear

Raniero Cantalamessa points out that although the Hebrew text contains six gifts rather than seven—including "fear" twice—the Septuagint and Latin Vulgate include piety as a substitute for one of the references to fear.[24] The Latin Vulgate, St. Jerome's translation of the proto-Masoretic text, stated: *et requiescet super eum spiritus Domini: spiritus sapientiæ et intellectus, spiritus consilii et fortitudinis, spiritus scientiæ et pietatis.* This has now been updated in the *Nova Vulgata*. The reference to *pietatis* has

23. *CCC*, sec. 1303.

24. Cantalamessa, *Come, Creator Spirit*, 175–76.

now been revised to the more precise translation—*et timoris Domini*.[25] This explains why piety is included in the original list of gifts, even if it is missing from more recent translations.

In the same section of the *Catechism*, there is a description of the fruits of the Spirit, taken from Galatians 5:22–23. The fruits of the Spirit are perfections that the Holy Spirit forms in us as the first fruits of eternal glory. The tradition of the Church lists twelve of them: "charity, joy, peace, patience, kindness, goodness, generosity, gentleness, faithfulness, modesty, self-control, chastity."[26]

What is curious here is that the fruits of the Spirit are taken from Paul's letter to the Galatians, but the gifts of the Spirit are taken from Isaiah. This is surprising, given that Paul also explicitly addresses the "gifts of the Spirit," (Rom 12:4–8; 1 Cor 12–14; Eph 4:4–13) and the text of Isaiah does not use the language of "gift," even if the text implies the effect of God's Spirit resting on the shoot that will come out "from the stump of Jesse" (Isa 11:1). In 1 Corinthians 12:4–11, Paul specifically speaks of the gifts of the Spirit and names eight, without suggesting that the list is exhaustive. Interestingly, when the *Catechism* refers to *gifts* such as tongues, it uses (most of the time) the language of *special graces* rather than gifts.[27] Moreover, though the *Catechism* acknowledges the Pentecost event of Acts 2 as foundational to the theology of confirmation, and the apostles were given the *special grace* of tongues at Pentecost, there is no explicit linking in the *Catechism* between the sacrament of confirmation and the receiving of *special graces*. There is some disharmony between the *Catechism* and the biblical texts in regard to what is understood as a "gift of the Spirit." This disparity may well provide some insight into the confusion around the difference between the work of the Spirit in baptism compared with confirmation and the difference between the Spirit's work of regeneration and the Spirit's work of empowerment for mission. Of relevance here is the fact that Paul references tongues as a gift of the Spirit and in the texts of Acts 2, 10, and 19 these gifts are received. The giving of these gifts of the Spirit in the book of Acts understood in relationship to the sacrament of confirmation also brings

25. Compare *Nova Vulgata Bibliorum Sacrorum Editio*, 1214, with *Biblia Sacra, Vulgata Editio Sixti V*, 543.

26. *CCC*, sec. 1832.

27. *CCC*, sec. 2003. The *Catechism* itself is not entirely consistent in its language regarding these "special graces." At times, it uses the language of "charismatic gifts" (*CCC*, sec. 768), "charisms" (*CCC*, sec. 798, 799), and also "gifts of the Holy Spirit" (*CCC*, sec. 800), but then it also refers to the seven "gifts of the Holy Spirit" as derived from Isaiah. Killian McDonnell and George T. Montague critique the language of "special graces" and state that "the baptism of the Spirit is not a special grace for some but common for all." McDonnell and Montague, *Christian Initiation*, 334.

into play the texts within the Pauline corpus that address the gifts of the Spirit (or special graces).

It is evident that the *gifts of the Spirit* for Paul are not the same as those proposed in the *Catechism*. For Paul, every believer receives one or more of these *gifts* of the Spirit and these Pentecost events in Acts 2, 10, and 19 appear to be the occasion by which these new believers receive at least one of these *gifts*, or *special graces*.[28] On these occasions, it is the *gift* of tongues (and also prophecy in Acts 19). By way of clarification, it is not suggested that the text implies that everyone who has received the Spirit necessarily speaks in tongues, but rather that everyone who has received the Spirit necessarily receives one or more of the special graces listed by Paul. By application to the sacrament of confirmation, it would be reasonable to presume that the infilling of the Spirit in confirmation is the occasion by which the newly confirmed receives these special graces, and that these graces are those listed as gifts in the New Testament. These special graces are for empowering the mission of the Church, rather than being related to regeneration. This is an important inference and one that raises questions about how the Church came to understand *gifts of the Spirit* in the first place.

Interestingly, though the *Catechism* does not include these gifts from Paul's letters in its list of *gifts of the Spirit*, Paul's list is cited and affirmed in *Lumen Gentium*:

> There is only one Spirit who, according to His own richness and the needs of the ministries, gives His different gifts for the welfare of the Church (cf. 1 Corinthians 12:1–12). What has a special place among these gifts is the grace of the apostles to whose authority the Spirit Himself subjected even those who were endowed with charisms.[29]

And again, in paragraph 12:

> It is not only through the sacraments and the ministries of the Church that the Holy Spirit sanctifies and leads the people of God and enriches it with virtues, but, "allotting his gifts to everyone according as He wills" (cf. [1] Cor. 12:11), He distributes special graces among the faithful of every rank. By these gifts He makes them fit and ready to undertake the various tasks and offices which contribute toward the renewal

28. For the sake of clarity, and in order to be consistent with the language of the *Catechism*, from this point on, the more charismatic gifts of the Spirit listed in the Pauline epistles and evidenced in Acts will be referred to as *special graces*, while *spiritual gifts* will refer to the seven gifts listed by the *Catechism* derived from Isaiah.

29. Second Vatican Council, *Lumen Gentium*, sec. 7.

and building up of the Church, according to the words of the Apostle: "The manifestation of the Spirit is given to everyone for profit" (1 Cor. 12:7). These charisms, whether they be the more outstanding or the more simple and widely diffused, are to be received with thanksgiving and consolation for they are perfectly suited to and useful for the needs of the Church.[30]

It is argued by some that Aquinas was likely the first to codify the seven *gifts* as seen in the *Catechism* today.[31] The seven gifts are explicitly affirmed in the *Summa*; interestingly, however, there is no discussion about why the Pauline gifts would be overlooked. Even more curious is the fact that there is one reference to the Pauline gifts (special graces) in Aquinas' discussion on gifts, but it is limited to wisdom and word of knowledge, without any mention of the rest.[32] Even so, it is clear that references to these seven gifts of the Spirit in relation to the book of Isaiah were recognized much earlier. In his commentary on the beatitudes, Augustine uses the language of *gifts* and draws a correlation between the *gifts* in Isaiah and those found in the beatitudes.[33] Ambrose also makes reference to these seven gifts, although he does not use the language of *gifts* but rather makes reference to the seal of the Spirit that grants the "spirit of wisdom and understanding."[34] Brian Gaybba makes the point that "systematic thinking on these gifts only began in mediaeval times" and that "relatively little is to be found about them in the western fathers."[35] As such, it is unclear why these seven gifts derived from Isaiah became so prominent when compared to those explicitly listed in Paul's letters.

In *Come, Creator Spirit*, Raniero Cantalamessa provides further insight into this distinction between the gifts referred to in Isaiah and the special graces referred to in the Pauline corpus. He notes that the Church Fathers

30. Second Vatican Council, *Lumen Gentium*, sec. 12.

31. Walters et al., *Feast of Corpus Christi*, 451.

32. In this section, Aquinas is refuting the use of the Pauline text to suggest that some people are given some gifts and not others, even though his point relates to the gifts from Isaiah rather than those listed in 1 Corinthians. He makes the point that we "are therefore not to understand that one gift can be without another; but that if understanding were without wisdom, it would not be a gift; even as temperance, without justice, would not be a virtue." Such an assertion makes sense in regard to the gifts of the Spirit derived from Isaiah, but the Pauline text is not referring to these gifts. See Aquinas, *Summa Theologica*, I–II, q. 68, a. 5.

33. Augustine, "Sermon on the Mount," 6.

34. Ambrose, "On the Mysteries," 322.

35. Gaybba, *Spirit of Love*, 88. Gaybba also points out that most scholarly work of this era was focused on the nature of these gifts and their relationship to the cardinal virtues.

can be seen to employ the same language of gifts for both "charisms given for the common good as well as charisms destined to personal sanctification."[36] He goes on to make a distinction between gifts and charisms (special graces) and writes that a "gift is sanctifying and ordered towards the perfecting of its recipient, while a charism is a disposition granted for the benefit of others."[37] This distinction is helpful to the extent that it acknowledges that the seven gifts referred to in Isaiah are primarily ordered towards the individual's own sanctification and regeneration. In this case, the individual referenced in Isaiah is the king, so the implication is the sanctification and regeneration of the whole community through the reign of this king. Again, in light of this discussion regarding the infilling of the Holy Spirit in the book of Acts, it is evident that what was received at Pentecost, and also in Acts 8, 10, and 19, was different to these sanctifying gifts. As such, there is more going on than simply an impartation or strengthening of the gifts that sanctify.[38]

Cantalamessa states that in the "generally accepted interpretation, these seven gifts do not belong in the charismatic sphere but to the area of sanctification in the strict sense, for they are not given to certain people only but offered exactly the same to everyone."[39] This is important in regard to how the Church understands confirmation. If these seven gifts—as listed in Isaiah—are received in baptism and confirmation is primarily to do with the strengthening of these gifts[40] and therefore primarily related to individual sanctification, then it makes sense for confirmation to precede the Eucharist as confirmation would appropriately prepare one for the Eucharist. But to the contrary, if confirmation perpetuates the grace of Pentecost and empowers the newly confirmed for mission, it makes sense for confirmation to follow the Eucharist as it is a sacrament ordered toward sending the newly confirmed out from the table of the Lord rather than preparing one for the table. It does not make sense to be empowering

---

36. Cantalamessa, *Come, Creator Spirit*, 174.

37. Cantalamessa, *Come, Creator Spirit*, 175. Pope John Paul II employed a similar definition regarding charism but fell short of commenting explicitly on gifts. He said that "the charisms, the ministries, the different forms of service exercised by the lay faithful exist in communion and on behalf of communion. They are treasures that complement one another for the good of all and are under the wise guidance of their Pastors." John Paul II, *Christifideles Laici*, 20.

38. This distinction of Cantalamessa, however, does not acknowledge that the "perfecting of the recipient" is also ordered towards the benefit of others. Indeed, the perfecting of the individual is a benefit to others. Holiness is primarily communal. See Adewuya, *Holiness and Community*, 1.

39. Cantalamessa, *Come, Creator Spirit*, 175. This is the point Aquinas makes in *Summa Theologica*, I–II, q. 68, a. 5.

40. *CCC*, sec. 1266 and 1303.

someone for the evangelization mission of the Church if they have not yet received the Eucharist. This would explain one of the reasons as to why Jesus instituted the Eucharist before (not after) the empowering of the Spirit at Pentecost.

Historically the order of initiation rites has not been consistent other than the recognition that baptism always comes first. Since the Council of Trent, and particularly in the nineteenth and twentieth centuries, the order of initiation rites has continued to vary. Paul Turner chronicles these movements in his article "Benedict XVI and the sequence of the sacraments of initiation."[41] He explains that in the mid-nineteenth century, bishops in France began to legislate for Eucharist before confirmation.[42] He points out that the Councils of Avignon, Sens, Rouen, Auch and Prague, as well as the Statutes of Mende, all legislated for this order.[43] In 1897, however, Pope Leo XIII gave instruction in reply to a letter from the Bishop of Marseille to administer confirmation before Eucharist as this prepared the confirmand "for receiving afterwards the Eucharist."[44] In 1910, the Sacred Congregation for the Discipline of the Sacraments produced the decree *Quam singulari*, which, with reference to confession and Eucharist, clarified the age of reason as being about the seventh year.[45] Barrett points out that this clarification led to confirmation again being administered after Eucharist, in part because a local priest could baptize, hear confession and administer the Eucharist but needed a bishop to confirm.[46] This disparity in the order of initiation rites is still yet to be clarified.[47]

As recently as 2007, Pope Benedict XVI raised the question of the order of initiation rites:

> Attention needs to be paid to the order of the sacraments of initiation. Different traditions exist within the Church. There is a clear variation between, on the one hand, the ecclesial customs of the East and the practice of the West regarding the initiation of adults, and, on the other hand, the procedure adopted for children. Yet these variations are not properly of

41. Turner, "Benedict XVI," 132.

42. Curiously, Turner's first example is a reference to the Council of Tours, the last of which took place in 1163. This appears to be an error, perhaps caused by the work he is citing being last printed in 1849. Nonetheless, the rest of his examples remain correct.

43. Turner, "Benedict XVI," 135–36.

44. Leo XIII, *Abrogata quae*, June 22, 1897, in Turner, "Benedict XVI," 136.

45. Pius X, *Quam Singulari*.

46. Barrett, "Confirmation," 703.

47. For a survey of the development of confirmation, see Pellicaan, "Theology of Confirmation," 47–54.

the dogmatic order, but are pastoral in character. Concretely, it needs to be seen which practice better enables the faithful to put the sacrament of the Eucharist at the centre, as the goal of the whole process of initiation. In close collaboration with the competent offices of the Roman Curia, Bishops' Conferences should examine the effectiveness of current approaches to Christian initiation, so that the faithful can be helped both to mature through the formation received in our communities and to give their lives an authentically eucharistic direction, so that they can offer a reason for the hope within them in a way suited to our times (cf. 1 Pet 3:15).[48]

Arguably a key factor in the ongoing confusion regarding the order of initiation regards the primary *telos* of the sacrament. When the biblical data is taken into account, a clearer picture emerges. Cantalamessa is explicit about this disconnect between the seven gifts of the Spirit and the biblical evidence. He states that the issue needs radical rethinking and that "the old theology of the seven gifts really does not have any biblical basis."[49] Though there is limited evidence of special graces in the early centuries of Christianity, Irenaeus makes a passing reference, stating that "we do also hear many brethren in the Church, who possess prophetic gifts, and who through the Spirit speak all kinds of languages."[50] In his commentary on 1 Corinthians, Charles Talbert provides a collection of references to supernatural spiritual gifts in the patristic period, which provides quotations from Hermas, Eusebius, Epiphanius, Justin, Irenaeus, Tertullian, Origen, Novatian, Cyril of Alexandria, and Gregory the Great.[51]

While Cantalamessa acknowledges the fact that the seven gifts identified from Isaiah and referenced throughout the Church's history do

48. Benedict XVI, *Sacramentum Caritatis*, sec. 18.

49. This is a remarkable statement from a theologian who, since 1980, has been the Preacher to the Papal Household. See Cantalamessa, *Come, Creator Spirit*, 175. Cantalamessa goes on to point out that the special graces, with the possible exception of speaking in tongues and interpreting tongues, were never lost from the Church's practice, which is in keeping with Pius XII's statement that "members gifted with miraculous powers will never be lacking in the Church." See Pius XII, *Mystici Corporis Christi*, sec. 17. In Cantalamessa's analysis of why the Church seemed to decline in its expression of the special graces, he argues that the interplay between community life, charism, and office was becoming imbalanced. He writes that the balance favored office to the point that charism became something understood to be conferred at ordination and therefore exercised by ordained ministers, which pushed the charisms (special graces) to the fringes of the Church as a result. See Cantalamessa, *Come, Creator Spirit*, 183.

50. Irenaeus, "Against Heresies," v, 6, 1.

51. See Talbert, *Reading Corinthians*, 105–6.

not have robust biblical foundations and promotes the special graces as listed (as gifts) by Paul, he falls short of identifying these gifts as being connected to the sacrament of confirmation. He shows that the special graces are being brought back into the center of the Church—that the special graces typical of Pentecost have come back—but he makes a distinction between sacrament and special grace. He says that the Church "lives not by sacrament alone but also by charism"[52]—the two lungs of the Church body—and implies that sacraments come from above (through the hierarchy) and charisms from below (through each member of the body).[53] This is where the understanding of the special graces being imparted in the sacrament of confirmation can enable a new understanding of the relationship between the sacraments and the special graces. Though this relationship between the sacraments and charisms can be understood as co-dependent, with one essential to the other. That is to say, in Acts 2, 10, and 19, the Holy Spirit is imparted, and each time the recipient receives a special grace. It has already been shown that Pentecost in Acts 2 is the central foundational text for the sacrament of confirmation and that the events of Acts 8:14–17, 10:44–48, and 19:1–6 are at some level "Pentecost" events. It follows then that the special graces have a strong relationship with the infilling of the Holy Spirit that takes place in the sacrament of confirmation. In this light the special graces flow from the sacraments, and especially from confirmation, rather than merely working in a kind of random collaboration with them. In light of this, it is proposed that not only are the seven gifts of the Holy Spirit—derived from Isaiah—strengthened in the sacrament of confirmation, but the special graces, or charismatic gifts of the Spirit, are also given to each person being confirmed as the Spirit determines (1 Cor 12:11).

CONCLUSION

In the five biblical texts consistently identified in *Divinae Consortium Naturae* (the *Apostolic Constitution on the Sacrament of Confirmation*), *The Order of Confirmation*, and the current *Catechism of the Catholic Church*, namely Luke 4:12–21, Acts 1:8, Acts 2, Acts 8:15–17, and Hebrews 6:2–5, it can be seen that the Pentecost event in Acts 2 can be understood as a kind of archetype of the sacrament of confirmation. In the book of Acts, Luke identifies three other "Pentecost events" whereby the Holy Spirit is imparted to new converts (Acts 8:14–17, 10:44–48, and 19:1–6). If the

---

52. Cantalamessa, *Come, Creator Spirit*, 184.

53. Cantalamessa, *Come, Creator Spirit*, 184.

sacrament of confirmation "perpetuates the grace of Pentecost"[54] then an examination of Pentecost and these three other "Pentecost events" in Acts can inform a theology of confirmation. What emerges from these texts is that empowerment for mission and the receiving of special graces are strong themes. Jesus makes clear that the power to be received is in order that the apostles can "be my witnesses" (Acts 1:8). When this power is received, the apostles receive one or more of the (special graces) gifts of the Spirit as identified in the Pauline corpus and referred to as special graces in the *Catechism*. At times these special graces can be thought of as an agenda of focus for those within charismatic renewal movements within the Church. Fortuitously, these special graces are given to everyone. St. Paul makes this clear when he writes:

> Now there are varieties of gifts, but the same Spirit; and there are varieties of services, but the same Lord; and there are varieties of activities, but it is the same God who activates all of them in everyone. To each is given the manifestation of the Spirit for the common good. (1 Cor 12:4–7)[55]

With this in view, it can be understood that the primary work of the Holy Spirit in what is now understood and experienced as the sacrament of confirmation is the empowering for mission. One of the effects of this empowerment in light of the biblical data can be understood as the giving of the Pauline spiritual gifts (or special graces), that are given for the welfare of the Church and its mission. The seven gifts of the Spirit as derived from Isaiah are indeed strengthened in the sacrament in order that the newly confirmed is adequately prepared to deploy the special graces and to engage in the mission of the Church. Such an understanding draws these special graces into the sacramental life of the Church whilst harmonizing the disparity between the seven gifts of the Spirit, the Pauline gifts of the Spirit (or special graces), and their relationship to the sacrament of confirmation which perpetuates the grace of Pentecost.

---

54. Paul VI, *Divinae Consortium Naturae*, ix.

55. It should also be noted that the gifts listed in the Pauline corpus are not limited to the more supernatural gifts such as tongues, prophecy, and healing, but also include wisdom, understanding, teaching, and so forth. See Rom 12:4–8, 1 Cor 12–14, and Eph 4:4–13. For an exegesis of these texts in regard to their relationship to confirmation, see Pellicaan, "Theology of Confirmation," 196–225.

BIBLIOGRAPHY

Adewuya, J. Ayodeji. *Holiness and Community in 2 Cor 6:14—7:1: Paul's View of Communal Holiness in the Corinthian Correspondence*. Eugene, OR: Wipf & Stock, 2011.

Ambrose. "On the Mysteries." In *Nicene and Post-Nicene Fathers, Second Series*, edited by Philip Schaff and Henry Wace, translated by H. de Romestin et al., 10:697–717. Grand Rapids, MI: Eerdmans, 1989.

Aquinas, Thomas. *Summa Theologica*. Translated by the English Dominican Fathers. New York: Christian Classics, 1981.

Augustine. "Sermon on the Mount." In *Nicene and Post-Nicene Fathers, First Series*, edited by Philip Schaff, translated by William Findlay, 4:1–63. Grand Rapids, MI: Eerdmans, 1991.

Bausch, William J. A. *New Look at the Sacraments*. Mystic, CT: Twenty-Third, 1983.

Barrett, Richard J. "Confirmation: A Discipline Revisited." *Jurist* 52 (1992) 697–714.

Behrens, James. *Confirmation, Sacrament of Grace*. Herefordshire: Wright, 1995.

Benedict XVI. *Summorum Pontificum*. https://www.vatican.va/content/benedict-xvi/en/letters/2007/documents/hf_ben-xvi_let_20070707_lettera-vescovi.html.

Biblia Sacra, Vulgata Editio Sixti V. Parisiis: Typis Jacobi Vincent, 1741.

Bohen, Marian. *The Mystery of Confirmation*. New York: Herder & Herder, 1963.

Cantalamessa, Raniero. *Come, Creator Spirit: Meditations on the Veni Creator*. Collegeville, MN: Liturgical, 2003.

Catechism of the Catholic Church. 2nd ed. Vatican City: Vatican, 1997.

Cessario, Romanus. "Introduction." In *Meeting Christ in the Sacraments*, edited by Colman E. O'Neill, revised by Romanus Cessario, xiii–xx. New York: Alba House, 1991.

Cunningham, Joseph. *Confirmation: Pastoral Concerns*. Collegeville, MN: Liturgical, 1973.

Diekmann, Godfrey. "The Laying on of Hands: The Basic Sacramental Rite." *Proceedings of the Catholic Theological Society of America* 29 (2012) 339–51. https://ejournals.bc.edu/index.php/ctsa/article/view/2812.

Fisher, John Douglas Close. *Confirmation Then and Now*. London: Alcuin Club, 1978.

Gaybba, Brian. *The Spirit of Love: Theology of the Holy Spirit*. London: Chapman,1987.

John Paul II. *Christifideles Laici*. https://www.vatican.va/content/john-paul-ii/en/apost_exhortations/documents/hf_jp-ii_exh_30121988_christifideles-laici.html.

Irenaeus. "Against Heresies." In *Ante-Nicene Fathers*, edited by Alexander Roberts et al., translated by Alexander Roberts and William Rambaut, 1:315–567. Buffalo, NY: Christian Literature, 1885.

Kavanagh, Aidan. "Confirmation: A Suggestion from Structure." In *Living Water, Sealing Spirit*, edited by Maxwell E. Johnson, 148–58. Collegeville, MN: Liturgical, 1995.

———. *Confirmation: Origins and Reform*. New York: Pueblo, 1988.

Keener, Craig S. *Acts: An Exegetical Commentary*. Vol. 2, *3:1—14:28*. Grand Rapids, MI: Baker Academic, 2013.

Leo XIII. "*Abrogata quae*, 22 June 1897." In *Codicis iuris canonici fonts*, edited by Peter Gasparri, 3:515–16. Rome: Typis Polyglottis Vaticanis, 1925.

Martinez, German. *Signs of Freedom: Theology of the Christian Sacraments*. New York: Paulist, 2003.

Martos, Joseph. *Doors to the Sacred*. New York: Image, 1982.

McDonnell, Kilian, and George T. Montague. *Christian Initiation and Baptism in the Holy Spirit: Evidence from the First Eight Centuries*. Collegeville, MN: Liturgical, 1991.

Milner, Austin P. *Theology of Confirmation*. Cork: Mercier, 1971.

Nova Vulgata Bibliorum Sacrorum Editio. https://www.vatican.va/archive/bible/nova_vulgata/documents/nova-vulgata_index_lt.html.

The Order of Confirmation. Strathfield: St. Paul's, 2015.

Oulton, John E. L. "The Holy Spirit, Baptism, and Laying on of Hands in Acts." *Expository Times* 66 (1955) 236–40.

Paul VI. "*Divinae consortium naturae*. Apostolic Constitution on the Sacrament of Confirmation, 15 August 1971." In *The Order of Confirmation*, vii–xiv. Strathfield: St. Paul's, 2015.

Pellicaan, Peter. "A Theology of Confirmation from the Canon of Scripture." PhD diss., University of Notre Dame Australia, 2021.

Pius XII. *Mystici Corporis Christi*. https://www.vatican.va/content/pius-xii/en/encyclicals/documents/hf_p-xii_enc_29061943_mystici-corporis-christi.html.

Pius X. *Quam Singulari*. https://www.papalencyclicals.net/pius10/p10quam.htm.

Rackham, Richard B. *The Acts of the Apostles*. Eugene, OR: Wipf & Stock, 2003.

Second Vatican Council. *Lumen Gentium*. In *Vatican Council II: The Conciliar and Post Conciliar Documents*, edited by Austin Flannery, 350–426. Collegeville, MN: Liturgical, 1975.

Talbert, Charles H. *Reading Corinthians: A Literary and Theological Commentary*. Chicago: Chicago Review, 2002.

Turner, Paul. "Benedict XVI and the Sequence of the Sacraments of Initiation." *Worship* 82 (2008) 132–40.

Vall, Gregory. *Ecclesial Exegesis: A Synthesis of Ancient and Modern Approaches to Scripture*. Washington, DC: The Catholic University of America Press, 2022.

Vanderkam, James C. "Covenant and Pentecost." *Calvin Theological Journal* 37 (2002) 239–54.

Walters, Barbara R., et al. *The Feast of Corpus Christi*. University Park, PA: Pennsylvania State University Press, 2006.

14

CONFIRMATION AND TRANSFIGURATION

Joseph Vnuk, OP

THE HOLY SPIRIT IS given in confirmation. This is obvious from the post-Vatican II formula and from the other prayers and elements of the rite, and it is a primary focus of the catechesis for the sacrament. This truth is undeniable, but it is also problematic, for two reasons. The first problem is that the Holy Spirit is also given in baptism, and we are left with the very good question of why we need a spiritual booster sacrament. As the saying goes, "Confirmation is a sacrament in search of a theology." The second problem can also be summed up in a saying: "Confirmation is the sacrament of leaving the Church." This reflects a pastoral problem rather than a theological one and reminds us that our theological question is not purely academic: we can hope that a good theology of the sacrament will inspire a pastoral practice that will help make a difference in the lives of those who receive the sacrament. We cannot leave this just to catechists or sacramental coordinators or liturgical historians; we must ask theological questions and seek answers in the Scriptures.[1]

The theological question will not be an immediately pneumatological one, but, following a healthy Trinitarian theology, it will be a Christological question, about Christ sent by the Father in the Holy Spirit. After looking a little at some evidence from the Fathers for this Christic side of confirmation, we shall then ask why our union with Christ in Christian initiation should be split into two. This will lead us to look at Christ's baptism and transfiguration,

---

1. See Peter Pellicaan's chapter, "Holy Spirit and the Sacrament of Confirmation," above.

to examine transfiguration symbolism in Christian initiation, and to see how it was understood by the Fathers, with a particular focus on illumination.

REFRAMING THE QUESTION: FROM PNEUMATOLOGY TO CHRISTOLOGY VIA THE TRINITY

The work of the Spirit cannot be separated from the work of the Son, indeed, any work of God in creation involves all three persons. You cannot have the Holy Spirit working solo, as that would imply a disunity in the God who is one in ways beyond our imagining. You cannot receive the Holy Spirit without at the same time receiving the Son, with both sent by the Father: this theological truth is the climax of Thomas' teaching on the Trinity.[2] Therefore, the question of why we need to receive the Holy Spirit again after baptism is also the question of why we should be united with Christ again after baptism. And that is an easier question to answer. It is hard to talk about separable aspects of the one, simple and undivided Spirit, but the incarnate Word shares the complexity of all human beings, and can be received, now in one way, now in another. Thomas Aquinas talks of the Word of God as not just any Word, but the *Verbum spirans Amorem*, the Word that breathes Love, that is, the Holy Spirit.[3] Can we talk about confirmation as primarily an engagement with Christ at a deeper level than at baptism, which is enabled by the Holy Spirit and leads to a new outpouring of that same Spirit?

WAS "CONFIRMATION" ORIGINALLY CHRISTIC?

The *Apostolic Tradition*

Given the uneasy status of confirmation as an independent sacrament, some liturgical historians have focused on the "pneumatic" tone of the rites that "consummated," "perfected," or "confirmed" the newly baptized. One can consider the discussion prompted by Aidan Kavanagh on the *Apostolic Tradition*.[4] He claims that in the earliest versions of the prayer in §22 said

2. Thomas Aquinas, *Summa Theologiae*, I, q. 43, especially a. 5. See also McGregor, "Introduction to Pneumatology at the Beginning of the Third Millennium," Ch. 1 and Rowland, "Milestones in Pneumatology from *Divinum Illud Munus* to *Dominum et Vivificantem*," Ch 14.

3. "Verbum, non qualecumque, sed spirans Amorem." Aquinas, *Summa Theologiae*, I, q. 43, a. 5, ad. 2.

4. Kavanagh, *Confirmation*, 44; Kavanagh, "Confirmation," 148–58. For a response, see Turner, "Origins of Confirmation," 238–58.

by the bishop before placing his hand on the neophyte's head, there was no distinctive reference to the Holy Spirit, and therefore this action was not proto-confirmation; nor was the anointing by the presbyter beforehand in §21, as the words were specifically Christic, not pneumatic. Indeed, he accuses Gregory Dix of inserting a reference to the Holy Spirit found in the later Ethiopic and Coptic versions to turn it into a precedent for the modern sacrament of confirmation.[5] But the bishop's words, like the baptismal formula, include all three Persons. If such a formula in baptism can unite us to Christ and give us the Spirit so that we can cry out *Abba!*, could not such a formula also unite us even more closely to Christ, the Son of the Father, and result in a further outpouring of the Spirit?

Augustine

But the eagerness of Gregory Dix—or the Ethiopic and Coptic copyists— to include a reference to the Holy Spirit is not without further precedent. Augustine is repeatedly arguing against those who, based on Acts 8, hold that the Holy Spirit is not given at all until the bishop lays hands. Augustine, acknowledging that this is the normal way things happen, argues further that the Holy Spirit is not given by human beings but by God who can give at any time, as at Pentecost, or with the centurion, or the Ethiopian eunuch; indeed, the Holy Spirit is given in baptism itself.[6] Augustine is in a sense warning us to be wary of how we interpret rites which have many parts that form an integral whole, of chopping up a unified rite into little bits doing totally separate things. As Paul Turner says, "The meaning of baptism is so rich that additional rites explore its wealth."[7] However, Augustine does not seem to give this laying on of hands any specific reference to Christ.

Cyprian

If we want to see a Christic significance at this point of the rite, we can go to Cyprian. On the basis of Acts 8, Cyprian seems to hold that the Holy Spirit is given by the laying on of hands, but he still sees the ceremony as related to Christ. He speaks of people being baptized in the Church and brought

5. See Dix, *Apostolic Tradition*, 38–39, where he adds a title "Confirmation" and includes the words "make them worthy to be filled with" between "laver of regeneration" and "Holy Spirit," which are not found in the earliest Latin version of the document.

6. Augustine, *Sermones*, 99.10–11 (PL 38:600–602); 266.3–4 (PL 38:1225–27); 269.2 (PL 38:1235).

7. Turner, "Origins of Confirmation," 255.

to the prelates, and "through our prayer and the imposition of hands, they obtain the Holy Spirit and *signaculo Dominico consummentur* (they are consummated with the little sign of the Lord)."[8] The "consummation" is not the "sign of the Holy Spirit," but the sign of the Lord, that is, Jesus.

Ambrose

Similarly, at the end of the rite of initiation, Ambrose, without indicating any extra ritual action, talks of Christ addressing his Church in the words of the Song of Songs, "Set me as a little seal (*signaculum*) on your heart, as a seal (*sigillum*) on your arm"—in other words, Christ himself is the seal. And then he asks the neophyte "Recall that you received the spiritual seal (*signaculum spiritale*), the spirit of wisdom and understanding, the spirit of counsel and virtue, the spirit of knowledge and piety, the spirit of holy fear: and preserve what you have received. God the Father has sealed (*signavit*) you, Christ the Lord has confirmed (*confirmavit*) you, and he has given [as] a pledge the Spirit in your hearts, as you learned in the reading from the Apostle."[9] The seal that makes the believer firm (confirms) is Christ, given by the Father (who seals); because the seal is Christ one can talk of a "spiritual seal," for Christ had the spirit of the Lord upon him, but the Spirit is not described as a seal, but as a pledge. Ambrose therefore repeats the basic ideas of Cyprian (a Christic seal and yet the bestowal of the Holy Spirit) and expands them.

Patrick

St. Patrick (c. 450) knows two separate parts of Christian initiation. In his *Confessio* he says "so that many people might through me be reborn into God and later consummated (*consummarentur*)," putting an interval of time between the two, and a little later in the same work we find the line "where no-one had ever come who might baptize or ordain clerics or consummate the people (*consummaret*)," where "consummation" is separated in the list from baptism by the sacrament of ordination.[10] That this consummation is Christic is clear from his *Letter to Coroticus*, where he talks of those "quos

8. Cyprian, *Ep.*, 73.9.

9. Ambrose, *De Mysteriis* 7.41–42 (SC 23*bis*, 178).

10. Patrick, *Confessio*, 38, 51, in Bieler, *Liber Epistolarum*, 78, 86.

ego in numerum Deo genui et in Christo confirmavi (whom I begot into the number [of the elect] for God and confirmed in Christ).”[11]

Thus we should not let early references to the bestowal of the Spirit at the end of Christian initiation hide the fact that these concluding rites were also Christic. When Thomas Aquinas maintains that all sacramental character—whether for baptism, for confirmation or for ordination—is participation in the character of Christ, he has solid patristic support.[12]

THE TWO FACES OF SONSHIP: BAPTISM AND TRANSFIGURATION

We have established that there is a basis in the tradition that in confirmation we are somehow joined to Christ, claimed as Christ's or made like Christ. But we are already joined to Christ, made members of his body, and sharers in his priestly, prophetic, and kingly office at baptism; we have gone into the grave with him and risen with him: what extra connection with Christ is added at confirmation? And why is this extra connection so important that it warrants a new sacrament?

Scriptural Support

Where we look for this new presence of Christ will in part depend on how we consider Christ to be present in baptism. Maxwell Johnson has convincingly presented the evidence that before Nicaea, and in many places for centuries afterwards, the principal scriptural texts used in conjunction with baptism did not include Romans 6, about dying and rising with Christ, but the accounts of Jesus' baptism in the Jordan.[13] And in all three synoptics this text, with the voice of the Father proclaiming Jesus' sonship, has its obvious double in the transfiguration. Thus, right from the beginning there is a recognition that the sonship of Jesus into which we are initiated has a two-fold aspect. Let us compare the way the sonship of Jesus is proclaimed in the various accounts.

---

11. Patrick, *Letter to Coroticus*, 3, in Bieler, *Liber Epistolarum*, 92.

12. Aquinas, *Summa Theologiae*, III, q. 63, a. 3.

13. Johnson, *Rites of Christian Initiation*, 47, 49, 53, 57–58, 64, 87.

	Baptism	**Transfiguration**
Mark	You are my son, the beloved	This is my son, the beloved,
	in whom I am well-pleased.	
1:1; 9:7		listen to him.
Luke	You are my son, the beloved	This is my son, the chosen,
	in whom I am well-pleased.	
3:22; 9:35		listen to him.
Matthew	This is my son, the beloved,	This is my son, the beloved,
	in whom I am well-pleased.	in whom I am well-pleased;
3:17; 17:5		listen to him.

Two main distinguishing features emerge. First of all, we must notice that, unlike Luke, Matthew has significantly altered the Marcan tradition, allowing the baptism and transfiguration texts to influence each other in a way that strengthens the connection between the two events; nonetheless, all three accounts distinguish the transfiguration from the baptism with a concluding "Listen to him." Luke has kept the Marcan text with one minor variant, and so in these two Gospels there is the second distinction: at the baptism the voice is directed towards Jesus himself, in contrast to the transfiguration, where it is directed towards the disciples.

A very common interpretation of "Listen to him" is that it harks back to the passion prediction, where Peter urged Jesus not to go to Jerusalem where arrest and execution awaited.[14] This is commonly corroborated by Jesus' remark in that passage that there are some present who will see the Son of Man in glory before they taste death, a prophecy some see fulfilled at the transfiguration.[15] As far as the disciples are concerned, the purpose of the transfiguration is to give them an assurance of Christ's final victory, so that they can listen to him and follow him through death to resurrection. We see this displayed in one of the few writers to offer an extensive comparison

---

14. For instance, Chrysostom, *Homiliae in Matthaeum* 56.2 (PG 58:552).

15. This idea that the prophecy is fulfilled at the transfiguration dates from at least the middle of the second century, for Clement of Alexandria gives it to us in a citation from Theodotus. See *Excerpta ex Scriptis Theodoti et Doctrina Quae Orientalis Vocatur* 4 (PG 9:656A–B). Origen reports some who have a similar interpretation, but this is too literal for Origen's liking, and is suitable for those who are still on milk rather than solid food; see *Commentarium in evangelium Matthaei* 12.31 (PG 13:1051C–1054B). That does not put an end to it, however, as we find it in Chrysostom, *Hom. Mat* 56.1 (PG 58:549).

and contrast the two scenes, Anselm of Laon in the *Glossa Ordinaria*, which I take as cited by Thomas in the *Catena Aurea*.

Scholastic Interpretations

First of all, Anselm interprets the shining clothes of Christ as the saints (an observation Thomas cites).[16] A little later he says:

> It should be noted that the mystery of the second regeneration (which will take place in the resurrection, when the flesh shall be brought to life) corresponds fittingly to the mystery of the first, which is in baptism, where the soul is brought to life. For in the baptism of Christ the working of the whole Trinity is shown, for there was the incarnate Son, the Holy Spirit appeared in the appearance of a dove, and the Father was there manifested in the voice; and similarly in the transfiguration, which is the sacrament of the second regeneration, the whole Trinity appeared: the Father in the voice, the Son in the human being, and the Holy Spirit in the cloud. But it is asked why the Holy Spirit was manifested there is the dove, and here in the cloud. The answer is that he is accustomed to manifest his gifts through the appearance. In baptism he gives simplicity, which is indicated through the simplicity of the bird. In the resurrection he will give glory and refreshment; therefore refreshment is indicated in the cloud, the glory of the rising bodies in the brightness of the cloud.[17]

Just because Anselm uses *sacramentum* with regard to the Transfiguration we should not jump to any conclusions. He is arguing for something different, and in the process he is using *sacramentum* as an equivalent of *mysterium*, talking of the "mysteries" of the life of Christ. His fundamental point seems to be the involvement of each Person of the Trinity in both our first, spiritual, regeneration (the sacrament of baptism) and our second, bodily, regeneration (the resurrection of the flesh). The parallel between the two mysteries and the two regenerations is not what it first seems to be, because while for Anselm our baptism corresponds to Christ's baptism, our resurrection corresponds, not to Christ's resurrection, but to the transfiguration. The solution is not to try somehow to assimilate the second to the first, but the first to the second. The baptism of Christ is not his birth, but a manifestation of his divine sonship, just as the

16. Aquinas, *Expositio in Matthaeum*, 17.1.

17. Aquinas, *Expositio in Matthaeum*, 17.2.

transfiguration is not the resurrection, but a pledge of it. Now, at Christ's baptism Jesus makes his sonship available to us (by "sanctifying the waters," a common patristic interpretation); at the transfiguration Jesus also shows his willingness to share his glory as Son with us, because even his clothes (which symbolize us) are made to shine.[18] And just as we use water symbolism in Christian initiation, so also we use the symbol of the white robe, which has an eschatological significance that is intimately connected with the transfiguration.

THE WHITE GARMENT

We should not underestimate the significance of the white robe in early Christianity. It was unthinkable that one should get baptized without one—when a large number of Jews in Agrigentinum in Sicily want to convert to the Christian faith, Gregory the Great instructs a certain Fantinus to go there and assist in various ways, including, for those who are poor, buying "a robe they can have at baptism," and to include it in his expenses.[19]

The symbolism of the white robe is twofold, as is clearly shown in the *De Mysteriis* of Ambrose.

> Then you received white garments as a sign that you had cast off the wrappings of sin and put on the chaste coverings of innocence, of which the prophet said: You will sprinkle me with hyssop and I shall be cleansed, you will wash me and I shall be made whiter than snow. One who is baptized is seen to be made clean in terms of the law and of the Gospel. In terms of the law, because with a bunch of hyssop Moses sprinkled the blood of the lamb; in terms of the Gospel, because Christ's garments were white as snow when in the Gospel he revealed the glory of his resurrection.[20]

Ambrose starts fairly naturally with the idea of the white robe signifying forgiveness and purity. But by quoting Psalm 50 with its reference to hyssop and "whiter than snow" Ambrose can lead into a reference to

18. John II of Jerusalem not only has the standard patristic comment that when Jesus is baptized, he is not purified, but sanctifies the waters so that we may be purified, but he uses this as a parallel to explain what is happening at the transfiguration, for Jesus, going up the mountain to pray, prays not to find mercy for himself, but so that he may gratify our prayers when we pray. See *Homily for the Feast of the Transfiguration*, in Coune, *Joie de la transfiguration*, 69.

19. Gregory the Great, *Register Epistolarum* 8.23 (PL 77:925A). See also *Reg.Ep.* 5.3 and 8.1 (PL 77:724C, 904D). These references are given in Pavan, "Veste bianca," 262.

20. Ambrose, *De Mysteriis* 7.34 (SC 23*bis*, 174; PL 16:399B–400A).

Moses and then to the one who is greater than Moses, who is Jesus himself. The whiteness of his robes is not about forgiveness, but rather they reveal the glory of his resurrection. This "revealing the glory" does not refer to the resurrection accounts themselves—none of the Gospels says that the risen Jesus wore white—but clearly to the transfiguration. This reference is necessary to bring out the eschatological significance of the white robe.

WHITE ROBES AND BEAUTIFUL FACES

We shall see a few other references linking white robes to the transfiguration, but we should not forget the full visual impact of the newly baptized. Consider St. Patrick's description of those whom, as noted above, he had "confirmed in Christ."

> Postera die qua crismati neophyti in candida veste—flagrabat in fronte ipsorum dum crudeliter trucidati atque mactati gladio supradictis—misi epistolam.

> The day after the neophytes in shining white clothes [had been] anointed with chrism—it was shining brightly on their foreheads when they were cruelly cut down and slain with the sword by the ones just mentioned—I sent a letter.[21]

Not only are they dressed in shining white, but their faces are blazing: the two features of the transfigured Jesus.

Texts that link the anointing of the face and the white robe are not easy to find, but one text so links the two as to make being anointed with chrism the equivalent of being clothed. The Gothic Missal (written between 690 and 710 in what is now eastern France) has a prayer used by the priest in the one post-baptismal anointing.[22]

> §261 Dum crisma eum tangis dicis

> Perungo te crisma sanctitatis tonicam immortalitatis qua dominus noster iesus Christus traditam a patre primus accepit ut eam integram et inlibatam perferas ante tribunal Christi et uiuas in saecula saeculorum.

> While you touch him with chrism you say

> I anoint you with the chrism of holiness, the tunic of immortality which, handed over by the Father, Our Lord Jesus Christ was the

---

21. Patrick, *Letter to Coroticus* 3, in Bieler, *Liber Epistolarum*, 53.
22. Els Rose, Introduction to *Missale Gothicum*, 15–16.

first to receive, that you may keep wearing it intact and unstained before the tribunal of Christ and may live for ever and ever.)[23]

Although some editors think that something has dropped out of the text just before the mention of the tunic,[24] more recent scholars hold that this is original, not a mistake. Bannister points to a possible Syrian influence, as a collection of Eastern prayers has one for the *Sancti unguenti officium* (Rite of holy anointing) that includes "Fac illud [unguentum] . . . esse incorruptionis indumentum (Make this [anointing] to be the clothing of incorruption)."[25] Another reason for holding this form as original is that there is an actual clothing in a white garment a little later at §263—only the washing of the feet intervenes.[26] Although the newly-baptized is asked to guard this "tunic" from tears and stains, the emphasis is on eternal life, which is referred to twice, but not at all in the prayer for the white garment. It is also a tunic given by the Father and first worn by Christ, thus holding a number of links to the transfiguration.

Indeed, the connection between chrism shining on the face and white garments is still made in the traditional Latin rite prayer for the consecration of the sacred chrism, retained in the current pontifical as the first option. This prayer twice mentions shining faces in connection with oil, "vultus nostros in oleo exhilarandos (our faces should be made glad with oil)" (citing Ps 103:15) and "hæc olei unctio vultus nostros iucundos efficit ac serenos (this anointing with oil makes our faces joyful and bright)" (referring to the use of the sacred chrism). A little later it talks of the anointing itself as a clothing: "regio et sacerdotali propheticoque honore perfusi, vestimento incorrupti muneris induantur (who have been poured over with royal, priestly and prophetic honor may be clothed with the robe of an uncorrupted gift)."[27]

---

23. *Missale Gothicum*, 450, with a note that a similar prayer in found in the Bobbio Missal, §253. The use "tonicam" for "tunicam" and "qua" for "quam" is typical of the state of Latin at that time and place: see Rose, Introduction to *Gothic Missal*, 43–44, 70–71; see also Bannister, "*Missale Gothicum*," 77, where the printed text gives "qua[m]."

24. Bannister's critical apparatus mentions Jean Mabillon (1685), Antonio Francesco Vezzosi (1747), and J. M. Neale and G. H. Forbes (1855), suggesting *induo te* (I clothe you with) or *induere* (put on). Bannister, "*Missale Gothicum*," 77.

25. Goar, *Euchologion*, in Bannister, "*Missale Gothicum*," 61.

26. Bannister, "*Missale Gothicum*," 77. This is simply a shining white (*candidam*) item of clothing (*vestimentum, vestem*) to be kept white until Christ's judgement.

27. *Ordo Benedicendi Oleum*, 13–15. I am grateful to Richard Conrad, who read a draft of this chapter, for directing me to this connection.

DIGRESSION: "TRANSFIGURATION" OR "TRANSFORMATION"?

Another writer to link the white robe and our face becoming Christ-like is Gregory of Nyssa. But as the argument will in places rely upon verbal links in the Greek, we need first to look at the Greek term used in the Synoptics, μεταμόρφόω, and its standard Latin (English) translation, "transfiguratio(n)."

The word μεταμόρφοωσις was an odd one to use for the event on Mount Tabor, as Jesus did not change in shape or form (μορφή), even if he did change in appearance. Simon Lee argues that even Mark's readers would have been familiar with the Hellenistic use of μεταμόρφοωσις for pagan stories of gods adopting another form, such as those by Lucius, Apuleius and Ovid, and also that in some of these the god becomes known by an overflow of glory. Given his argument elsewhere that both Mark and Paul are drawing on a prior tradition, one could propose that their shared use of the verb μεταμόρφόω may reflect an early borrowing from pagan literature to talk about the event. As the only change in Jesus was in his appearance, and as it was not a change of shape, but of brightness,[28] it is not a surprise that the Latin translators of Gospels did not use the obvious *transformatio* but opted for the weaker *transfiguratio* (which would normally translate words related to the Greek μετασχηατίζω.[29] But even here there are problems, and Thomas needs to explain that Jesus' *figura* (outward shape) does not change.[30]

The result of all this is that when μεταμόρφόω occurs in other places in the Bible it is translated, appropriately, as "transformed," and the verbal link to the transfiguration is lost to English readers. The obvious example is 2 Cor 3:18, and indeed the pericope which contains that verse is often seen as the earliest reference to the transfiguration, with the comparison to Moses and the reference to gazing upon the glory on the face of Christ offered as further evidence.[31] The verbal links are even harder to notice when related words are used. A word like συμμορφωθέντες would normally be translated "conformed," but in what follows below I shall use "conformed/configured" to make the link clear.

---

28. Simon Lee, *Jesus' Transfiguration*, 24–29, 50.

29. On the other hand, if the transfiguration causes *us* to change, we do not want the mere surface change denoted by μετασχηματίζω, but a deep and real μεταμόρφωσις. See Ramsey, *Glory of God*, 54.

30. Aquinas, *Summa Theologiae*, III, q. 47, a. 1, obj. 1 and ad. 1.

31. Dorothy Lee, *Transfiguration*, 111–13.

WHITE ROBES AND BEAUTIFUL FACES AGAIN

Gregory of Nyssa

The Gothic Missal had a face made to shine at initiation by chrism that symbolized the robe of immortality, but it lacked an explicit link to the transfiguration. Gregory of Nyssa starts with a metaphorical robe of immortality which he links explicitly to the transfiguration and by allusion to sacramental initiation, but then goes on to talk about the beauty of the face. At the beginning of his homilies on the Song of Songs, Gregory of Nyssa tells his readers to aim for the deeper meaning of this book:

> You who have followed the advice of Paul and have put off the old human being like dirty clothes and have wrapped yourself in the luminous cloaks of the Lord, which he showed at the transfiguration (μεταμορφώσις) on the mountain, through purity of life, or more correctly those who have put on (ἐνδυσάμενοι) our Lord Jesus Christ himself with his holy robe and have been "conformed/configured" (συμμορφωθέντες) to him to what is not swayed by emotion (*apathes*) and more divine, hear the mysteries of the Song of Songs.[32]

The "putting off of the old man" is a reference to Eph 4:22, but "putting on of our Lord Jesus Christ" as the equivalent of putting on clothes of light uses very much the same language as Rom 13: 12, 14: "let us put on (ἐνδυσώμεθα) the armor of light . . . put on (ενδύσασθε) the Lord Jesus Christ." Furthermore, this language, which encourages behavior in the present, is related to what ritually took place at their Christian initiation, as Paul reminds his readers in Galatians 3:26 "for all of you who were baptized into Christ have put on (ἐνεδύσασθε) Christ." It is our Christian initiation that enables us to receive what the transfigured Jesus offers us.

According to one ancient theory of vision, the object seen makes an impression on the one who sees and in this way vision takes place.[33] Indeed, if you stare into someone's eyes, you can see your face in their pupils. And therefore, in the Song of Songs the lover praises the beloved's eyes, and "the image (ἔίδος) of the dove which appears in her pupils becomes the praise of the beauty (εὐμορφίας) of her eyes." A few lines later, citing St. Paul (Gal 5:16), Gregory argues that having "the image of the Dove in her eyes is a sign of a soul set free from all bodily attachment." Moreover, "able to receive

32. Gregory of Nyssa, *In Cantica Canticorum* 1.1 (PG 44:764).

33. See Kevin Wagner's chapter, "Spirit as Dove in Patristic Interpretations of the Canticle of Canticles," above. This treatment of vision makes ample use of Wagner's work.

the imprint of the dove, her soul has the capacity to contemplate the beauty of the bridegroom. For now the virgin first gazes on the form (μορφή) of the bridegroom, when she took possession of the dove with her eyes—'No-one can say "Jesus is Lord" except in the Holy Spirit.'"[34]

He takes up the idea again in Homily 5, explaining the verse "Arise, come, my neighbor, my beautiful one, my dove." This time he also includes the idea of a mirror (κατόπτριον), a word-root that occurs only once in Scripture as κατοπτρίζομαι (reflecting, as in a mirror), namely, at 2 Corinthians 3:18—the passage that contains the verb for transfiguration. "For how is it possible to see a beautiful face in a mirror, unless it receives the reflection of someone with a beautiful figure (μορφῆς). And so the mirror of human nature only becomes beautiful when it comes close to the beautiful one, and it is inwardly formed (ἐνεμορφώθη) by the image of the divine beauty." Gregory then says that when it lies on the ground (has earthly desires) it can only see the serpent, when it rises it can see the divine beauty and be transformed (σχηματίζεται) into what it sees.[35]

Origen

This interpretation of the Song of Songs needs to be read along with Origen's. Origen also repeatedly says that we only understand the spiritual sense of the Scriptures if we read them with the eyes of the dove.[36] The extra point Origen makes is that the spiritual reading goes beyond the historical: it is to read the Scriptures as being fulfilled not only historically in the time of Christ, but also today, in us.

> If you understand the Law spiritually, your eyes are those of a dove; so too if you understand the Gospel as the Gospel means itself to be understood and preached, seeing Jesus not only having healed "all sickness and infirmity" at the time when those things happened in the flesh, but also healing today, and

34. Gregory of Nyssa, *Cant.* 4 (PG 44:833D–836A). Ambrose offers a similar exposition of this passage when talking of those who have just been clothed in white after baptism. "But Christ, seeing in shining white clothes his Church, on behalf of whom he, as you have in the book of Zechariah the Prophet [Zech 3:5], took on *dirty clothes*, or [seeing] the soul white and washed clean in the laver of regeneration, says: *Behold, you are beautiful, my neighbor, behold you are beautiful, your eyes are like doves*; in whose image (*specie*) the Holy Spirit descended from heaven. The eyes [are] beautiful, as we said above, because he descended like a dove." *Myst.* 7.37 (SC 23*bis*, 176) (italics in the original to indicate scriptural quotes).

35. Gregory of Nyssa, *Cant.* 5 (PG 44:867 C–D).

36. Wagner, "Spirit as Dove."

[realizing] not only that he came down then to human beings, but that today also he comes down and is present; for "Behold, I am with you all days, even to the consummation of the world."[37]

The links become even clearer when we recall that the idea of a "spiritual" as opposed to a "literal" reading of the Scriptures comes from 2 Cor 3:6, "The letter kills, but the Spirit gives life," which is the occasion for Paul to make the comparison between the fading shine of the face of Moses and the ever-brightening shine on the believer who turns to the "Lord who is Spirit."

TRANSFIGURATION AND CHRISTIAN INITIATION

We could put the themes together this way. To come to perfection, our faith in Christ must follow him through death to eternal life, but, like Peter, we are afraid to follow and would prefer that Christ did not lead us into Jerusalem; we are unable to listen to him, and therefore are unable to understand the Scriptures as fulfilled in him and to be fulfilled in us. In the transfiguration, Jesus reveals his future glory and, by letting his clothes shine as well, promises that we will share that glory too. If we can trust that promise, then we can bear to listen to him, and we can understand the Scriptures as the promise to us of eternal life if we take the path of Christ. Then we can contemplate the mysteries of his glory, a glory that does not fade but rather one that we enter more and more deeply, becoming like him in glory. Although we are not on the mountain, that promise and therefore that enlightenment or illumination are given to us symbolically in our Christian initiation, when we are given the white robe of immortality and our faces are made to shine with the sacred chrism.

These themes are already present in 2 Corinthians 3, which, as we have seen, many scholars take as a reference to the transfiguration. These same themes are also found in the Church Fathers, who repeatedly call Christian initiation "illumination" and who take the ascent of Mount Tabor as a penetration of the mysteries through the ascent of contemplation. The few texts presented here are those most useful for arguing the connection between the various themes.

To put it another way, something takes place in Christian initiation which requires us to go beyond the baptism accounts to those of the transfiguration, and which is symbolized in Christian initiation by the white robe and the anointing. This "extra" does not require any additional

---

37. Origen, *Homiliae in Canticum Canticorum* 2.4 (SC 37:87–88).

rite (Ambrose does not seem to have one), but it is weighty enough, and sufficiently grounded in the Gospels, that Christian initiation can be divided into what we in the Latin rite call baptism and confirmation.

A POSSIBLE PASTORAL APPROACH

Much more could be said. We still have not even touched the witness of the book of Revelation, which begins with the voice of the One whose face shines like the sun, and in which those who prove victorious are clothed in white and are sealed on the forehead with the seal of the living God. However, we do have enough of a theology of confirmation to give a few pastoral ideas about how to prepare for the sacrament.

If confirmation is not given along with infant baptism or soon after, then it should be delayed until the young believer is humanly capable of interpreting a text both literally and symbolically. Preparation for the sacrament would focus on learning to read Scripture (and put it into practice), just as in the early Church a great deal of the instruction of catechumens was focused on seeing the Old Testament as fulfilled in Christ. Key foundational texts would be 2 Corinthians 3 and the Synoptic transfiguration accounts. The standard four senses of Scripture—literal, allegorical, tropological, and anagogical—would be taught, although the terminology may need to be adapted for work with adolescents.[38] Through the historical (literal) sense, they would learn the history of God's saving work; through the allegorical sense they would learn to find Christ on every page of the Scriptures, and so move beyond any deadly interpretation that could be stuck merely on the blessings of this world, or still caught up in cycles of violence. The anagogical sense would give them the hope of sharing in Christ's glory, so that they would not be afraid of the tropological or moral sense whereby they apply the example of Christ to their own behavior. It may even be appropriate to give examples of all these techniques in the interpretation of the Song of Songs.

But the catechesis would also be focused on the symbolism of the sacrament. The candidates would be clothed in white robes, recalling their baptismal gown, but now with the meaning of innocence and purity extended to being the pledge of immortality. The chrism would be presented as making their face shine like Christ (which would mean a lavish anointing, rather than just a dab). The gifts of the Holy Spirit would be linked to the Spirit of Jesus being upon us as well, with the intellectual gifts focusing on

---

38. See Aquinas, *Summa Theologiae*, I, q. 1, a. 10.

the interpretation of Scripture, and the moral gifts on living as Jesus did (putting Scripture into practice).[39]

As all sacraments are ordered towards the Eucharist, the catechesis at confirmation should make the connection as well. For it is by receiving the Word become flesh that we are transformed into the one we read about in the Scripture. And if they study the Song of Songs, it can also be presented as the wedding feast.

BIBLIOGRAPHY

Ambrose. *De sacramentis. De mystères. Explications do symbole.* Edited by Bernard Botte. Sources Chrétiennes, 25 bis. Lyons: Sources Chrétiennes, 1991.

Aquinas, Thomas. *Catena Aurea in Quatuor Evangelia.* Vol. 1, *Expositio in Matthaeum et Marcum.* Edited by Angelico Guarienti. Turin: Marietti, 1953.

———. *Summa Theologiae.* Vol. 1, *Prima Pars.* Edited by Pontifical Institute of Medieval Studies, Ottawa. 2nd rev. ed. Ottawa: Commissio Piana, 1953.

———. *Summa Theologiae.* Vol. 2, *Prima Secundae.* Edited by Pontifical Institute of Medieval Studies, Ottawa. 2nd rev. ed. Ottawa: Commissio Piana, 1953.

———. *Summa Theologiae.* Vol. 3, *Secunda Secundae.* Edited by Pontifical Institute of Medieval Studies, Ottawa. 2nd rev. ed. Ottawa: Commissio Piana, 1953.

———. *Summa Theologiae.* Vol. 4, *Tertia Pars.* Edited by Pontifical Institute of Medieval Studies, Ottawa. 2nd rev. ed. Ottawa: Studium Generale OP, 1944.

Bannister, H. M., ed. *"Missale Gothicum": A Gallican Sacramentary MS Vatican Regin. Lat. 317.* Vol. 1, *Text and Introduction.* London: Bradshaw Society, 1917.

Bieler, Ludwig, ed. *Liber Epistolarum Sancti Patricii Episcopi: Introduction, Text, and Commentary.* Dublin: Royal Irish Academy, 1993.

Coune, Michel, ed. *Joie de la transfiguration d'après les pères d'orient.* Bégrolles-en-Mauges, Maine-&-Loire: Abbaye de Bellefontaine, 1983.

Cyprian. *Epistularium. Epistulae 58–81.* Edited by G. F. Diercks. Corpus Christianorum Series Latina 3b. Turnhout: Brepols, 1996.

Dix, Gregory, ed. *The Treatise on the Apostolic Tradition of St. Hippolytus of Rome Bishop and Martyr.* Vol. 1. London: SPCK, 1937.

Johnson, Maxwell, ed. *Living Water, Sealing Spirit: Readings on Christian Initiation.* Collegeville, MN: Liturgical, 1995.

———. *The Rites of Christian Initiation: Their Evolution and Interpretation.* Collegeville, MN: Liturgical, 1999.

Kavanagh, Aidan. *Confirmation: Origins and Reform.* New York: Pueblo, 1988.

———. "Confirmation: A Suggestion from Structure." In *Living Water, Sealing Spirit: Readings on Christian Initiation,* edited by Maxwell Johnson, 148–58. Collegeville, MN: Liturgical, 1995.

39. Thomas Aquinas, who draws attention to the fact that these are first of all gifts that Christ enjoyed and that Scripture calls them spirits rather than gifts, emphasizes their role in the interpretation of Scripture; see *Summa Theologiae* I–II, q. 68, a. 1 cor; II–II, qq. 8–9, especially II–II, q. 8, a. 6 cor, where he talks of the role of the gifts in understanding what is revealed to us to be believed, which is the whole of Scripture (cf. II–II, q. 1, a. 1, ad. 2).

Lee, Dorothy. *Transfiguration.* London: Continuum, 2004.

Lee, Simon S. *Jesus' Transfiguration and the Believers' Transformation.* Tübingen: Mohr Siebeck, 2009.

Missale Gothicum e codice Vaticano Reginensi latino 317 editum. Edited by Els Rose. Corpus Christianorum Series Latina 159D. Turnhout: Brepols, 2005.

Origen. *Homélies sur le Cantique.* Edited by Olivier Rousseau. Translated by St. Jerome. Sources Chrétiennes, 37 bis. Lyons: Sources Chrétiennes, 2007.

Ordo Benedicendi Oleum Catechumenorum et Infirmorum et Conficiendi Chrisma: Editio Typica. Roma: Typis Polyglottis Vaticana, 1971.

Patrologia Latina. Edited by J.-P. Migne. 217 vols. Paris, 1844–64.

Patrologia Graeca. Edited by J.-P. Migne. 162 vols. Paris, 1857–86.

Pavan, Vincenzo. "La veste bianca battesimale, *indicium* escatologico nella Chiesa dei primi secoli." *Augustinianum* 18 (1978) 257–71.

Ramsey, Arthur Michael. *The Glory of God and the Transfiguration of Christ.* London: Longmans, 1949.

Turner, Paul. "The Origins of Confirmation: An Analysis of Kavanagh's Hypothesis." In *Living Water, Sealing Spirit: Readings on Christian Initiation,* edited by Maxwell Johnson, 238–58. Collegeville, MN: Liturgical, 1995.

15

MILESTONES IN PNEUMATOLOGY FROM *DIVINUM ILLUD MUNUS* TO *DOMINUM ET VIVIFICANTEM*

Tracey Rowland

BETWEEN 1897 AND 1986 only two papal encyclicals directly addressed the subject of pneumatology. Almost one century of theological scholarship is bookended by Leo XIII's *Divinum Illud Munus* (*On the Holy Spirit*) and John Paul II's *Dominum et Vivificantem* (*The Lord, the Giver of Life*).

Divinum Illud Munus emphasized the unity of the persons of the Trinity. In the third paragraph which is the heart of the encyclical, Leo XIII declared that the Persons of the Trinity are not to be honored separately in divine worship nor are they considered as acting separately in the work of sanctification. He noted that even if the three Persons are mentioned separately in prayers such as litanies, such prayers should always end with an invocation to the Blessed Trinity. Leo XIII also made reference to St. Augustine's comment in *De Trinitate*, that the words "of Him, and by Him, and in Him" are not to be taken indiscriminately; but rather "of Him refers to the Father, by Him to the Son, and in Him to the Holy Ghost" (*De Trin.* 1. vi., c. 10; 1. i., c. 6). Pope Leo then affirmed the custom of the Church of attributing to the Father those works of the Divinity in which power excels, to the Son those in which wisdom excels, and to the Holy Spirit those in which love excels. Notwithstanding this appropriation he quickly added the caveat that all perfections and external operations are common to the Divine Persons because the "operations of the Trinity are indivisible."

The sequel to this 1897 encyclical is the 1943 encyclical of Pius XII titled *Mystici Corporis Christi* (*The Mystical Body of Christ*). Paragraph 57 of *Mystici Corporis Christi* refers back to the statement of *Divinum Illud* to the effect that while Christ is the Head of the Church, the Holy Spirit is her soul. This principle is defended in paragraphs 56 and 57 where the various works of the Holy Spirit in the life of Christ and in the Church are enumerated. Included here is the statement that it is the Holy Spirit who makes the members of the Church adopted sons of God, and who assists them in proportion to their various duties and offices and in proportion to the greater or lesser degree of spiritual health which they enjoy. The Holy Spirit is described as "the principle of every supernatural act in all parts of the Body of Christ."[1]

In both of these encyclicals the Holy Spirit is treated primarily in the context of the Spirit's relationship to the other two Persons of the Trinity, secondly, in the context of the Spirit's work in the life of the Church, and thirdly, in the context of the Spirit's work in the souls of individual members of the body of Christ. These contexts correspond to the fields of Trinitarian theology, and what Yves Congar was to call *ecclésiologie pneumatologique* and *anthropologie pneumatologique* or pneumatological ecclesiology and pneumatological anthropology.

In the field of Catholic Trinitarian theology arguably the most seminal work of the twentieth century was Karl Rahner's 1967 publication in the *Mysterium Salutis* series, and its reprint three years later as a stand-alone volume, simply titled *The Trinity*. This publication is famous for Rahner's criticism that Catholics had become "almost mere monotheists" and for his axiom: The economic Trinity is the immanent Trinity and the immanent Trinity is the economic Trinity. This axiom has spawned so many publications that it could be said to have opened up its own sub-field of Trinitarian theology. Although it was in the 1967 publication that the axiom first appears as such, it was foreshadowed in Rahner's earlier works, including his 1939 article published in *Zeitschrift für katholische Theologie*.[2] While various authors have sought to criticise the second half of the axiom, that the immanent Trinity is the economic Trinity, there has been something like universal agreement that Rahner was correct in his general judgment about there being a constructive, unwitting, monotheism in much pre-Conciliar era Catholic theology.

Consistent with Rahner's concern about an unintentional monotheism throughout the decades of the second half of the twentieth century many

---

1. Pius XII, *Mystici Corporis*, sec. 57.
2. Rahner, "Zur scholastiischen Begrifflichkeit," 137–57.

scholarly monographs appeared examining the salvific work of one particular Person of the Trinity. Most notable in this genre is Louis Bouyer's trilogy *The Eternal Son*, *The Invisible Father*, and *The Consoler*, first published in their French versions between 1973 and 1980.

In the second and third abovementioned fields of pneumatological ecclesiology and pneumatological anthropology, the "lion" was Yves Congar with his *I Believe in the Holy Spirit* trilogy and the later short monograph titled "The Word and the Spirit" which included material on the Holy Spirit as "co-instituting the Church" and the charisms as structuring principles of the Church. One of Congar's recurring themes was the idea that institution and charism are not opposed to one another, notwithstanding the tension between the two. Congar's work was a milestone because it sought to unify the pneumatological ecclesiology with a pneumatological anthropology. In his summary of this work of unification Cornelis van Vliet argued that Congar examined the relationship between the ecclesiological and anthropological work of the Holy Spirit through the lens of three biblical motifs: the mystical Body of Christ, the People of God, and the Temple of the Holy Spirit. Vliet further argued that the mystical body motif dominated Congar's ecclesiology between 1931 and 1944; the theology of the People of God motif dominated between 1959 and 1968; and the theology of the Temple of the Holy Spirit came to the fore between 1969 and 1991.[3] All three of these motifs are given extensive treatment by Benoît-Dominique de La Soujeole, in his *Introduction to the Mystery of the Church*. They also appear in the Conciliar Constitution on the Church, known as *Lumen Gentium* (1964). The ecclesiology of Vatican II is both Christological and Pneumatological. Speaking of the Pneumatological dimension Aloys Grillmeier wrote:

> The Church is a unity of communion in the holy Eucharist, in the Holy Spirit, in the (visible) hierarchical government and in the various forms of service. It is an animated bodily unity in the variety of its members and their functions. And the hierarchical order is a self-communication of the Spirit just as are charismatic endowments. Thus the Spirit is embodied in the Church, where he produces a mystical person from many persons.[4]

In his treatment of the Conciliar understanding of the Church as the Temple of the Holy Spirit, Benoît-Dominique de La Soujeole emphasizes that

---

3. Vliet, *Communio sacramentalis*, 83–87, 200–8, 244–46. See also Groppe, *Yves Congar's Theology of the Holy Spirit*, ch. 4.

4. Grillmeier, "Mystery of the Church," 142.

> Unity among Christians is received from the Holy Spirit in
> Person; it is not "produced" by human initiative. . . . The pastors
> do not bring about the deepest unity of the Church as a colonel
> brings about the unity of a regiment—in other words, principally
> by commanding and by being obeyed.[5]

Unity is, rather, the fruit of the gifts of the Holy Spirit, the "hierarchy is not 'productive' of the fundamental unity (as in a socio-juridical scheme), but rather the servant of the gift of unity."[6] In short, unity cannot be coerced by Petrine or episcopal decree.

Discerning what the will of the Holy Spirit is, is not, however, an easy task. In his introduction to the first volume of *I Believe in the Holy Spirit* subtitled *The Experience of the Spirit*, Congar observed that "revelation and knowledge of the Spirit are affected by a certain lack of conceptual mediation."[7] While the idea of a Father and a Son are easy to understand, the "Spirit" is much less accessible. He suggested that "the Holy Spirit empties himself, in a kind of kenosis of his own personality, in order to be in a relationship, on the one hand, with 'God' and Christ and, on the other, with men, who are called to realise the image of God and his Son."[8] The Holy Spirit is therefore revealed to us and known to us not in himself, but through what he brings about in us.[9] This makes sense of Christ's principle that "by their fruits you will know them" (Matt 7:15–20).[10] A key element of any pneumatological anthropology is therefore a person's receptivity to the gifts of the Holy Spirit.

In the context of his pneumatological anthropology, Congar, following St. Thomas Aquinas, affirmed the importance of the seven gifts of the Holy Spirit for moral theology. He described the gifts as "dispositions" that make the Christian ready to grasp and follow and inspirations of the Holy Spirit "beyond the power of the virtues, beyond his reason as animated by faith, beyond his supernatural prudence, by another who is infinitely superior and has sovereign freedom."[11] The "another" here is the Holy Spirit. For Congar the gifts are not superior to the theological virtues of faith, hope, and love, but are at the service of the virtues, "enabling them to be practiced

---

5. La Soujeole, *Introduction to the Mystery of the Church*, 189.

6. La Soujeole, *Introduction to the Mystery of the Church*, 189.

7. Congar, *Experience of the Spirit*, vii.

8. Congar, *Experience of the Spirit*, vii.

9. Congar, *Experience of the Spirit*, viii.

10. Biblical references in this chapter are from the NABRE.

11. Congar, *Experience of the Spirit*, 119–20.

perfectly."[12] Congar further argued that "this is a position far removed from a purely rational moral attitude, or from an attitude often imputed to Thomas, that is, a morality based on models derived from a nature of things that is established outside time."[13] On the contrary, "Thomas allows for the *event* of the Spirit; for him, morality is based on the saving and sanctifying will of God, according to norms which go beyond human and even supernatural reason."[14] While reason and a conception of natural law both have their place in Thomistic moral teaching, such teaching cannot be reduced to arguments based upon reason and natural law alone.[15]

In addition to building bridges between pneumatological ecclesiology and pneumatological anthropology, Congar also spent time criticizing Joachimism—the idea that there can be a relatively autonomous and new time of the Holy Spirit, transcending the time of Christ, as put forward by Joachim of Fiore (c. 1135–1202), the founder of the monastic order of San Giovanni in Fiore. According to Congar, Thomas Aquinas was "resolutely, severely and radically critical of Joachim's teaching. He regarded Joachim as a lout playing with theology; 'in *subtilibus fidei dogmatibus rudis*,' and his theology of the Trinity in particular as wrong."[16] Congar wrote:

> Joachim introduced into the history of this world, which was for him, of course, the history of the Church, an eschatology that was characterized by the great novelty of a rule of the inner life and of freedom. Joachim in his way opened the flood-gates to admit what could well become the torrent of human hopes. This could at any time result in social protest, a polarized attempt to reform the Church, or many different searches for freedom and novelty. It could take the form of philosophies of reason, of progress, of the "spirit." . . . There have been, parallel to what Etienne Gilson called "metamorphoses of the City of God," a series of metamorphoses of Joachimism which have often been forms of secularization of the Spirit. I summarise the most important.[17]

Congar's summary then ran for two pages and included Kant, Hegel, Schelling, and Adolf Hitler as examples of those infected with the spirit of

12. Congar, *Experience of the Spirit*, 120.

13. Congar, *Experience of the Spirit*, 120.

14. Congar, *Experience of the Spirit*, 120.

15. For a treatment of these issues, see Melina, *Sharing in Christ's Virtues*.

16. Congar, *Experience of the Spirit*, 127. For a criticism of Joachimism, see also La Soujeole, *Introduction to the Mystery of the Church*, 143–44.

17. Congar, *Experience of the Spirit*, 129.

Joachimism, before he ended his summary with a quotation from Thomas Altizer as an example of where the dangerous trajectory of Joachmite ideas can end. Altizer, an Episcopalian theologian associated with the "death of God" movement, declared:

> The radical Christian also inherits both the ancient prophetic belief that revelation continues in history and the eschatological belief of the tradition following Joachim of Floris. This tradition maintains that we are now living in the third and final age of the Spirit, that a new revelation is breaking into this age and that this revelation will differ as much from the New Testament as the New Testament itself does from its Old Testament counterpart. ... We can learn from earlier radical Christians the root radical principle that the movement of the Spirit has passed beyond the revelation of the canonical Bible and is now revealing itself in such a way as to demand a whole new form of faith. To refuse such a new revelation of the Spirit would be to repudiate the activity of the Word which is present and to bind oneself to a now empty and lifeless form of the Word. Nor can we expect the new revelation to be in apparent continuity with the old. ... Yet this should by no means persuade us that no new revelation has occurred. We can only judge by the fruits of the Spirit and if a new vision has arisen recoding a universal and eschatological form of the Word, a form of the Word pointing to a total redemption of history and the cosmos, then we should be prepared to greet it with the full acceptance of faith.[18]

Congar was strongly critical of such a way of thinking which in Catholic circles often arises in the context of discussions about reading the signs of the times. Congar addressed the subject of what Christ meant about reading the signs of the times in Volume II of *I Believe in the Holy Spirit*, subtitled *Lord and Giver of Life*. He wrote:

> However useful and indeed necessary the work of sociologists may be, these indications should not be interpreted purely sociologically, but rather in the light of the gospel, inspired by faith and led by the Holy Spirit. ... I do not deny that God acts in the history of the secular world or that historical events and movements can tell us something of what God wants for us and therefore of what he is. What is difficult, however, is the interpretation of those events. Interpretation is able to go further than mere conjecture and personal conviction only if the meaning of the facts is tied to and illuminated by the positive

18. Congar, *Experience of the Spirit*, 133.

revelation of God's plan with Jesus Christ at its centre. And here we need to bear in mind that the salvation and the kingdom that God's plan envisages include the world of creation and are God's response to creation's groaning and its hope (see Romans 8:20–24).[19]

A few pages later, as if to underscore the point, Congar declared:

The Spirit, however, is the Spirit of Jesus Christ. He does no other work but that of Jesus Christ. There is no time of the Paraclete that is not the time of Jesus Christ, contrary to what Joachim of Fiore, who misinterpreted the original and correct idea that he had of history as open to hope and newness, seemed to believe. The catholicity of the Church is the catholicity of Christ. The soundness of any pneumatology is its reference to Christ.[20]

Congar thus insisted that the Spirit does not invent or introduce a new and different economy. Rather he gives life to the flesh and words of Jesus (cf. John 6:63). He recalls those words to mind and penetrates the whole truth: "He will not speak on his own account, but whatever he hears he will speak. . . . He will glorify me."[21]

Congar also concurred with St. Augustine's idea that the Church exists in two orbs or circles. The first of these is the *communio sacramentorum*, which is the work of Christ, and the second is the *societas sanctorum*, which is the work of the Holy Spirit.[22] Following the line of argumentation in the magisterial documents Congar also noted that for Augustine, the Holy Spirit performs in the Church that function that is carried out in the body by the soul.[23]

The opposition to Joachimism was also strong in the theology of Hans Urs von Balthasar. While Rahner, Bouyer, Congar and others contributed to the field of pneumatology by exploring the economic Trinity, Hans Urs von Balthasar and the mystic Adrienne von Speyr went exploring in the opposite direction with their speculations on the work of *kenosis* within the immanent Trinity. One of the best examinations of this aspect of Balthasarian thought is Michele M. Schumacher's *A Trinitarian Anthropology: Adrienne von Speyr and Hans Urs von Balthasar in Dialogue with Thomas Aquinas*, published in 2014. In this work, Schumacher seeks to promote dialogue between

19. Congar, *Lord and Giver of Life*, 32.

20. Congar, *Lord and Giver of Life*, 35.

21. Congar, *Experience of the Spirit*, 56–57.

22. Congar, *Experience of the Spirit*, 80.

23. Congar, *Experience of the Spirit*, 80.

disciples of Balthasar (d. 1988) and those of Aquinas (d. 1274) on the critical theological question of how analogies and metaphors drawn from the philosophy and theology of the person (that is, from anthropology) may rightly be used to address the mystery of the Trinity. For those seeking to understand Balthasar's pneumatology the books to read are the last volume of the Theo-logic titled *The Spirit of Truth*, and the third volume of his *Explorations in Theology*, titled *Creator Spirit*. In *Creator Spirit* Balthasar offered his analysis of the problems with Joachimism. In a pithy statement Balthasar declared:

> The only thing that must be set down as certain for the moment is that the trinitarian Spirit will never let his divine freedom blow elsewhere than in the sphere of the love between Father and Son, and that he will not encounter and direct the human spirit in any other way than by judging it and redeeming it and giving it admittance to this love of which he is the fruit and the witness.[24]

In *The Trinitarian Theology of Hans Urs von Balthasar*, Brendan McInerny argues that Balthasar's description of the immanent Trinity provides a way to speak of how "God is love" in himself, beyond his relationship to creatures.[25] He then shows how Balthasar's speculation into the immanent Trinity serves as the substructure of his theology of deification. One might say that pneumatology is the bridge between spirituality and dogmatic theology for Balthasar.

A work that drills deep into the relationship between Balthasar's Trinitarian theology and his theology of deification is *Kenosis in Theosis: An Exploration of Balthasar's Theology of Deification* by Sigurd Lefsrud. Lefsrud argues that in the theology of Balthasar "becoming like God" goes beyond simply being "like Christ" to participating in the kenotic relations of the three Persons of the Trinity.[26] In other words, he argues, in Balthasar's theology there is a movement from describing humanity as the *imago dei* to characterizing this image as the *imago Christi*, and finally to considering humanity as the *imago trinitatis*.[27]

Running, in a sense, parallel with the work of Balthasar was Jean Daniélou's 1968 book *La Trinité et la Mystère de l'existence* that was published in English under the title *God's Life in Us*. Marc Nicholas has described it as offering a doxological humanism, highlighting the place of pneumatology

---

24. Balthasar, *Creator Spirit*, 156.

25. McInerny *Trinitarian Theology of Hans Urs von Balthasar*.

26. Lefsud, *Kenosis in Theosis*, 141.

27. Lefsud, *Kenosis in Theosis*, 141.

in theological anthropology. The book offers a theological reflection upon the words, "Through Him, with Him, in Him, in the unity of the Holy Spirit, all glory and honour is yours, almighty Father, for ever and ever." Daniélou (1905–74) concurred with Leonce de Grandmaison's statement that the continuing work of the Word and the Spirit in the world aims at "all men becoming Christians and all Christians becoming saints."[28] In other words, "the primary goal of missionary activity is the expansion of Trinitarian life through the believer's sharing in the divine life of the triune God."[29]

While Daniélou represented the Jesuit tradition, his fellow countryman Marie-Joseph le Guillou (1920–90) represented the Dominican tradition. In the post-Conciliar era Guillou followed in the footsteps of Congar in producing works on the Holy Trinity including *Les Témoins sont parmi nous. L'expérience de Dieu dans l'Esprit Saint* and the posthumous publication *L'expérience de l'Esprit-Saint en Orient et en Occident*. Guillou also contributed an essay on the development of the doctrine of the Holy Spirit in the books of the New Testament at the Congress titled *Credo in Spiritum Sanctum* held in Rome in 1982 to celebrate the 1600th anniversary of the Council of Constantinople and the 1550th anniversary of the Council of Ephesus.[30] The Congress brought together the leading scholars in pneumatology from around the world, including Congar, whose contribution, "Actualité de la Pneumatologie" was a passionate affirmation of the reality of work of the Holy Spirit in the contemporary world, Ignace de La Potterie who contributed a paper on the Holy Spirit and the Church, and John Zizioulas, who contributed an essay on the teaching of the Second Ecumenical Council on the Holy Spirit in Historical and Ecumenical Perspective.[31] Guillou also followed in the footsteps of Bouyer and Congar in working in the field of ecumenism, especially Catholic-Orthodox ecumenism, where pneumatology is the axial issue.

Arriving now at the papacy of St. John Paul II (1978–2005), just one decade after the publication of Rahner's *The Trinity*, St. John Paul II began his quarter-century teaching pontificate with a suite of encyclicals on each of the Divine Persons. *Redemptor Hominis* on God the Son was published in 1979, *Dives in Misericordia* on God the Father followed in 1980 and *Dominum et Vivificantem* on God the Holy Spirit completed the trilogy in 1986. This pattern of highlighting the specific role of each of the Divine

28. Daniélou, "Missionary Nature of the Church," 14.

29. Nicholas, *Jean Daniélou's Doxological Humanism*, 89.

30. Guillou, "Développement de la doctrine," 729–39.

31. Congar, "Actualité de la Pneumatologie," 15–28; La Potterie, "L'Esprit Saint et l'Église," 791–808; Zizioulas, "Teaching of the Second Ecumenical Council," 29–53.

Persons in the economy of salvation was then followed in the second decade of the Wojtyłian pontificate with the declaration of 1997 as the Year of God the Son, 1998 as the Year of the Holy Spirit, and 1999 as the Year of God the Father. These years of reflection on each of the Divine Persons were preparations for the celebration of the second millennium of Christianity.

The second of our bookend encyclicals, *Dominum et Vivificantem*, of 1986, begins in its early sections with references to the inseparable relationship between Christ and the Holy Spirit, echoing Leo XIII, Congar, Balthasar, and many others concerned about Joachimist tendencies to separate the two.[32] Paragraph 7 declares: "Between the Holy Spirit and Christ there thus subsists, in the economy of salvation, an intimate bond, whereby the Spirit works in human history as 'another Counsellor,' permanently ensuring the transmission and spreading of the Good News revealed by Jesus of Nazareth."

The emphasis on the Holy Spirit as both love and gift which is also strong in the theology of Balthasar appears in §41. Here St. John Paul II wrote:

> The Holy Spirit as Love and Gift comes down, in a certain sense, into the very heart of the sacrifice which is offered on the Cross. Referring here to the biblical tradition, we can say: He consumes this sacrifice with the fire of the love which unites the Son with the Father in the Trinitarian communion. And since the sacrifice of the Cross is an act proper to Christ, also in this sacrifice he "receives" the Holy Spirit. He receives the Holy Spirit in such a way that afterwards—and he alone with God the Father—can "give him" to the Apostles, to the Church, to humanity. He alone "sends" the Spirit from the Father. He alone presents himself before the Apostles in the Upper Room, "breathes upon them" and says: "Receive the Holy Spirit; if you forgive the sins of any, they are forgiven," as John the Baptist had foretold: "He will baptize you with the Holy Spirit and with fire." With those words of Jesus, the Holy Spirit is revealed and at the same time made present as the Love that works in the depths of the Paschal Mystery, as the source of the salvific power of the Cross of Christ, and as the gift of new and eternal life.

Another strong motif in the encyclical is the idea that the Holy Spirit will convince the world concerning sin. St. John Paul II links this concept to theological anthropology so that it becomes an exercise in what Congar called pneumatological anthropology. In §43 John Paul II declared:

32. For an overview of the Trinitarian theology of St. John Paul II, see Nachef, *Mystery of the Trinity.*

> The Gospel's "convincing concerning sin" under the influence of
> the Spirit of truth can be accomplished in man in no other way
> except through the conscience. If the conscience is upright, it
> serves "to resolve according to truth the moral problems which
> arise both in the life of individuals and from social relationships";
> then "persons and groups turn aside from blind choice and try
> to be guided by the objective standards of moral conduct."

The theme of the Holy Spirit being both gift and love is repeated in §52
where reference is made to the human person becoming a partaker in the
divine nature through the action of the Holy Spirit who grants access to
God the Father for the human person. §53 then follows through the logic
of this by stating that grace bears within itself both a Christological and a
pneumatological aspect. These principles of a pneumatological anthropology
are then drawn together in §55 that declares:

> In the texts of St. Paul there is a superimposing—and a mutual
> compenetration—of the ontological dimension (the flesh
> and the spirit), the ethical (moral good and evil), and the
> pneumatological (the action of the Holy Spirit in the order of
> grace). His words (especially in the *Letters to the Romans* and
> *Galatians*) enable us to know and feel vividly the strength of the
> tension and struggle going on in man between openness to the
> action of the Holy Spirit and resistance and opposition to him,
> to his saving gift.

Returning then to the mission of the Holy Spirit to convince the world
concerning sin, §56 concludes with the judgment that:

> The resistance to the Holy Spirit which St. Paul emphasizes
> in the interior and subjective dimension as tension, struggle
> and rebellion taking place in the human heart, finds in every
> period of history and especially in the modern era, its external
> dimension, which takes concrete form as the content of culture
> and civilization, as a philosophical system, an ideology, a
> program for action and for the shaping of human behaviour.

Concretely, John Paul II identified materialism, including its
manifestation in varieties of Marxism, as the dominant ideology of the era
of the late twentieth century resistant to the work of the Holy Spirit. This
materialism underpins what the philosopher Rémi Brague calls an exclusive
humanism, a humanism that excludes Christ.[33]

---

33. Brague, *Kingdom of Man.*

From this brief review of the milestones in pneumatology between the two encyclicals it may be argued that a common theme cascading down the decades is that of the inseparable relationship between Christology and Pneumatology and the importance of understanding the bridges or links between pneumatology and ecclesiology and pneumatology and theological anthropology. Included within this is a recognition of the recurring attraction for some of new forms of Joachimism which may be yet another manifestation of resistance to the Holy Spirit taking a concrete form in both the culture of the world and the culture of the Church.

BIBLIOGRAPHY

Balthasar, Hans Urs von. *Explorations in Theology*. Vol. 3, *Creator Spirit*. San Francisco: Ignatius, 1993.

Brague, Rémi. *The Kingdom of Man: Genesis and Failure of the Modern Project*. South Bend, IN: University of Notre Dame Press, 2018.

Congar, Yves. "Actualité de la Pneumatologie." In *Credo in Spiritum Sanctum: Atti del Congresso teologico internazionale pneumatologia in occasione del 1600 anniversario del I Concilio di Constantinopoli e del 1550 anniversario del Concilio di Efeso: Roma, 22-26 marzo, 1982*, edited by J. Saraiva Martins, 1:15-28. Rome: Libreria Editrice Vaticana, 1983.

———. *I Believe in the Holy Spirit*. Vol. 1, *The Experience of the Spirit*. London: Chapman, 1983.

———. *I Believe in the Holy Spirit*. Vol. 2, *Lord and Giver of Life*. London: Chapman, 1983.

Daniélou, Jean. "The Missionary Nature of the Church." In *The Word in the Third World*, edited by James P. Cotter, 11-43. Washington DC: Corpus, 1968.

Grillmeier, Aloys. "The Mystery of the Church." In *Commentary on the Documents of Vatican II*, edited by Herbert Vorgrimler, 1:138-52. New York: Herder & Herder, 1969.

Groppe, Elizabeth Teresa. *Yves Congar's Theology of the Holy Spirit*. Oxford: Oxford University Press, 2004.

John Paul II. *Dominum et Vivificantem*. http://www.vatican.va/content/john-paul-ii/en/encyclicals/documents/hf_jp-ii_enc_18051986_dominum-et-vivificantem.html.

Le Guillou, Marie-Joseph. "Le développement de la doctrine sur l'Esprit Saint dans les écrits du Nouveau Testament." In *Credo in Spiritum Sanctum: Atti del Congresso teologico internazionale pneumatologia in occasione del 1600 anniversario del I Concilio di Constantinopoli e del 1550 anniversario del Concilio di Efeso: Roma, 22-26 marzo, 1982*, edited by J. Saraiva Martins, 1:729-39. Rome: Libreria Editrice Vaticana, 1983.

———. *L'expérience de l'Esprit-Saint en Orient et en Occident*. Saint-Maur: Parole et Silence, 2000.

———. *Les témoins sont parmi nous: L'expérience de Dieu dans l'Esprit Saint*. Paris: Fayard, 1976.

La Potterie, Ignace de. "L'Esprit Saint et l'Église." In *Credo in Spiritum Sanctum: Atti del Congresso teologico internazionale pneumatologia in occasione del 1600 anniversario del I Concilio di Constantinopoli e del 1550 anniversario del Concilio di Efeso: Roma, 22–26 marzo, 1982*, edited by J. Saraiva Martins, 1:791–808. Rome: Libreria Editrice Vaticana, 1983.

La Soujeole, Benoît-Dominique de. *Introduction to the Mystery of the Church.* Washington, DC: The Catholic University of America Press, 2014.

Lefsrud, Sigurd. *Kenosis in Theosis: An Exploration of Balthasar's Theology of Deification.* Eugene, OR: Pickwick, 2020.

Melina, Livo. *Sharing in Christ's Virtues: For the Renewal of Moral Theology in the Light of "Veritatis Splendor."* Washington, DC: The Catholic University of America Press, 2001.

McInerny, Brendan. *The Trinitarian Theology of Hans Urs von Balthasar: An Introduction.* South Bend, IN: University of Notre Dame Press, 2020.

Nachef, Antoine E. *The Mystery of the Trinity in the Theological Thought of Pope John Paul II.* New York: Lang, 1999.

Nicholas, Marc. *Jean Daniélou's Doxological Humanism: Trinitarian Contemplation and Humanity's True Vocation.* Eugene, OR: Pickwick, 2012.

Pius XII. *Mystici Corporis Christi.* https://www.vatican.va/content/pius-xii/en/encyclicals/documents/hf_p-xii_enc_29061943_mystici-corporis-christi.html.

Rahner, Karl. *The Trinity.* New York: Herder & Herder, 1970.

———. "Zur scholastiischen Begrifflichkeit der ungeschaffenen Gnade." *Zeitschrift für katholische Theologie* 63 (1939) 137–57.

Schumacher, Michele M. *A Trinitarian Anthropology: Adrienne von Speyr and Hans Urs von Balthasar in Dialogue with Thomas Aquinas.* Washington, DC: The Catholic University of America Press, 2014.

Vliet, Cornelius Th. M. van. *Communio sacramentalis: Das Kirchenverständis von Yves Congar-genetisch und systematisch betrachtet.* Mainz: Matthias-Grünewald, 1995.

Zizioulas, John. D. "The Teaching of the Second Ecumenical Council on the Holy Spirit in Historical and Ecumenical Perspective." In *Credo in Spiritum Sanctum: Atti del Congresso teologico internazionale pneumatologia in occasione del 1600 anniversario del I Concilio di Constantinopoli e del 1550 anniversario del Concilio di Efeso: Roma, 22–26 marzo, 1982*, edited by J. Saraiva Martins, 1:29–53. Rome: Libreria Editrice Vaticana, 1983.

16

HE HAS SPOKEN THROUGH THE PROPHETS

Sr. Susanna Edmunds, OP

"ALL SCRIPTURE IS INSPIRED," St. Paul declares to Timothy (1 Tim 3:16). Yet the modern appreciation for Scripture's historical and literary context has necessitated a renewal in the theology of inspiration, searching out who, how, and what the Holy Spirit "inspired." *The Interpretation of the Bible in the Church*, produced in 1993 by the Pontifical Biblical Commission (PBC), chose not to pursue this question.[1] However, following the 2008 synod on the "The Word of God in the Life and Mission of the Church" and the subsequent post-synodal apostolic exhortation *Verbum Domini*, the PBC devoted several years to the "fuller and more adequate study" of inspiration and truth in relationship to Scripture requested by Pope Benedict XVI, who identified these concepts as central to "an ecclesial hermeneutic of the sacred Scriptures."[2]

Before the twentieth-century, Catholic approaches to the theology of inspiration were largely based on St. Thomas Aquinas's epistemology of prophetic knowledge.[3] However, the discussion revolved around nuanced distinctions which became too technical to engage the broader exegetical community, and seemed far removed from the prophets' dramatic and personal experiences of the Word and the Spirit.[4] Thus, in the Pontifical Biblical Commission's document on the subject, *The Inspiration and*

1. Pontifical Biblical Commission, *Interpretation of the Bible*, Introduction, B.
2. Benedict XVI, *Verbum Domini*, sec. 19.
3. Burtchaell, *Biblical Inspiration Since 1810*, 239.
4. Burtchaell, *Biblical Inspiration Since 1810*, 244.

Truth of Sacred Scripture (2014), no reference is made to the legacy of Aquinas, and systematic theology is set aside in favor of a more biblical and phenomenological approach.

This chapter aims to highlight areas of continuity and discontinuity between the work of the PBC and the Thomistic tradition, which agree that the figure of the prophet is crucial for understanding the human authors of Scripture but differ in their applications of this prophetic framework. The first section will outline the theology of inspiration proposed by the PBC, followed by an introduction to the Thomistic approach as found in the writings of Fr. Pierre Benoit, OP (1906–87), and recently revived by Matthew Ramage in his book *Dark Passages of the Bible: Engaging Scripture with Benedict XVI and Thomas Aquinas*. The second section will outline the theology of inerrancy implied by this prophetic approach to inspiration, as found in the descriptions of biblical "truth" proposed in Part II of the PBC's document and in Ramage's version of Benedict XVI's "Method C" exegesis.[5]

The third section will consider the implications of this understanding of inerrancy for understanding difficult Scripture passages, comparing the PBC's case-studies to those of Ramage to highlight the role of philosophical presuppositions in exegesis. The PBC's case-studies indicate that an over-emphasis on the practical and pedagogical dimension of inspiration can shed doubt on the historicity of key moments in salvation history. This can be remedied by coupling prophetic epistemology with Thomistic metaphysics. In this way, remembering the Holy Spirit to be "the Lord, the giver of life" becomes a fruitful context for exegesis based on his "speaking through the prophets."

THE INSPIRATION OF SACRED SCRIPTURE

A Prophetic Phenomenology: Pontifical Biblical Commission

The Pontifical Biblical Commission's investigation *The Inspiration and Truth of Sacred Scripture* is an intentional attempt to bring biblical exegesis and theology into dialogue. It opens by considering the Scriptures in their liturgical setting, which establishes a hermeneutic of faith and an ecclesial framework for the exegesis.[6] This setting "constitutes the most adequate

5. Ramage follows Benedict XVI in calling for a synthesis of traditional ("Method A") and modern ("Method B") exegetical tools and in designating this approach as "Method C."

6. In *Verbum Domini*, Benedict XVI uses the phrase "hermeneutic of faith" to summarize the framework proposed in *Dei Verbum* sec. 11: the context of the canon, tradition, and the analogy of faith. It is opposed to the "hermeneutic of suspicion"

context for studying [Scripture's] inspiration and truth."[7] Within this theological framework, however, the methodology of the PBC is biblical: "We set ourselves the task of establishing what the biblical writings themselves say about their divine provenance . . . [and] about God and his project of salvation."[8] It does this by investigating the "phenomenology" of the relationship between God and the human authors of Scripture,[9] with phenomenology understood in a loose sense.[10]

The first part of the document concerns the biblical witnesses to the phenomena of inspiration. The PBC examines a range of passages in which the scriptural authors disclose their experiences of God revealing himself, with the overall finding that while biblical revelation is propositional, it occurs always in the context of relationship. Indeed, the letter to the Hebrews begins with the declaration "God spoke," followed not by a direct object (what he said), but rather by a series of indirect objects: our ancestors, the prophets, us.[11] This experience of revelation is not limited to the scriptural authors but is experienced by the whole People of God. What is unique in the experience of the scriptural authors is the inspiration to communicate their experience in writing. In various ways throughout the two testaments, they "implicitly affirm that their texts constitute the final expression and stable deposit of the revelatory acts of God."[12] Two graces received by the scriptural authors can thus be distinguished: hearing the Word and committing it to writing.[13]

The PBC proposes a distinction between revelation and inspiration that reflects this two-fold experience.[14] The document *Inspiration and Truth* defines revelation as the grace whereby God simultaneously "communicates who he is, and the mystery of his will" and enables the recipient to receive

---

employed by some secular exegetical approaches but does not exclude critical approaches or legitimate questioning of the text. Benedict XVI, *Verbum Domini*, sec. 3.

7. Pontifical Biblical Commission, *Inspiration and Truth*, Introduction, II, 3.

8. Pontifical Biblical Commission, *Inspiration and Truth*, Introduction, II, 3.

9. Pontifical Biblical Commission, *Inspiration and Truth*, Part One, 1.2.6.

10. It seems that the Pontifical Biblical Commission's approach is consistent with the "East Coast" interpretation of Husserl, as represented in the writings of Robert Sokolowski, which does not divorce the study of the "phenomena" from true knowledge of the "noumena." This approach has been used fruitfully in theological exegesis. Wright and Martin, *Encountering the Living God in Scripture*, 183–87.

11. Pontifical Biblical Commission, *Inspiration and Truth*, Part One, 3.6.1.

12. Pontifical Biblical Commission, *Inspiration and Truth*, Part One, 1.2.7.

13. The language of "grace" is my own but is in keeping with the Pontifical Biblical Commission's later reference to "charism."

14. This chapter will follow the Pontifical Biblical Commission's definitions of revelation and inspiration unless otherwise specified.

this communication with the certainty of faith. Inspiration is a subsequent grace, whereby "God enables certain persons . . . to transmit his revelation faithfully in writing."[15] Furthermore, the document suggests that "the charism of inspiration spreads in various ways," a claim based on the variety of ways in which the scriptural authors' describe their experiences of revelation and inspiration.[16] This suggests that the distinct but interrelated charisms of revelation and inspiration play out in various ways throughout the history of salvation, "according to the specific phase of the 'plan' of revelation."[17] This variety highlights the importance of understanding both revelation and inspiration not as univocal but analogical terms.[18]

While acknowledging the analogous experiences of inspiration attested in the Scriptures, the PBC proposes the prophet as the model of the scriptural author. Like most contemporary exegetes, it defines prophecy as a "social mission,"[19] and use the term "prophet" to designate those men called by God to participate in the transmission of public revelation during key periods in the history of ancient Israel. Hidden within this definition, however, lies the key to opening the concept of "prophet" to all those involved with the composition, redaction, and transmission of Scripture. It is in the prophetic call that "the reality of inspiration is formally expressed as the intimate awareness of some men who declare that they are able to understand the words of God and have received the mandate to transmit them faithfully."[20] The prophet thus epitomizes not only the experience of revelation, but also the grace of inspiration.

In proposing the classic figure of the prophet as the model of all biblical authors, one could argue that the PBC implies that it is not unscriptural to suggest that all biblical authors experienced, in some sense, the charism of prophecy.[21] Furthermore, the PBC notes that the redactors of the Old Testament paint the scriptural authors in the model of the prophets to

---

15. Pontifical Biblical Commission, *Inspiration and Truth*, Part One, 1.2.6.

16. Pontifical Biblical Commission, *Inspiration and Truth*, General Conclusion, II.143.

17. Pontifical Biblical Commission, *Inspiration and Truth*, Part One, 1.4.10.

18. Pontifical Biblical Commission, *Inspiration and Truth*, General Conclusion, II.142. "Analogical" is used here and throughout as an alternative to "univocal" and "equivocal." In contrast, "analogous" refers to an analogical relationship between two realities.

19. Benoit, *Inspiration and the Bible*, 97.

20. Pontifical Biblical Commission, *Inspiration and Truth*, General Conclusion, II.142.

21. While this conclusion does not follow necessarily from the argument, is it not incompatible with the line of reasoning.

convey the divine provenance of their writings. Thus, the legislative books are attributed to Moses, the wisdom books to Solomon and the apocalyptic traditions to Daniel.[22] In doing so, the redactors create "a kind of general uniformity, almost like a seal of guarantee to confirm for the readers the nature of the writing as deriving from a single divine source."[23] This is ratified by the declaration of the letter to the Hebrews, that "God spoke to our ancestors in many and various ways by the prophets" (Heb 1:1).[24] The prophet can thus become a doorway to understanding the unity of Scripture as the inspired word of God, with the prophetic charism underlying all of the canon and uniting the various figures who participate in its transmission.

A Prophetic Epistemology: Fr. Pierre Benoit, OP

This connection between the prophet and the scriptural author is at the heart of the Thomistic theology of inspiration, especially as promoted in the 1960s by Fr. Pierre Benoit, then-director of the École Biblique in Jerusalem. Aquinas's writings on prophecy are found particularly in the *Summa Theologica* (II-II, Q. 171–78) and *De Veritate* (Q. 12, a. 12).[25] Benoit's adaptations of the Thomistic framework were widely debated and disputed, with Benoit himself often revising his definitions and hypotheses from one publication to the next. They received little attention between 1980 and 2010. However, interest in his writings has increased as part of the contemporary search for a theology of inspiration.[26]

According to Aquinas, the gift of prophecy is the gratuitous grace, given for the upbuilding of the Church, whereby a person is drawn into a participation in the divine knowledge. Contrary to common parlance, it does not apply only to the knowledge of future contingents.[27] All knowledge— natural knowledge, matters of faith, and mysteries higher still—can be the

---

22. Pontifical Biblical Commission, *Inspiration and Truth*, General Conclusion, II.142.

23. Pontifical Biblical Commission, *Inspiration and Truth*, General Conclusion, II.142.

24. Biblical references in this chapter are from the NRSV-CE.

25. Additionally, Aquinas's commentary on 1 Corinthians 14 may provide an explicit link between prophecy and scriptural interpretation. Rogers, "Prophecy and the Moral Life," 200.

26. In addition to Ramage's work, examples include Blankenhorn, "God Speaks," and Bonino, "Saint Thomas Aquinas."

27. Bonino, "Saint Thomas Aquinas," 1211. See also Aquinas, *Summa Theologica*, II–II, q. 171, a. 3.

objects of prophecy.[28] What distinguishes prophecy is the cause of knowing. Unlike natural knowledge, which comes to humans through the senses, and *sacra doctrina*, which is imparted by the Holy Spirit through human mediators, prophecy is knowledge given by the Holy Spirit, through the mediation of angels.[29]

Aquinas's explanation of the mechanism of prophetic knowledge builds on his epistemology, using a three-fold analogy of light.[30] In the physical realm, light illumines the object of sight so that it can be grasped by the senses. So too, an intellectual light is needed for the intellect to grasp concepts. This intellectual light consists in the abiding knowledge of first principles, such as the principle of non-contradiction, which perfect the intellect and enable it to abstract concepts from sense impressions. Receiving prophetic knowledge likewise requires light. While prophetic knowledge may be of things that lie within the grasp of human reason, it most properly consists in knowledge of supernatural truths;[31] and in either case, the manner of knowing is supernatural. Thus, the prophetic light must be proportionally supernatural. It is a transitory grace given by the Holy Spirit, elevating the intellect by a participation in God himself, who is "the principle of things pertaining to supernatural knowledge."[32] What the Blessed possess habitually, the prophet possesses in a transitory and partial manner.[33]

The experience of the prophet consists in two distinct actions of the Holy Spirit.[34] The mind is elevated by the imparting of the prophetic light (*lumen*), and it is thus able to receive the prophetic knowledge (*species*) which God wishes to communicate.[35] On both levels, the prophet becomes

28. Aquinas, *Summa Theologica*, II–II, Introduction to the Treatise on Prophecy.

29. Aquinas, *Summa Theologica*, II–II, q. 172, a. 1, 2.

30. Aquinas, *Summa Theologica*, II–II, q. 171, a. 2.

31. Aquinas, *Summa Theologica*, II–II, q. 174, a. 3.

32. Aquinas, *Summa Theologica*, II–II, q. 171, a. 2. This emphasis on participation in the divine essence may be another fruitful point of dialogue between Aquinas's systematic approach to inspiration and revelation and the phenomenological approach of the Pontifical Biblical Commission, which emphasizes the prophet's encounter and relationship with God.

33. Aquinas, *Summa Theologica*, II–II, q. 171, a. 2. This connection between the enlightenment of the intellect and participation in the divine intellect is emphasized by Aquinas's teaching that a vision given by a demon would not be a prophetic enlightenment of the intellect but only an infused phantasm in the imagination. Aquinas, *Summa Theologica*, II–II, q. 172, a. 5, ad. 2.

34. Aquinas, *Summa Theologica*, II–II, q. 172, a. 1.

35. Aquinas, *Summa Theologica*, II–II, q. 171, a. 1, ad. 4. Aquinas uses Scripture to illustrate this argument, analyzing the experience of Ezekiel (Ezek 2:1). See also Synave and Benoit, *Inspiration and the Bible*, 17. While these two actions may seem to

a secondary cause of divine revelation.[36] The *lumen* does not override the intellect, but rather elevates it, so that the knowledge imparted—even if it is of the highest mysteries—is still received in a human manner.[37] The prophet does not see the divine essence, but rather beholds the mysteries "afar off," imperfectly, as if in a mirror.[38] Likewise, the *species* is received by the prophet in an appropriately human mode, either through the senses, the imagination, or directly impressed on the mind.[39] This robust understanding of causality is of central importance for the Thomistic approach to Scripture's dual authorship, and the questions of inspiration and inerrancy. This approach also, like the PBC's definitions of revelation and inerrancy, points to a likely spectrum of experiences within the charism of prophecy.

THE TRUTH OF SACRED SCRIPTURE

Since "the God who speaks cannot, in fact, deceive," the theology of scriptural inspiration is intimately tied to that of scriptural inerrancy.[40] By treating revelation and inspiration as analogical realities, the PBC and the Thomistic tradition are both able to explicate the truth of Sacred Scripture while taking seriously the apparent contradictions therein. They link prophetic phenomenology and epistemology with the two tools for interpretation proposed by *Dei Verbum*: awareness of literary form and the wisdom of the divine pedagogy.[41] As the contemporary followers of Benoit are more explicit in their methodology and in linking prophetic inspiration and inerrancy, their work will be considered first.[42] Their findings will then be compared

---

correspond respectively to "revelation" and "inspiration," Aquinas does not use these words in a technical sense in the *Summa*; the closest he comes to this precise usage is in *De Veritate* q. 12, a. 12. The nuances of the distinction are at the heart of the twentieth-century Thomistic debates regarding biblical interpretation. See Benoit, "Revelation and Inspiration."

36. I will refer to the author as a "secondary" cause to avoid the passivity associated in English with "instrument." Aquinas's approach is that of a "twofold efficient causality," by which "instrumental causality is nothing less than a participatory causality." Hahn, "For the Sake of Our Salvation," 32. See also Aquinas, *Quodlib.* 7, q. 6, a. 1, ad. 1.

37. Aquinas, *Summa Theologica*, II–II, q. 174, a. 2, ad. 3. See also Ramage, *Dark Passages*, 125.

38. Aquinas, *Summa Theologica*, II–II, q. 173, a. 1.

39. Aquinas, *Summa Theologica*, q. 173, a.2.

40. Pontifical Biblical Commission, *Interpretation of the Bible in the Church*, 63.

41. *Dei Verbum*, sec. 12–13.

42. Ramage, *Dark Passages*, as well as Bonino, "Saint Thomas Aquinas." I am indebted to Fr. John Martin Ruiz, OP, for translating this article from French and alerting me to its existence. See also Blankenhorn, "God Speaks."

with the conclusions reached by the PBC in *Inspiration and Truth*, as found in Part II, "The Testimony of the Biblical Writings to their Truth."

Divine Pedagogy: Benoit on Inerrancy

Central to Benoit's understanding of prophetic epistemology is the distinction between the illumination of the intellect (*lumen*) and the reception of concepts (*species*). While both these steps are generally grouped by the PBC under the term "revelation," distinguishing them highlights the possibility of analogous experiences of revelation, varying in two ways. The first difference concerns the degree of *lumen* given. Just as the prophet does not "receive the light of inspiration in such a way that he pierces the depths of what God is revealing to him," so too, the authors of Scripture may have had different levels of awareness of the truth contained in their words.[43] The experience may also differ according to the type of *species* given. The *species* may be infused, or it may be known by natural means but now understood in its supernatural dimension by the light of inspiration. The analogical nature of revelation is furthered by the Thomistic distinction between the speculative and practical ends of the intellect. The *lumen* generally enlightens the intellect for a speculative end, but can also serve a practical end, such as "for the purpose of discerning truthfully and efficaciously what is to be done."[44] In this way, a text may serve a practical purpose beyond the human author's imagining, although not incongruous with his own human ends.[45]

This distinction between the speculative and practical ends of the intellect, and thus of the charism of inspiration, has implications for scriptural inerrancy.[46] If a scriptural statement was inspired primarily for the purpose of moving the reader to a practical end, such as contrition, compassion, or conversion, then perhaps it is "inerrant" in achieving this end, even if

---

43. Ramage, *Dark Passages*, 128.

44. Aquinas, *Summa Theologica*, II–II, q. 173, a. 2. Aquinas refers to Isaiah 63:14 ("The Spirit of the Lord was their guide").

45. This approach is akin to the Pontifical Biblical Commission's awareness of the "dynamic literal sense" of Scripture, as well as its *senus plenior*, and deserves more attention than I can give it here. Pontifical Biblical Commission, *Interpretation of the Bible in the Church*, II, B, 1. As a beginning, see also Brown, "Sensus Plenior."

46. Benoit, writing in 1954, hypothesized that "inerrancy . . . follows upon inspiration only insofar as the author's speculative judgment comes into play." Burtchaell, *Biblical Inspiration Since 1810*, 240. However, he later revised his position, holding that they are coterminous. Benoit, *Aspects of Biblical Inspiration*, 40; Ramage, *Dark Passages*, 125. This is in line with the teaching of *Spiritus Paraclitus*. Benedict XV, *Spiritus Paraclitus*, sec. 19.

it seems to our Enlightenment-shaped factual mindset to contain errors.[47] This view is consistent with the patristic tradition of the "condescension of Moses" or divine "accommodation," whereby God communicated with the people through Moses using the "language of the tribe," that is, in a manner appropriate to their stage in salvation history.[48]

Reading Scripture, especially the Old Testament, thus requires an awareness of the divine pedagogy, whereby God has led his people through a gradual unfolding of divine revelation.[49] The scriptural authors, acting as secondary causes, at times communicated supernatural truths that had been directly revealed by God (revelation in the strict sense), but at other times, presented truths known by a natural mode, but "in light of God's plan" and thus produced supernatural lessons (revelation in the broad sense).[50] They received a degree of revelation "proportioned both in quality and quantity" to God's purpose.[51] If these "lessons" included historical or scientific facts which are known today to be erroneous, the text remains inspired and inerrant, as it achieves its purpose of "asserting" all that the authors

---

47. Ramage distinguishes between formal errors, "when what an author asserts for its own sake does not conform to reality," and material errors, which he prefers to call "imperfections." Ramage, *Dark Passages*, 137. In these cases, the author may be "using" a proposition (e.g., in accordance with literary or cultural conventions), but not "teaching" it. See also the explanation of Second Vatican Council member Cardinal Raúl Silva Henríquez on the use of *docere* in *Dei Verbum*, sec. 11, in Harrison, "Restricted Inerrancy," 235. The acceptance of "material errors" is not to be confused with the acceptance of "material limitations," characteristic of a theology of restricted inerrancy, whereby "a certain number of the affirmations made by the sacred authors are immune from error, while the rest are not." Harrison, "Restricted Inerrancy," 235. The concept of a "material error" is also distinct from the terminology of "matter" (content) and "form" (genre or structure); in that usage, it is the "matter" that is inspired, with the form useful in so far as it points towards the correct interpretation. Harrison, "Restricted Inerrancy," 243.

48. Bonino, "Saint Thomas Aquinas," 1217. *Dei Verbum*, sec. 13n11 cites St. John Chrysostom as the most relevant patristic witness to this concept, referring specifically to his Homily 17 on Genesis 3:8, on God strolling in the garden with Adam and Eve. The term translated in *Dei Verbum*, sec. 11 as "condescension" is in Greek "*synkatabasis*," and in Latin, "*attemperatio*," which the footnote renders literally as "suitable adjustment." This concept, especially as used by Chrysostom, can also be understood as "considerateness," "adaptability," or "accommodation." Hill, "Chrysostom's Teachings on Inspiration," 56–70. See also Rylaarsdam, *Chrysostom on Divine Pedagogy*. Despite the contemporary pejorative sense of "condescension," it captures the kenotic dimension of *synkatabasis* and thus needs to be held in tension with the other renderings (with gratitude to Kevin Wagner for this insight).

49. Bonino, "Saint Thomas Aquinas," 1218.

50. Ramage, *Dark Passages*, 126.

51. Benoit, *Inspiration and the Bible*, 78.

(both human and divine) wished to assert, "for the sake of salvation."[52] This approach requires a robust understanding of divine causality, human freedom, and providence, with God "grant[ing] spiritual significance to the events, persons and things mentioned by the writer"[53] and choosing to work through his incomplete understanding.[54]

From the perspective of the human author's analogical experiences of revelation and the pedagogical purpose of the divine author, the Scriptures can be read as the record of "God's revelation ... slowly and painfully trying to assert itself" in the darkness of human apathy.[55] Passages that lack the fullness of revelation serve the divine pedagogy precisely in their limitations, through which exegesis can illuminate not only the literal sense of the passage but truths about the divine pedagogy itself. The role of the exegete, then, is "to discern what precisely constitutes the inerrant message Scripture's authors are intending to teach us in each of their writings and as a whole."[56]

52. Second Vatican Council, *Dei Verbum*, sec. 11. This approach is not to be confused with the approach implied by Roderick MacKenzie in his commentary on *Dei Verbum* (Abbott edition). MacKenzie proposes that all scriptural affirmations are inspired, but that the human and divine authors only intend affirmations about the "revelation of God and the history of salvation." This leads to the sifting of biblical propositions based on their content, requiring presuppositions about what is relevant for salvation (a closed approach). Harrison, "Restricted Inerrancy," 239–40. Ramage's approach is also distinct from methods which would distinguish between scriptural assertions and non-assertions based on their linguistic modality. Harrison, "Restricted Inerrancy," 242. While Ramage uses content (that is, apparent doctrinal discrepancies) to identify problematic texts, he then uses literary form and cultural context to identify the type of affirmations the text is making. Although this may arrive at similar conclusions (acknowledging erroneous propositions in Scripture, but denying that they are "asserted"), Ramage's is an open method, which does not limit the types of content which have a bearing on salvation. The inherent risk in MacKenzie's approach is exemplified in Raymond Brown's hesitation in describing the virginal conception of Jesus as a biblical "affirmation," because its facticity is not necessary for salvation. Given Brown's acknowledgement that both Matthew and Luke clearly believed that Jesus was conceived without a human father, his conclusion that this doctrine cannot be deduced from Scripture alone seems to be not based on the text (either its content or form) but rather on hermeneutical presuppositions. Harrison, "Restricted Inerrancy," 241.

53. McGuckin, "Saint Thomas Aquinas," 209.

54. Synave and Benoit, *Prophecy and Inspiration*, 142.

55. Burtchaell, *Biblical Inspiration Since 1810*, 301.

56. Ramage, *Dark Passages*, 139. Given that one of Benoit's critics proposed an alternative approach based on awareness of literary form, it is worth noting that this attentiveness to pedagogy and purpose is precisely the hermeneutical presupposition undergirding the study of literary forms. See Zerafa, "Limits of Biblical Inerrancy."

The Word Who Speaks: The PBC on Inerrancy

Part II of the PBC's document *The Inspiration and Truth of Sacred Scripture* is devoted to a biblical investigation of the nature of "truth" and the type of truth to be found in the Scriptures. This follows directly from the conclusions made in Part I about the nature of biblical inspiration and inerrancy. The document explicitly rejects any approach which would limit the truth of Scripture to "those parts of the Sacred Books that are necessary for faith and morality, to the exclusion of other parts," reminding the reader that this was the reason why the expression "saving truth" (*veritatis salutaris*) of *Dei Verbum*'s fourth schema was replaced with "the truth which God wanted put into the sacred writings for the sake of our salvation."[57] All parts of Scripture communicate truth. But the inspired nature of Scripture means that this truth is both less and more than the "common" understanding of truth implies.[58] Its nature is not that of empirical data, but knowledge of God and his ways with his people. Unlike empirical data, Scripture is only true "insofar as it relates to our salvation." Yet as such, it reveals the very essence of truth and the source of the truthfulness of all empirical knowledge: God Himself, steadfast and true, and Jesus Christ, "the Amen incarnate of all God's promises."[59] This is the truth "communicated and confirmed by the Holy Spirit and handed on in the Church."[60]

In this light, the PBC surveys key biblical texts to sketch a portrait of truth, considering both its form (the nature of truth) and its content (what Scripture claims to be true). In both the Old and New Testaments, truth takes the form of an unveiling of the nature of God as one who is both close to men and yet infinitely beyond them. In his dealings with humanity, he is both just and merciful, Creator and Savior, and his self-revelation calls forth a response of fear, faith, conversion, and observance.[61] The core content of the truth recorded "for the sake of salvation" is the testimony to the economy of creation and salvation, culminating in the person of Jesus in whom the message becomes the messenger. In him, the Creator is

---

57. Pontifical Biblical Commission, *Inspiration and Truth*, 63. See also *Dei Verbum*, sec. 11. "For the sake of our salvation" functions in the Latin text as an adverbial phrase, modifying the verb phrase translated here as "wanted put into the sacred writings," not an adjective modifying "truth." Hahn, "For the Sake of Our Salvation," 35. This modification of the verb phrase points towards the inextricable link between the inspiration of Scripture and its salvific purpose.

58. Pontifical Biblical Commission, *Inspiration and Truth*, 64.

59. Pontifical Biblical Commission, *Inspiration and Truth*, 64.

60. Pontifical Biblical Commission, *Inspiration and Truth*, 64.

61. Pontifical Biblical Commission, *Inspiration and Truth*, 83.

revealed to have the nature of a Word. The PBC highlights the capacity of a word to cause a transformation in the one who receives it, "implanting . . . newness."[62] Thus, to receive the Word as truth is to encounter Truth himself. This inextricable connection between the form and content of saving truth is consistent with the document's earlier conclusions about the prophet's experience of Revelation encompassing both the encounter with God and the understanding of His Word.

THE INTERPRETATION OF THE WORD OF GOD AND ITS CHALLENGES

The understanding of biblical truth presented by the PBC is largely consistent with the divine pedagogy proposed by Matthew Ramage. The truth of any individual passage can only be known in light of its *telos*, its relationship to the Paschal Mystery. The PBC calls this "canonical logic."[63] This hermeneutic both requires and surpasses the tools of historical criticism.[64] A passage must be studied in light of its historical and literary context in order to ascertain the author's communicative intent, that is, the speculative knowledge that he desires to impart and/or his inspired practical purpose.[65] Depending on the genre, a passage may reveal inspired propositional truth (Benoit's "revelation in the strict sense"). Some passages, however, may be primarily practical, and not reveal any new propositional truth ("revelation in the broad sense").[66] In either case, the truth presented by the passage is only fully understood when placed within the trajectory of the divine pedagogy as it has been revealed throughout salvation history, leading to an encounter with Truth Himself.

Having demonstrated the overall coherence of the canon, the PBC and Matthew Ramage both proceed to consider passages in Scripture that do not seem consistent with the biblical proclamation. The PBC focus on difficulties arising from three sources: historical inaccuracy, narrative implausibility, and ethical contradictions. These are largely contradictions

---

62. Pontifical Biblical Commission, *Inspiration and Truth*, 100.

63. Pontifical Biblical Commission, *Inspiration and Truth*, 103.

64. There is no one definition of the historical-critical method. Ayres and Fowl, "(Mis)Reading the Face of God," 516n10. I am following the broad outline provided by the Pontifical Biblical Commission, describing it as the "scientific study of the meaning of ancient texts," applied to Scripture in light of its genuine human authorship. Pontifical Biblical Commission, *Interpretation of the Bible in the Church*, I.A.

65. Levering, *Participatory Biblical Exegesis*, 84.

66. Ramage, *Dark Passages*, 125.

between scriptural and secular truth claims. Ramage acknowledges these difficulties, but chooses to focus instead on internal contradictions, where contradictory claims concerning faith and morality are presented in different parts of the canon. He implies that using the divine pedagogy to resolve these faith-based difficulties will also highlight avenues for resolving the questions raised by secular sciences.[67] To test this claim, Ramage's work will be considered first, followed by that of the PBC.

Internal Contradictions

Ramage groups the most serious internal biblical contradictions into three categories: the nature of God,[68] the nature of good and evil,[69] and the nature of the afterlife.[70] In each of these categories, there are multiple (largely Old Testament) passages which seem to contain errors, not regarding historical or scientific facts but indeed truths of faith and morality.

Ramage applies Benoit's prophetic epistemology to show that these passages do not contradict the doctrines of inspiration and inerrancy. The human authors of Scripture were inspired, always with prophetic *lumen* and sometimes with prophetic *species*, to communicate "solidly, faithfully and without error that truth which God wanted put into sacred writings for the sake of salvation."[71] In accordance with the divine condescension, the meaning they had in mind retains its historical and literary conditioning, which can be stripped back using the tools of historical criticism.[72] Allowing his "prophets" to be genuine secondary causes, God chose to speak through their limitations and "environmental glitches."[73] Yet through all this, the

67. Ramage, *Dark Passages*, 39.

68. Difficulties include traces of polytheism (Gen 3:22; 6:1–4; Josh 24:2, 14–15; Pss 82:1; 86:8), divine mutability (Gen 22:12; Exod 32:14), and the femininity of divine wisdom (Prov 1–9).

69. Difficulties include God commanding or commending evil actions (Gen 7:23; Exod 12:29; 32:27; Num 21:17–18; Deut 20:16–17; 1 Sam 16:14; Hos 13:16), the imprecatory psalms (Ps 137:8–9), and the relationship between God and the devil (Gen 3; Job 1–2).

70. Difficulties include the nature of Sheol, the absence of reward for the righteous, and the lack of hope in the resurrection (Job 7:9, 14:11; Ps 88:4–5; Isa 38:18; Sir 17:28–30; Eccl 3:19–20).

71. Second Vatican Council, *Dei Verbum*, sec. 11.

72. Ramage, *Dark Passages*, 86, 277.

73. These "glitches" are logical conclusions reached by the authors based on the (imperfect) data at their disposal. The charism of inspiration ensured that although these can be glimpsed in the text, it was never the intention of the author to express them. Thus, they remain merely "material," not "formal," errors. Ramage, *Dark Passages*, 145.

divine author's intentions can be discerned through the intentions of the human author and the trajectory of the canon.[74]

While this approach is a helpful apologetic for the inerrancy of Scripture, it is most fruitful when embedded within the divine pedagogy. Rather than discarding the Old Testament as historically conditioned, materially erroneous, and substantially replaced by the New, Ramage proposes that the very trajectory from the Old to the New is also part of Divine Revelation. To use his most developed example, the passages which seem to convey despair over the fate of the dead are evidence of a stage in salvation history in which God purified Israel from the hedonistic, materialistic concept of the afterlife held by her Egyptian neighbors.[75] Out of this salutary despair, God gradually led Israel to develop a healthy theology of the goodness of creation, of finding one's "immortality" in the endurance of the covenant community, and eventually, of an afterlife in which the just are rewarded not with earthly pleasures but with spiritual delight.[76] Studying this trajectory not only reveals God's ways with men, but also draws the reader into the very dynamics of the pedagogy. We must go through "the same process of discovery and commitment" as our forbearers.[77] The divine pedagogy thus becomes a continuation of the prophetic charism, whereby the reader, like the author, encounters the living God and is empowered to bear witness to his truth.[78]

External Contradictions

In its case studies, the PBC focuses on contradictions between the claims of Scripture and those of historical criticism, literary criticism, and the conventions of Western culture. While the PBC notes that the divine condescension accounts for the presence of "imperfect and temporary things" in the Old Testament, it primarily focuses on the other method proposed by Dei Verbum, the study of literary genre.[79]

---

74. Ramage, Dark Passages, 152.

75. For example, Isaiah 38:18 and Psalm 88:4–5. Ramage, Dark Passages, 197.

76. Ramage, Dark Passages, 208.

77. From paragraph 69 of the document Dialogue and Proclamation by the Pontifical Council for Inter-Religious Dialogue, 1991, as quoted in Ramage, Dark Passages, 15n19.

78. Ramage, Dark Passages, 13.

79. Pontifical Biblical Commission, Inspiration and Truth, 105, quoting Dei Verbum, sec. 15. This choice is not explained but it is consistent with the stated desire to find the "truth" of difficult passages, rather than dismissing them as a stage in the divine pedagogy. Pontifical Biblical Commission, Inspiration and Truth, 104.

Following the methodology of its earlier document *The Interpretation of the Bible in the Church*, the PBC explores difficult passages using historical-critical tools within a hermeneutic of faith. For its example of "historical inaccuracy," it chooses the Abraham cycle, dating its final redaction to the Persian Period in accordance with "the majority of exegetes."[80] Based on redaction criticism, it identifies Genesis 15 as an example of a later addition to the earlier "clan narratives," and indicates that as such, it "does not describe the events in the precise way in which they took place."[81] Rather, it is to be read as an expression of the faith of the post-exilic generation, who are coming to understand the miraculous survival of their nation and culture as a testimony to the fidelity of God. Texts like Genesis 15 are a rereading (and rewriting) of ancient traditions to serve as instruction in the "normative behavior willed by God" and to "invite their compatriots to believe."[82] For the PBC, the "today" of this actualization "counts more than the facts themselves."[83] While it acknowledges the historical roots of the patriarchal narratives, the PBC's analysis implies that the core truth of the texts lies not in history but in the human author's inspired interpretation. This is consistent with the earlier consideration of the experience of the prophet and is a possible application of Benoit's theory of the inspiration of the practical intellect.

In the same section, the PBC investigates cases of narrative implausibility, which can prove difficult for readers to accept as factual. The chosen examples are: the crossing of the Red Sea, the books of Tobit and Jonah, the Gospel infancy narratives, the miracle narratives (OT and NT), and the Easter accounts. Each is judged to contain implausible elements, with either their content or their structural form indicating a need for investigation with the tools of literary criticism. The mirroring between the Red Sea texts and the Creation narratives, for example, points to their highly literary character, and indicate that they contain, inseparably, an "ancient account" and its "actualization" in light of the "new creation" experienced in the return from the Babylonian Exile.[84] Literary tools are likewise used to

---

80. Pontifical Biblical Commission, *Inspiration and Truth*, 106.

81. Pontifical Biblical Commission, *Inspiration and Truth*, 106.

82. Pontifical Biblical Commission, *Inspiration and Truth*, 107.

83. Pontifical Biblical Commission, *Inspiration and Truth*, 107.

84. Pontifical Biblical Commission, *Inspiration and Truth*, 108. Whether this "ancient account" is based on a historical event is left ambiguous. The Commission does say that "the Exodus account does not intend primarily to transmit a record of ancient events in the manner of an archival document but rather to call to mind a tradition which attests that today, as yesterday, God is present along with his people to save them."

separate core historical events from theological commentary in the infancy narratives and the Easter accounts. This is proposed as a necessary strategy to avoid two extreme approaches to discrepancies: trying to harmonize the factual details of the accounts or rejecting the historicity of the accounts altogether. Since it is now acknowledged that, like all texts, the Gospels present interpretation along with the facts, the "theological comment" is to be considered of "normative import," while "the purely historical elements have a subordinate function."[85]

A separate section is devoted to the ethical and social problems encountered in Scripture. The two focus issues are violence[86] and the role of women.[87] The PBC proceeds methodically to consider each problematic text in light of its literary genre, cultural context, and canonical function. While acknowledging that these passages are genuinely confusing for contemporary readers, it provides plausible explanations of their "didactic, paraenetic and theological purpose."[88] This section balances the historical reality of these difficult issues with pedagogical interpretations in light of the whole of Revelation.[89]

The PBC concludes the chapter by acknowledging the difficulty of some scriptural passages for the average Christian but insists that as long as the "fundamental orientation of the reader" is towards what the text is saying about God and salvation, his or her inability to discern the historicity of the event in question is immaterial.[90]

---

85. Pontifical Biblical Commission, *Inspiration and Truth*, 123.

86. For example, the violent actions of the Chosen People (Gen 4:8, 23–24; 6:11, 13), the violent sanctions recommended in the Law (Exod 21:24; Lev 24:20; Deut 17:12; 19:21; 22:21), the law of extermination (Deut 7:1–2; 20:16–18; Josh 6–12; 1 Sam 15), and the imprecatory psalms (Pss 35; 88; 109; 137).

87. For example, the expectation that they be subordinate to their husbands (Col 3:18; Eph 5:22–33; Titus 2:5), not speak in the assembly (1 Cor 14:33–35) and be blamed for the Fall (Sir 25:24; 1 Tim 2:11–15).

88. Pontifical Biblical Commission, *Inspiration and Truth*, 104.

89. The only example in which historicity is not balanced with pedagogy but rather replaced by it is the document's brief consideration of the conquest wars, which are deemed to be historically implausible. On this basis, the Pontifical Biblical Commission interprets the law of extermination as more of a parable than a historical reality. Pontifical Biblical Commission, *Inspiration and Truth*, 127.

90. Pontifical Biblical Commission, *Inspiration and Truth*, 136.

Evaluation

Despite the convergence of the PBC and Ramage regarding an analogical approach to revelation and inspiration, their divergent philosophical frameworks are made manifest in their case studies. In accordance with the workings of the divine pedagogy and the inspiration of the prophet's practical intellect, the PBC finds the truth of Scripture primarily in the human author's theological purpose, not in the events or realities themselves. This could be seen as an application of Aquinas's teaching that truth lies not in the words themselves, but in their "sense," that is, in the meaning intended by the author.[91]

This method has proved most fruitful when dealing with passages which are difficult primarily due to their enculturation. Both the PBC and Ramage use historical-critical tools to unpack the pedagogy at work in Old Testament passages which seem contrary to Christian ethics, and thus demonstrating their ongoing relevance for Christian readers. Ramage also applies these tools to passages which seem contrary to Christian doctrine, highlighting avenues by which these passages can be understood in the light of the development of doctrine, and continue to function as Revelation by bringing the reader into an encounter with God that is both propositional and relational, speculative and practical.

Perhaps presuming the widespread acceptance of doctrinal development, the PBC focuses instead on passages which are perceived as difficult in light of secular historical-critical scholarship. This is an important endeavor, especially for apologetics and evangelization. However, it is inherently dependent on the hypothetical nature of historical-critical findings, which, as in any empirical science, always remain subject to revision in light of subsequent data.[92] There is a temptation for historical-critical analysis to "over-play its hand."[93] This risk is increased when the secular approaches being employed are not functioning within the hermeneutic of faith and instead seek "neutral" ground.[94] The PBC's approach is open

---

91. Aquinas, *Summa Theologica*, II–II, q. 110, a. 3, ad. 1. However, "sense" as used here by Aquinas may refer more to the text's teleological thrust than to the author's communicative intent. Ratzinger, "Biblical Interpretation in Conflict," 24. This is an English publication of Ratzinger's 1988 Erasmus lecture, based on the published German text. It is longer than the original lecture and includes several explicit calls to complement contemporary exegetical methods with Thomistic metaphysics.

92. Ramage, *Dark Passages*, 51.

93. Ratzinger, *Jesus of Nazareth*, 303.

94. For a critique of this quest, see the essays by Jon Levenson, who argues that Christians can only do historical-critical work in so far as they lay aside their Christianity and thus "cast the truth claims of [their] tradition in doubt." Levenson,

to this risk, especially if it holds to its 1993 proposal that the historical-critical method "when used in an objective manner, implies of itself no a priori."[95] This presupposition has been challenged by recent "criticisms of the criticism," which highlight the philosophical assumptions underlying the historical-critical method.[96]

One presupposition which seems to underlie some of the PBC's analysis is Troeltsch's "analogy of history." In his authoritative essay "On Historical and Dogmatic Method in Theology" (1898), Troeltsch called for an "analogical" understanding of history, claiming that the "rules" of existence as we experience them today apply equally in all times and places, and thus must be applied in the study of ancient texts. While this may be true, Troeltsch fails to explicate the presupposition underlying his conclusions, that is, that the rules of being should be reduced to that which can be explained by mathematics and science. It is this premise, not the analogical nature of history, which underlies Troeltsch's conclusion that all supernatural occurrences must be explained in natural ways.[97] In contrast, Fr. Francis Martin calls for an "analogy of historical being," which acknowledges God's ability and desire to be actively involved in human history, both in the past and in the present, and is open to the real possibility of the miraculous.[98]

Despite its deliberate efforts to work within the hermeneutic of faith, the PBC's chapter on "Historical Problems" seems influenced by Troeltsch's approach. It does highlight some literary evidence which indicates the highly practical and pedagogical purpose of the books of Tobit and Jonah, the Red Sea account, and the miracle narratives of both Old and New Testament. However, unlike the Abraham narrative, these are identified as difficult passages not because of their redaction history or literary genre, but precisely because they contain events which are "implausible." This is a judgement based on philosophical presuppositions, not on the text itself.[99]

Hebrew Bible, 29, 50.

95. Pontifical Biblical Commission, *Interpretation of the Bible in the Church*, I.A.4.

96. For example, Levering, *Participatory Biblical Exegesis*; Carbajosa, *Faith*; Hahn and Wiker, *Politicizing the Bible*.

97. Hahn and Wiker, *Politicizing the Bible*, 10.

98. Martin, "Historical Criticism," 266.

99. A more moderate approach is seen in the work of Fr. Francis Martin, who acknowledges that plenary inerrancy leaves room for historical discrepancies, but points to more limited examples, such as Caesar Augustus' census in Luke 2:1, the date of the siege of Jerusalem, and mistaken attributions when New Testament authors quote the prophets. Martin, "Revelation and Its Transmission," 67n56. An even more conservative route would be that of St. Augustine, who, in a letter to St. Jerome, outlined his three preferred explanations for "anything that appears to me opposed to

In contrast, Ramage's work combines Thomistic epistemology with Aquinas's metaphysics of moderate realism. Although the illumination of the practical intellect is an important aspect of inspiration, and can help in uncovering the divine pedagogy, it is the text itself, handed down through the ministry of the Church, which transmits Revelation to each generation. As highlighted in his article on the senses of Scripture, Aquinas holds that words are primarily intended to point to realities, not to authorial intention.[100] And while authorial intention (both human and divine) is important for discerning the literal sense of the words, it is in God's power to signify meaning not only in words, but in things themselves.[101] This is what gives Scripture its spiritual senses, which distinguish it from other historical texts and mark it as belonging to Divine Revelation. As such, it must be interpreted in the broader context of Revelation, which includes the created world, the events of history, and the tradition of the Church.[102]

The fruitfulness of this approach can be glimpsed in comparing the PBC's exegesis of the Abraham cycle to that obtained through the traditional senses of Scripture, to which Ramage points.[103] The PBC does well to acknowledge the somewhat disjointed literary style of patriarchal history found in Genesis and the occasional factual discrepancies, and to attribute these to a long redaction history.[104] This approach can highlight the pedagogical choices made by redactors, which point towards the divine pedagogy. However, the evidence of a process of redaction and theological interpretation does not require a dismissal of the historical event, which is implied especially in the PBC's exegesis of Genesis 15.[105] Nor does it justify introducing a divide between the event and the author's interpretation of the event.

In contrast, the metaphysical approach is capable of harnessing the four-fold senses of Scripture to bring the contemporary reader not only into an epistemological encounter with the God of Abraham, but a metaphysical encounter. The inspired Word mediates the vertical participation of the original event, the inspired authors, the reader today, and our eschatological

---

truth": a faulty manuscript, an imperfect translation, or the limitations of the reader's understanding. Pitre, "Mystery of God's Word," 60.

100. Aquinas, *Summa Theologica*, I, q. 1, a. 10.

101. Aquinas, *Summa Theologica*, I, q. 1, a. 10, corpus.

102. Benedict XVI, *Verbum Domini*, sec. 7.

103. Ramage, *Dark Passages*, 60.

104. Pontifical Biblical Commission, *Inspiration and Truth*, 106.

105. Pontifical Biblical Commission, *Inspiration and Truth*, 107.

destiny in the one *mysterion* of Christ and His Paschal Mystery.[106] Compared with the somewhat apologetic approach of the PBC, this metaphysical exegesis is a far more fruitful avenue for facilitating the ongoing work of Revelation as an encounter with the living God.[107]

CONCLUSION

In this dialogue between the Pontifical Biblical Commission's document *The Inspiration and Truth of Sacred Scripture* and Matthew Ramage's revival of the Thomistic approaches to inspiration and inerrancy, two dimensions of pneumatology's ongoing relevance have emerged. The first is the Holy Spirit's gift of prophecy. The biblical witness as explored by the PBC and the dogmatic approach of the Thomists both point to the figure of the prophet as the model of the scriptural author. The prophet is filled with the Holy Spirit, who enables his encounter with God, participation in supernatural knowledge and judgement, and divine mandate to proclaim the Word. The second is the Holy Spirit's instrumental causality. As with all the gifts and charisms, the Spirit elevates man into a secondary cause, and works through his human limitations, not in spite of them. The charism of prophecy, and thus the graces of revelation and inspiration, are analogical realities, which function differently according to the phase of salvation history and the wisdom of the divine pedagogy. This analogical approach allows the PBC and Ramage to discern the truth recorded "for the sake of salvation" which runs through the whole biblical canon, holding in fruitful tension the inerrancy of Scripture and its human limitations.

However, while upholding the doctrine of inerrancy, this epistemological approach leaves the historicity of biblical events in ambiguity. It must be complemented with a metaphysics of moderate realism, which places scriptural revelation within the broader context of the "analogy of the Word"—Revelation as encountered in the created world, the events of salvation history, and the tradition of the Church. The Holy Spirit, giver of life, hovered over the waters of creation, giving it a participation in the transcendental perfections of its Creator. He is likewise the Lord of salvation history, drawing each event, person, and institution into the *telos* of divine providence and the wisdom of the divine pedagogy. Thus, confidence in the revelatory power of creation and history, and the awareness that divine intervention is not a rare occurrence but rather a constant reality, is

---

106. This is the approach proposed in Martin, "Historical Criticism."

107. The metaphysics of this encounter is well explained in Wright and Martin, *Encountering the Living God in Scripture*, Part Two.

necessary for a truly prophetic hermeneutic. Just as the prophets' experience included both encounter and knowledge, and just as they were instructed to bear witness to their experience both in speech and in their prophetic acts, so too, God reveals himself in words and deeds, which are to be appreciated as "equi-primordial."[108]

In this context, the human limitations of scriptural revelation can be understood not as a necessary evil from which the truth of salvation must be abstracted, but as a providential facet of Revelation. Apparent "material errors" or "environmental glitches" can be used by God to draw people into an encounter with Him.[109] This is an extension of the *analogia entis* ("analogy of being"), and the mysterious way in which created essences limit and yet manifest existence; it is also an extension of the Incarnation, by which "the divine is made known and rendered comprehensible through the human."[110] Both the divine wisdom and the divine pedagogy are manifested in the limited yet lifegiving ways in which Revelation is received and expressed by each scriptural author. Without insisting that every statement in Scripture is empirically factual, it is possible to affirm with *Dei Verbum* that "everything asserted by the inspired authors or sacred writers must be held to be asserted by the Holy Spirit."[111]

BIBLIOGRAPHY

Aquinas, Thomas. *Summa Theologica*. Translated by Fathers of the English Dominican Province. New York: Benziger Brothers, 1911–25.

Ayres, Lewis, and Stephen E. Fowl. "(Mis)Reading the Face of God: The Interpretation of the Bible in the Church." *Theological Studies* 60 (1999) 513–28.

Benedict XV. *Spiritus Paraclitus*. https://www.vatican.va/content/benedict-xv/en/encyclicals/documents/hf_ben-xv_enc_15091920_spiritus-paraclitus.html.

Benedict XVI. *Verbum Domini: The Word of God in the Life and Mission of the Church*. https://www.vatican.va/content/benedict-xvi/en/apost_exhortations/documents/hf_ben-xvi_exh_20100930_verbum-domini.html.

Benoit, Pierre. *Aspects of Biblical Inspiration*. Translated by J. Murphy-O'Connor and S. K. Ashe. Chicago: Priory, 1965.

———. *Inspiration and the Bible*. Translated by J. Murphy-O'Connor and M. Keverne. London: Sheed & Ward, 1965.

Blankenhorn, Bernhard. "God Speaks: Divine Authorship of Scripture in Karl Rahner and Pierre Benoit." *Angelicum* 93 (2016) 445–61.

108. Ratzinger, "Biblical Interpretation in Conflict," 25.

109. Following the approach of Cardinal Augustin Bea, this is the understanding of *Dei Verbum*, sec. 11, proposed in Waldstein, "Analogia Verbi," 94–96.

110. Hahn, "For the Sake of Our Salvation," 38.

111. Second Vatican Council, *Dei Verbum*, sec. 11.

Bonino, Serge-Thomas. "Saint Thomas Aquinas Exegete of the Hexaemeron: Bible and Philosophy." *Nova et Vetera* 18 (2020) 1207–34.

Brown, Raymond E. "The History and Development of the Theory of a Sensus Plenior." *Catholic Biblical Quarterly* 15 (1953) 141–62.

Burtchaell, James Tunstead. *Catholic Theories of Biblical Inspiration Since 1810: A Review and Critique.* London: Cambridge University Press, 1969.

Carbajosa, Ignacio. *Faith, the Fount of Exegesis: The Interpretation of Scripture in Light of the History of Research on the Old Testament.* Translated by Paul Stevenson. San Francisco: Ignatius, 2011.

Hahn, Scott W. "For the Sake of Our Salvation: The Truth and Humility of God's Word." *Letter & Spirit* 6 (2010) 21–46.

Hahn, Scott W., and Benjamin Wiker. *Politicizing the Bible: The Roots of Historical Criticism and the Secularization of Scripture (1300–1700).* New York: Crossroads, 2013.

Harrison, Brian W. "Restricted Inerrancy and the 'Hermeneutic of Discontinuity.'" *Letter & Spirit* 6 (2010) 225–46.

Hill, Robert C. "St. John Chrysostom's Teachings on Inspiration in His Old Testament Homilies." PhD diss. Pontificiam Universitatem S. Thomae in Urbe, 1981.

Levenson, Jon D. *The Hebrew Bible, the Old Testament, and Historical Criticism: Jews and Christians in Biblical Studies.* Louisville, KY: Presbyterian, 1993.

Levering, Matthew. *Participatory Biblical Exegesis: A Theology of Biblical Interpretation.* South Bend, IN: University of Notre Dame Press, 2008.

Martin, Francis. "Historical Criticism and New Testament Teaching on the Imitation of Christ." *Anthropotes: rivista di studi sulla persona e la famiglia* 6 (1990) 261–87.

———. "Revelation and Its Transmission." In *Vatican II: Renewal within Tradition*, edited by Matthew L. Lamb and Matthew Levering, 55–75. Oxford: Oxford University Press, 2008.

McGuckin, Terence. "Saint Thomas Aquinas and Theological Exegesis of Sacred Scripture." *New Blackfriars* 74 (1993) 197–211.

Pitre, Brant. "The Mystery of God's Word: Inspiration, Inerrancy, and the Interpretation of Scripture." *Letter & Spirit* 6 (2010) 47–66.

Pontifical Biblical Commission. *The Inspiration and Truth of Sacred Scripture: The Word That Comes from God and Speaks of God for the Salvation of the World.* Translated by Thomas Esposito and Stephen Gregg. Collegeville, MN: Liturgical, 2014.

———. *The Interpretation of the Bible in the Church.* https://catholic-resources.org/ChurchDocs/PBC_Interp.htm.

Ramage, Matthew J. *Dark Passages of the Bible: Engaging Scripture with Benedict XVI and Thomas Aquinas.* Washington, DC: The Catholic University of America Press, 2013.

Ratzinger, Joseph. "Biblical Interpretation in Conflict: On the Foundations and the Itinerary of Exegesis Today." In *Opening Up the Scriptures: Joseph Ratzinger and the Foundations of Biblical Interpretation*, edited by José Granados et al., translated by Adrian Walker, 1–29. Grand Rapids, MI: Eerdmans, 2008.

———. *Jesus of Nazareth: From the Baptism in the Jordan to the Transfiguration.* Translated by Adrian J. Walker. New York: Doubleday, 2007.

Rogers, Paul M. "Prophecy and the Moral Life in Thomas Aquinas's Commentary on 1 Corinthians." In *Towards a Biblical Thomism: Thomas Aquinas and the Renewal of*

Biblical Theology, edited by Piotr Roszak and Jörgen Vijgen, 197–218. Pamplona: Ediciones Universidad de Navarra, 2018.

Rylaarsdam, David. *John Chrysostom on Divine Pedagogy: The Coherence of His Theology and Preaching*. Oxford: Oxford University Press, 2014.

Second Vatican Council. *Dei Verbum: Dogmatic Constitution on Divine Revelation*. https://www.vatican.va/archive/hist_councils/ii_vatican_council/documents/vat-ii_const_19651118_dei-verbum_en.html.

Synave, Paul, and Pierre Benoit. *Prophecy and Inspiration: A Commentary on the Summa Theologica II-II, Questions 171–178*. Translated by Avery R. Dulles and Thomas L. Sheridan. New York: Desclee, 1961.

Waldstein, Michael Maria. "Analogia Verbi: The Truth of Scripture in Rudolf Bultmann and Raymond Brown." *Letter & Spirit* 6 (2010) 93–140.

Wright, William M., IV, and Francis Martin. *Encountering the Living God in Scripture: Theological and Philosophical Principles for Interpretation*. Grand Rapids, MI: Baker Academic, 2019.

Zerafa, Peter Paul. "The Limits of Biblical Inerrancy." *Letter & Spirit* 6 (2010) 359–76.

17

SERVAIS PINCKAERS AND THE NEW LAW IN THE SPIRIT

A Pneumatological Approach to Morality

Rev. Dr. Paschal M. Corby OFM Conv.

UNTIL HIS DEATH IN 2008, the great Belgian Dominican theologian, Servais Pinckaers, was a prominent herald for the renewal of moral theology. He simultaneously recognized the deficiencies of the post-Tridentine manualist tradition, with its "morality of obligation," as well as the deficiencies of the consequentialist and proportionalist moralities that marked post-conciliar attempts at renewal.[1] In response, Pinckaers promoted a turn towards the subject in the pursuit of beatitude, with particular concern for the place of virtue and the interior working of grace through the Holy Spirit.

One of the key elements of Pinckaers' scholarship was his identification of the fourteenth-century Nominalist "shift," associated with the figure of William of Ockham, in the relationship of freedom to nature. In Pinckaers' analysis, this shift led to two polar theories of morality: a morality of *happiness*, and a morality of *obligation*.[2] Before the fourteenth century, from Antiquity into the Middle Ages, questions of the moral life concerned the

1. Pinckaers, "Rediscovering Virtue," 361.
2. Pinckaers, *Morality*, 65.

path to happiness. But from Ockham onwards, the moral question changed, no longer concerned with what leads to beatitude, but focused rather "on the obligations imposed by law as the expression of the divine will."[3]

Foundational to these distinct moral theories, Pinckaers further identifies two models of freedom: *freedom for excellence*, which arouses moralities of happiness and virtue, and the *freedom of indifference*, which is the basis of moralities of obligation.[4] According to Aquinas, freedom flowed from reason and will, "quickened by the inclinations to truth, goodness, and happiness."[5] For Ockham, instead, freedom was prior to all things. Stated otherwise, "according to Aquinas, free will *proceeds from* reason and will; according to Ockham, free will *precedes* reason and will, like a first faculty."[6] Ockham's theory therefore severed any connection between reason and nature, revolutionizing our understanding of the person and his or her actions.[7] Nature was no longer the source of freedom but was rendered subordinate and external to choice. The famous maxim, *sequi naturam* (follow nature) lost meaning, and a new vision emerged: *dominari naturam*.[8] Thus subordinated, human nature found itself disconnected from its roots in divine creation, such that only an exterior relationship to God through "law" remained. Morality therefore became a choice between autonomy and heteronomy. As Pinckaers writes: "Either a moral system was autonomous, centered on the human person, and precisely on his freedom to claim radical independence in his choice of external things, or it was heteronomous and subjected his freedom, in one way or another, to a rule, a law, to alien obligations."[9]

INTERIORITY OF THE NEW LAW

To renew moral theology, therefore, Pinckaers counsels moving away from obligation towards self-fulfilment in beatitude. To this end, he reclaims the subjectivity of the acting person as the locus of morality. He recognizes two levels of action: *exterior* action which operates at the level of purpose and circumstance; and *interior* action which "stems from our capacity to reflect upon ourselves, our personal dispositions, desires, intentions, and

3. Pinckaers, *Morality*, 66.

4. Pinckaers, *Morality*, 68.

5. Pinckaers, *Morality*, 68.

6. Pinckaers, "Aquinas on Nature and the Supernatural," 361.

7. Dupré, *Passage to Modernity*, 39.

8. Pinckaers, *Morality*, 69.

9. Pinckaers, "Aquinas and Agency," 169.

feelings."[10] Of these, Pinckaers acknowledges the deeper significance of the interior dimension.

> Human action is directly moral at the level of the interior act.
> ... The moral plane is constituted by the qualities of the human
> person at the level of reason, will, and heart, where she has
> mastery over her actions. That is the domain of the virtues, the
> virtues that make both the act and the one who does it good.[11]

However, Pinckaers cannot be pigeon-holed as just any virtue ethicist. Nor does he coincide with other Thomists who regard interiority in terms of the human person's rational integration of virtue with the natural law. In this context, Pinckaers stands in contrast to the thought of Swiss philosopher Martin Rhonheimer. According to his brand of Thomism, Rhonheimer expresses confidence in "the profound continuity of unassisted practical reason, as unfolded in natural law, with revealed Christian morality"—a continuity that recognizes practical reason's intrinsic capacity to grasp the good, though admittedly "not in its *full* intelligibility, which precisely stem from revealed Christian morality."[12] The order of revelation is consonant with reason. It stands in progressive relation to the natural law. It serves to complete that which is lacking in natural rationality.

Such reductive conflation of reason and revelation has been widely criticized, especially from a member of the *Communio* School. A young Joseph Ratzinger, commenting on the confused anthropology contained in the Conciliar document *Gaudium et Spes*, rejects this "juxtaposition" of nature and supernature which proceeds from "the fiction that it is possible to construct a rational philosophical picture of man intelligible to all and on which all men of goodwill can agree, the actual Christian doctrines being added to this as a sort of crowning conclusion."[13]

Hans Urs von Balthasar also challenges the "continuity" thesis between natural reason and revelation, practical reason and Christian morality. The logic of the Incarnation, while possessing "an intelligibility that illuminates the pure facticity of the historical as a necessity," remains "at the same time an intelligibility that cannot be reduced to that which the human being demands or (for whatever reason) anticipates."[14] He is, therefore, guarded in his language of human potentiality. In upholding the gratuity of divine

10. Pinckaers, "Rediscovering Virtue," 364.

11. Pinckaers, "Scripture and the Renewal of Moral Theology," 61.

12. Rhonheimer, "Is Christian Morality Reasonable?," 544n13.

13. Ratzinger, "Dignity of the Human Person," quoted in Rowland, "Natural Law," 378.

14. Balthasar, *Love Alone Is Credible*, 55.

grace, he stresses its freedom from pre-existing potentialities within the human person or structures of recognition. While grace completes nature, it does so on God's terms. As he writes, "the love of God, which is of course grace, necessarily includes in itself its own conditions of recognizability."[15]

The content of God's action in human history "cannot in any essential way be derived from or anticipated a priori on the basis of created nature, because it arises from the Other *as* Other in unfathomable freedom toward his other; no preliminary bridge of understanding can be built on similarity or, for that matter, on identity."[16] We may hope for it and we strive after it. Our whole lives are orientated towards it. But the revelation of our end in Jesus Christ—our filial adoption as sons-in-the-Son—is something beyond our expectations, beyond what human reason can comprehend. As Balthasar writes: "Only in infinite reverence (Phil 2:12) can we participate in the saving work of God, whose absolute love towers infinitely above us—in the *maior dissimilitudo*."[17]

In continuity with this respect for the *maior dissimilitudo*, Pinckaers rejects Rhonheimer's attempt to extract Aquinas' philosophical method and content from his theological synthesis.[18] Instead, Pinckaers firmly holds to Aquinas' twofold foundation of interiority through the natural law *and* the Evangelical Law, the latter "written by the Holy Spirit in the human heart by means of faith and defined as the very grace of the Holy Spirit operating through charity."[19]

> The moral law thus has its source in the profound interiority of the human being, where the Holy Spirit encounters human nature to heal, vivify, and sanctify it, and to create progressively a dynamic harmony which will find expression chiefly in the fruits of the Spirit.[20]

"This is why Christian theology must begin with faith and the Gospel," writes Pinckaers, "which reveal to us, beyond sin, our heart and our true nature, such as they were in the beginning and as they shall once more become through the grace of Christ."[21]

15. Balthasar, *Love Alone Is Credible*, 75.

16. Balthasar, *Love Alone Is Credible*, 70.

17. Balthasar, "Nine Propositions on Christian Ethics," 80.

18. Rhonheimer, *Perspective of Morality*, 2.

19. Pinckaers, "Aquinas on Nature and the Supernatural," 368.

20. Pinckaers, "Aquinas on Nature and the Supernatural," 368.

21. Pinckaers, *Sources of Christian Ethics*, 464.

A DISTINCTIVELY CHRISTIAN MORALITY

Flowing from this priority of the New Law, written by the Holy Spirit on the heart of those who believe, Pinckaers insists on the distinctiveness of Christian morality. Christianity does not merely adopt the morality of the human good but reorientates it. The Christian novelty lies in the fact that "the first source of moral excellence is no longer located in the human person, but in God through Christ."[22] In response to the young man's question in the Gospel, "What good must I do to gain eternal life?," Christ directs us to the only One who is good (Matt 19:16–17).[23] Indeed, as Pinckaers attests, "one cannot give a fully satisfactory answer to the question of 'what is good,' and the desire for happiness, without bringing in God."[24] God exists both as the standard of excellence and the means of achieving it through the grace of the Holy Spirit.

When applied to virtue ethics, Pinckaers therefore contends that the classical doctrine is radically transformed by divine revelation. A Christian virtue ethic is different from the classical model. The mean of the virtue fixed by human reason, and the mean of the virtue determined by Divine rule, are different. The latter, in its broader vision infused by love, demands something more. It possesses "a new criterion of judgment and proportion."[25] In this broadened context, grace empowers the subject to act in view of his or her supernatural end. It is concerned with the natural virtues, but gives them "a more perfect, characteristic mode of concrete action."[26] While he coincides with a classical definition of virtue "as a dynamic interiority that causes us to act in a personal way with ease and joy," Pinckaers more explicitly emphasizes that they are exercised "according to the movement of love"[27] within the context of the New Law. He recognizes this in the theology of St. Paul, who in preaching the priority of faith, inaugurates a new morality.

> In the face of Jewish justice and Greek wisdom [Paul] proclaimed a new virtue: [the virtue of] faith in Jesus, crucified and risen and become for all the source of God's justice and wisdom. [Paul] was laying the foundation stone of morality, a virtue the Greeks did not know and the Jews misunderstood: faith, and

22. Pinckaers, *Morality*, 71.
23. Biblical references in this chapter are from the NABRE.
24. Pinckaers, "Encyclical for the Future," 21.
25. Pinckaers, *Sources of Christian Ethics*, 180.
26. Pinckaers, *Sources of Christian Ethics*, 180.
27. Pinckaers, "Aquinas and Agency," 181.

faith in Jesus. He did not reject the desire for justice and wisdom but gave them a new source: no longer human virtue, but what might be called the virtue of God acting through Jesus Christ. He did not hide the fact that the exchange was traumatic: this faith seemed a scandal to the Jews and folly to the Greeks.[28]

The scandal, the folly, of faith underscores its newness. It challenges the independent pride of human wisdom. It demands "a humble, docile opening to the Spirit"—the Spirit who "brings forth a justice, a virtue, a holiness that comes from God through Jesus Christ."[29]

In this new morality, Pinckaers speaks of the priority of the theological virtues, likening this priority to the ordering of the head to its body.[30] In this analogy, "faith, hope, and charity constitute the head of the Christian organism of the virtues and impart life from within, like a vital impulse, to the human virtues so that they can be ordered to divine beatitude, but not without transforming them to some extent."[31] Of the theological virtues, it is charity in particular that acts to "inform" the other virtues, penetrating them "so deeply" that they "become aspects or forms of *agape*."[32] Charity enlivens the other virtues and conforms them to itself to become "ways of loving."[33] St. Paul thus refers to a love that is in all things—"bears all things, believes all things, hopes all things, endures all things" (1 Cor 13:4–7). In this sense, Pinckaers speaks of "the virtues grouped around charity," and of "the attitudes of heart" that lead towards beatitude.[34]

As Pinckaers elaborates, the application of the theological virtue of love to moral action is concretely illustrated in the same Letter to the Corinthians, in St. Paul's teaching on fraternal charity in relation to food sacrificed to idols (1 Cor 8:1–13). The Apostle establishes a norm that Christians may eat such food, since faith and reason tells us that idols do not exist. But "this material, external judgment does not go far enough."[35] For freedom [in this scenario] is secondary to the duty to love. As Pinckaers interprets, "a more basic criterion" is established through "the consideration of charity toward the weak."

---

28. Pinckaers, *Sources of Christian Ethics*, 114.
29. Pinckaers, *Sources of Christian Ethics*, 115.
30. Pinckaers, *Sources of Christian Ethics*, 178–81.
31. Pinckaers, "Place of Philosophy in Moral Theology," 67.
32. Pinckaers, "Scripture and the Renewal of Moral Theology," 58.
33. Pinckaers, *Sources of Christian Ethics*, 28.
34. Pinckaers, "Scripture and the Renewal of Moral Theology," 53.
35. Pinckaers, "Role of Virtue in Moral Theology," 293.

The concern to avoid scandal and to practice fraternal charity modifies the practical judgment and calls for abstinence from the idol offerings. Thus reflection rises to the decisive level of personal interiority, which opens out to others and to the common good. The quality of the Christian's actions and his or her perfection will depend more on charity than on abstract knowledge.[36]

We therefore recognize that the perfection [that is the end of the moral life] is dependent on grace. Accompanied by the gifts of the Holy Spirit, the natural virtues are propelled towards their perfection in beatitude. In Pinckaers' words, the gifts of the Spirit "add a receptivity to the virtues, a docility to spiritual impulses. In this way the Holy Spirit's action, like the virtues, can affect all that the Christian does."[37] To this end, St. Thomas (in the *Secunda Secundae*) couples each of the virtues with a specific gift "that disposes us to receive divine inspirations that empower us to act according to a higher measure."[38] The virtue of Faith with the gifts of knowledge and intelligence; Hope with the corresponding gift of fear; Love with the gift of wisdom. Prudence perfected by the gift of counsel; Justice with the gift of piety; Courage with the gift of courage; and Temperance with the gift of fear.

BEYOND THE NATURAL LAW: COMPENETRATION OF FAITH AND REASON

In stressing the priority of the New Law and the grace of the Holy Spirit, Pinckaers is both corrective of a morality that was exclusively bound to the natural law, and critical of contemporary moralities that propose "love" independent of reason, with their "strong attraction for love and spontaneity, without due regard for the demands of integrity and truth."[39] In response, Pinckaers speaks of a "compenetration" between grace and reason. He finds it in the morality of the New Testament, in St. Paul's treatment of fornication in 1 Corinthians. The Apostle begins with an appeal to the natural law, the recognition of the truth of the human person discerned by reason: "Every other sin which a man commits is outside the body; but the immoral man sins against his own body" (1 Cor 6:18); but he then shifts emphasis, when

---

36. Pinckaers, "Rediscovering Virtue," 366–67.
37. Pinckaers, "Place of Philosophy in Moral Theology," 68.
38. Pinckaers, "Sources of the Ethics," 23.
39. Pinckaers, *Sources of Christian Ethics*, 29.

he adds: "Do you not know that your body is a temple of the Holy Spirit?" (1 Cor 6:19).

From this Pinckaers adds:

> We thus see here an intimate link between the understanding of the human and the understanding of Christ. Each penetrates and reinforces the other, but the Christian criteria become predominant, particularly through the work of charity which unites believers as brothers and sisters, as members of the same Body by the impulse of the Spirit.[40]

Such compenetration is again corrective of distorted relations between philosophy and theology, nature and grace. While philosophy humbly recognizes that our final end in the vision of God is fulfilled only in the light of Revelation, theology needs reason to provide "the necessary categories and language for a sound explanation of the riches of the Gospel and Christian experience."[41] Yet Pinckaers, following the teaching of Aquinas and the Fathers, insists on a proper order. He speaks of two "moments" in which the faith is first implanted and reasoned later. Philosophical wisdom at the service of faith comes only after faith has been established.[42] In the context of the ordering of these "moments," Pinckaers makes a distinction regarding the Thomistic maxim that *gratia non tollit naturam, sed perficit.*[43]

> The principle should not be understood in the sense that philosophy, as a work of reason, must first be constructed while saying to oneself that in any case it will be confirmed by grace, but rather in the opposite sense: we must have the boldness to believe in the Word of God and to abandon ourselves to grace, in the assurance that, far from destroying whatever is true, good, and reasonable in philosophy, grace will teach us how to make it our own, to develop it and to perfect it, while revealing to us a broader and more profound wisdom than any human thought,

40. Pinckaers, "Scripture and the Renewal of Moral Theology," 58.

41. Pinckaers, "Place of Philosophy in Moral Theology," 72. However, it would appear that Pinckaers is speaking of the pedagogical role of philosophy in relation to theology, rather than as a foundation for revelation. This is made more explicit when elsewhere he writes that those who have "received the gift and charge of teaching from the Spirit and the Church . . . may and indeed should return to human wisdom and the teaching of the philosophers to discern the truth and goodness they contain and subject it to the wisdom of God for the service of evangelical preaching." Pinckaers, "Aquinas's Pursuit of Beatitude," 110–11.

42. Pinckaers, "Aquinas's Pursuit of Beatitude." 110.

43. Aquinas, *Summa Theologiae*, I, q. 1, a. 8, ad. 2.

the wisdom given by the Holy Spirit who unites us with the person of Christ and his Cross by teaching us to "live in Christ."[44]

Pinckaers stresses what the perfecting of nature by grace should not be "taken as a guarantee to reason and the natural virtues" working "according to their own rules and methods, even independently of faith" and receiving some "additional perfection" by the application of grace.[45] In Pinckaers' analysis, the priority of grace is not just in the completion of beatitude, as something added to the work of reason, but as intrinsic to the reasoning process itself through the wisdom of the Holy Spirit. Or as Michael Sherwin writes: "We do not become well ordered with regard to eternal beatitude by first being well ordered toward the temporal community. Instead, we become well ordered to our temporal community by first becoming citizens of heaven in the gift of grace."[46]

CENTRALITY OF THE FIGURE OF CHRIST

In advocating "boldness to believe in the Word of God and to abandon ourselves to grace," Pinckaers acknowledges that at the heart of the morality of the Gospels stands the figure of Christ.[47] He writes that "an essential condition for any true renewal of the teaching of moral theology is the reestablishment of a profound and sustained contact with that primary source of inspiration for Christian life and theology that is the Word and Person of Christ."[48] In responding to the Christocentric focus of *Veritatis Splendor*, Pinckaers confirms that "Christian morality cannot be reduced

44. Pinckaers, "Place of Philosophy in Moral Theology," 72. See also Pinckaers, "Revisionist Understandings," 269: "Do not be afraid to surrender to grace, faith, and revelation, for far from harming your nature and reason they will confirm, develop, and perfect them."

45. Pinckaers, "Aquinas on Nature and the Supernatural," 366–67.

46. Sherwin, "Infused Virtue," 51.

47. Pinckaers takes seriously the Council's call for the renewal of moral theology. The Decree on Priestly Training specified that the "scientific exposition" of moral theology, "nourished more on the teaching of the Bible, should shed light on the loftiness of the calling of the faithful in Christ and the obligation that is theirs of bearing fruit in charity for the life of the world." Second Vatican Council, *Optatam Totius*, sec. 16. This theological and distinctively scriptural emphasis was reinforced in the Dogmatic Constitution on Divine Revelation which decreed that the Gospel of Christ is "the source of all saving truth and moral teaching." Second Vatican Council, *Dei Verbum*, sec. 7. It was confirmed in the encyclical *Veritatis Splendor* when John Paul confesses that "Sacred Scripture remains the living and fruitful source of the Church's moral doctrine." John Paul II, *Veritatis Splendor*, sec. 28.

48. Pinckaers, "Encyclical for the Future," 13.

to a code of commands and prohibitions. It consists basically in "holding fast to the very person of Jesus . . . sharing in his free and loving obedience to the will of the Father."[49] As the encyclical explicitly states: "the decisive answer to every one of man's questions, his religious and moral questions in particular, is given by Jesus Christ, or rather is Jesus Christ himself."[50] Thus Pinckaers contends that the moral rule of the Christian life consists in *imitation of Christ*,[51] which as he explains is *"an interior following*, at the level of heart and morality, under the impulse of the Spirit; it means *being conformed to Christ*."[52] It is conformation to the image of Christ as found in the Gospels, above all in the Beatitudes in which "it is possible to discern the spiritual physiognomy of Christ"[53]—"a sort of *self-portrait of Christ*"[54]— which invite us to follow him in discipleship and communion.

Building on this theme of imitation, Pinckaers draws on the Pauline theology of being "in Christ" through the Holy Spirit's communication of the new life flowing from the resurrection. He notes that for the Apostle, the concept of imitation is far more profound than simply copying.

> Imitation rooted in faith operates at a deeper level, for it is the work of the Holy Spirit. He conforms us interiorly to the image of Christ and engraves "the sentiments of Christ Jesus" so profoundly upon our souls that we can ourselves become models for others, the model always being in the end the image of Christ, who is all in all.[55]

A parallel may be drawn with Balthasar's identification of Christ as "concrete categorical imperative."

> Christ's concrete existence—his life, suffering, death and ultimate bodily resurrection—surpasses all other systems of ethical norms. In the final analysis it is to this norm alone, which is itself the prototype of perfect obedience to God the Father, that the moral conduct of Christians has to answer.[56]

49. Pinckaers, "Encyclical for the Future," 20; John Paul II, *Veritatis Splendor*, sec. 19.

50. John Paul II, *Veritatis Splendor*, sec. 2.

51. Pinckaers, "Encyclical for the Future," 20.

52. Pinckaers, "Encyclical for the Future," 33.

53. Pinckaers, "Encyclical for the Future," 28.

54. John Paul II, *Veritatis Splendor*, sec. 16.

55. Pinckaers, *Sources of Christian Ethics*, 121.

56. Balthasar, "Nine Propositions on Christian Ethics," 82.

In the words of Balthasar, this perfect obedience of Christ is "eschatological" and "unsurpassable," and as such "universally normative."[57] But more than a mere model or paradigm for imitation, Christ is a "personal" norm, "who, in virtue of his suffering for us and his eucharistic surrender of his life for us (which imparts it to us—*per ipsum et in ipso*), empowers us inwardly to do the Father's will together with him (*cum ipso*)."[58] He is himself the means of overcoming the distance between the particular and the universal, the personal and the "other." Through our communion with him, we take on the Christ-form of filial obedience; we love with his own love.

Accordingly, for Balthasar, as for Pinckaers, configuration to Christ as moral norm through the internal working of the grace of the Holy Spirit, does not undermine human subjectivity or moral autonomy. Pinckaers explains: "The more one submits to God in accordance with one's natural inclinations to truth and goodness, the more capable one becomes of self-direction and the freer one becomes also as a person, sharing in the divine freedom."[59] That is to say, "the more one submits to the divine heteronomy, the more autonomous one becomes."[60] In this context, Pinckaers makes a further distinction regarding the meaning of *gratia non tollit naturam, sed perficit*, noting that human fulfillment comes through surrender to grace, and "the more fully one gives oneself to God, the more fully one becomes oneself."[61]

Through an encounter with Christ—who, according to Balthasar, is "the self-interpreting revelation-form of love itself"[62]—the complete realization of the human person created in his image is revealed. Grace changes us. "The Christian has glimpsed in faith a singular fullness: to be loved by God the Father as he loves Christ, the Son, and to love as Christ himself loves."[63] By realizing the depths of God's love for us, and the heights to which we are called, we are transformed. Pinckaers maintains that insertion into the Body of Christ brings about a radical change within the human person. It is "the source of a grace that changes the human in his very being—he becomes a new man—and in his behavior is inspired henceforth by the *agape* under the movement of the Holy Spirit."[64] Thus, the image of God within us is not

---

57. Balthasar, "Nine Propositions on Christian Ethics," 83.

58. Balthasar, "Nine Propositions on Christian Ethics," 79.

59. Pinckaers, "Aquinas and Agency," 169–70.

60. Pinckaers, "Aquinas and Agency," 170.

61. Pinckaers, "Aquinas and Agency," 170.

62. Balthasar, *Love Alone Is Credible*, 56.

63. Melina, *Sharing in Christ's Virtues*, 32.

64. Pinckaers, "Body of Christ," 34.

exhausted by creation but is "re-created" in us by grace. Transfigured by grace, the human person becomes a sign and instrument of Christ's love in the world.

According to Pinckaers, this offers a more radical way of appropriating nature and grace.

> The idea of the image of God presupposes a certain link that we might call natural between humans and God. This link can be seen from the viewpoint of the creator of human beings in the image and likeness of God, and through natural inclinations to truth and goodness that come from God and render humans *capax Dei*. It can also be envisioned from the viewpoint of beatitude, through the actualization of this capacity under the action of grace, faith, and charity, principally by way of imitation and growing likeness.[65]

This Christological perspective therefore offers "something more" for our understanding of the human person, and of the moral life. "The Christian perspective does not eliminate or substitute the principles of the natural law, but in keeping them, integrally gives them *a new definitive interpretation*, with consequences also on the normative level."[66] Revelation does not do away with reason, but transforms it through new vision and expanded possibilities.

In the universality of the New Law in Christ through the Holy Spirit, Pinckaers thus finds confidence to again boldly proclaim the Gospel. He writes: "In order to discuss Christian morality properly, therefore, we must go straight to the point and begin with the Gospel teaching that harmonizes with the moral aspirations inscribed in the heart and mind of every human person."[67] He thus reawakens our confidence in the power of grace to speak to the human heart. As Pinckaers exhorts: "The universalism of Christian morality calls for what we might call "faith in faith," precisely, faith in the action of the Holy Spirit that works through faith and charity."[68]

CONFORMATION TO CHRIST THROUGH LOVE

Finally, I would suggest that one can recognize a profound harmony between Pinckaers' conception of the interiorization of the New Law and Benedict

---

65. Pinckaers, "Ethics and the Image of God," 141.

66. Melina, *Sharing in Christ's Virtues*, 85; emphasis added.

67. Pinckaers, "Aquinas and Agency," 176.

68. Pinckaers, "Aquinas and Agency," 175.

XVI's presentation in *Deus Caritas est* of the perfection of our likeness to God in love. Benedict bases his reflection in Sacred Scripture, drawing on the nuptial imagery used to convey the loving relationship between God and his chosen people. From the Old Testament, God's spousal love for Israel is revealed through the gift of the Torah. Through faithfulness to this word, man "comes to experience himself as loved by God and discovers joy in truth and in righteousness—a joy in God which becomes his essential happiness."[69]

In the New Covenant, it is the cross which reveals the depths of God's love, Christ giving himself completely for his bride/Church "in order to make her holy" (Eph 5:26). Benedict confesses that in "contemplating the pierced side of Christ" (cf. John 19:37) we are brought to the realization that "God is love" (1 John 4:8).[70] "It is there that this truth can be contemplated. It is from there that our definition of love must begin. In this contemplation the Christian discovers the path along which his life and love must move."[71]

This sacrificial love, as Benedict points out, is perpetuated in Christ's gift of the blessed Eucharist, prefigured in the blood which flowed from his pierced side. And in its dynamism of making us one with him, the Eucharist "draws us into Jesus' act of self-oblation."[72] Through the action of the Holy Spirit, working through the Sacrament, we are made participants in the love of God. In a very real sense, we become "lovers" like God, and are enabled to fulfil his command to love as he himself loves (cf. John 15:12).[73] This eucharistic orientation fosters humanity's movement from commandment to love. It moves us beyond morality as obedience to norms that "could exist apart from and alongside faith in Christ and its sacramental re-actualization."[74] Worship and ethics are united. "Faith, worship and *ethos* are interwoven as a single reality which takes shape in our encounter with God's *agape*."[75] Eucharistic communion thus includes both the vertical realization of being loved and the horizontal call to love others in return.

---

69. Benedict XVI, *Deus Caritas Est*, sec. 9.

70. Benedict XVI, *Deus Caritas Est*, sec. 12.

71. Benedict XVI, *Deus Caritas Est*, sec. 12.

72. Benedict XVI, *Deus Caritas Est*, sec. 13.

73. "More than just statically receiving the incarnate *Logos*, we enter into the very dynamic of his self-giving. The imagery of marriage between God and Israel is now realized in a way previously inconceivable: it had meant standing in God's presence, but now it becomes union with God through sharing in Jesus' self-gift, sharing in his body and blood." Benedict XVI, *Deus Caritas Est*, sec. 13.

74. Benedict XVI, *Deus Caritas Est*, sec. 14.

75. Benedict XVI, *Deus Caritas Est*, sec. 14.

This integration points to the fact that the human person finds his fulfillment in love. Love "calls into play all man's potentialities,"[76] engaging the whole man, intellect and will. This engagement signifies that love is not irrational, but that human reason finds its context within love. The person is moved beyond his human limitations to reach the heights of the divine.

> The love-story between God and man consists in the very fact that this communion of will increases in a communion of thought and sentiment, and thus our will and God's will increasingly coincide: God's will is no longer for me an alien will, something imposed on me from without by the commandments, but it is now my own will, based on the realization that God is in fact more deeply present to me than I am to myself.[77]

Here again, any sense of heteronomy is overcome in our conformation to God's love. It harmonizes with Pinckaers' thought:

> By means of charity the Holy Spirit does away with the distance that exists between our free will and the moral law expressed in the Gospel, inclining our heart to love God and neighbor in Christ by its own movement, with a personal thrust, to such a point that we recognize in the Gospel teaching the desires and exigencies of our own love as well as Christ's.[78]

Pinckaers speaks of "an intimate correspondence between our heart and the New Law"[79] such that it becomes our own. And Benedict, before his election to Peter's chair, writes that "through communion with Christ, I can find myself again and, entering into myself, I can find God and my *theosis*, my true essence, my true autonomy."[80] Again, this idea of "participated theonomy" as communion goes far beyond a participation of the divine law implanted in the human mind in the form of the natural law.[81] According to Pinckaers and Benedict, it would seem that it is not simply a rational participation, but a true identification with the living God—a relationship of love, in which, through the Holy Spirit, we become one with Christ.

---

76. Benedict XVI, *Deus Caritas Est*, sec. 17.

77. Benedict XVI, *Deus Caritas Est*, sec. 17. See Augustine, *Confessions* III, 6, 11.

78. Pinckaers, "Aquinas and Agency," 179–80.

79. Pinckaers, "Aquinas and Agency," 180.

80. Ratzinger, "Renewal of Moral Theology," 366.

81. See Rhonheimer, *Natural Law and Practical Reason*, 66.

CONCLUSION

The chapter has considered the pneumatological approach to the discipline of moral theology as contained in the scholarship of Servais Pinckaers. Consistent with contemporary trends in moral theology that move away from obligation towards self-fulfilment in beatitude, Pinckaers' work centers around themes of subjectivity, interiority, and virtue. However, unlike some of his contemporaries who would conceive of interiority as the rational integration of virtue with the natural law, Pinckaers speaks in terms of the compenetration of grace and reason, of the New Law of the Holy Spirit written on the heart of those who believe and working through charity.

Pinckaers constructs his pneumatological morality on patristic and Scholastic principles, in which the beatitudes—the foundation of New Testament morality—are accompanied by the gifts of the Holy Spirit. As Pinckaers notes, the gifts of the Spirit "add a receptivity to the virtues, a docility to spiritual impulses."[82] The priority of faith in Pinckaers' morality challenges the pride of human wisdom. It relativizes the independent claims of reason. It demands "a humble, docile opening to the Spirit"—the Spirit who "brings forth a justice, a virtue, a holiness that comes from God through Jesus Christ."[83]

BIBLIOGRAPHY

Aquinas, Thomas. *Summa Theologiae*. Translated by the English Dominican Fathers. Charlottesville, VA: InteLex, 1993.

Balthasar, Hans Urs von. *Love Alone Is Credible*. Translated by D. C. Schindler. San Francisco: Ignatius, 2004.

———. "Nine Propositions on Christian Ethics." In *Principles of Christian Morality*, translated by G. Harrison, 77–104. San Francisco: Ignatius, 1986.

Benedict XVI. *Deus Caritas Est*. https://www.vatican.va/content/benedict-xvi/en/encyclicals/documents/hf_ben-xvi_enc_20051225_deus-caritas-est.html.

Dupré, Louis. *Passage to Modernity: An Essay in the Hermeneutics of Nature and Culture*. New Haven, CT: Yale University Press, 1993.

John Paul II. *Veritatis Splendor*. https://www.vatican.va/content/john-paul-ii/en/encyclicals/documents/hf_jp-ii_enc_06081993_veritatis-splendor.html.

Melina, Livio. *Sharing in Christ's Virtues: For a Renewal of Moral Theology in Light of "Veritatis Splendor."* Translated by William E. May. Washington, DC: The Catholic University of America Press, 2001.

Pinckaers, Servais. "Aquinas and Agency: Beyond Autonomy and Heteronomy?" In *The Pinckaers Reader: Renewing Thomistic Moral Theology*, edited by J. Berkman and

82. Pinckaers, "Place of Philosophy in Moral Theology," 68.

83. Pinckaers, *Sources of Christian Ethics*, 115.

C. S. Titus, 167–84. Washington, DC: The Catholic University of America Press, 2005.

———. "Aquinas on Nature and the Supernatural." In *The Pinckaers Reader: Renewing Thomistic Moral Theology*, edited by J. Berkman and C. S. Titus, 359–68. Washington, DC: The Catholic University of America Press, 2005.

———. "Aquinas's Pursuit of Beatitude: From the *Commentary on the Sentences* to the *Summa Theologiae*." In *The Pinckaers Reader: Renewing Thomistic Moral Theology*, edited by J. Berkman and C. S. Titus, 93–114. Washington, DC: The Catholic University of America Press, 2005.

———. "The Body of Christ: The Eucharistic and Ecclesial Context of Aquinas's Ethics." In *The Pinckaers Reader: Renewing Thomistic Moral Theology*, edited by J. Berkman and C. S. Titus, 26–45. Washington, DC: The Catholic University of America Press, 2005.

———. "An Encyclical for the Future: *Veritatis Splendor*." In *"Veritatis Splendor" and the Renewal of Moral Theology*, edited by J. A. Di Noia and R. Cessario, 11–71. Chicago: Midwest Theological Forum, 1999.

———. "Ethics and the Image of God." In *The Pinckaers Reader: Renewing Thomistic Moral Theology*, edited by J. Berkman and C. S. Titus, 130–43. Washington, DC: The Catholic University of America Press, 2005.

———. *Morality: The Catholic View*. Translated by M. Sherwin. South Bend, IN: St. Augustine's, 2001.

———. "The Place of Philosophy in Moral Theology." In *The Pinckaers Reader: Renewing Thomistic Moral Theology*, edited by J. Berkman and C. S. Titus, 64–72. Washington, DC: The Catholic University of America Press, 2005.

———. "Rediscovering Virtue." *Thomist* 60 (1996) 361–78.

———. "Revisionist Understandings of Actions in the Wake of Vatican II." In *The Pinckaers Reader: Renewing Thomistic Moral Theology*, edited by J. Berkman and C. S. Titus, 236–70. Washington, DC: The Catholic University of America Press, 2005.

———. "The Role of Virtue in Moral Theology." In *The Pinckaers Reader: Renewing Thomistic Moral Theology*, edited by J. Berkman and C. S. Titus, 288–303. Washington, DC: The Catholic University of America Press, 2005.

———. "Scripture and the Renewal of Moral Theology." In *The Pinckaers Reader: Renewing Thomistic Moral Theology*, edited by J. Berkman and C. S. Titus, 46–63. Washington, DC: The Catholic University of America Press, 2005.

———. *The Sources of Christian Ethics*. Translated by M. T. Noble. Washington, DC: The Catholic University of America Press, 1995.

———. "The Sources of the Ethics of St. Thomas Aquinas." In *The Ethics of Aquinas*, edited by Stephen J. Pope, 17–29. Washington, DC: Georgetown University Press, 2002.

Ratzinger, Joseph. "The Dignity of the Human Person." In *Commentary on the Documents of Vatican II*, edited by H. Vorgrimler, 5:115–63. London: Burns and Oates, 1969.

———. "The Renewal of Moral Theology: Perspectives of Vatican II and *Veritatis Splendor*." *Communio* 32 (2005) 357–68.

Rhonheimer, Martin. "Is Christian Morality Reasonable? On the Difference between Secular and Christian Humanism." *Annales Theologici* 15 (2001) 529–49.

———. *Natural Law and Practical Reason: A Thomist View of Moral Autonomy.* Translated by G. Malsbary. New York: Fordham University Press, 2000.

———. *The Perspective of Morality: Philosophical Foundations of Thomistic Virtue Ethics.* Translated by G. Malsbary. Washington DC: The Catholic University of America Press, 2011.

Rowland, Tracey. "Natural Law: From Neo-Thomism to Nuptial Mysticism." *Communio* 35 (2008) 374–96.

Second Vatican Council. *Dei Verbum.* https://www.vatican.va/archive/hist_councils/ii_vatican_council/documents/vat-ii_const_19651118_dei-verbum_en.html.

———. *Optatam Totius.* https://www.vatican.va/archive/hist_councils/ii_vatican_council/documents/vat-ii_decree_19651028_optatam-totius_en.html.

Sherwin, Michael S. "Infused Virtue and the Effects of Acquired Vice: A Test Case for the Thomistic Theory of Infused Cardinal Virtues." *Thomist* 73 (2009) 29–52.

18

PROCESSION OF THE HOLY SPIRIT AND ECCLESIOLOGY

Some Contemporary Perspectives

Mariusz Biliniewicz

THE QUESTION ABOUT THE procession of the Holy Spirit in the Trinity is perceived by many as one of a high level of abstraction and no practical value. How can we really know for sure whether the Spirit proceeds from the Father and the Son, as the Western tradition maintains it? Or from the Father only, as many Eastern Orthodox theologians believe? Or maybe from the Father through the Son, as the Cappadocian Fathers thought and as the most ancient Greek tradition attests to? If the Spirit proceeds from the Father *through* the Son, does this mean the same as proceeding from the Father *and* the Son, as Aquinas thought? Or does it mean something different, and if so, what exactly is the difference? Many also ask whether the question of the procession of the Holy Spirit really needs to be a Church-dividing matter, given that there are no immediate implications of either of the existing views? Is it not just another example of an overly scholastic dispute that has no immediate relevance, of some Trinitarian celestial mathematics that no one really understands, and no one can pass a final judgment on?

In 1967, Karl Rahner, SJ, famously complained that the doctrine of the Trinity receives very little attention in Christian, or at least Catholic, spirituality. He opined that "should the doctrine of the Trinity have to be dropped as false, the major part of religious literature could well remain virtually unchanged."[1] One could rephrase this statement and refer it to the doctrine of the procession of the Holy Spirit in the Trinity: if we were to admit that the Western doctrine of the Spirit's procession from the Father and the Son was actually wrong and that the Spirit proceeds only from the Father, would anyone notice? Would anything change in the Church's core teachings on faith and morality? Would this have any influence on Christian spirituality?

Theologians would frequently respond to such questions by pointing out the need of pursuing the truth for the sake of knowing it, regardless of how difficult this pursuit may be, and how abstract and disconnected with our daily life this truth may appear to be. "Knowing for the sake of knowing" has been a well-known ancient Greek axiom which the Catholic intellectual tradition happily adopted and absorbed as its own. As the magisterium of the Catholic Church tirelessly reminds us, the human mind does have the capacity to know and communicate the truth, even if imperfectly and sometimes with great difficulty. Despite the existence of the mystery, we nevertheless do want to know and understand. And since this is a desire that is instilled in us by God himself, we should not extinguish this instinct of wanting to know and explore, but rather cherish and celebrate it.[2]

At the same time, it is worth noting that according to some theologians, the question of the *filioque*, the Latin word meaning "and the Son" which the Catholic Church added in the Middle Ages to the original creed from the Council of Constantinople from 381, actually does have at least one important practical consequence, and this consequence is to be found in the area of ecclesiology. The purpose of this chapter is to look at this claim and some of its possible implications, and to offer some critical reflections on it.

In this chapter, the question about the possible ecclesiological ramifications of the *filioque* will not address the matter of papal jurisdiction and its limits. The question whether the Pope has legitimate authority to change ancient conciliar creeds without consulting an ecumenical council, and whether the Catholic Church can expect the whole Christian world to accept such change under the pain of heresy and excommunication is an

---

1. Rahner, *Trinity*, 10–11.

2. One of the most eloquent expositions of the importance of pursuing the truth in the Catholic tradition is John Paul II's encyclical letter *Fides et Ratio* from 1998.

important one, and it deserves attention.[3] However, it will not be the topic of this chapter. Rather, this chapter will only address the question of whether our understanding of the procession of the Holy Spirit has any impact on our perception of the nature of the Church and how the Church operates in and of itself. In other words, it will address the question whether there is a link between our understanding of the procession of the Spirit and our understanding of the nature and the mission of the Church.

FILIOQUE AND ECCLESIOLOGY IN SOME EASTERN ORTHODOX LITERATURE

In his article on Orthodox perspectives on the ecclesiological ramifications of the *filioque* clause, Viorel Coman argues that the question of ecclesiological consequences of either accepting or rejecting the doctrine of *filioque* was first raised in a serious manner by the Greek Orthodox theologian Vladimir Lossky.[4] In the first part of the twentieth century, Lossky argued that acceptance or rejection of the filioque is central to Catholic and Orthodox ecclesiologies. Lossky famously wrote that:

> Whether we like it or not, the question of the procession of the Holy Spirit has been the sole dogmatic grounds for the separation of East and West. All the other divergences which, historically, accompanied or followed the first dogmatic controversy about the Filioque, in the measure in which they too had some dogmatic importance, are more or less dependent upon this original issue.[5]

In other words, according to Lossky, Western ecclesiology is guilty of an incorrect understanding of the Church because it has an incorrect understanding of the Trinity, at least with regard to the question of the procession of the Holy Spirit. Lossky believes that the West subordinated the Spirit to the Son, made him dependent on the Son, and therefore, by doing so, it subjected pneumatology to Christology. In this model, Christology in ecclesiology stands for the "objective, unchangeable, perfectly stable and immovable dimension," whereas pneumatology stands for "dynamic,

---

3. There is no shortage of works that deal with these topics and also with the whole history of the controversy. Some most important sources include Congars' three volumes of *I Believe in the Holy Spirit*; Siecienski, *Filioque*; Habets, *Ecumenical Perspectives*.

4. Coman, "Different Orthodox Perspectives," 4.

5. Coman, "Different Orthodox Perspectives," 7, quoting Lossky, *In the Image and Likeness of God*, 71.

continuous, and progressive dimension."[6] If the procession of the Spirit from the Son really means the Spirit's subordination to the Son, then this explains all the problems and distortions that Orthodox theologians identify in the Roman Catholic Church: the subordination of charism to institution, of personal freedom to Church authority, of the prophetic to the juridical, of mysticism to scholasticism, of common priesthood to hierarchical priesthood, and finally, of episcopal collegiality to the primacy of Rome.[7]

In his article, Coman looks at another Orthodox theologian, Dumitru Stăniloae, who, despite some nuancing of Lossky's stark vision of "two independent economies"—that of the Son and that of the Spirit acting somehow autonomously—nevertheless shares Lossky's main intuition regarding the impact of *filioque* on ecclesiology. Coman reports that in Stăniloae's view "the Western doctrine of the *filioque*, which subordinates the Spirit to the Son, leads in practice to ecclesiological Christomonism and to the development of an exaggeratedly institutionalized Church," and to an ecclesiology which is "impersonal," "juridical" and "strictly rational."[8] Stăniloae believes that

> the character of a juridical society has been imprinted upon the Church. This society is conducted rationally and in absolutist fashion by the Pope, and it neglects both the active permanent presence of the Spirit within her and within all the faithful, as well as the presence of Christ bound indissolubly to the presence of the Spirit.[9]

In this same article, Coman compares Lossky and Stăniloae to two other twentieth century Greek Orthodox theologians who adopted a different point of view on this issue, John Zizoulas[10] and Georges Florovsky.[11] By looking at their ecclesiologies Coman comes to the conclusion that unlike Lossky and Stăniloae, Zizoulas' and Florovsky's understanding of the Church is not anchored in pneumatology, or in Trinitarian theology, but rather in the event of the sacrament of the Eucharist. Their point of

6. Coman, "Different Orthodox Perspectives," 7.

7. Coman, "Different Orthodox Perspectives," 7–8.

8. Coman, "Different Orthodox Perspectives," 11, referring to Stăniloae, *Theology and the Church*, 107.

9. Coman, "Different Orthodox Perspectives," 11. Coman notes that later in his career Stăniloae adopted a more conciliatory approach towards the issue.

10. The main works of Florovsky that Coman refers to in his analysis are Florovsky, "Corpus Mysticum"; Florovsky, "Christ and His Church"; Florovsky, "Image of the Church"; Florovsky, "Church."

11. The main works of Zizoulas that Coman refers to in his analysis are Zizoulas, *Being as Communion*; Zizoulas, *Eucharist, Bishop, Church*.

departure is not the question of how the Church reflects the inner life of the Trinity, but how the Church reflects and is built by the celebration of the mystery of Christ's Body and Blood in the sacrament of the altar. This does not mean that Zizoulas and Florovsky pay no attention to the Trinitarian dimension of the Church—they do, however in their ecclesiologies this Trinitarian dimension is not as dominant as it is for Lossky and Stăniloae.

According to Coman, this different point of departure results in a different point of arrival. For Florovsky, the Western belief in the Spirit's procession from the Father and the Son does not influence what he labels as "papism." He argues that historically "papism" existed well before the *filioque* even became an issue, and so it could have hardly been caused by it. For Zizoulas, the Western preference for Christology-oriented ecclesiology does not necessarily lead to ecclesiological Christomonism, and even less can it be derived from the *filioque* clause.[12]

Coman, therefore, ascribes the different views of these four Orthodox theologians to different understandings of the relationship between ecclesiology, Christology, pneumatology and liturgy. If ecclesiology is derived from Trinitarian theology, some Orthodox theologians tend to ascribe significant weight to the importance of the *filioque*. If it is derived from sacramentology, or more specifically from the Eucharist, not so much. This observation is very useful and insightful and the rest of this chapter will be devoted to adding some additional points to Coman's reflections, primarily from the point of view of Western theology.

FILIOQUE AND ECCLESIOLOGY IN THE WEST

The first point that seems to be worth raising is that it is not only a feature of Eastern Orthodox theology to build ecclesiology on Trinitarian theology, and to link the doctrine of the procession of the Spirit with ecclesiology.[13]

12. Coman, "Different Orthodox Perspectives," 19–21.

13. Apart from Lossky and Stăniloae, another Eastern Orthodox who subscribes to the position that the Western acceptance of the *filioque* does influence the Western ecclesiology is Oliver Clément, *L'Eglise orthodoxe*, 50, quoted by Congar, *I Believe in the Holy Spirit*, 208. At 211, Congar quotes Clément's opinion: "Filioquism, according to which the 'fontal' privilege which is peculiar to the Person of the Father alone is also shared by the Son, this placing the Spirit, in his hypostatic existence, in a position of dependance on the Son, has certainly contributed to an increase in the authoritarian and institutional aspect of the Roman Church. The Trinitarian theology of the Orthodox Church, on the other hand, teaches that procession and begetting condition each other. . . . That is why there is also a mutual conditioning in a reciprocity of service between sacrament and inspiration, the institution and the event, the economy of the Son and that of the Spirit."

Roman Catholic theologian Bertrand de Margerie, SJ, also sees a close connection between these two realities, and also argues that St. Thomas Aquinas also saw this relationship.[14] According to Ralph Del Colle, de Margerie "contends that the triadology of the Greek Fathers necessitates the more mature speculative theology of the Latin scholastics (especially the psychological analogy) in order to resolve the relationship between the Son and the Spirit in the divine triunity."[15]

Whether Aquinas indeed believed that the understanding of the procession of the Holy Spirit influences ecclesiology is a subject for discussion. In *Contra Errores Graecorum* the Angelic Doctor states that:

> The error of those who deny the primacy of the Vicar of Christ over the universal Church bears a resemblance to the denial of the procession of the Holy Spirit with regard to the Son. In fact, it is Christ himself, the Son of God, who consecrates his Church and seals it by the Holy Spirit as by a character and a seal. . . . And similarly the Vicar of Christ, by his primacy and his solicitude as a faithful servant, keeps the universal Church subject to Christ.[16]

From this text alone it is not evident that Aquinas links the issue of the *filioque* and the primacy of Rome in the way that there would be a *causal* relationship between the two. A close reading of this text of Aquinas does not necessitate this, since Thomas may be speaking here simply about yet another error of the Greeks that is similar to the error that he had just discussed in the previous section of his work. He does not clearly state that the ecclesiological error is a *result* of the pneumatological error, even if he does speak about one error resembling the other. In any case, regardless of whether Aquinas saw a causal relationship here, it is certain that de Margerie sees it, and therefore shares Lossky's and Stăniloae's intuition about the influence of the *filioque* on ecclesiology. As a Roman Catholic, he differs from them in their assessment of this influence, but he does not deny its existence.[17]

The second point is that despite the conviction of some Orthodox and Catholic theologians about the influence of the *filioque* on ecclesiology, experience seems to be showing that such influence is not at all evident.

---

14. Margerie, *Christian Trinity in History*, 177.

15. Del Colle, "Reflections on the Filioque," 203.

16. Aquinas, *Contra Errores Graecorum*, 32.

17. Interestingly, Congar seems to agree with de Margerie's reading of Aquinas, even if he ultimately rejects his conclusion and does not see any obvious link between the *filioque* clause and ecclesiology; see Congar, *I Believe in the Holy Spirit*, 208–11.

If it was, Christian denominations that profess the *filioque* would easily and automatically recognize the primacy of the See of Rome, because they would all share in the apparent Western Christomonistic ecclesiology where charism is subordinated to institution, personal freedom to Church authority, the prophetic to the juridical, mysticism to scholasticism, and common priesthood to hierarchical priesthood. However, this is not the case. The majority of Western, Protestant Christian communities either continue to profess the *filioque* in their creed or have been professing it until very recently. And yet, it would be difficult to accuse them of practicing a Christomonic, hierarchical, and juridical ecclesiology that ultimately leads to "papism." The same goes *a fortiori* for Protestant theologians whose thought is at the bases of these non-Catholic, Western Christian denominations. Luther and Calvin accepted and supported the *filioque*, and so did many of their followers, including Karl Barth, who vigorously defended the *filioque* and its indispensable character for the Trinitarian faith, but was also critical of the Catholic idea of the papacy and some other aspects of Catholic ecclesiology.[18]

Furthermore, the Pentecostal renewal that has been sweeping through the Western Christian world, both Catholic and Protestant, strongly emphasizes the subjective, personal, emotional, volitional, diverse, charismatic aspect of the Church. This aspect is obviously associated with the person of the Holy Spirit, and rather than being linked with unity and institution, it is identified with diversity and charism. It is interesting to note that it is precisely in the Western tradition, the tradition that has always upheld the *filioque*, that this Spirit-oriented movement has originated and continues to attract many Christians and Christians-to-be. If the *filioque* clause was so repressive of the charismatic dimension of the Church, and the lack of *filioque* so conducive to its thriving, how could it be that the charismatic stream of Christianity originated and continues to flourish in the West, but finds little fertile ground in the East? To be sure, other factors may play a role here, but this phenomenon should give something to ponder to those who want to swiftly identify the acceptance of the rejection of *filioque* with the acceptance or rejection of the charismatic aspect of the Church.

---

18. For a detailed analysis of Barth's take on the *filioque*, see Guretzki, *Karl Barth on the Filioque*. For Barth's views on the Roman Catholic tradition and the evolution of his thought in this regard, see Norwood, *Reforming Rome*. For a general overview of the most important topics in Barth's ecclesiology, see Bender, *Karl Barth's Christological Ecclesiology*. With regard to the general point about the Protestant acceptance of the *filioque*, a similar point is made in Congar, *I Believe in the Holy Spirit*, 210–11.

Finally, there is something to be said about the general methodological presupposition that seems to lurk from behind these attempts to link the doctrine of the procession of the Holy Spirit with ecclesiology. This presupposition assumes, at least implicitly, that the whole doctrine of the Trinity in general, not just the *filioque*, exercises some significant influence on ecclesiology, and that is has some "practical" import to other areas of theology.

This conviction about the general influence of Trinitarian theology on ecclesiology is shared not only by many Eastern Orthodox theologians, but also by many Catholic and Protestant scholars in the West. On the Catholic side, one can point to such authors as Leonardo Boff,[19] Catherine Mowry LaCugna,[20] Walter Kasper,[21] or Neil Ormerod[22] as examples of theologians who argue that the Church's community is, or at least should be, *in one way or another* a reflection of the divine community of the Father, Son and Holy Spirit. Arguably, this kind of Trinitarian ecclesiology has even entered the Catholic magisterial teaching in the works of Popes John Paul II, Benedict XVI and Francis.[23] On the Protestant side, examples are even more numerous: Jurgen Moltmann,[24] Miroslav Volf,[25] or Colin Gunton[26] stand out as some of the most eminent examples of authors who, like Lossky or Stăniloae, think that the doctrine of the Trinity does have some real practical impact on other areas of theology and the life of the Church, even if they do not talk explicitly about the *filioque*. Volf has famously announced that "the Trinity is our social program" and with such authors as Boff or Zizoulas argued that our understanding of the Trinity impacts not only on our understanding of the Church, but of everything.[27] Moltmann and Gunton agree. Moltmann sees in the traditional, Western version of the doctrine of

---

19. Boff, *Holy Trinity, Perfect Community*; Boff, *Trinity and Society*.

20. LaCugna, *God for Us*.

21. Kasper, *Catholic Church*, 75–77.

22. Ormerod, "A (Non-*Communio*) Trinitarian Ecclesiology."

23. This is a topic for a separate essay, but for an overview of John Paull II's trinitarian theology see Nachef, *Mystery of the Trinity*. Also, for some anthropological implications of this vision, see Zimmermann, "John Paul II." With regard to Francis, see his Angelus Address on the Trinity Sunday on June 12, 2022.

24. Moltmann, *Trinity and the Kingdom of God*.

25. Volf, *After Our Likeness*.

26. Gunton, *One, the Three, and the Many*; also, Gunton, *Promise of Trinitarian Theology*.

27. Volf, "Trinity Is Our Social Program." Boff, *Trinity and Society*; Zizoulas, *Being and Communion*.

the Trinity a vehicle of oppression and inequality,[28] and Gunton a source of Western individualism and demolition of community.[29] Therefore, they would concur with their Eastern Orthodox colleagues that "one needs to get the Trinity right in order to get everything else right."

However, this general proposition that the doctrine of the Trinity has, or should have, a real influence on the other areas of theology, the life of the Church, and even the society is not without its critics. Authors such as Karen Kilby,[30] Stephen Holmes,[31] or Mark Husbands[32] prefer to stress the limits of human understanding of divine realities and caution against making too bold claims about matters regarding which the Scriptures and the vast majority of Christian tradition tell us very little. Hence, they are rather uncomfortable with any attempts to make the doctrine of the Trinity "useful," "relevant" or "influential," regardless of whether, in their opinion, it is understood as a vehicle of oppression in the Church and the society (Moltmann, Boff), or of liberation and radical equality (LaCugna). They prefer to understand the doctrine of the Trinity as a form of grammar that helps us to establish what can and cannot be said about God, and consider it a stretch to overly extend this grammar to ecclesiology, or, even more, to make it a social program. Once one understands that Jesus is the revelation of the Father and that he is the way to the Father, and once one understands that we know this thanks to the Holy Spirit, one has more or less understood what the doctrine of the Trinity is all about. In the opinion of these theologians, if one links the *taxis* of the Trinitarian life with the structure of the Church, it can be a risky exercise to speak with great confidence of matters about which we should be rather restrained. Speaking about the Trinity and its impact on other aspects of theology, or of everyday life, could lead into a "double projection" that Kilby warns against. We first observe the reality of community and reciprocity among people, then project it on God as the being in which this reciprocity must be present in the perfect way, and then we project it back on ourselves, trying to build our earthly realities on the view of heavenly realities which we have previously constructed.[33]

28. Moltmann, *Trinity and the Kingdom*, 195–96.

29. Gunton, *Promise of Trinitarian Theology*.

30. Kilby, "Perichoresis and Projection"; Kilby, "Aquinas."

31. Holmes, "Three versus One?"; Holmes, *Quest for the Trinity*.

32. Husbands, "Trinity Is *Not* Our Social Program."

33. Kilby, "Perichoresis and Projection," 439–43. For a critical appraisal of the work of Kilby and Holmes, see Brink, "Social Trinitarianism." Kilby's stance is not exactly the same as Holmes' and Husband's, and it would take a separate study to analyze their thought on this matter in detail. The purpose of clustering these scholars together in this chapter is simply to make the point that they all are quite critical of certain contemporary readings of the Trinitarian doctrine and its "relevance."

There are other authors, such as Matthew Levering[34] or Keith E. Johnson,[35] who would also at least caution against far reaching attempts to make the doctrine of the Trinity "relevant." They may differ regarding some particular aspects of the way the Trinitarian doctrine is understood and applied in various contexts. However, they do not differ in their general concern and restraint in their efforts to make the Trinity immediately and evidently "useful" in some practical sense. Should the fact that for centuries no one has seriously thought that the Christian understanding of the Trinity should be "relevant" in the way that many contemporary theologians propose give us pause for thinking? Could it be that the doctrine of the Trinity is "useful" enough when it tells us that we have access to the Father through Christ in the Holy Spirit (Kilby) and when it helps us to contemplate God and think about him in a way that would be both scriptural and metaphysical (Levering)? Is seeking the intelligibility of the doctrine in and of itself not a preliminary condition for any attempts to relate it to any other areas of theology (Ormerod)?[36] Is it not concerning that so many different, and sometimes mutually exclusive "practical conclusions" are derived from allegedly the same doctrine (Holmes)?[37]

CONCLUSION

These deliberations bring us to the conclusion that the answer to the main question of this chapter: Does the doctrine of the procession of the Holy Spirit from the Father and the Son influence ecclesiology? It depends on who is asked. Catholic scholar Yves Congar, OP, thought that this discussion was of "doubtful value,"[38] and Orthodox author Sergius Bulgakov thought

---

34. Levering, *Scripture and Metaphysics*, especially Conclusion (236–41) where he agrees with Kilby's criticism of some contemporary attempts to make the doctrine of the Trinity "useful," but at the same time proposes that our understanding of the Trinity should be more than just a way of speaking about God (a "grammar"), but an exercise in contemplation which, in the spirit of Aquinas, engages both Scripture and philosophical enquiry, and ultimately brings us closer to God.

35. Johnson, *Rethinking the Trinity*, 185–219, where he criticizes the tendency to see the doctrine of the Trinity as "relevant" to areas where this "relevance" is not at all clear (in this book the argument is primarily directed at the area of theology of religions). At the same time, Johnson does think that the doctrine of the Trinity has "practical relevance," and he lists six "purposes" of the Augustinian presentation of it: theological, doxological, hermeneutical, anthropological, formative, soteriological.

36. Ormerod, *Trinity*, 93–94.

37. Holmes, "Three versus One?," 82.

38. Congar, *I Believe in the Holy Spirit*, 210–11.

that it was "sterile and empty."[39] Generally speaking, some theologians are more restrained than others with regard to defining the degree to which the doctrine of the Trinity in general, and the *filioque* clause in particular, influences other areas of theology.

In this context, one could make a final, sociological observation. In theology we have long been accustomed to thinking about theologians along denominational lines: Catholic, Protestant, Orthodox. However, Trinitarian theology is an example of an area in which these lines are not really helpful anymore. There are Protestant theologians whose views are closer to their Catholic counterparts than to their fellow Protestants, and vice versa. The same could be said about scholars working in the Orthodox tradition: in each of these groups there are theologians who would answer the main question of this chapter affirmatively, and scholars who would answer in the negative.

The question about the *filioque* clause and ecclesiology differentiates scholars not so much according to denominational lines, but according to issues of theological methodology, or fundamental theology. The matter of the "practical impact" of the clause "and the Son" invites some more general questions, such as ones concerning the inner relationship between the various Christian doctrines: How necessary, or how casual, is this relationship? What kind of influence should all doctrines have on other doctrines? To what extent do these teachings need to impact the everyday life of Christians, and do they have to have some importance for believers' spirituality and prayer life? Do all doctrines need to be immediately "relevant"? If so, exactly how "relevant" should they be, and how can one judge the degree of this relevance? Even if no one would seriously argue that the more immediately "relevant" the given doctrine is considered to be, the more prominence it should have in theological exploration and in pastoral planning, it is not hard to imagine that those doctrines which appear to be more abstract and divorced from "everyday life" are more likely to be perceived as an unnecessary "splitting of the hair" and as semantic quarrels over matters that are well beyond our human comprehension. In general, to a great extent the question about the ecclesiological import of the doctrine of the procession of the Holy Spirit is linked to questions about the relationship between logos and ethos, Christian belief and Christian praxis, faith and spirituality, contemplation and action.

Given the length and the depth of the millennium old conversation between the East and the West about the *filioque*, finding an ecumenical solution that would satisfy all sides of the discussion is, and will remain,

---

39. Bulgakov, *Comforter*, 148.

a very difficult task. Experience shows that finding a formula that all sides of the discussion would be ready to endorse often does not result in the complete solution of the problem. Examples for this could range from the 325 Nicaean acceptance of the *homousion* to the 1999 Joint Declaration on the Doctrine of Justification between the Lutheran World Federation and the Pontifical Council for Promoting Christian Unity. However, regardless of the difficulties, it needs to be noted that some laudable attempts can be found in the writings of individual theologians and ecumenical working groups, as well as in magisterial documents.[40]

What is worth remembering is that the discussion about the *filioque* and ecclesiology does more than just help us to understand where the various theologians and Churches taking part in this discussion actually stand on this matter and why. They also help us to think about deeper issues of how we do theology and what kind of fundamental presuppositions we bring into our theologizing. From this point of view, even if the doctrine of the *filioque* may not be that relevant for ecclesiology, the question of this relevance is certainly relevant because it stimulates a reflection on theological methodology that is always beneficial for theologians of all stripes: Catholic, Orthodox, Protestant, Trinitarian, ecclesiological, pneumatological, and many other.

BIBLIOGRAPHY

Aquinas, Thomas. *Contra Errores Graecorum.* https://isidore.co/aquinas/english/ContraErrGraecorum.htm.
Bender, Kimlyn J. *Karl Barth's Christological Ecclesiology.* Eugene, OR: Cascade, 2013.
Boff, Leonardo. *Holy Trinity, Perfect Community.* Maryknoll, NY: Orbis, 2000.
———. *Trinity and Society.* Maryknoll, NY: Orbis. 1988.
Brink, Gijsbert van den. "Social Trinitarianism: A Discussion of Some Recent Theological Criticisms." *International Journal of Systematic Theology* 16 (2014) 321–50.
Bulgakov, Sergius. *The Comforter.* Translated by Boris Jakim. Grand Rapids, MI: Eerdmans, 2004.
Clément, Oliver. *The Church of Orthodoxy.* New York: Chelsea House, 2001.
———. *L'Eglise orthodoxe.* Paris: Presses Universitaires de France, 1961.
Coman, Viorel. "Different Orthodox Perspectives on the Ecclesiological Ramifications of the *Filioque*: Trinitarian Ecclesiology and Eucharistic Ecclesiology." *Logos* 58 (2017) 1–22.

40. See Del Colle, "Reflections on the Filioque"; Habets, *Ecumenical Perspectives on the Filioque.* On the Roman Catholic side, the most significant official documents include the Pontifical Council for Promoting Christian Unity, "Greek and Latin Traditions" and the North American Orthodox-Catholic Theological Consultation, "Filioque."

Congar, Yves. *I Believe in the Holy Spirit*. Vol. 3, *The River of the Water of Life (Rev 22:1) Flows in the East and in the West*. Translated by David Smith. New York: Seabury, 1983.

Del Colle, Ralph. "Reflections on the Filioque." *Journal of Ecumenical Studies* 34 (1997) 202–17.

Florovsky, Georges. "Christ and His Church: Suggestions and Comments." In *L'Eglise et les Églises 1054–1954: Neuf Siècles de douloureuse Séparation entre l'Orient et l'Occident*, edited by Yves Congar et al., 159–70. Chevetogne: Collection Irénikon, 1955.

———. "The Church: Her Nature and Task." In *Bible, Church, Tradition: An Eastern Orthodox View*, 57–72. Collected Works of Georges Florovsky 1. Belmont, MA: Norland, 1972.

———. "Corpus Mysticum: The Eucharist and Catholicity." *Church Service Society Annual* 9 (1936–37) 38–46.

———. "The Image of the Church." In *John XXIII Lectures*, 96–104. New York: Fordham University Press, 1969.

Francis. "Angelus Address. June 12, 2022." https://www.vatican.va/content/francesco/en/angelus/2022/documents/20220612-angelus.html.

Gunton, Colin. *The One, the Three, and the Many*. Cambridge: Cambridge University Press, 1983.

———. *The Promise of Trinitarian Theology*. Edinburgh: T. & T. Clark, 1991.

Guretzki, David. *Karl Barth on the Filioque*. London: Routledge, 2009.

Habets, Myk, ed. *Ecumenical Perspectives on the Filioque for the 21st Century*. London: Bloomsbury T. & T. Clark: 2014.

Holmes, Stephen R. *The Quest for the Trinity: The Doctrine of God in Scripture, History, and Modernity*. Downers Grove, IL: InterVarsity, 2012.

———. "Three versus One? Some Problems of Social Trinitarianism." *Journal of Reformed Theology* 3 (2009) 77–89.

Husbands, Mark. "The Trinity Is *Not* Our Social Program. Volf, Gregory of Nyssa, and Barth." In *Trinitarian Theology for the Church: Scripture, Community, Worship (Wheaton Theology Conference Series)*, edited by Daniel J. Treier and David Lauber, 120–41. Downers Grove, IL: InterVarsity, 2009.

John Paul II. *Fides et Ratio*. https://www.vatican.va/content/john-paul-ii/en/encyclicals/documents/hf_jp-ii_enc_14091998_fides-et-ratio.html.

Johnson, Keith E. *Rethinking the Trinity and Religious Pluralism: An Augustinian Assessment*. Downers Grove, IL: IVP Academic, 2011.

Kasper, Walter. *The Catholic Church: Nature, Reality, and Mission*. London: Bloomsbury T. & T. Clark, 2015.

Kilby, Karen. "Perichoresis and Projection: Problems with Social Doctrines of the Trinity." *New Blackfriars* 81 (2000) 432–43.

———. "Aquinas, the Trinity, and the Limits of Understanding." *International Journal of Systematic Theology* 7 (2005) 414–27.

LaCugna, Catherine Mowry. *God for Us: The Trinity and Christian Life*. San Francisco: Harper & Row, 1991.

Levering, Matthew. *Scripture and Metaphysics: Aquinas and the Renewal of Trinitarian Theology*. Oxford: Blackwell, 2004.

Lossky, Vladimir. *In the Image and Likeness of God*. Crestwood, NY: St. Vladimir's Seminary Press, 1974.

Margerie, Bertrand de. *The Christian Trinity in History*. Translated by Edmund J. Fortmann. Still River, MA: St. Bede's, 1982.

Menelaou, Iakovos. "The Interpretation of the Filioque Clause by Orthodox Ecclesiology and Biblical Exegetical Methodology." *Scriptura* 116 (2017) 1–10.

Moltmann, Jürgen. *The Trinity and the Kingdom of God*. San Francisco: Harper & Row, 1981.

Nachef, Antoine. *The Mystery of the Trinity in the Theological Thought of Pope John Paul II*. New York: Lang, 1999.

North American Orthodox-Catholic Theological Consultation. "The Filioque: A Church Dividing Issue?: An Agreed Statement." https://www.usccb.org/resources/filioque-a-church-dividing-issue.pdf.

Norwood, Donald W. *Reforming Rome: Karl Barth and Vatican II*. Grand Rapids, MI: Eerdmans, 2015.

Ormerod, Neil. "A (Non-*Communio*) Trinitarian Ecclesiology: Grounded in Grace, Lived in Faith, Hope, and Charity." *Theological Studies* 76 (2015) 448–67.

———. *Trinity: Retrieving the Western Tradition*. Milwaukee, WI: Marquette University Press, 2004.

Pontifical Council for Promoting Christian Unity. "The Greek and Latin Traditions Regarding the Procession of the Holy Spirit." *L'Osservatore Romano*, September 20, 1995.

Rahner, Karl. *The Trinity*. Translated by Joseph Donceel. London: Burns & Oates, 1970.

Siecienski, Edward A. *The Filioque: History of a Doctrinal Controversy*. New York: Oxford University Press, 2010.

Stăniloae, Dumitru. *Theology and the Church*. Crestwood, NY: St. Vladimir's Seminary Press, 1980.

Volf, Miroslav. *After Our Likeness: The Church as an Image of the Trinity*. Grand Rapids, MI: Eerdmans, 1998.

———. "'The Trinity Is Our Social Program': The Doctrine of the Trinity and the Shape of Social Engagement." *Modern Theology* 14 (1998) 403–23.

Zimmermann, Nigel. "John Paul II and the Significance of the Trinity for Human Dignity: 'Ipsa autem iam hic in terris adest.'" *Australian eJournal of Theology* 20 (2013) 108–21.

Zizoulas, John. *Being as Communion: Studies in Personhood and the Church*. Crestwood, NY: St. Vladimir's Seminary Press, 1985.

———. *Eucharist, Bishop, Church: The Unity of the Church in the Divine Eucharist and the Bishop during the First Three Centuries*. Translated by Elizabeth Theokritoff. Brookline, MA: Holy Cross Orthodox, 2001.

19 ···

THE NET AND THE PNEUMATIC BODY OF CHRIST

Matthew John Paul Tan

INTRODUCTION

In the pastorally minded drive to engage the Church in online outreach, there is the temptation to justify that outreach on the basis of its efficacy, substantiated by a series of statistics concerning impact, reach, potential audiences and so on. This metrics-based approach to gauging pastoral efficacy may miss a more fundamental pastoral question: Is the key pastoral goal of encountering the person of Jesus Christ attainable in a real way in cyberspace? If the answer to this pastoral question is in the affirmative, another dogmatic question arises. This dogmatic question constitutes the focus of this chapter: is there a proper dogmatic basis on which we can justify an internet end-user having a real encounter with the body of Jesus Christ on the net? Here, we propose an answer in the affirmative.

More generally, we argue that what is encountered on the net is indeed the body of Christ, but the body that is encountered is what we would call, in a way analogous to the terminology used by Romano Guardini, a "pneumatic body of Christ."[1] By this we mean a body that, through the Spirit, becomes extended, disseminated and distributed at Christ's solicitation. The distribution of His body extends across all space and, more to the point, extends to the digital space of the net. We further argue that this remains the case even if we concede that the net does not constitute a space at all, but

---

1. Guardini, *Last Things*, 76.

rather what Graham Ward calls a "utopia," "a 'nowhere' without a place."[2] To establish our case, this chapter will be broken up into three sections.

The first section will lay the dogmatic foundation, identifying sources within the Church's magisterium that tie Christology to Pneumatology, or more specifically, that tie Christ's Incarnation to the Holy Spirit's operations. The upshot of laying such a foundation is to establish a basis for arguing that the body of the second person of the Trinity is never to be construed in isolation from the works of the third.

Having looked at Christ's embodiment, the second section focuses on the extension of Christ's body beyond the purely biological. Although, as Ward observes, this extension of Christ's body will implicate social and cultural bodies, the focus will be on the social dimension of this extension, with a particular focus on the socialization in Christ's body in the Church. As in the first section, we argue that this socialization of Christ's body is only possible because of the Holy Spirit's work. In arguing this point, the chapter will provide the scriptural foundation for this tie-in between Christ's dissemination of His body and the formation of the Church.

It is only after establishing the link between the Spirit and Christ's extended, that is ecclesial, body in the first two sections that we can in the third section problematize the Spirit's extension of Christ's body in the net. In this section, we explore two things. We need to briefly consider the literature that explores whether cyberspace is a space at all, or whether it is devoid of any spatiality. The answer is more complex than a simple yes or no, and we will need to briefly explore whether the dispersal of the body of Christ can take place in each nuance of complexity. In addition, we will also explore how the body of Christ's extension across all space can still be possible if we take the extreme position and argue that cyberspace is indeed a spatial vacuum. In this context, we will consider the insights from Chiara Lubich, the founder of the ecclesial movement Focolare. The chapter will have a particular focus on her conception of Christ Abandoned, and we argue that this insight can underpin the extension of Christ, in whom we have our being, even in cyberspace, a spatial vacuum that is devoid of being. As in the previous two sections, this third section will establish how the Spirit is at work in this final stage of His body's extension.

INCARNATION

Articulating the Trinitarian formula on the distinction of persons in the Trinity could tempt one to make each person so distinct as to assume each

2. Ward, *Cities of God*, 226.

one operates separately from the other two. To correct this tendency, the tradition handed down by the Church holds that God was "indivisible in being and therefore in activity.[3] It will be beyond the remit of this chapter to exhaustively review the literature on this facet of trinitarian dogma. In any case, any attempt here will fall far short of more comprehensive expositions on this point undertaken elsewhere.[4] Because of this, for the purpose of this chapter, reference to this point will be made in summary form, with particular reference to the *Catechism of the Catholic Church.*

Paragraph 743 of the *Catechism* foregrounds this point when speaking of the joint mission of all three persons. "Whenever God sends His son," the *Catechism* says, "He always sends His Spirit," making the mission of all three "conjoined and inseparable."[5] Against the backdrop of the joint activity of the three persons, paragraph 689 articulates a more specific tie in between the Son and Spirit. This is summarized in a pithy line that says that "when the Father sends His Word, he always sends His breath, that is His spirit." Even more interesting is the final part of paragraph 689 which says: "To be sure, it is Christ who is seen, the visible image of the invisible God, but it is the Spirit who reveals him."[6]

This is interesting for the purposes of this chapter because by saying that the Spirit reveals the Son, it highlights the indispensable role the Spirit plays in *manifesting* the Son. While we can speak of the revelation as the revelation of Jesus as the Son of God,[7] this line in paragraph 689 underscores a more fundamental point that the very *manifestation* of the Divine Word in the flesh and blood reality of Jesus of Nazareth is only possible because of the work of the Spirit.

Another dogmatic source that substantiates the above claim are the creeds. In their recitation, the focus tends to be on Jesus Christ, and less reflected upon is the role the Spirit plays in the embodiment of the Word to manifest Jesus Christ. The Nicene-Constantinopolitan creed, more directly than the Apostles' creed, points to a relationship between the Spirit and Christ in the Incarnation by explicitly stating that it is "by the power of the Holy Spirit" that Christ "was incarnate of the Virgin Mary and became man." John Paul II's *Dominum et Vivificantem* picks up on this point. As a manifestation of the divine, John Paul II says, the entire activity of Jesus is

3. Wittman, "Unity," 359.

4. See for instance, Wittman, "Unity."

5. *CCC*, sec. 743.

6. *CCC*, sec. 689.

7. See, for instance, Matthew 16:16–17, in which Peter declares the person of Jesus to be also "the Son of the living God," which Jesus confirms as a truth revealed by God.

always carried out "in the active presence of the Holy Spirit."[8] Read together, the creed and encyclical suggest that the embodiment of the Son is only possible because of the action of the Spirit. Set against the backdrop of the ongoing joint mission and activity of all three persons of the Trinity mentioned in paragraph 743, any action undertaken by the body of the Son in the fulfillment of *His* mission by necessity implicates the Spirit and *Its* mission. The Divine Word's self-emptying into the empirical facticity of Jesus of Nazareth and, with that, His body's ability to work within the confines of empirical fact, is only possible because of the Holy Spirit and never occurs independently of It.

If we accept that the empirical fact of Jesus' embodiment is in itself a work of the Spirit, we then must ask if the Spirit would also be at work in instances where Jesus' embodiment *transcends* the limitations of empirical fact. Scripture records instances that give witness to this transcendent dimension of the body, particularly in the Gospel of John, which records the various theophanies demonstrated in Jesus' miracles. Through the works of the Spirit, the body of Jesus is able to alter the chemical composition of substances as at the Wedding at Cana (John 2:1–12), heal unhealable illness as when He heals the paralytic at Siloam (John 5:1–18), circumvent material scarcity in feeding the multitude (John 6:1–14), and overcome the laws of physics as when He walks on water (John 6:15–25), just to name a few. In Jesus' passion, death, and resurrection, we not only see a decisive turning point in the narrative of Jesus' embodiment; they also mark a turning point in the relationship between His body and the Spirit. These are hinted at in *Dominum et Vivificantem* when John Paul II says that: "The Paschal events—the Passion, Death and Resurrection of Christ—are also the time of the new coming of the Holy Spirit. . . . They are the time of the 'new beginning' of the self-communication of the Triune God to humanity in the Holy Spirit through the work of Christ the Redeemer."[9]

Here, we need to deal with a particular temptation that might arise when reading this paragraph, as well as the Scripture passages tied to these Paschal events in which Jesus speaks of bestowing His Spirit at the Last Supper (John 14:16) and also gives up His Spirit on the Cross (John 19:30). Read together, there might arise a temptation to treat the Spirit as a gift imparted by Jesus, which will suggest a separation between the second and third persons. This chapter will suggest, however, that there is a more intimate link between the Spirit and Jesus. Flowing from this link, there

---

8. John Paul II, *Dominum et Vivificantem*, sec. 20.

9. John Paul II, *Dominum et Vivificantem*, sec. 23.

are more radical implications for the latter's embodiment because of the former's work, especially following the resurrection.

The starting point for this post-resurrection narrative is Mark 16:3, where the women who desire to anoint Jesus' dead body express their concerns about finding someone to roll away the stone covering Jesus' tomb, only to find it rolled away and the tomb evacuated of His body. Within this passage are two seemingly distinct events, the rolling away of the stone and the resurrection. These two otherwise distinct occurrences can be read as two dimensions of a single new manifestation, one that points to a new stage in Christ's embodiment. This new, post-resurrection body goes beyond its capabilities recorded prior to the Passion. Having demonstrated His ability to overcome *occasional* empirical limitations, Christ's post-resurrection body is now able to transcend *all* limitations. These include the most decisive of empirical barriers: physical barriers like the stone or physiological barriers like death. If the Father's Word is indeed only made manifest because of the work of His Spirit, then we can argue that the resurrected body of Jesus, now able to overcome all limitations, is similarly made manifest only because of the work of the Spirit. Indeed, if God's word and breath are paired on an ongoing basis, then the post-resurrection body of Jesus declares a new phase in this pairing; it is a pairing that redefines embodiment itself, where the body is manifested insofar as it is socialized and distributed. To substantiate this claim, this chapter will explore the course of Jesus' embodiment in the events between the Resurrection and Pentecost.

DISSEMINATION

It must be said at the outset that the post-resurrection dissemination of Christ's body, while in and of itself a decisive event in that body's biography, did not emerge out of a vacuum. A keen reader of Scripture might notice pre-passion foretastes of Christ's dissemination in His miracles where the works of His body involve an extension of power generated by His body (such as the healing of the woman with the hemorrhage in Mark 5:30 or Luke 8:46) or exponential proliferation of something already there in limited supply (such as the feeding of the multitude mentioned above). While these miracles meet an obvious pastoral need, what is less obvious is how these miracles are also statements about the body performing them. In Ward's words, these miracles show how the body is, in Christ, undergoing a shift from the purely physical to the figurative. It should be said that figuration here is not a removal of the body and replacing it with a mere cypher. On the contrary, Ward's use of the body's figuration is intended to accentuate the presence of Christ's body, but in a way that extends embodiment beyond the purely biological. To underwrite the presence of this type of body, Ward uses "figuration" to highlight how Christ's body "is represented in the Scriptures, and the tradition's reflection upon the Scriptures, as being continuously displaced," that is, distributed and disseminated.[10]

What should also be said from the outset is that, in light of the inextricable pairing of God's word and breath, the dissemination of Christ's body in these episodes, as in all movements of Christ's body, are only made possible because of a concomitant movement by the Spirit. To elaborate, let us look at the post-resurrection encounter between Jesus and the disciples in John 20:19–22. For the purposes of this chapter, we could analyze this encounter with reference to five constitutive parts. First, Jesus comes and stands among His disciples, despite the fact that the doors were locked (v. 19), demonstrating again His post-resurrection body's capacity for overcoming limit. Second, He imparts His peace to His disciples (v. 19). Third, Jesus presents His hands and side to them, putting the disciples into contact with His post-resurrection body. Fourth, after repeating the imparting of His peace, Jesus tells the disciples that are about to be sent out on mission (v. 21). Finally, Jesus breathes the Holy Spirit upon His disciples (v. 22). Read together, these five moments can be seen to constitute a microcosm of Christ's redefinition of embodiment, whereby He disseminates His body, crossing the border between one body and another, relocating His body in the bodies of His apostles, and orienting it towards its further extension through their mission.

Christ's ability to enter into a locked room carries over the events of the resurrection and its demonstration of His body's capacity to overcome all limits, with the only difference being that this capacity is now put on display before His disciples. This overt example of dissemination then takes a subtle turn when we get to the imparting of peace to His disciples. At first blush, peace and dissemination do not look like related categories. We need to understand, however, that the condition of peace facilitates this dissemination by establishing a relation between one and another. This social dimension is crucial to the dissemination of Christ's post-resurrection body, because in the Christian tradition, the body's dissemination is synonymous with its extension from an individualized body into a socialized body.[11] The physiological body thereby makes a shift into the relational. As Ward suggests, Christ's post-resurrection embodiment situates His body within a set of relations which are both the result of human construction and divine

10. Ward, *Cities of God*, 97.

11. Ward, *Christ and Culture*, 175–78.

enactment.[12] Furthermore, it will be "in and through the movement of these relations that [Christ's] salvation announces itself."[13] At one level, Christ's presentation of His body to the disciples might seem to reinforce the point that this is no mere spirit. At another level, however, the presentation of His hands and side are particularly significant. Christ putting His apostles in contact with His post-resurrection body, puts them in turn into contact with their—it is really John's—last bodily encounter with Christ's body, namely at the crucifixion. To put the disciples in contact with His post-crucifixion body thereby reinforces the point that it is a body, His body alone, that bears this capacity to overcome limits and be socially distributed. The Apostles' sending out is an indication of that social distribution's orientation and trajectory. This socialized body does not exist for itself, but is subordinate to a missionary *telos*, presenting a proposal to others whereby salvation is coupled with incorporation into this web of relations, first with Christ and then with the communion of believers. In Christ's imparting of the Spirit to the apostles, the coupling of relation and salvation becomes sealed. For it is Christ's Spirit that guarantees that the enactment of His body's socialization is of divine origin, and this pneumatological underwriting becomes definitive at Pentecost. Under the Spirit's jurisdiction, Christ's body becomes definitively re-situated and now operates within an ecclesial body.[14] Quoting *Ad Gentes*, John Paul II reminds us in *Dominum et Vivificantem* that even though the Spirit was already present before Pentecost, it "came upon the disciples to remain with them forever" at Pentecost.[15] Put another way, Pentecost represents a definitive bringing together of the pneumatological, the christological and the ecclesial. We see confirmation of this threefold convergence in the Acts of the Apostles when, in speaking to Saul, Jesus affirms the pneumatological link with believers by squarely identifying himself in the bodies of members of the persecuted Church, exclaiming to Saul "I am Jesus, whom you are persecuting" (Acts 8:5).

DETERRITORIALIZATION

While the above sought to establish the dogmatic basis for the dissemination of Christ's body, we get into more contestable territory when we speak of a distribution that is also oriented towards deterritorialization. Put another way, while we have explored the bases for the distribution of the Church

12. Ward, *Christ and Culture*, 22.

13. Ward, *Christ and Culture*, 151.

14. Ward, *Christ and Culture*, 177.

15. John Paul II, *Dominum et Vivificantem*, sec. 25.

through space and time, we have not yet demonstrated the basis for the distribution of the Church in the digital space which, at least on its face, is characterized by a compression and even outright negation of space and time.

The puzzle comes into sharper relief when we consider Manuel Castells' descriptor for cyberspace as the endless production of what he calls "timeless time."[16] This is the production of an ever-expanding zone of simultaneity or, in Castells' own words, a "universe of undifferentiated temporality," where what might be far off and require time to bridge can be brought close to the user in an instant.[17] Along with this compression in time comes the production of a reformatted space, indeed a virtual space. While we may not be able to comprehensively explore the nuances of the debate concerning the reality behind this virtual space, what might help us cut a path through the corpus of literature is the drawing of a distinction between place or space. This distinction follows Michel de Certeau's distinction between a more intimate and delicate habitation of space (tactical), because it plays on a locus not of its own making, and a surveilled and controlled management of a place (strategic).[18] The reason for drawing out this distinction is that, as Castells suggests, the production of "timeless time" is only possible because of the expansion of networks of ever-accelerating information flows to create online avatars, shopfronts and communities. The infrastructure to support these flows are only made possible by the ever-increasing production of information management infrastructure, constituted by an array of data systems (which survey the information) as well as hardware (which store or distribute the information). This management is possible when intimacy has been replaced by the drive towards seizure, surveillance, and even domination, or de Certeau's "strategic" mode of managing a place. Tim Jordan gives a more specific term—technopower—to describe the management of the flows of information and calibration of the terms of online lives.[19] As the volume of information and the speed of its transfer, and the concomitant networks an individual can be immersed in, continues to grow exponentially, it would become difficult, if not impossible, to have the kind of intimate engagement consonant with de Certeau's conception of a "tactical" engagement of space.[20] Be that as it may, the desire to either gain or produce more information and the drive to control the access to that

16. Castells, *Network Society*, 462.
17. Castells, *Network Society*, 462.
18. Certeau, *Practice of Everyday Life*, 36–38.
19. Jordan, *Cyberpower*, 115.
20. Jordan, *Cyberpower*, 117–18.

information, combined with the techniques of management that mediate between them, demonstrate the strategic control of place as defined by de Certeau, even if the place is not strictly speaking territorial.[21] If we accept that the place within the internet is nonetheless real, we face the question of establishing the grounds for the body of Christ to be further disseminated by the Spirit within this place.

To address this question, we need to revisit the Gospel passage where Jesus bestows both peace and the Spirit in the same movement. We already submitted above that the condition of peace is always coupled with the establishment of a relation between persons. If this coupling holds true, then insofar as one can establish relations, however fleeting, with another online, one can fulfill the conditions of peace and the bestowal of the spirit, and thereby extend Christ's body. What we must establish here is whether such relations are indeed possible in a digital context, that is, the non-territorial place of the internet. Theorists such as Heidi Campbell and Stephen Garner acknowledge that the theologian faces a tension between conceptions of community in the online and offline contexts, with attempts for one to replicate the other being difficult, if not impossible.[22] In spite of the difficulty, other theorists such as Dwight Friesen and Kester Brewin argue that it does not negate the possibility for relational connections to still be made between users across online networks with built-in feedback loops.[23] We can go further and argue that such relations are possible even in the context of a lone user reading texts and symbols of a post left by another on a static site for, as Jodi Dean argues, the exchange of symbols across what she calls "affective networks" are in themselves sufficient to establish relations between persons, even though the only thing they share is a digital network connecting disparate ISP addresses.[24] Against this position some, like Ward, might argue that these relations are illusory because their disembodied nature and the forests of avatars block out any meaningful access to real persons.[25] Against that, however, we argue that even if these affective networks establish a simulated relation, the presence of persons working behind the simulation could form the foundation, however shaky, of a substantive relation between persons, making possible the conditions of peace, the bestowal of the Spirit and the extension of Christ's body. The

21. See Schmidt, *Virtual Communion*, 12–13.

22. Campbell and Garner, *Networked Theology*, 85.

23. Friesen, *Thy Kingdom Connected*, 112–17; Brewin, *Complex Christ*, 82–85.

24. Dean, *Blog Theory*, 95. See also Ward, *Cities of God*, 250.

25. Ward, *Cities of God*, 251. See also Pontifical Council for Social Communications, "Church and the Internet," sec. 3.

relation holds because even the disseminations of what Dean calls "affective nuggets" feed back to an actual body of Christ, which solicited and produced those disseminations in the first place.[26]

Even if we concede that the relations *per se* can be real, we can problematize this even further if we turn our attention to the place—or more specifically the lack thereof—within which these relations emerge. To problematize this, let us assume with Ward that cyberspace does *not* even constitute de Certeau's place, and that its virtuality equates to a spatial vacuity, which makes cyberspace a negative place devoid of any *topos*. Because of this vacuum, it can be argued that any real basis to undergird any social relations gets erased. The question that arises is whether the dissemination of the body of Christ across time and space can extend even into a negative place, such that we can meaningfully couple spatial vacuity with social relation. In labelling cyberspace as a "pseudo-space," Ward paints a stark dichotomy between the terrestrial and the digital and suggests that bridging this gap is impossible.[27] Theology is a resource for the interrogation *of* cyberspace, but not a foundation that enables a meaningful habitation or relation *within* it. In response, we put forward the thought of Chiara Lubich; more specifically, the focus will be on her theme of Jesus Forsaken, which forms the core of the spirituality of Focolare. Space only permits a brief coverage of this most central tenet of Lubich's thought. However, we submit that even these broad contours provide ample material to speak into the coupling of spatial vacuity with social relation mentioned above.

Although the spirituality of Focolare is centered on the theme of unity, which is the peaceable relation in a state of communion, Lubich says that it was Jesus abandoned—manifested in His cry of dereliction (Matt 27:46)—which was the vital key for accomplishing this unity.[28] Indeed, Lubich states quite plainly that:

> Jesus had suffered that tremendous sense of abandonment, of separation from the Father, precisely in order to reunite all human beings to God, detached as they were by sin, and to reunite them to one another. It was evident, therefore, that that boundless suffering had something to do with the mystery of unity.[29]

We see in Lubich's statement a deep coupling of Jesus' abandonment and the peaceable relations the theme of unity seeks to capture, which

---

26. Ward, *Christ and Culture*, 177.
27. Ward, *Cities of God*, 250.
28. Lubich, "Unity and Jesus Forsaken," 88.
29. Lubich, "Unity and Jesus Forsaken," 88.

we will need to unpack here. In Christ's cry of dereliction, Lubich wrote that Jesus goes beyond articulating a *feeling* of forsakenness. His cry of dereliction is not just an exclamation of a specific internal response to a particular situation. It is a cry describing an *ontological* state which is woven into the fiber of every imaginable reality. Lubich draws on Sergei Bulgakov's argument that Christ's being left alone constitutes a divine and spiritual death;[30] in entering this divine death Christ, through whom all things have their being, entered the *negation* of being itself. God's entry into the negation of being is a paradox, in which Lubich argues that it is precisely in the negation of being that Christ unlocks the reality of being. Writing on Lubich's thought on Christ Forsaken, Crescencia Gabijan argues that Lubich follows the thought of St. Paul, for whom Jesus Crucified is also "the fullness [*sic*] manifestation of the 'mystery of God' to the world."[31] Flowing from that, Lubich defines Christ's entry into the negation of being as being in its essence, "the acknowledgement of the great ocean of existence in which human beings are in communion with everyone and everything."[32] This forms the core of Lubich's coupling of Christ forsaken with unity, and we submit that this coupling has implications for our consideration of space and sociality. Even if space requires being, and even if the negation of being amounts to a negation of space, in Christ, that negation of space does not negate sociality. Rather, it paradoxically forms the very basis for that sociality. What is more, the condition of Christ forsaken is only possible through the Spirit because in Christ's being stricken from the communion with the Triune God, Christ does not simply give His life, but also yields His Spirit (John 19:30), who the Creeds confess to be the "Lord and giver of life." Thus, it is in the Spirit that Jesus can demonstrate how non-being no longer negates being but reveals it. In Lubich's words, Christ is one who "makes himself nothing to make us everything."[33]

How might Lubich's reflection on Christ Forsaken help us make sense of the extension of Christ's body in the negative place of the net? Even if we concede that cyberspace is a negative place devoid of any substance, and thus any substantive territory, it is still possible to extend the body of Christ. We need to return to Ward's construal of the dissemination of Christ's body. Apart from distribution and expansion, Ward draws on Deleuze and Guattari to use another term, "deterritorialization," wherein the body is "reaching the furthest limits of the decomposition of the socius [that is the social

---

30. Lubich, "Unity and Jesus Forsaken," 89.
31. Gabijan, "Jesus Forsaken," 550.
32. Gabijan, "Jesus Forsaken," 551.
33. Lubich, "A Little Harmless Manifesto," cited in Gabijan, "Jesus Forsaken," 549.

body] on the surface of His own body without organs."[34] One question to ask is whether this deterritorialization could also encompass the extension of Christ's body, even where any territory to underwrite the "socius" is negated. Ward does not take His explanation of deterritorialization any further, and there are grounds for arguing that it is unlikely that he would extend the concept in this manner. This is because this extended concept of deterritorialization we propose sits in tension with the sharp distinction Ward makes between physical and digital space, as mentioned above. Such a distinction acts as a barrier to the ability of Christ's body to be substantially present online. Lubich is helpful in breaking this impasse, speaking into and extending the scope of Ward's deterritorialization of Christ's body. Because Lubich embraces the paradox of the negation of being and its very revelation in Christ's entry into divine death, it is still possible for the body of Christ to inhabit what we have problematized as a vacuum of being—the negative space of the net—and still reveal Himself to be encountered by us. As outlined above, this revelation in negation is only possible because of the Spirit, who facilitates the unfolding of a body even within the context of negative space. It is this body that we call the "pneumatic body."

CONCLUSION

To circle back to this chapter's original question, we explored how it is possible to meaningfully encounter Christ on the internet, not just in a vaguely spiritual sense, but in a substantial corporeal sense as well. This is possible not because of some sophistry through which the body *per se* is over-coded or sidestepped, but because of an attention to what Christ has done to embodiment itself, in light of the expansion and distribution of His own body from the purely physical into the disseminated.

It is on this basis that we proposed that the body of Christ encountered on the net was a pneumatic body. After exploring the dogmatic basis for the Spirit's role in the very embodiment of the Son, we also looked into how Jesus' redefinition of embodiment is also facilitated by the Spirit as it extends Christ's body. It is because of the Spirit's role in the body's extension that, even in seemingly disembodied spaces like the internet, it is possible for Christ's body to inhabit negative space. While Ward provides invaluable work to underwrite the dissemination of the body of Christ, that underwriting shows its limits when we arrive at the threshold of the body's deterritorialization, wherein the virtuality of cyberspace appears to negate Christ's corporeality. At this juncture, Lubich's conception of Christ

---

34. Deleuze and Guattari, *Anti-Oedipus*, 35.

abandoned appears to fill this theoretical gap insofar as it secures an ability for Christ's body to be present even in negation. Thus, even when cyberspace could be problematized to inhabit a negative place, it is still possible to speak of encountering Christ in the conceptual void of the digital context.

BIBLIOGRAPHY

Brewin, Kester. *The Complex Christ: Signs of Emergence in the Urban Church*. London: SPCK, 2004.

Campbell, Heidi A., and Stephen Garner. *Networked Theology: Negotiating Faith in Digital Culture*. Grand Rapids, MI: Baker Academic, 2016.

Castells, Manuel. *The Rise of the Network Society*. Oxford: Blackwell, 1996.

Certeau, Michel de. *The Practice of Everyday Life*. Berkeley, CA: University of California Press, 1984.

Dean, Jodi. *Blog Theory: Feedback and Capture in the Circuits of Drive*. Cambridge: Polity, 2010.

Deleuze, Gilles, and Felix Guattari. *Anti-Oedipus: Capitalism and Schizophrenia*. London: Athlone, 1984.

Friesen, Dwight. *Thy Kingdom Connected: What the Church Can Learn from Facebook, the Internet, and Other Networks*. Grand Rapids, MI: Baker Academic, 2009.

Gabijan, Crescencia C. "Jesus Forsaken in Chiara Lubich: Locus of Encounter for Philosophy, Religions, and Transcendence." *Philippiana Sacra* 43 (2008) 545–55.

Guardini, Romano. *The Last Things*. Providence, RI: Cluny, 2019.

John Paul II. *Dominum et Vivificantem*. https://www.vatican.va/content/john-paul-ii/en/encyclicals/documents/hf_jp-ii_enc_18051986_dominum-et-vivificantem.html.

Jordan, Tim. *Cyberpower: The Culture and Politics of Cyberspace and the Internet*. London: Routledge, 1999.

Lubich, Chiara. "Unity and Jesus Crucified and Forsaken: Foundation of a Spirituality of Communion." *Ecumenical Review* 55 (2003) 87–95.

Pontifical Council for Social Communications. "The Church and the Internet." https://www.vatican.va/roman_curia/pontifical_councils/pccs/documents/rc_pc_pccs_doc_20020228_church-internet_en.html.

Schmidt, Katherine G. *Virtual Communion: Theology of the Internet and the Catholic Sacramental Imagination*. Lanham, MD: Lexington, 2020.

Ward, Graham. *Christ and Culture*. Cambridge: Blackwell, 2005.

———. *Cities of God*. London: Routledge, 2000.

Wittman, Tyler R. "On the Unity of the Trinity's External Works: Archaeology and Grammar." *International Journal of Systematic Theology* 20 (2018) 359–80.

20

THE "AGE OF THE SPIRIT"

An Idea That Refuses to Die

David Patrick Collits

INTRODUCTION

"The world grows old [and] hastens towards its death."[1]

St. Gregory the Great preached these words at St. Peter's Basilica, Rome within months of his accession to the papacy, on a Sunday of Advent in AD 590.[2] His words reflect an Augustinian view of history, in which the world is understood to be in its final stage of development prior to Christ's Parousia.[3] This chapter juxtaposes the Augustinian view of the history's old age against the spiritualist vision presented in the visions of twelfth-century abbot, Joachim of Fiore. His intellectual progeny within contemporary theology and philosophy maintain a Joachimite hope of a Third Age of the Holy Spirit.

---

1. Duffy, *Ten Popes*, 50.

2. Gregory the Great, "Homily 1."

3. Cf. the argument of John Green that Gregory the Great "translated" Augustinian spirituality to match the demands of the sixth and seventh centuries: Green, "St. Gregory the Great," 167: "Gregory, the great preacher, simplified and popularised Augustine's teaching, harmonising a most cogent and all-embracing intellectual system with a practical rule of life."

A desire for the Third Age raises pneumatological questions. Having briefly compared the Augustinian and Joachimite visions of salvation history and commented upon Joachimism's continuing appeal today, this chapter will analyze the response of the recently deceased Joseph Ratzinger/Pope Benedict XVI's (1927–2022) to Joachimism.[4] Importantly, Ratzinger argues that Joachim's revival of chiliast expectation presents a "systematic doctrine of God."[5] Theological reflection on the Holy Spirit and his role in history must be rooted in the dogmatic understanding of the Church. Touching on Ratzinger's own Christological theology of history, the paper examines Ratzinger's Augustinian pneumatology as a response to the Joachimite vision of a Third Age of the Spirit. While Augustine's pneumatology may have "the disadvantage of less relevance," according to Ratzinger, the saint remains an "objective" and "great witness of the tradition."[6]

Joachim's expectation of an Age of the Spirit breaks the nexus between Trinitarian dogmatics, Christology, pneumatology, and ecclesiology; between Christ, Spirit, and Church. In light of an understanding of the Holy Spirit, which names Him properly as Love and Gift, it can be perceived that Joachimite expectation threatens the unity of the Church. Ratzinger's pneumatological critique of Joachimism serves as a continuing warning of the danger of seeking the "true" Church in a spiritual reality outside the sacramental, hierarchical one. It is a reminder of the fundamental importance of living in communion with the Spirit, in the Church, despite temptations to flee the manifold failures, weakness, and wickedness of her leaders and members.

HISTORY IN ITS OLD AGE

Occasioned by historical crises and in the face of overturned verities,[7] St. Augustine and St. Gregory the Great present what became a typical Catholic understanding of the meaning and direction of history and the Church's place within it.[8] A key to unlocking this conception is in their use of the word "old" or *senescens* in referring to the current state of history. A fuller

---

4. Tracey Rowland's chapter in this volume touches on the critique of Joachimism in other twentieth-century Catholic thinkers such as Yves Congar and Hans Urs von Balthasar. Joachimism can be described generally as a view of history that expects a level of eschatological fulfillment within history.

5. Ratzinger, *Eschatology*, 13.

6. Ratzinger, "Holy Spirit as Communio," 325.

7. Cf. Ratzinger, *Theology of History*, v; Ratzinger, *Eschatology*, 1.

8. O'Callaghan, *Christ Our Hope*, 65, who well points out the parallelism of Augustine and Gregory.

rendering of St. Gregory's words quoted at the outset is as follows: "Now, on the contrary, the world is sinking under the weight of his own old age, and as if his death were approaching, he is overwhelmed by ever increasing trials. So, my brothers, do not love this world, which can not, as you see, survive long."[9] The pericope from St. Luke's Gospel proclaimed that Sunday of Advent was particularly appropriate for St. Gregory's eschatological mood.[10] Two centuries of war, famine and disease had reduced the once mighty Rome's population of a million souls to fewer than one hundred thousand.[11] The part-pagan and part-Arian Lombard tribes from Austria ruled half of the Italian peninsula. Rome was isolated.[12] Commenting on the decimated Roman population and the challenges of invasion, St. Gregory applied the Gospel to his and his hearers' situation, confronted daily by unexpected disaster.[13] History, bowed down by old age and in "its final agony," contained within itself no hope for historical improvement.[14] Hope instead was based on the promise of the Lord's enduring words ("my words will not pass away," Luke 21:33), which pointed to eschatological realization outside history.[15]

A similarly grim context faced St. Augustine when he penned his *De civitate Dei contra paganos* as invasion challenged the "orderly and apparently definitive form" of Roman life.[16] Augustine emphasized the pilgrim character of earthly existence for the Christian, who was not to love the world, while being in it.[17] In language that anticipated Gregory the Great by almost two centuries, he exhorted his listeners "not [to] hold on to the old man, the world" because "it is full of pressing tribulations."[18] Historical calamity underscored that Christian fulfillment was beyond history.

Augustine, in developing his juxtaposition of the City of God and the city of man, distinguishes between profane history and sacred history. The sacred history of the City of God develops alongside and in counterpoint to the history of the rise, decline and fall of empires. Importantly, "only

9. Gregory the Great, "Homily 1," 5.

10. Luke 21:25–33, the proper Gospel of the First Sunday of Advent according to the *Missale Romanum*, 2.

11. Duffy, *Ten Popes*, 50, Duffy, *Saints and Sinners*, 60.

12. Duffy, *Ten Popes*, 50, Duffy, *Saints and Sinners*, 60.

13. Gregory the Great, "Homily 1," 5.

14. O'Callaghan, *Christ Our Hope*, 65.

15. Biblical references in this chapter are from the RSV.

16. Ratzinger, *Theology of History*, v; Löwith, *Meaning in History*, 167.

17. Green, "St. Gregory the Great," 184–85; Gregory the Great, "Homily 1," 5.

18. *Sermo*, 81, 8 quoted in O'Callaghan, *Christ Our Hope*, 65.

transcendental history, including the earthly pilgrimage of the church, has direction towards its eschatological fulfilment."[19] Sacred history is thus the story of the supra-historical progress of the City of God, in which the citizens of that city, including the Church, will be redeemed at history's consummation.[20]

Augustine discerns a threefold development in the "spiritual progress" of sacred history.[21] Like the progression of human life, history can be divided into the period before the law (childhood), the period under the law (manhood), and the period of *mundus senescens*, the old age of grace. Importantly, sacred history's turning point is the Incarnation, which "culminates in the appearance of Christ and the establishment of the church."[22] Additionally, Augustine detects six epochs in history, corresponding to the six days of creation. The last epoch is the period in which we now live on the cusp of the "eternal sabbath,"[23] inaugurated at the first coming of Christ and concluding at his second.[24] The period between Christ's first and second comings, in fact, contains the *adventus medius* of Christ, a middle coming in which he is present in the Church in "spirit and in power," in sacrament and liturgy.[25] The "most real and most hidden substance of history" therefore becomes the accomplishment, "by preaching and the sacraments," of the great works of God in the Church.[26] Thus, on the Augustinian view of history, the chiliast millennium is already found in Christ, which began in his Incarnation and extends in parallel to the movement of profane history.[27]

In contrast to the advance of the City of God, secular history contains its own senescence and progresses towards its termination. Profane history is *saeculum senescens*, an age that grows old in anticipation of its termination.[28] It contains no hope of chiliast renewal. Importantly the world (and history) is "created and transient."[29] The "historical process as such, the *saeculum*,

19. Voegelin, *New Science of Politics*, 118.

20. Voegelin, *New Science of Politics*, 118.

21. Löwith, *Meaning in History*, 171.

22. Voegelin, *New Science of Politics*, 118.

23. Voegelin, *New Science of Politics*, 118.

24. Löwith, *Meaning in History*, 170–71.

25. Ratzinger, *Holy Week*, 240–41, quoting St. Bernard of Clairvaux, *In Adventu Domini*, Serm. III, 4.

26. Rowland, *Benedict XVI*, 97, quoting Daniélou, "Conception of History," 174–75.

27. Reeves, "Originality and Influence of Joachim of Fiore," 273.

28. Voegelin, *New Science of Politics*, 118.

29. Löwith, *Meaning in History*, 171.

shows only the hopeless succession and cessation of generations."[30] The *saeculum* is inherently unable to contain human and therefore historical fulfillment.[31] Augustine's view of history was mirrored in a strain of the medieval Western conceptions of the progress of history as fundamentally pessimistic, limited and dying: Gregory's "old age of the world," *mundus senescit*.[32] The possibilities inherent to history itself are ultimately checked and confined.

JOACHIM'S VISION OF HISTORY

Joachim's spiritualist interpretation of history's movement opposes Augustine's. In contrast to the "Augustinian defeatism" regarding the senescent, "mundane sphere of existence," Joachim predicted the establishment within history of an "Age of the (Holy) Spirit."[33] The Third Age would see the "Church living in spontaneous fulfillment of the Sermon on the Mount, through the universally efficacious action of the Holy Spirit."[34] Chiliasm seeks to "synthesize eschatology with action" and hopes for an *eschaton* of the beyond to be brought into history, "so that even within history there must be an end-time in which everything will be as it should have been all along."[35] History itself is expected now to contain a period of eschatological perfection, in which the Holy Spirit directly reigns.

Joachim understood history to follow a Trinitarian structure, culminating in the eschatological perfection of the Age of the Spirit. He thus presented his well-known tripartite division of history corresponding to the Persons of the Blessed Trinity. History was not a duality between the City of God and city of man, but the progression through three successive ages, each its own status, corresponding with the Persons of the Blessed Trinity and the increasing spiritualization of humanity. The first age was that of the Father, which corresponded with the age of married laymen, undertaking "labor and work."[36] The second was that of the Son, characterized by the "active contemplative life of the priest" involving "learning and discipline."[37] This

30. Löwith, *Meaning in History*, 170.

31. Reeves, "Originality and Influence of Joachim of Fiore," 273.

32. Le Goff, *Medieval Civilization, 400–1500*, 166, quoted in Weimann, "*Mundus senescit*," 25.

33. Voegelin, *New Science of Politics*, 119.

34. Ratzinger, *Eschatology*, 13.

35. Ratzinger, *Church, Ecumenism, and Politics*, 226.

36. Löwith, *Meaning of History*, 148. Newheiser, "Conceiving Transformation," 652.

37. Voegelin, *New Science of Politics*, 111; Löwith, *Meaning in History*, 148.

Second, clerical age of the Son will be superseded by the Third Age of the monks and the "ultimate historical phase of the history of salvation."[38] In the apocalyptic vein of the twelfth century, Joachim "announced the coming of a new age, the age of the Spirit and the Eternal Gospel in which the Church will be renewed in the liberty of the Spirit under the leadership of the new order of Spiritual Contemplatives."[39] The Third Age would culminate in the "perfect spiritual life of the monk" and would begin in 1260 when the *Dux e Bablyone* would appear.[40]

Joachim's tripartite division of history, in which an overlapping but dialectical progression of history is presented, relativizes Christ's role. Significantly, on this scheme, Christ would lead the Second Age and thereby rank equally with Abraham as the leader of the First Age and the yet to be unveiled leader of the Third Age.[41] History moves from the Old and New Testament letter to the Spirit, and the dispensations of law and grace themselves are preparatory to the new Age of the Spirit. The New Testament "merely" concords with (rather than fulfills) the Old Testament, in which New Testament figures and events match and supersede the corresponding figures from the Old.[42] Unlike the Age of the Son, there will be "full freedom of the Spirit" in the Third Age.[43] Tavard well points out the spiritualist character of the dialectical progression of history according to Joachim's ideas: "After God the Father and the Old Testament there has been God the Son, who became flesh and gave us the New Testament. It was Joachim's doctrine that there must soon be God the Spirit, who will bring the Eternal Gospel and will lead the Church from its present monastic status."[44] Tavard importantly highlights the differentiated role of the Divine Persons in Joachim's economy, in which "God's relation to creation, and in particular humanity, keeps evolving."[45] There is a progression of salvation history with respect to each Person, from the "imperfect" under the Old Testament, through the "beginners" who follow Christ's precepts to the "better and more advanced state" given by the Holy Spirit.[46] Joachimism

---

38. Löwith, *Meaning in History*, 151.

39. Dawson, *Religion and the Rise of Western Culture*, 204.

40. Voegelin, *New Science of Politics*, 111.

41. Voegelin, *New Science of Politics*, 111.

42. Löwith, *Meaning in History*, 149.

43. Joachim of Fiore, "*Expositio in Apocalypsum*," quoted in Newheiser, "Conceiving Transformation," 652.

44. Tavard, *Contemplative Church*, 9.

45. Tavard, *Contemplative Church*, 9.

46. Tavard, *Contemplative Church*, 9.

thus expects Christ's Church—at least in its clerical form—to give way to a spiritual Church. The historical Church is "not an everlasting foundation but an imperfect configuration" of that to come.[47] Joachim's vision left therefore "an ambiguous legacy about the future of the institutional papacy, [which] was associated both with absolute evil and with angelic good."[48] However, on the logic of the scheme, the sacraments, hierarchy and papacy will be rendered obsolete by the Kingdom of the Spirit in time: *contra* Augustine, the sacraments do not mediate transcendent reality but shows a potentiality to be fulfilled within history.[49]

Accordingly, the eschatological perfection of the Age of the Spirit supersedes the defective Age of Christ. The "unredeemed and defective history [that continued] after Christ" would be replaced by the Third Age.[50] Joachim hoped for the advent of the "redeemed history," which had been growing in secret and would imminently "burst forth in the open."[51] During the Kingdom of the Spirit, "the life of the monks will be like rain watering the face of the earth in all perfection and in the justice of brotherly love."[52] In "the future age of the Holy Spirit, an earthly Sabbath . . . would transform the world into an irenic kingdom for the faithful followers of the Lord," absent war, scandal, worry, or terror, as a result of God's direct sanctification.[53] Joachim's predictions are temporal yet reflect the eschatological promises of Christ in the Book of Revelation (Rev 21:1–8). History's imperfections, including those of the Age of the Son, will be overcome within history in the Third Age.

THE "AGE OF THE SPIRIT" TODAY

Joachim revolutionized approaches to the meaning of history. Whalen argues that, "Never before [Joachim] had any Christian thinker dared to imagine such a process of historical transformation with this sort of audacious precision and boldness."[54] His "anticipation of . . . millennial

47. Löwith, *Meaning in History*, 150; cf. Newheiser, "Conceiving Transformation," 652–53.

48. Whalen, *Dominion of God*, 123.

49. Löwith, *Meaning in History*, 149.

50. Ratzinger, *Theology of History*, 108.

51. Ratzinger, *Theology of History*, 108.

52. Joachim, "*Expositio*," 134, quoted in Newheiser, "Conceiving Transformation," 658.

53. Whalen, *Dominion of God*, 100.

54. Whalen, *Dominion of God*, 123.

transformations" have become an abiding, secularized idea in modernity.[55] Henri de Lubac concluded that "Joachim's major orientations" have "resurfaced time and time again" in secular utopian movements.[56] These span the political spectrum from the workers' paradise promised in communism to Hitler's Third Reich and Mussolini's *Duce*.[57] Joachim's desire for a new historical epoch continues to appeal.

The "forward-thrusting" reading of history present in Joachim has long been recognized as a feature of contemporary theology and philosophy. Joachim had combined chiliast expectation with the utopia of the monks. In so doing, he fatefully incorporated human agency into eschatological expectation, setting the ground for progressive philosophies in modernity.[58] Hegel and Marx's philosophies of history in particular share structural features with Joachimism, *viz.* the premise that history moves forward according to dialectical stages, culminating in a stage of perfection admitting of no further historical progress.[59] Their respective views of history as being "a forward-thrusting process, in which man actively works at his salvation" according to a logic of history, is an end-product of this Joachimite tendency.[60] As Ratzinger puts it: "Via Hegel, Marxism, too, adopted something of [Joachim's] vision: the idea of history that marches forward in triumph, infallibly reaching its goal, and hence the idea of the definitive realization of salvation within history."[61] In the modern period, Joachimism is married to philosophies of history expectant of an Age of the Spirit, in whatever guise.

Twentieth century theologian, Jürgen Moltmann, exemplifies the continuing influence of Joachim on contemporary theology. Although not citing Joachim in his well-known *Theologie der Hoffnung* (1964), the Joachimite influence on Moltmann is clear. Joachim's scheme reflects dissatisfaction with the state of history and the Church, which marks the twentieth century theology of which Moltmann is representative. A contemporary eschatological reading of the Gospel contrasts the Kingdom of God, which Christ preached, and the "pathetic" reality of the Church.[62]

---

55. Whalen, *Dominion of God*, 100–1.

56. Tavard, *Contemplative Church*, 139.

57. Tavard, *Contemplative Church*, 9.

58. Ratzinger, *Eschatology*, 13.

59. Fukuyama, *End of History*, serves as a well-known example of an application of Hegel's historical dialecticism. See Collits, "Hope and History Debate," 1.2.1.

60. Ratzinger, *Church, Ecumenism, and Politics*, 235.

61. Ratzinger, *God of Jesus Christ*, 117.

62. Ratzinger, *From the Baptism*, 48.

Moltmann's recasting of eschatology away from the future eternity "beyond [history]," towards the transformation of history exemplifies this Joachimite expectation of radically renewed history.[63] In a contrasting attitude to the historical sensibility present in St. Augustine and St. Gregory the Great, Moltmann wrote in a letter to Karl Barth that, for the contemporary period, "Joachim is more alive than Augustine."[64] He confirmed a "belief in the Age of the Spirit."[65] Thomas Joseph White, on this exchange, contrasted Moltmann's Joachimite expectation with Augustine's ecclesiology. The former sought "deinstitutionalized spirituality," which needed not the Church's "fixed creeds, sacraments and hierarchy."[66] The latter viewed the Church as not being conformed to the world and bearing witness for the world "to the perennial truths that endure."[67] Moltmann's clearly expressed preference for Joachim's "Age of the Spirit" showed his attachment to a form of Christian thinking that wanted to "raz[e] the bastions of institutional stability and eliminat[e] references to traditional authority."[68] The spiritualizing thrust of Joachim's Age of the Spirit is apparent in Moltmann's theology of hope, which places eschatological expectation within an historical framework and seeks thereby to supersede the Church.

Moltmann's own reading of Joachim bears out the historical, messianic thrust of his conception of Christian hope. Responding to Henri de Lubac and Hans Urs von Balthasar's criticisms of his theology of hope, he clarified that what he wrote to Barth was as follows: "In modern times the doctrine of the Holy Spirit has had a thoroughly enthusiastic and chiliast stamp to it. Joachim is more alive than Augustine."[69] Moltmann's comment to Barth evidences a Joachimite inflexion of pneumatology in contemporary theology. He argues that, for Joachim, the Gospel is not the fulfillment of the Old Law but rather, along with the Old Testament, promises "the future of God."[70] Importantly, the eschatological fulfillment promised by the Old and New Testaments are historicized: "This fulfilling history, which puts an end to all of the preliminary action of salvation history, is an historical future for Joachim, a future which can be physically experienced and temporally

63. Moltmann, *Theology of Hope*, 15.

64. Sutton, "Elie Kedourie and Henri de Lubac," 730, quoting Lubac, *La Postérité spirituelle de Joachim de Flore*, Vol I, 7.

65. Sutton, "Elie Kedourie and Henri de Lubac," 730.

66. White, "Metaphysics of Democracy," 30.

67. White, "Metaphysics of Democracy," 30.

68. White, "Metaphysics of Democracy," 30.

69. Moltmann, "Christian Hope," 329.

70. Moltmann, "Christian Hope," 331.

calculated."[71] Moltmann, therefore, interprets Joachim through a historical-eschatological lens, arguing for a position in which hope is historicized. Moltmann's concern is "to liberate the Christian hope from its speculative translation into a chronology of world history."[72] Joachim's chiliasm supports a conception of hope as "*messianic . . . within the horizon of eschatological expectation*."[73] Joachim impels the development of a progressive historical consciousness, driven forward by Christian hope.

Further, in Moltmann, Joachim's historical scheme tends to make the Trinity chronological and therefore to historicize God. Moltmann's appropriation of Joachim emphasizes the historical-eschatological character of the latter's tripartite scheme of history, over and against Thomas Aquinas. Thomas's "doctrine of the Trinity neutralizes and shuts down the eschatological dynamism of the biblical history of promise."[74] Moltmann accuses Thomas of reductionist thinking, by using the categories of time and eternity, with little interest "in the progression of the ages."[75] Conversely, Joachim instigated a perspective in which history and the Trinity are seen together in an eschatological light: "such that the history of the kingdom is determined in a trinitarian fashion and the Trinity is conceived as the consummation of its own trinitarian history in the kingdom of its own glory."[76] In Moltmann's estimation, the Trinity has its own history, which culminates in the kingdom. Eternity and metaphysics are consequently elided in an historical-eschatological conception of the end of salvation history.

Furthermore, implicit in Moltmann's discussion of Joachim is an apparently sharper distinction between the economic roles or missions of the Son and Holy Spirit than present in traditional expositions. For example, the *Catechism of the Catholic Church* states that "the Spirit is inseparable from [the Father and the Son], in both the inner life of the Trinity and *his gift of love for the world*."[77] The Son and the Spirit's mission is "joint" and "the mission of the Spirit of adoption is to unite them to Christ and make them live in him."[78] On Moltmann's contrasting reading of Joachim, the promises of the Old Law and New Law will be fulfilled in the coming kingdoms of

71. Moltmann, "Christian Hope," 331.
72. Moltmann, "Christian Hope," 348.
73. Moltmann, "Christian Hope," 348; emphasis in original.
74. Moltmann, "Christian Hope," 344.
75. Moltmann, "Christian Hope," 344.
76. Moltmann, "Christian Hope," 344.
77. *CCC*, sec. 689; emphasis added.
78. *CCC*, sec. 690.

Christ and the Holy Spirit. These are simultaneously historical and chiliast fulfillments, the transitional age from history to the eschaton, in which the Church is surpassed "in the future of the Spirit" and the kingdom of God realized.[79] Moltmann argues that there cannot be objection to distinguishing the law of Christ from the law of the Spirit or of appropriating to the Holy Spirit the *intellectus spiritualis*.[80] Moreover, the Holy Spirit cannot "be equated with Christ" to any extent greater than the Son is "equated with the Father."[81] Moltmann thereby differentiates Thomas's view of the progression of history from the Old Law to the New Law from Joachim's tripartite scheme.[82] A "distance between the Son and the Spirit" is, therefore, arguably implied in Joachim's view of history, in which the Church founded by Christ is superseded within history, albeit in a transitional stage to the eschaton, by the Age of the Holy Spirit.[83]

THE RESPONSE OF RATZINGER TO JOACHIMISM

Ratzinger considers the idea of the Age of the Spirit to be problematic in a number of ways and he believes it to carry dangerous ecclesiological implications. First, the expectation of an intra-historical definitive epoch, even if transitional, contradicts the nature of history as being characterized by freedom and peccability.[84] As Ratzinger argues, "the Christian hope knows no idea of an inner fulfilment of history."[85] To expect a historical Age of the Spirit, in which there is complete spiritual freedom, ignores that history *qua* history is characterized by the exercise of human agency and carries a postlapsarian inclination to sin.

Secondly, Joachim's scheme undermines a specifically Christological reading of the movement of salvation history. In this regard, a classic expression of theological opposition to Joachim can be seen in Thomas Aquinas.[86] Directly confronting the line of thought originating in Joachim and seen later in Moltmann, Aquinas argues that the state of the world can

---

79. Moltmann, "Christian Hope," 331, 344.

80. Moltmann, "Christian Hope," 344.

81. Moltmann, "Christian Hope," 344.

82. Moltmann, "Christian Hope," 344.

83. Cf. *CCC*, sec. 690, quoting Gregory of Nyssa, *De Spiritu Sancto*, 16.

84. For more on this, including references, see Collits, "Hope and History Debate," 2.2.3.

85. Ratzinger, *Eschatology*, 213.

86. For further on Thomas's critique of Joachim and the historical context, see Tavard, *Contemplative Church*, 77–90.

only change with a change of law (as from the Old Law to the New), or as humanity is placed *vis-à-vis* the prevailing law (as for example the extent to which people cooperate with grace). The transition from the Old Law to the New Law was a change in the state of the world. The New succeeded the Old as a more perfect law. Importantly, the New Law cannot be improved upon, as it is that whereby humanity is brought to its last end.[87] Underpinning Aquinas's argument is an eschatological sensibility, shared by Ratzinger, that history cannot, on its own terms and while remaining history proper, be perfected. Perfection will be realized in the *eschaton*, which is humanity's last end and is outside history. The New Law, as succeeding the Old, places humanity in the position whereby it is apt to enter into that eschatological state. As applicable to history, however, the New Law is not the perfect realization of the *eschaton* but the closest to it that can be in history: the "Law of the Gospel ... has brought things to perfection."[88] As to the argument that a status (i.e., a change in the state of the world and history) corresponds to each of the Persons of the Trinity, Aquinas states that it is inaccurate to attribute the Old Law solely to the Father, as it corresponded also to the Son, insofar as he was foreshadowed in the Old Law. Likewise, the New Law corresponds not just to the Son but also the Holy Spirit.[89]

In this regard, Moltmann's argument that there cannot be objection to distinguishing between the Law of Christ and the Law of the Spirit and Joachim's expectation of inner-historical fulfillment are shown to be misconceived.[90] The Law of Christ *is* the New Law, which is the grace of the Holy Spirit.[91] Nor is it simply a matter of appropriating to each status a Person of the Trinity, as Moltmann argues, because each status involves a fundamental change in the nature of historical reality.[92] The Age of the Spirit, in which there is monkish spiritual contemplation, without mediation of hierarchy or sacrament, would mark such a fundamental change in history, but is in fact historically impossible. The latest stage of history (which remains characterized by freedom and peccability) is that in which the New Law of Christ, the grace of the Holy Spirit, prepares humanity for the *eschaton*.

---

87. Aquinas, *ST*, I–II, q. 106, a. 4, resp.

88. Aquinas, *On the Power of God*, q. 5, a. 6, ad. 9.

89. Aquinas, *ST*, I–II, q. 106, a. 4, ad. 3.

90. Cf. Moltmann, "Christian Hope," 344.

91. Cf. Aquinas, *ST*, I–II, q. 106, a. 2, resp.; q. 106, a. 4, ad. 4; Moltmann, "Christian Hope," 344.

92. Cf. Moltmann, "Christian Hope," 343.

Ratzinger's critique of Joachim partly rests on Aquinas's (and also Bonaventure's) Christo-centric view of the relationship between the Old and New Testaments. Aquinas rejected Joachim's exegesis whereby particular events of the Old Testament were said to prefigure particular events in the New Testament period. To suggest that Old Testament history would anticipate New Testament history is to suggest that the Old Testament determines—and therefore in some senses controls and suppresses—the New Testament. Rather, the whole of the Old Testament points to and is fulfilled in Christ, who does not parallel any Old Testament figure. Instead, in his Church is found the perfection of the Old Law in the New Law, as that which immediately presses up against the promised eschatological reality. On this view, Christ is the turning-point of history and ushers in a new status. For Bonaventure, Joachim's Third Age of the Spirit "destroyed the central position of Christ in the Joachimite view."[93] Rather, the seventh age "of the New Testament Christ-time ... endures up to the end."[94] For Bonaventure, as for Thomas, "Christ is the center of all," that on which history turns as on an axis.[95] He is not one dividing point among others as he is for Joachim, whose concern was to "[bring] out the movement of the second age to the third."[96] Rather, he is the fulfillment of the Old Testament and ushers in the final days before the eschaton (cf. Acts 2:17).

Thirdly, because it undermines a Christological reading of history, a Joachimite theology of history reflects a pneumatology untethered from Christology. Consistent with the Christological centre of his theology, Ratzinger critiques Joachim's schema because it tends to treat the Spirit not only as distinct but separate from the Son.[97] Although recognizing merit in Joachim's work, the speculations of Joachim "distorted" the insight that "the Christianity of the Spirit *is* the Christianity of the lived Word."[98] Against the backdrop of the Church's dogmatic reflection on the mystery of the Trinity, Ratzinger sketches an "initial outline of a theology of the Holy Spirit,"

93. Ratzinger, *Theology of History*, 116–17; quotation on 117.

94. Ratzinger, *Theology of History*, 118.

95. Ratzinger, *Theology of History*, 118.

96. Ratzinger, *Theology of History*, 118.

97. Cf. Gaál, *Theology of Pope Benedict XVI*, x. This is notwithstanding arguments of Moltmann that the undivided Trinity is not divided in Joachim and that the tripartite scheme of history is nothing more than a matter of appropriation: "Joachim simply transferred these three great appropriations to ages and sites in salvation history," Moltmann, "Christian Hope," 343. Ratzinger notes that Joachim considered the stages of history to overlap and that his desire for a "spiritual" form of Christianity emerged from the depths of the Word and not in opposition to it: *God of Jesus Christ*, 116.

98. Ratzinger, *God of Jesus Christ*, 115–18; quotation on 118; emphasis added.

making clear that the Spirit is located *in* the Word and that for a Christian to become truly spiritual requires immersion in the Word, where the Spirit is found.[99] A Christianity of the Spirit as a Christianity of the Word reflects the inner life of the Trinity and the procession of the Holy Spirit from the Father and the Son, who together as one principle spirate Him: "The Spirit dwells in the Word, not in a departure from the Word. The Word is the location of the Spirit; Jesus is the source of the Spirit."[100] Ratzinger here reflects the perichoretic communion of God's life whereby the Holy Spirit proceeds from the Father and the Son *within* and not "outside" the Father and the Son.[101] The preposition "*in*" may also express Aquinas's notion of the dynamic of *impressio-inclinatio* in the life of the Trinity. Analogous to the human experience whereby what is loved is "impressed" upon the will of the lover, such that the lover's will is "inclined" to the beloved, the Holy Spirt is "in" the Son and the Father. Thomas Joseph White explains it thus: "The Spirit is the eternal term of the love of the Son within the Father and of the love of the Father within the Son, and accordingly is their shared reciprocal impression of love."[102] The Spirit, as the consubstantial communion of the Father and the Son, lives in and with the Son, not outside of Him.[103] To separate the Son and the Spirit, as Ratzinger detects in Joachim, misapprehends the life of God and the Holy Spirit's dwelling in the Son.

To approach the Spirit, therefore, we must live in the Son, who gives access to the Father, in the Spirit, in the economy of salvation. Ratzinger writes, "the more we enter into him [Jesus], the more really do we enter into the Spirit, and the Spirit enters into us."[104] The Christian is in the Spirit insofar as he is in the Son. Ratzinger uses John 20:19–23 as his scriptural warrant for connecting closely the Son and Spirit and for suggesting that the Son is the source of life in the Spirit. This is the account of the Risen Christ's interaction with the disciples on Easter Sunday night. After giving the disciples his peace, the Lord states that the disciples would be sent as the Father had sent him. Importantly, Jesus breathes on [*enephusēsen*] the disciples and gives them the Holy Spirit [*Labete pneuma hagion*] (v. 22). The account contains an important detail: the Son is the source of the gift of the Holy Spirit to the apostles in the economy (the Holy Spirit proceeds from

99. Ratzinger, *God of Jesus Christ*, 118.

100. Ratzinger, *God of Jesus Christ*, 118. Cf. The Second Council of Lyons, "Constitution on the Blessed Trinity and on the Catholic Faith," in Neuner and Dupuis, *Christian Faith*, n321.

101. Emery, *Trinity*, 89.

102. White, *Trinity*, 488.

103. Cf. Emery, *Trinity*, 143.

104. Ratzinger, *God of Jesus Christ*, 118.

the Son and the Father as the "principle without principle").[105] Underscoring the close connection between Son and Spirit, it is the Spirit, in turn, who allows Christians to live in the Son and return to the Father. The purpose of the sending of the Spirit of adoption is to configure Christians to Christ, as sons in the Son.[106] As the *Catechism* points out, the Son reveals the Father and the Holy Spirit reveals Father and Son (precisely, it could be added, as the communion of the Father and the Son).[107]

A Joachimite scheme of history inverts this order. For Ratzinger, St. Irenaeus of Lyon contains a "[much more correct] trinitarian logic of history" than Joachim.[108] According to Irenaeus, history does not progress in successive stages from Father, Son to the Holy Spirit. Rather, the Holy Spirit, present at the beginning of creation (Gen 1:2), instructs and guides humanity, leading us to the Son, and through him, to the Father whom the Son reveals (cf. John 14:6). Further, the Irenaean logic of salvation history more appropriately reflects the *taxis* within the Trinity, whereby the Father is the source and origin of Son and Holy Spirit but also the end to which the immanent processions in God move. In the words of Romanus Cessario, the inner-life of God consists of: "intra-Trinitarian coming forth in the Word [from the Father] and *recoil* in Personal Love ... God as Father utters a Word with whom he breathes forth the force of *loving recoil* who is the Holy Spirit."[109] Implicitly Joachim's scheme shows the Holy Spirit proceeding out from the Father and the Son, without "springing back."

Sundering pneumatology from Christology (and implicitly, Trinitarian theology) also separates ecclesiology from pneumatology. Ratzinger observes the tendency of contemporary theology to contrast Christology with pneumatology, and Incarnation/sacrament from the charismatic. Although it is correct "to distinguish Christ and the Pneuma," Word and Spirit, they are properly distinguished in order to underscore their unity.[110] Likewise, it is mistaken to consider the Trinity as a fellowship or "communion" of three Gods. Rather, the Persons must be considered "as one single God in the relative Trinity of Persons."[111] It is only in that relative distinction in unity that the Persons can begin to be understood: neither Christ nor Spirit

---

105. Cf. Emery, *Trinity*, 148, quoting *CCC*, sec. 248. There is of course the etymological connection between the concepts of "breath" and "spirit": Jesus breathes the Holy Spirit as the Father and Son breathe forth the Holy Spirit. Cf. *CCC*, sec. 691.

106. Cf. Ratzinger, *Eschatology*, 62, 64–65.

107. *CCC*, sec. 238–48.

108. Ratzinger, *God of Jesus Christ*, 119.

109. Cessario, "Theology at Fribourg," 332–33; emphases added.

110. Ratzinger, *Pilgrim Fellowship of Faith*, 183.

111. Ratzinger, *Pilgrim Fellowship of Faith*, 183.

can be understood without the other. Citing St. Paul in 2 Corinthians 3:17 ("The Lord is the Spirit"), Ratzinger argues that St. Paul does not mean that Christ and Spirit are personally identical, but that Christ's Lordship continues in and after the Incarnation, which is "not his [Christ's] last word."[112] The Incarnation is "perfected" in Christ's death on the Cross and his Resurrection.[113] Having lived the life of the Spirit, Christ "shares himself [to the Church] through him and in him."[114] St. Paul's "pneumatological Christology" and the Johannine farewell discourses underpin the reality that Christ is made present in the Church through the sacraments, which themselves are the work of the Holy Spirit. Linking back to the Resurrection account John 20, the once-for-all redemptive sacrifice offered on the Cross, made victorious in the Resurrection, "is the gift of the Holy Spirit, which is the Spirit of the Risen Christ."[115] The Risen flesh of Christ, the culmination of the Incarnation, is communicated through time and space "in the power of the Holy Spirit."[116] In Ratzinger, there is a resultant "synthesis of Christology and pneumatology."[117] In the economy, the Holy Spirit, far from establishing a spiritual reality separate from the visible Church, is He who communicates Christ in history in the sacramental life of the Church.

Accordingly, another important reality revealed in John 20 is that the Holy Spirit is not only necessary for the Church's mission, but in fact animates the life of the Church. The flipside is that the Holy Spirit cannot be found apart from the Church. Following on, and closely connected to, Christ's statement that he was sending the disciples as he had been sent by the Father, was the act of breathing forth the Holy Spirt on them. The Incarnate Word, Holy Spirit and Church are inextricably linked in the economy of salvation.[118] It is the Holy Spirit, as Christ's gift, which empowers the disciples to engage in ecclesial mission (cf. Acts 1:8). Ratzinger highlights thus the "false element in Joachim, namely, the utopia of a [spiritual] Church that would depart from the Son and rise higher than him and the irrational expectation that portrays itself as a real and rational program."[119] Rather, the Church, which receives the power of the Holy Spirit, continues the Son's

112. Ratzinger, *Pilgrim Fellowship of Faith*, 183.

113. Ratzinger, *Pilgrim Fellowship of Faith*, 183.

114. Ratzinger, *Pilgrim Fellowship of Faith*, 183–84.

115. Ratzinger, *Pilgrim Fellowship of Faith*, 184.

116. Ratzinger, *Pilgrim Fellowship of Faith*, 185.

117. Ratzinger, *Pilgrim Fellowship of Faith*, 185.

118. John Paul II uses the expression of the Holy Spirit, "the soul of the Church," in *Dominum et Vivificantem*, 26. Thomas Aquinas also uses the expression in *Homilies on the Apostles' Creed*, art. 9 (no. 971), quoted in Emery, *Trinity*, 155–56n82.

119. Ratzinger, *God of Jesus Christ*, 118.

mission. In his address at the Vigil of World Youth Day in Sydney, 2008 (the theme of which was based on Acts 1:8), Pope Benedict XVI warned against constructing such "a spiritual utopia" over and against the visible structure of the Church. To do so risks undermining the unity of the Church, a unity caused by the Holy Spirit:

> To separate the Holy Spirit from Christ present in the Church's institutional structure would compromise the unity of the Christian community, which is precisely the Spirit's gift! It would betray the nature of the Church as the living temple of the Holy Spirit (cf. 1 Cor 3:16). It is the Spirit, in fact, who guides the Church in the way of all truth and unifies her in communion and the in the works of ministry (cf. *Lumen Gentium*, 4).[120]

A spiritualized Christianity, apart from the visible structures of the Church, mistakes the nature of Christ's gift of the Spirit.

AN AUGUSTINIAN PNEUMATOLOGY

Benedict's concern with a non-ecclesial, spiritual Christianity rests upon an Augustinian pneumatology. Ratzinger utilizes the Doctor of Grace to explore this "physiognomy" of the Holy Spirit.[121] In the World Youth Day address, he noted that the proper name of the "Holy Spirit" refers to what is common between the Father and the Son. The personal property of the Holy Spirit as he who proceeds is to be their communion: "he is that which is common, the unity of the Father and the Son, the unity in Person. The Father and the Son are one with each other by going out beyond themselves; it is in the third Person, in the fruitfulness of their act of giving, that they are One."[122] The names "Holy" and "Spirit" refer not to the giving and receiving proper to the Father and the Son, but to what is common to the Godhead. That is, "essential to the description of God" in his essence is that he is holy and spirit, designations which could equally be applied to the Father and the Son as much as to the Holy Spirit.[123] However, the "paradox [which is] characteristic of [the Holy Spirit]" is this "mutuality," whereby he is "the *communio* of the Father and the Son."[124] Importantly, the dyad of Father and

---

120. Benedict XVI, *Dear Young People*, 55.

121. Ratzinger, "Holy Spirit as Communio," 326. Matthew Levering describes this essay as "influential"; Levering, *Engaging the Doctrine of the Holy Spirit*, 71.

122. Ratzinger, *God of Jesus Christ*, 119, Benedict XVI, *Dear Young People*, 58.

123. Ratzinger, "Holy Spirit as Communio," 326.

124. Ratzinger, "Holy Spirit as Communio," 326.

Son remains a dialogue in the unity of the Trinity (i.e., without distance or separation) because the "Spirit is Person as unity, unity as Person."[125] This is another way, perhaps, of saying that the Holy Spirit is that "loving recoil" that does not simply come out from the Father and the Son, but is the Person who, precisely in his Personhood, is the unity of the Father and the Son by which God finds His term.[126]

Augustinian pneumatology, in naming the Holy Spirit as Gift and Love, underscores the connection between Christology, pneumatology and ecclesiology. Joachimism threatens this connection. In his justification of the term "Gift" "as an essential designation of the Holy Spirit," Augustine refers to John 4:7–14, John 7:37, 39, and 1 Cor 12:13.[127] These passages relate Christ's interaction with the Samaritan woman at Jacob's well, his invitation at the Feast of Tabernacles for people to drink "living water" from himself, and St. Paul's comment that Christians "drink of the one Spirit."[128] Augustine argues that Christ's promise to give "living water" to those who ask of it and St. John and St. Paul's identification of that living water with the Spirit show that those who receive the living water from him are receiving the Holy Spirit. Accordingly, "Christology and pneumatology" are deeply connected for Augustine (and Ratzinger) because "Christ is the well of living water . . . the crucified Lord is the generative source of life for the world. The well of the Spirit is the crucified Christ."[129] As the Risen Christ gifts the Holy Spirit by breathing on the disciples after the Resurrection, so is Jesus the source of the living water, which is the Holy Spirit. Again, to live in the Holy Spirit and to have humanity's "ultimate thirst" sated, is to live in Christ from whom the gift of the Holy Spirit is received.[130]

Similar to Christology's connection to pneumatology in Augustine, so too is pneumatology connected to ecclesiology. The proper name for the Holy Spirit indicates the mutuality and communion of the Father and the Son and thus bears "a fundamentally ecclesiological meaning."[131] Ratzinger

125. Ratzinger, "Holy Spirit as Communio," 326.

126. It should be noted that Ratzinger comments that the Holy Spirit, as "Gift" is that which in a sense comes out from God and is the point of contact, as it were, between God and creation: Ratzinger, "Holy Spirit as Communio," 331. The point, though, is that God the Holy Spirit, as the communion of the Father and the Son, leads back to the Son and through him the Father, precisely as that communion.

127. Ratzinger, "Holy Spirit as Communio," 329–30. See also Levering's discussion of Augustine's exegesis: Levering, *Doctrine of the Holy Spirit*, 55–67.

128. Ratzinger, "Holy Spirit as Communio," 330.

129. Ratzinger, "Holy Spirit as Communio," 330.

130. Ratzinger, "Holy Spirit as Communio," 330.

131. Ratzinger, "Holy Spirit as Communio," 327.

argues that the Christian mode of existence is to "[enter] into the mode of being of the Holy Spirit" and enter into communion.[132] True spirituality—truly being led by the Holy Spirit—is to be "unifying, communicating."[133] Moreover, as it is appropriate to designate the Holy Spirit as "Love," which "proves itself in constancy," a truly spiritual life is an ecclesial life, one focused on the unity that is the Holy Spirit.[134] The spiritual Christian lives in the heart of the Church: "Clearly anyone who looks for *pneuma* only on the outside, in the always unexpected, is on the wrong path. He or she fails to appreciate the basic activity of the Holy Spirit: unifying love entering into abiding."[135] A fundamental relationship between the Holy Spirit and the Church exists. An almost "dogmatic thesis for [Augustine]" is the claim that the "Church is love."[136] The following quotation underscores the consequent connection between the concepts of communion, love, and gift, and how the Holy Spirit proceeds from the Word to build up the Church: "As a creation of the Spirit, the Church is the body of the Lord built up by the *pneuma*, and thus also becomes the body of Christ when the *pneuma* forms men and women for '*communio*.' This creation, this Church, is God's 'gift' in the word, and this 'gift' is love."[137] That is, the gift of the Gift that is the Holy Spirit (the "*gift* of God is God himself") is to bring humanity into the communion and love of the Church, which is the body of Christ.[138] Augustine consequently equates true possession of the Holy Spirit with one's love of the Church and with "ecclesial patience."[139] To be in the Holy Spirit is to be in the Church.

Although not mentioned in this context directly, Joachimism is clearly a target of Ratzinger's Augustinian pneumatological ecclesiology. Spiritual dreams of "an earthly kingdom of God" and schismatic separation from the Church, such as might have animated Augustine's opponents, the Donatists, is "a pneumatological heresy."[140] Rather, the Church cannot be divided between "spirit" and "institution":

132. Ratzinger, "Holy Spirit as Communio," 327.

133. Ratzinger, "Holy Spirit as Communio," 327.

134. Ratzinger, "Holy Spirit as Communio," 328–29, quotation on 328. On Augustine's exegesis on naming the Holy Spirit "Love," see Ratzinger, "Holy Spirit as Communio," 328; Levering, *Doctrine of the Holy Spirit*, 55–67.

135. Ratzinger, "Holy Spirit as Communio," 329.

136. Ratzinger, "Holy Spirit as Communio," 332.

137. Ratzinger, "Holy Spirit as Communio," 332.

138. Ratzinger, "Holy Spirit as Communio," 331.

139. Ratzinger, "Holy Spirit as Communio," 333.

140. Ratzinger, "Holy Spirit as Communio," 333; first quotation from Meer, *Augustinus der Seelsorger*.

The Church is the house of the Spirit, visible and "empirical," in the sacraments and in the word. The Spirit is given precisely in the concrete community of those who derive from Christ their support and bear with one another. . . . Whoever looks for the Spirit only externally, Augustine would say, misunderstands the fundamental activity of *pneuma*: unifying love entering into abiding.[141]

Christ's gift is the Gift of the Spirit in the Church, which is the "continuation of the humanity of Jesus."[142] Spiritual existence is to live the unity and love offered in the Church, which are the characteristic of the Holy Spirit.[143]

CONCLUSION

To much fanfare, the Church in Australia in 2022 held a Plenary Council. One attendee, Professor Hayden Ramsay, pointed out the danger of the spiritualizing positions put by some at the Council to the integrity of the Church's structure and life. He states:

One effect of this approach, where you spiritualise everything, is that nothing can be critiqued. When we find that what we feel the spirit saying to us or hear the spirit saying to the group is at odds with other parts of the tradition (Scripture, doctrine, law) or plain fact, we can simply assert we are being spiritual. Accountability to canons of faith and reason or interaction with other perspectives doesn't apply to us.[144]

Joachimism undergirds various arguments either to move beyond Christianity altogether or beyond the concrete, visible, sacramental and therefore hierarchical structure of the Church. This chapter has offered a critique of the Joachimite vision of history and defended the enduring value of the Augustinian vision of history. An Augustinian eschatology understands that history cannot be perfected within itself and is rather in a state of senescence, awaiting its redemption from beyond history. In contrast, the Joachimite vision of history expects a period, even if transitional, of perfection within history. For many, this will involve moving past Christianity and its tangible expressions.

141. Ratzinger, "Holy Spirit as Communio," 334.
142. Ratzinger, "Holy Spirit as Communio," 335.
143. Cf. Ratzinger, "Holy Spirit as Communio," 337.
144. Ramsey, "What Was Not on the Agenda," par. 13.

By positing a Trinitarian movement, which culminates in an Age of the Spirit, the Joachimite theology of history squarely raises issues of pneumatology. Promoting an Age of the Holy Spirit raises questions of the Holy Spirit's role in the economy of salvation and, more fundamentally, the Holy Spirit's relationship with the Son and the Church he founded. Ratzinger's pneumatology, if implicitly based on classic expressions of Trinitarian doctrine, St. Irenaeus and St. Augustine, demonstrates the intimate relationship between Christology and pneumatology, and an appropriate theology of history. Reflecting a perichoretic understanding of the Holy Spirit's procession from the Father and the Son, within the Father and the Son, Ratzinger "locates" the Holy Spirit "in" the Word. Son and Spirit "belong together" (human language only barely grasps the distinction in unity of the Divine Persons). Spirit is not separate from Word but is breathed forth from the Son (and Father). Simultaneously, the Spirit is "loving recoil," the unity of Father and Son. Salvation history does not follow a progression towards a terminus in an Age of the Spirit, on the way to an eschatological future. Instead, it follows an *exitus-reditus* pattern proceeding forth from the Father and returning through the Son *in* the Spirit.[145] The grace of the Holy Spirit, which is the New Law, is the highest state of historical development for the human person. The believer enters into communion with God therefore through the Spirit of adoption, who configures Christians to the Son as coheirs of the Father.

A Christologically informed pneumatology in turn is closely connected to ecclesiology. The Spirit proceeds as breath from the Son, given as Gift by Christ on Resurrection Sunday. Ratzinger here applies Augustine's pneumatological exegeses to the life of the Church. Properly named Holy Spirit, the Third Person of the Trinity is what is common to the Godhead. In so being, he is the unity and communion of the Father and the Son. Likewise, the Holy Spirit is properly called Love and Gift. As Love (Communion) and Gift, the Holy Spirit promotes abiding and effects the communion that is the Church.

It remains the constant temptation of Catholics to seek a spiritual Church outside the visible Church. The Joachimite progression of history even sees the visible, hierarchical, sacramental Church as to be superseded. But, for Augustine, failure to abide results in schism, a sin against communion. Ultimately, schism amounts to a failure to abide in the Holy Spirit with ecclesial patience. The truly spiritual Christian will live in the

---

145. On the *exitus-reditus* scheme of Thomas's *Summa*, see Torrell, *Aquinas's Summa*, 27–29. See also Ratzinger's discussion of the importance of this scheme in Ratzinger et al., *End of Time?*, 17–25.

bosom of the concrete reality of the Church, where the Holy Spirit configures us to Christ, as we wait expectantly for the full realization of divine filiation.

BIBLIOGRAPHY

Aquinas, Thomas. *On the Power of God.* Translated by the English Dominican Fathers. 3 vols. London: Burns, Oates, and Washbourne, 1932–34.

———. *Summa Theologica.* Translated by English Dominican Province. 5 vols. London: Benziger Brothers, 1948.

Beiser, Frederick. *Hegel.* London: Routledge, 2005.

Benedict XVI. *Dear Young People: Homilies and Addresses of Pope Benedict XVI: Apostolic Journey to Sydney, Australia, on the Occasion of the 23rd World Youth Day, Sydney, 12 to 21 July 2008.* Strathfield: St. Pauls, 2008.

Catechism of the Catholic Church. 2nd ed. Strathfield: St. Pauls, 2000.

Cessario, Romanus. "Theology at Fribourg." *Thomist* 51 (1987) 325–66.

Collits, David Patrick. "The Hope and History Debate in Fundamental Theology." PhD diss., University of Notre Dame, 2020. https://researchonline.nd.edu.au/theses/283/.

Copleston, Frederick. *A History of Philosophy.* Vol 7, *18th and 19th Century German Philosophy.* London: Bloomsbury, 1963.

Daniélou, Jean. "The Conception of History in the Christian Tradition." *Journal of Religion* 30 (1950) 171–79.

Dawson, Christopher. *Religion and the Rise of Western Culture.* New York: Doubleday, 1991.

Duffy, Eamon. *Saints and Sinners: A History of the Popes.* 3rd ed. New Haven, CT: Yale University Press, 2006.

———. *Ten Popes Who Shook the World.* New Haven, CT: Yale University Press, 2011.

Emery, Gilles. *The Trinity: An Introduction to Catholic Doctrine on the Triune God.* Translated by Matthew Levering. Washington DC: The Catholic University of America Press, 2011.

Fukuyama, Francis. *The End of History and the Last Man.* London: Penguin, 1992.

Gaál, Emery de. *The Theology of Pope Benedict XVI: The Christocentric Shift.* New York: Palgrave Macmillan, 2010.

Green, John. "St. Gregory the Great and the Pastoral Transvaluation of Augustinian Spirituality." *Australasian Catholic Record* 83 (2006) 167–85.

Gregory the Great. "Homily 1." Patristic Bible Commentary. https://sites.google.com/site/aquinasstudybible/home/luke-commentary/gregory-the-great-homily-1.

John Paul II. *Dominum et Vivificantem.* https://www.vatican.va/content/john-paul-ii/en/encyclicals/documents/hf_jp-ii_enc_18051986_dominum-et-vivificantem.html.

Levering, Matthew. *Engaging the Doctrine of the Holy Spirit: Love and Gift in the Trinity and the Church.* Grand Rapids, MI: Baker Academic, 2016.

Löwith, Karl. *Meaning in History.* Chicago: University of Chicago Press, 1949.

Missale Romanum. New York: Benziger Bros, 1962.

Moltmann, Jürgen. "Christian Hope: Messianic or Transcendent? A Theological Discussion with Joachim of Fiore and Thomas Aquinas." *Horizons* 12 (1985) 328–48.

———. *Theology of Hope: On the Grounds and the Implications of a Christian Eschatology*. Translated by James W. Leitch. Minneapolis, MN: Fortress, 993.

Neuner, J., and J. Dupuis. *The Christian Faith in the Doctrinal Document of the Catholic Church*. Edited by Jacques Dupuis. 7th ed. New York: Society of St. Paul, 2001.

Newheiser, David. "Conceiving Transformation without Triumphalism: Joachim of Fiore against Gianni Vattimo." *Heythrop Journal* 55 (2014) 650–62.

O'Callaghan, Paul. *Christ Our Hope: An Introduction to Eschatology*. Washington, DC: The Catholic University of America Press, 2011.

O'Collins, Gerald. *The Tripersonal God: Understanding and Interpreting the Trinity*. 2nd ed. Mahwah. NJ: Paulist, 2013.

Ramsey, Hayden. "What Was Not on the Agenda." *Catholic Weekly*, July 13, 2022. https://www.catholicweekly.com.au/hayden-ramsay-what-was-not-on-the-agenda/.

Ratzinger, Joseph. *Church, Ecumenism, and Politics: New Endeavours in Ecclesiology*. Translated by Michael J. Miller et al. San Francisco: Ignatius, 2008.

———. *Eschatology: Death and Eternal Life*. 2nd edition. Translated by Michael Waldstein and Aidan Nichols. Washington DC: The Catholic University of America Press, 1988.

———. *The God of Jesus Christ: Meditations on the Triune God*. 2nd ed. Translated by Brian McNeil. San Francisco: Ignatius, 2008.

———. "The Holy Spirit as Communio: Concerning the Relationship of Pneumatology and Spirituality in Augustine." *Communio* 25 (1998) 324–37.

———. *Jesus of Nazareth: From the Baptism in the Jordan to the Transfiguration*. Translated by Adrian J Walker. London: Bloomsbury, 2007.

———. *Jesus of Nazareth: Holy Week: From the Entrance into Jerusalem to the Resurrection*. Translated by Vatican Secretariat of State. San Francisco: Ignatius, 2011.

———. *Pilgrim Fellowship of Faith: The Church as Communion*. Translated by Henry Taylor. San Francisco: Ignatius, 2005.

———. *The Theology of History in St. Bonaventure*. Translated by Zachary Hayes. Chicago: Franciscan Herald, 1989.

Ratzinger, Joseph Cardinal, et al. *The End of Time? The Provocation of Talking about God*. Edited by Tiemo Rainer Peters and Claus Urban. Edited and translated by J. Matthew Ashley. Mahwah, NJ: Paulist, 2004.

Reeves, Majorie. "The Originality and Influence of Joachim of Fiore." *Traditio* 36 (1980) 269–316.

Rowland, Tracey. *Benedict XVI: A Guide for the Perplexed*. London: T. & T. Clark International, 2010.

Scruton, Roger. *Conservatism*. London: Profile, 2017.

———. *A Short History of Modern Philosophy: From Descartes to Wittgenstein*. 2nd ed. London: Routledge, 2002.

Škof, Lenart. "The Third Age: Reflections on Our Hidden Material Core." *Sophia* 59 (2020) 83–94.

Sutton, Michael. "Elie Kedourie and Henri de Lubac: Anglo-French Musings on the Progeny of Joachim of Fiore." *Middle Eastern Studies* 1 (2005) 717–33.

Tavard, George H. *Contemplative Church: Joachim and His Adversaries*. Milwaukee, WI: Marquette University Press, 2005.

Torrell, J. P. *Aquinas's Summa: Background, Structure, and Reception*. Translated by Benedict M. Guevin. Washington DC: The Catholic University of America Press, 2005.

Vattimo, Gianni. *After Christianity*. New York: Columbia University Press, 2002.

Voegelin, Eric. *The New Science of Politics: An Introduction*. Chicago: University of Chicago Press, 1987.

Weimann, Dirk. "*Mundus senescit*: Is Tolkien's Medievalism Victorian or Modernist?" *Hither Shore* 8 (2011) 24–39.

Whalen, Brett E. *Dominion of God: Christendom and Apocalypse in the Middle Ages*. Cambridge, MA: Harvard University Press, 2009.

White, Thomas Joseph. "The Metaphysics of Democracy." *First Things* 280 (2018) 25–30.

———. *The Trinity: On the Nature and Mystery of the One God*. Washington DC: The Catholic University of America Press, 2022.